Amiel's Journal

Henri-Frederic Amiel

(Translated by Mrs Humphrey Ward)

DODO PRESS

AMIEL'S JOURNAL

THE JOURNAL INTIME OF HENRI-FREDERIC AMIEL

TRANSLATED, WITH AN INTRODUCTION AND NOTES

By

Mrs. HUMPHREY WARD

PREFACE TO THE SECOND EDITION.

In this second edition of the English translation of Amiel's "Journal Intime," I have inserted a good many new passages, taken from the last French edition (*Cinquieme edition, revue et augmentee.*) But I have not translated all the fresh material to be found in that edition nor have I omitted certain sections of the Journal which in these two recent volumes have been omitted by their French editors. It would be of no interest to give my reasons for these variations at length. They depend upon certain differences between the English and the French public, which are more readily felt than explained. Some of the passages which I have left untranslated seemed to me to overweight the introspective side of the Journal, already so full—to overweight it, at any rate, for English readers. Others which I have retained, though they often relate to local names and books, more or less unfamiliar to the general public, yet seemed to me valuable as supplying some of that surrounding detail, that setting, which helps one to understand a life. Besides, we English are in many ways more akin to Protestant and Puritan Geneva than the French readers to whom the original Journal primarily addresses itself, and some of the entries I have kept have probably, by the nature of things, more savor for us than for them.

M. A. W.

PREFACE.

This translation of Amiel's "Journal Intime" is primarily addressed to those whose knowledge of French, while it may be sufficient to carry them with more or less complete understanding through a novel or a newspaper, is yet not enough to allow them to understand and appreciate a book containing subtle and complicated forms of expression. I believe there are many such to be found among the reading public, and among those who would naturally take a strong interest in such a life and mind as Amiel's, were it not for the barrier of language. It is, at any rate, in the hope that a certain number of additional readers may be thereby attracted to the "Journal Intime" that this translation of it has been undertaken.

The difficulties of the translation have been sometimes considerable, owing, first of all, to those elliptical modes of speech which a man naturally employs when he is writing for himself and not for the public, but which a translator at all events is bound in some degree to expand. Every here and there Amiel expresses himself in a kind of shorthand, perfectly intelligible to a Frenchman, but for which an English equivalent, at once terse and clear, is hard to find. Another difficulty has been his constant use of a technical philosophical language, which, according to his French critics, is not French—even philosophical French—but German. Very often it has been impossible to give any other than a literal rendering of such passages, if the thought of the original was to be preserved; but in those cases where a choice was open to me, I have preferred the more literary to the more technical expression; and I have been encouraged to do so by the fact that Amiel, when he came to prepare for publication a certain number of "Pensees," extracted from the Journal, and printed at the end of a volume of poems published in 1853, frequently softened his phrases, so that sentences which survive in the Journal in a more technical form are to be found in a more literary form in the "Grains de Mil."

In two or three cases—not more, I think—I have allowed myself to transpose a sentence bodily, and in a few instances I have added some explanatory words to the text, which wherever the addition was of any importance, are indicated by square brackets.

My warmest thanks are due to my friend and critic, M. Edmond Scherer, from whose valuable and interesting study, prefixed to the French Journal, as well as from certain materials in his possession which he has very kindly allowed me to make use of, I have drawn by far the greater part of the biographical material embodied in the Introduction. M. Scherer has also given me help and advice through the whole process of translation—advice which his scholarly knowledge of English has made especially worth having.

In the translation of the more technical philosophical passages I have been greatly helped by another friend, Mr. Bernard Bosanquet, Fellow of University College, Oxford, the translator of Lotze, of whose care and pains in the matter I cherish a grateful remembrance.

But with all the help that has been so freely given me, not only by these friends but by others, I confide the little book to the public with many a misgiving! May it at least win a few more friends and readers here and there for one who lived alone, and died sadly persuaded that his life had been a barren mistake; whereas, all the while—such is the irony of things—he had been in reality working out the mission assigned him in the spiritual economy, and faithfully obeying the secret mandate which had impressed itself upon his youthful consciousness: "*Let the living live; and you, gather together your thoughts, leave behind you a legacy of feeling and ideas; you will be most useful so.*"

MARY A. WARD.

Amiel's Journal

INTRODUCTION

It was in the last days of December, 1882, that the first volume of Henri Frederic Amiel's "Journal Intime" was published at Geneva. The book, of which the general literary world knew nothing prior to its appearance, contained a long and remarkable Introduction from the pen of M. Edmond Scherer, the well-known French critic, who had been for many years one of Amiel's most valued friends, and it was prefaced also by a little *Avertissement*, in which the "Editors"— that is to say, the Genevese friends to whom the care and publication of the Journal had been in the first instance entrusted—described in a few reserved and sober words the genesis and objects of the publication. Some thousands of sheets of Journal, covering a period of more than thirty years, had come into the hands of Amiel's literary heirs. "They were written," said the *Avertissement*, "with several ends in view. Amiel recorded in them his various occupations, and the incidents of each day. He preserved in them his psychological observations, and the impressions produced on him by books. But his Journal was, above all, the confidant of his most private and intimate thoughts; a means whereby the thinker became conscious of his own inner life; a safe shelter wherein his questionings of fate and the future, the voice of grief, of self-examination and confession, the soul's cry for inward peace, might make themselves freely heard.

"... In the directions concerning his papers which he left behind him, Amiel expressed the wish that his literary executors should publish those parts of the Journal which might seem to them to possess either interest as thought or value as experience. The publication of this volume is the fulfillment of this desire. The reader will find in it, *not a volume of Memoirs*, but the confidences of a solitary thinker, the meditations of a philosopher for whom the things of the soul were the sovereign realities of existence."

Thus modestly announced, the little volume made its quiet *debut*. It contained nothing, or almost nothing, of ordinary biographical material. M. Scherer's Introduction supplied such facts as were absolutely necessary to the understanding of Amiel's intellectual history, but nothing more. Everything of a local or private character that could be excluded was excluded. The object of the editors in their choice of passages for publication was declared to be simply "the reproduction of the moral and intellectual physiognomy of their friend," while M. Scherer expressly disclaimed any biographical intentions, and limited his Introduction as far as possible to "a study of the character and thought of Amiel." The contents of the volume, then, were purely literary and philosophical; its prevailing tone was a tone of introspection, and the public which can admit the claims and overlook the inherent defects of introspective literature has always been a small one. The writer of the Journal had been during his lifetime wholly unknown to the general European public. In Geneva itself he had been commonly regarded as a man who had signally disappointed the hopes and expectations of his friends, whose reserve and indecision of character had in many respects spoiled his life, and alienated the society around him; while his professional lectures were generally pronounced dry and unattractive, and the few volumes of poems which represented almost his only contributions to literature had nowhere met with any real cordiality of reception. Those concerned, therefore, in the publication of the first volume of the Journal can hardly have had much expectation of a wide success. Geneva is not a favorable starting-point for a French book, and it may well have seemed that not even the support of M. Scherer's name would be likely to carry the volume beyond a small local circle.

But "wisdom is justified of her children!" It is now nearly three years since the first volume of the "Journal Intime" appeared; the impression made by it was deepened and extended by the publication of the second volume in 1884; and it is now not too much to say that this remarkable record of a life has made its way to what promises to be a permanent place in literature. Among those who think and read it is beginning to be generally recognized that another book has been added to the books which live—not to those, perhaps, which live in the public view, much discussed, much praised, the objects of feeling and of struggle, but to those in which a germ of permanent life has been deposited silently, almost secretly, which compel no homage and excite no rivalry, and which owe the place that the world half-unconsciously yields to them to nothing but that indestructible sympathy of man with man, that eternal answering of feeling to feeling, which is one of the great principles, perhaps the greatest principle, at the root of literature. M. Scherer naturally was the first among the recognized guides of opinion to attempt the placing of his friend's Journal. "The man who, during his lifetime, was incapable of giving us any deliberate or conscious work worthy of his powers, has now left us, after his death, a book which will not die. For the secret of Amiel's malady is sublime, and the expression of it wonderful." So ran one of the last paragraphs of the

Introduction, and one may see in the sentences another instance of that courage, that reasoned rashness, which distinguishes the good from the mediocre critic. For it is as true now as it was in the days when La Bruyere rated the critics of his time for their incapacity to praise, and praise at once, that "the surest test of a man's critical power is his judgment of contemporaries." M. Renan, I think, with that exquisite literary sense of his, was the next among the authorities to mention Amiel's name with the emphasis it deserved. He quoted a passage from the Journal in his Preface to the "Souvenirs d'Enfance et de Jeunesse," describing it as the saying *"d'un penseur distingue, M. Amiel de Geneve."* Since then M. Renan has devoted two curious articles to the completed Journal in the *Journal des Desbats*. The first object of these reviews, no doubt, was not so much the critical appreciation of Amiel as the development of certain paradoxes which have been haunting various corners of M. Renan's mind for several years past, and to which it is to be hoped he has now given expression with sufficient emphasis and *brusquerie* to satisfy even his passion for intellectual adventure. Still, the rank of the book was fully recognized, and the first article especially contained some remarkable criticisms, to which we shall find occasion to recur. "In these two volumes of *pensees*," said M. Renan, "without any sacrifice of truth to artistic effect, we have both the perfect mirror of a modern mind of the best type, matured by the best modern culture, and also a striking picture of the sufferings which beset the sterility of genius. These two volumes may certainly be reckoned among the most interesting philosophical writings which have appeared of late years."

M. Caro's article on the first volume of the Journal, in the *Revue des Deux Mondes* for February, 1883, may perhaps count as the first introduction of the book to the general cultivated public. He gave a careful analysis of the first half of the Journal—resumed eighteen months later in the same periodical on the appearance of the second volume—and, while protesting against what he conceived to be the general tendency and effect of Amiel's mental story, he showed himself fully conscious of the rare and delicate qualities of the new writer. *"La reverie a reussi a notre auteur,"* he says, a little reluctantly—for M. Caro has his doubts as to the legitimacy of *reverie*; *"Il en aufait une oeuvure qui restera."* The same final judgment, accompanied by a very different series of comments, was pronounced on the Journal a year later by M. Paul Bourget, a young and rising writer, whose article is perhaps chiefly interesting as showing the kind of effect produced by Amiel's thought on minds of a type essentially alien from his own. There is a leaven of something positive and austere, of something which, for want of a better name, one calls Puritanism, in Amiel, which escapes the author of "Une Cruelle Enigme." But whether he has understood Amiel or no, M. Bourget is fully alive to the mark which the Journal is likely to make among modern records of mental history. He, too, insists that the book is already famous and will remain so; in the first place, because of its inexorable realism and sincerity; in the second, because it is the most perfect example available of a certain variety of the modern mind.

Among ourselves, although the Journal has attracted the attention of all who keep a vigilant eye on the progress of foreign literature, and although one or two appreciative articles have appeared on it in the magazines, the book has still to become generally known. One remarkable English testimony to it, however, must be quoted. Six months after the publication of the first volume, the late Mark Pattison, who since then has himself bequeathed to literature a strange and memorable fragment of autobiography, addressed a letter to M. Scherer as the editor of the "Journal Intime," which M. Scherer has since published, nearly a year after the death of the writer. The words have a strong and melancholy interest for all who knew Mark Pattison; and they certainly deserve a place in any attempt to estimate the impression already made on contemporary thought by the "Journal Intime."

"I wish to convey to you, sir," writes the rector of Lincoln, "the thanks of one at least of the public for giving the light to this precious record of a unique experience. I say unique, but I can vouch that there is in existence at least one other soul which has lived through the same struggles, mental and moral, as Amiel. In your pathetic description of the *volonte qui voudrait vouloir, mais impuissante a se fournir a elle-meme des motifs*—of the repugnance for all action—the soul petrified by the sentiment of the infinite, in all this I recognize myself. *Celui qui a dechiffre le secret de la vie finie, qui en a lu le mot, est sorti du monde des vivants, il est mort de fait.* I can feel forcibly the truth of this, as it applies to myself!

"It is not, however, with the view of thrusting my egotism upon you that I have ventured upon addressing you. As I cannot suppose that so peculiar a psychological revelation will enjoy a wide popularity, I think it a duty to the editor to assure him that there are persons in the world whose souls respond, in the depths of their inmost nature, to the cry of anguish which makes itself heard in the pages of these remarkable confessions."

So much for the place which the Journal—the fruit of so many years of painful thought and disappointed effort; seems to be at last securing for its author among those contemporaries who in his lifetime knew nothing of him. It is a natural consequence of the success of the book that the more it penetrates, the greater desire there is to know something more than its original editors and M. Scherer have yet told us about the personal history of the man who wrote it—about his education, his habits, and his friends. Perhaps some day this wish may find its satisfaction. It is an innocent one, and the public may even be said to have a kind of right to know as much as can be told it of the personalities which move and stir it. At present the biographical material available is extremely scanty, and if it were not for the kindness of M. Scherer, who has allowed the present writer access to certain manuscript material in his possession, even the sketch which follows, vague and imperfect as it necessarily is, would have been impossible.

[Footnote: Four or five articles on the subject of Amiel's life have been contributed to the *Revue Internationale* by Mdlle. Berthe Vadier during the passage of the present book through the press. My knowledge of them, however, came too late to enable me to make use of them for the purposes of the present introduction.]

Henri Frederic Amiel was born at Geneva in September, 1821. He belonged to one of the emigrant families, of which a more or less steady supply had enriched the little republic during the three centuries following the Reformation. Amiel's ancestors, like those of Sismondi, left Languedoc for Geneva after the revocation of the Edict of Nantes. His father must have been a youth at the time when Geneva passed into the power of the French republic, and would seem to have married and settled in the halcyon days following the restoration of Genevese independence in 1814. Amiel was born when the prosperity of Geneva was at its height, when the little state was administered by men of European reputation, and Genevese society had power to attract distinguished visitors and admirers from all parts. The veteran Bonstetten, who had been the friend of Gray and the associate of Voltaire, was still talking and enjoying life in his *appartement* overlooking the woods of La Batie. Rossi and Sismondi were busy lecturing to the Genevese youth, or taking part in Genevese legislation; an active scientific group, headed by the

Pictets, De la Rive, and the botanist Auguste-Pyrame de Candolle, kept the country abreast of European thought and speculation, while the mixed nationality of the place—the blending in it of French keenness with Protestant enthusiasms and Protestant solidity—was beginning to find inimitable and characteristic expression in the stories of Toepffer. The country was governed by an aristocracy, which was not so much an aristocracy of birth as one of merit and intellect, and the moderate constitutional ideas which represented the Liberalism of the post-Waterloo period were nowhere more warmly embraced or more intelligently carried out than in Geneva.

During the years, however, which immediately followed Amiel's birth, some signs of decadence began to be visible in this brilliant Genevese society. The generation which had waited for, prepared, and controlled, the Restoration of 1814, was falling into the background, and the younger generation, with all its respectability, wanted energy, above all, wanted leaders. The revolutionary forces in the state, which had made themselves violently felt during the civil turmoils of the period preceding the assembly of the French States General, and had afterward produced the miniature Terror which forced Sismondi into exile, had been for awhile laid to sleep by the events of 1814. But the slumber was a short one at Geneva as elsewhere, and when Rossi quitted the republic for France in 1833, he did so with a mind full of misgivings as to the political future of the little state which had given him—an exile and a Catholic—so generous a welcome in 1819. The ideas of 1830 were shaking the fabric and disturbing the equilibrium of the Swiss Confederation as a whole, and of many of the cantons composing it. Geneva was still apparently tranquil while her neighbors were disturbed, but no one looking back on the history of the republic, and able to measure the strength of the Radical force in Europe after the fall of Charles X., could have felt much doubt but that a few more years would bring Geneva also into the whirlpool of political change.

In the same year—1833—that M. Rossi had left Geneva, Henri Frederic Amiel, at twelve years old, was left orphaned of both his parents. They had died comparatively young—his mother was only just over thirty, and his father cannot have been much older. On the death of the mother the little family was broken up, the boy passing into the care of one relative, his two sisters into that of another. Certain notes in M. Scherer's possession throw a little light here and there upon a childhood and youth which must necessarily have been a little bare and forlorn. They show us a sensitive, impressionable boy, of health rather delicate than robust, already disposed to a more or less melancholy and dreamy view of life, and showing a deep interest in those religious problems and ideas in which the air of Geneva has been steeped since the days of Calvin. The religious teaching which a Genevese lad undergoes prior to his admission to full church membership, made a deep impression on him, and certain mystical elements of character, which remained strong in him to the end, showed themselves very early. At the college or public school of Geneva, and at the academie, he would seem to have done only moderately as far as prizes and honors were concerned. We are told, however, that he read enormously, and that he was, generally speaking, inclined rather to make friends with men older than himself than with his contemporaries. He fell specially under the influence of Adolphe Pictet, a brilliant philologist and man of letters belonging to a well-known Genevese family, and in later life he was able, while reviewing one of M. Pictet's books, to give grateful expression to his sense of obligation.

Writing in 1856 he describes the effect produced in Geneva by M. Pictet's Lectures on Aesthetics in 1840—the first ever delivered in a town in which the Beautiful had been for centuries regarded as the rival and enemy of the True. "He who is now writing," says Amiel, "was then among M. Pictet's youngest hearers. Since then twenty experiences of the same kind have followed each other in his intellectual experience, yet none has effaced the deep impression made upon him by these lectures. Coming as they did at a favorable moment, and answering many a positive question and many a vague aspiration of youth, they exercised a decisive influence over his thought; they were to him an important step in that continuous initiation which we call life, they filled him with fresh intuitions, they brought near to him the horizons of his dreams. And, as always happens with a first-rate man, what struck him even more than the teaching was the teacher. So that this memory of 1840 is still dear and precious to him, and for this double service, which is not of the kind one forgets, the student of those days delights in expressing to the professor of 1840 his sincere and filial gratitude."

Amiel's first literary production, or practically his first, seems to have been the result partly of these lectures, and partly of a visit to Italy which began in November, 1841. In 1842, a year which was spent entirely in Italy and Sicily, he contributed three articles on M. Rio's book, "L'Art Chretien," to the *Bibliotheque Universelle de Geneve*. We see in them the young student conscientiously writing his first review—writing it at inordinate length, as young reviewers are apt to do, and treating the subject *ab ovo* in a grave, pontifical way, which is a little naive and inexperienced indeed, but still promising, as all seriousness of work and purpose is promising. All that is individual in it is first of all the strong Christian feeling which much of it shows, and secondly, the tone of melancholy which already makes itself felt here and there, especially in one rather remarkable passage. As to the Christian feeling, we find M. Rio described as belonging to "that noble school of men who are striving to rekindle the dead beliefs of France, to rescue Frenchmen from the camp of materialistic or pantheistic ideas, and rally them round that Christian banner which is the banner of true progress and true civilization." The Renaissance is treated as a disastrous but inevitable crisis, in which the idealism of the Middle Ages was dethroned by the naturalism of modern times—"The Renaissance perhaps robbed us of more than it gave us"—and so on. The tone of criticism is instructive enough to the student of Amiel's mind, but the product itself has no particular savor of its own. The occasional note of depression and discouragement, however, is a different thing; here, for those who know the "Journal Intime," there is already something characteristic, something which foretells the future. For instance, after dwelling with evident zest on the nature of the metaphysical problems lying at the root of art in general, and Christian art in particular, the writer goes on to set the difficulty of M. Rio's task against its attractiveness, to insist on the intricacy of the investigations involved, and on the impossibility of making the two instruments on which their success depends—the imaginative and the analytical faculty—work harmoniously and effectively together. And supposing the goal achieved, supposing a man by insight and patience has succeeded in forcing his way farther than any previous explorer into the recesses of the Beautiful or the True, there still remains the enormous, the insuperable difficulty of expression, of fit and adequate communication from mind to mind; there still remains the question whether, after all, "he who discovers a new world in the depths of the invisible would not do wisely to plant on it a flag known to himself alone, and, like Achilles, 'devour his heart in secret;' whether the greatest problems which have ever been guessed on earth had not better have remained buried in the brain which had found the key to them, and whether the deepest thinkers—those whose hand has been boldest in drawing aside the veil, and their eye keenest in fathoming the mysteries beyond it—had not better, like the prophetess of Ilion, have kept for heaven, and heaven only, secrets and mysteries which human tongue cannot truly express, nor human intelligence conceive."

Curious words for a beginner of twenty-one! There is a touch, no doubt, of youth and fatuity in the passage; one feels how much the vague sonorous phrases have pleased the writer's immature literary sense; but there is something else too—there is a breath of that same speculative passion which burns in the Journal, and one hears, as it were, the first accents of a melancholy, the first expression of a mood of mind, which became in after years the fixed characteristic of the writer. "At twenty he was already proud, timid, and melancholy," writes an old friend; and a little farther on, "Discouragement took possession of him *very early.*"

However, in spite of this inbred tendency, which was probably hereditary and inevitable, the years which followed these articles, from 1842 to Christmas, 1848, were years of happiness and steady intellectual expansion. They were Amiel's *Wanderjahre*, spent in a free, wandering student life, which left deep marks on his intellectual development. During four years, from 1844 to 1848, his headquarters were at Berlin; but every vacation saw him exploring some new country or fresh intellectual center—Scandinavia in 1845, Holland in 1846, Vienna, Munich, and Tuebingen in 1848, while Paris had already attracted him in 1841, and he was to make acquaintance with London ten years later, in 1851. No circumstances could have been more favorable, one would have thought, to the development of such a nature. With his extraordinary power of "throwing himself into the object"—of effacing himself and his own personality in the presence of the thing to be understood and absorbed—he must have passed these years of travel and acquisition in a state of continuous intellectual energy and excitement. It is in no spirit of conceit that he says in 1857, comparing himself with Maine de Biran, "This nature is, as it were, only one of the men which exist in me. My horizon is vaster; I have seen much more of men, things, countries, peoples, books; I have a greater mass of experiences." This fact, indeed, of a wide and varied personal experience, must never be forgotten in any critical estimate of Amiel as a man or writer. We may so easily conceive him as a sedentary professor, with the ordinary professorial knowledge, or rather ignorance, of men and the world, falling into introspection under the pressure of circumstance, and for want, as it were, of something else to think about. Not at all. The man who has left us these microscopic analyses of his own moods and feelings, had penetrated more or less into the social and intellectual life of half a dozen European countries, and was familiar not only with the books, but, to a large extent also, with the men of his generation. The meditative and introspective gift was in him, not the product, but the mistress of circumstance. It took from the outer world what that world had to give, and then made the stuff so gained subservient to its own ends.

Of these years of travel, however, the four years spent at Berlin were by far the most important. "It was at Heidelberg and Berlin," says M. Scherer, "that the world of science and speculation first opened on the dazzled eyes of the young man. He was accustomed to speak of his four years at Berlin as 'his intellectual phase,' and one felt that he inclined to regard them as the happiest period of his life. The spell which Berlin laid upon him lasted long." Probably his happiness in Germany was partly owing to a sense of reaction against Geneva. There are signs that he had felt himself somewhat isolated at school and college, and that in the German world his special individuality, with its dreaminess and its melancholy, found congenial surroundings far more readily than had been the case in the drier and harsher atmosphere of the Protestant Rome. However this may be, it is certain that German thought took possession of him, that he became steeped not only in German methods of speculation, but in German modes of expression, in German forms of sentiment, which clung to him through life, and vitally affected both his opinions and his style. M. Renan and M. Bourget shake their heads over the Germanisms, which, according to the latter, give a certain "barbarous" air to many passages of the Journal. But both admit that Amiel's individuality owes a great part of its penetrating force to that intermingling of German with French elements, of which there are such abundant traces in the "Journal Intime." Amiel, in fact, is one more typical product of a movement which is certainly of enormous importance in the history of modern thought, even though we may not be prepared to assent to all the sweeping terms in which a writer like M. Taine describes it. "From 1780 to 1830," says M. Taine, "Germany produced all the ideas of our historical age, and during another half-century, perhaps another century, *notre grande affaire sera de les repenser*." He is inclined to compare the influence of German ideas on the modern world to the ferment of the Renaissance. No spiritual force "more original, more universal, more fruitful in consequences of every sort and bearing, more capable of transforming and remaking everything presented to it, has arisen during the last three hundred years. Like the spirit of the Renaissance and of the classical age, it attracts into its orbit all the great works of contemporary intelligence." Quinet, pursuing a somewhat different line of thought, regards the worship of German ideas inaugurated in France by Madame de Stael as the natural result of reaction from the eighteenth century and all its ways. "German systems, German hypotheses, beliefs, and poetry, all were eagerly welcomed as a cure for hearts crushed by the mockery of Candide and the materialism of the Revolution.... Under the Restoration France continued to study German philosophy and poetry with profound veneration and submission. We imitated, translated, compiled, and then again we compiled, translated, imitated." The importance of the part played by German influence in French Romanticism has indeed been much disputed, but the debt of French metaphysics, French philology, and French historical study, to German methods and German research during the last half-century is beyond dispute. And the movement to-day is as strong as ever. A modern critic like M. Darmstetter regards it as a misfortune that the artificial stimulus given by the war to the study of German has, to some extent, checked the study of English in France. He thinks that the French have more to gain from our literature—taking literature in its general and popular sense—than from German literature. But he raises no question as to the inevitable subjection of the French to the German mind in matters of exact thought and knowledge. "To study philology, mythology, history, without reading German," he is as ready to confess as any one else, "is to condemn one's self to remain in every department twenty years behind the progress of science."

Of this great movement, already so productive, Amiel is then a fresh and remarkable instance. Having caught from the Germans not only their love of exact knowledge but also their love of vast horizons, their insatiable curiosity as to the whence and whither of all things, their sense of mystery and immensity in the universe, he then brings those elements in him which belong to his French inheritance—and something individual besides, which is not French but Genevese—to bear on his new acquisitions, and the result is of the highest literary interest and value. Not that he succeeds altogether in the task of fusion. For one who was to write and think in French, he was perhaps too long in Germany; he had drunk too deeply of German thought; he had been too much dazzled by the spectacle of Berlin and its imposing intellectual activities. "As to his *literary* talent," says M. Scherer, after dwelling on the rapid growth of his intellectual powers under German influence, "the profit which Amiel derived from his stay at Berlin is more doubtful. Too long contact with the

German mind had led to the development in him of certain strangenesses of style which he had afterward to get rid of, and even perhaps of some habits of thought which he afterward felt the need of checking and correcting." This is very true. Amiel is no doubt often guilty, as M. Caro puts it, of attempts "to write German in French," and there are in his thought itself veins of mysticism, elements of *Schwaermerei*, here and there, of which a good deal must be laid to the account of his German training.

M. Renan regrets that after Geneva and after Berlin he never came to Paris. Paris, he thinks, would have counteracted the Hegelian influences brought to hear upon him at Berlin, [Footnote: See a not, however, on the subject of Amiel's philosophical relationships, printed as an Appendix to the present volume.] would have taught him cheerfulness, and taught him also the art of writing, not beautiful fragments, but a book. Possibly—but how much we should have lost! Instead of the Amiel we know, we should have had one accomplished French critic the more. Instead of the spiritual drama of the "Journal Intime," some further additions to French *belles lettres*; instead of something to love, something to admire! No, there is no wishing the German element in Amiel away. Its invading, troubling effect upon his thought and temperament goes far to explain the interest and suggestiveness of his mental history. The language he speaks is the language of that French criticism which— we have Sainte-Beuve's authority for it—is best described by the motto of Montaigne, "*Un peu de chaque chose et rien de l'ensemble, a la francaise*," and the thought he tries to express in it is thought torn and strained by the constant effort to reach the All, the totality of things: "What I desire is the sum of all desires, and what I seek to know is the sum of all different kinds of knowledge. Always the complete, the absolute, the *teres atque rotundum*." And it was this antagonism, or rather this fusion of traditions in him, which went far to make him original, which opened to him, that is to say, so many new lights on old paths, and stirred in him such capacities of fresh and individual expression.

We have been carried forward, however, a little too far by this general discussion of Amiel's debts to Germany. Let us take up the biographical thread again. In 1848 his Berlin apprenticeship came to an end, and he returned to Geneva. "How many places, how many impressions, observations, thoughts—how many forms of men and things—have passed before me and in me since April, 1843," he writes in the Journal, two or three months after his return. "The last seven years have been the most important of my life; they have been the novitiate of my intelligence, the initiation of my being into being." The first literary evidence of his matured powers is to be found in two extremely interesting papers on Berlin, which he contributed to the *Bibliotheque Universelle* in 1848, apparently just before he left Germany. Here for the first time we have the Amiel of the "Journal Intime." The young man who five years before had written his painstaking review of M. Rio is now in his turn a master. He speaks with dignity and authority, he has a graphic, vigorous prose at command, the form of expression is condensed and epigrammatic, and there is a mixture of enthusiasm and criticism in his description of the powerful intellectual machine then working in the Prussian capital which represents a permanent note of character, a lasting attitude of mind. A great deal, of course, in the two papers is technical and statistic, but what there is of general comment and criticism is so good that one is tempted to make some melancholy comparisons between them and another article in the *Bibliotheque*, that on Adolphe Pictet, written in 1856, and from which we have already quoted. In 1848 Amiel was for awhile master of his powers and his knowledge; no fatal divorce had yet taken place in him between the accumulating and producing faculties; he writes readily even for the public, without labor, without affectations. Eight years later the reflective faculty has outgrown his control; composition, which represents the practical side of the intellectual life, has become difficult and painful to him, and he has developed what he himself calls "a wavering manner, born of doubt and scruple."

How few could have foreseen the failure in public and practical life which lay before him at the moment of his reappearance at Geneva in 1848! "My first meeting with him in 1849 is still vividly present to me," says M. Scherer. "He was twenty-eight, and he had just come from Germany laden with science, but he wore his knowledge lightly, his looks were attractive, his conversation animated, and no affectation spoiled the favorable impression he made on the bystander—the whole effect, indeed, was of something brilliant and striking. In his young alertness Amiel seemed to be entering upon life as a conqueror; one would have said the future was all his own."

His return, moreover, was marked by a success which seemed to secure him at once an important position in his native town. After a public competition he was appointed, in 1849, professor of esthetics and French literature at the Academy of Geneva, a post which he held for four years, exchanging it for the professorship of moral philosophy in 1854. Thus at twenty-eight, without any struggle to succeed, he had gained, it would have seemed, that safe foothold in life which should be all the philosopher or the critic wants to secure the full and fruitful development of his gifts. Unfortunately the appointment, instead of the foundation and support, was to be the stumbling block of his career. Geneva at the time was in a state of social and political ferment. After a long struggle, beginning with the revolutionary outbreak of November, 1841, the Radical party, led by James Fazy, had succeeded in ousting the Conservatives—that is to say, the governing class, which had ruled the republic since the Restoration—from power. And with the advent of the democratic constitution of 1846, and the exclusion of the old Genevese families from the administration they had so long monopolized, a number of subsidiary changes were effected, not less important to the ultimate success of Radicalism than the change in political machinery introduced by the new constitution. Among them was the disappearance of almost the whole existing staff of the academy, then and now the center of Genevese education, and up to 1847 the stronghold of the moderate ideas of 1814, followed by the appointment of new men less likely to hamper the Radical order of things.

Of these new men Amiel was one. He had been absent from Geneva during the years of conflict which had preceded Fazy's triumph; he seems to have had no family or party connections with the leaders of the defeated side, and as M. Scherer points out, he could accept a non-political post at the hands of the new government, two years after the violent measures which had marked its accession, without breaking any pledges or sacrificing any convictions. But none the less the step was a fatal one. M. Renan is so far in the right. If any timely friend had at that moment succeeded in tempting Amiel to Paris, as Guizot tempted Rossi in 1833, there can be little question that the young professor's after life would have been happier and saner. As it was, Amiel threw himself into the competition for the chair, was appointed professor, and then found himself in a hopelessly false position, placed on the threshold of life, in relations and surroundings for which he was radically unfitted, and cut off by no fault of his own from the *milieu* to which he rightly belonged, and in which his sensitive individuality might have expanded normally and freely. For the defeated upper class very naturally shut their doors on the nominees of the new *regime*, and as this class represented at that moment almost everything that was intellectually distinguished in Geneva, as it was the guardian, broadly speaking, of the scientific and literary traditions of the little state, we can easily imagine how galling such a social ostracism must have been to the young professor, accustomed to the stimulating atmosphere, the common intellectual interests of Berlin, and tormented with perhaps more than the ordinary craving of youth for sympathy and for affection. In a great city, containing within it a number of different circles of life, Amiel would easily have found his own circle, nor could political discords have affected his social comfort to anything like the same extent. But in a town not much larger than Oxford, and in which the cultured class had hitherto formed a more or less homogeneous and united whole, it was almost impossible for Amiel to escape from his grievance and establish a sufficient barrier of friendly interests between himself and the society which ignored him. There can be no doubt that he suffered, both in mind and character, from the struggle the position involved. He had no natural sympathy with radicalism. His taste, which was extremely fastidious, his judgment, his passionate respect for truth, were all offended by the noise, the narrowness, the dogmatism of the triumphant democracy. So that there was no making up on the one side for what he had lost on the other, and he proudly resigned himself to an isolation and a reserve which, reinforcing, as they did, certain native weaknesses of character, had the most unfortunate effect upon his life.

In a passage of the Journal written nearly thirty years after his election he allows himself a few pathetic words, half of accusation, half of self-reproach, which make us realize how deeply this untowardness of social circumstance had affected him. He is discussing one of Madame de Stael's favorite words, the word *consideration*. "What is *consideration*?" he asks. "How does a man obtain it? how does it differ from fame, esteem, admiration?" And then he turns upon himself. "It is curious, but the idea of consideration has been to me so little of a motive that I have not even been conscious of such an idea. But ought I not to have been conscious of it?" he asks himself anxiously—"ought I not to have been more careful to win the good opinion of others, more determined to conquer their hostility or indifference? It would have been a joy to me to be smiled upon, loved, encouraged, welcomed, and to obtain what I was so ready to give, kindness and goodwill. But to hunt down consideration and reputation —to force the esteem of others—seemed to me an effort unworthy of myself, almost a degradation. A struggle with unfavorable opinion has seemed to me beneath me, for all the while my heart has been full of sadness and disappointment, and I have known and felt that I have been systematically and deliberately isolated. Untimely despair and the deepest discouragement have been my constant portion. Incapable of taking any interest in my talents for their own sake, I let everything slip as soon as the hope of being loved for them and by them had forsaken me. A hermit against my will, I have not even found peace in solitude, because my inmost conscience has not been any better satisfied than my heart."

Still one may no doubt easily exaggerate this loneliness of Amiel's. His social difficulties represent rather a dull discomfort in his life, which in course of time, and in combination with a good many other causes, produced certain unfavorable results on his temperament and on his public career, than anything very tragic and acute. They were real, and he, being what he was, was specially unfitted to cope with and conquer them. But he had his friends, his pleasures, and even to some extent his successes, like other men. "He had an elasticity of mind," says M. Scherer, speaking of him as he knew him in youth, "which reacted against vexations from without, and his cheerfulness was readily restored by conversation and the society of a few kindred spirits. We were accustomed, two or three friends and I, to walk every Thursday to the Saleve, Lamartine's *Saleve aux flancs azures*; we dined there, and did not return till nightfall." They were days devoted to *debauches platoniciennes*, to "the free exchange of ideas, the free play of fancy and of gayety. Amiel was not one of the original members of these Thursday parties; but whenever he joined us we regarded it as a fete-day. In serious discussion he was a master of the unexpected, and his energy, his *entrain*, affected us all. If his grammatical questions, his discussions of rhymes and synonyms, astonished us at times, how often, on the other hand, did he not give us cause to admire the variety of his knowledge, the precision of his ideas, the charm of his quick intelligence! We found him always, besides, kindly and amiable, a nature one might trust and lean upon with perfect security. He awakened in us but one regret; *we could not understand how it was a man so richly gifted produced nothing, or only trivialities.*"

In these last words of M. Scherer's we have come across the determining fact of Amiel's life in its relation to the outer world— that "sterility of genius," of which he was the victim. For social ostracism and political anxiety would have mattered to him comparatively little if he could but have lost himself in the fruitful activities of thought, in the struggles and the victories of composition and creation. A German professor of Amiel's knowledge would have wanted nothing beyond his *Fach*, and nine men out of ten in his circumstances would have made themselves the slave of a *magnum opus*, and forgotten the vexations of everyday life in the "*douces joies de la science.*" But there were certain characteristics in Amiel which made it impossible—which neutralized his powers, his knowledge, his intelligence, and condemned him, so far as his public performance was concerned, to barrenness and failure. What were these characteristics, this element of unsoundness and disease, which M. Caro calls "*la maladie de l'idéal?*"

Before we can answer the question we must go back a little and try to realize the intellectual and moral equipment of the young man of twenty-eight, who seemed to M. Scherer to have the world at his feet. What were the chief qualities of mind and heart which Amiel brought back with him from Berlin? In the first place, an omnivorous desire to know: "Amiel," says M. Scherer, "read everything." In the second, an extraordinary power of sustained and concentrated thought, and a passionate, almost a religious, delight in the exercise of his power. Knowledge, science, stirred in him no mere sense of curiosity or cold critical instinct—"he came to his desk as to an altar." "A friend who knew him well," says M. Scherer, "remembers having heard him speak with deep emotion of that lofty serenity of mood which he had experienced during his years in Germany whenever, in the early morning before dawn, with his reading-lamp beside him, he had found himself penetrating once more into the region of pure thought, 'conversing with ideas, enjoying the inmost life of things.'" "Thought," he says somewhere in the Journal, "is like opium. It can intoxicate us and yet leave us broad awake." To this intoxication of thought he seems to have been always specially liable, and his German experience—unbalanced, as such an experience generally is with a young man, by family life, or by any healthy commonplace interests and pleasures—developed the intellectual passion in him to an abnormal degree. For four years he had devoted himself to the alternate excitement and satisfaction of this passion. He had read enormously, thought enormously, and in the absence of any imperative claim on the practical side of him, the accumulative, reflective faculties had grown out of all proportion to the rest of the personality. Nor had any special subject the power to fix him. Had he been in France, what Sainte-Beuve calls the French "*imagination de detail*" would probably have attracted his pliant, responsive nature, and he would have found happy occupation in some one of the innumerable departments of research on which the French have been patiently spending their analytical gift since that general widening of horizons which accompanied and gave value to the Romantic movement. But instead he was at Berlin, in the center of that speculative ferment which followed the death of Hegel and the break-up of the Hegelian idea into a number of different and conflicting sections of philosophical opinion. He was under the spell of German synthesis, of that traditional, involuntary effort which the German mind makes, generation after generation, to find the unity of experience, to range its accumulations from life and thought under a more and more perfect, a more and more exhaustive, formula. Not this study or that study, not this detail or that, but the whole of things, the sum of Knowledge, the Infinite, the Absolute, alone had value or reality. In his own words: "There is no repose for the mind except in the absolute; for feeling except in the infinite; for the soul except in the divine. Nothing finite is true, is interesting, is worthy to fix my attention. All that is particular is exclusive, and all that is exclusive repels me. There is nothing non-exclusive but the All; my end is communion with Being through the whole of Being."

It was not, indeed, that he neglected the study of detail; he had a strong natural aptitude for it, and his knowledge was wide and real; but detail was ultimately valuable to him, not in itself, but as food for a speculative hunger, for which, after all, there is no real satisfaction. All the pleasant paths which traverse the kingdom of Knowledge, in which so many of us find shelter and life-long means of happiness, led Amiel straight into the wilderness of abstract speculation. And the longer he lingered in the wilderness, unchecked by any sense of intellectual responsibility, and far from the sounds of human life, the stranger and the weirder grew the hallucinations of thought. The Journal gives marvelous expression to them: "I can find no words for what I feel. My consciousness is withdrawn into itself; I hear my heart beating, and my life passing. It seems to me that I have become a statue on the banks of the river of time, that I am the spectator of some mystery, and shall issue from it old, or no longer capable of age." Or again: "I am a spectator, so to speak, of the molecular whirlwind which men call individual life; I am conscious of an incessant metamorphosis, an irresistible movement of existence, which is going on within me—and this phenomenology of myself serves as a window opened upon the mystery of the world. I am, or rather my sensible consciousness is, concentrated upon this ideal standing-point, this invisible threshold, as it were, whence one hears the impetuous passage of time, rushing and foaming as it flows out into the changeless ocean of eternity.

After all the bewildering distractions of life—after having drowned myself in a multiplicity of trifles and in the caprices of this fugitive existence, yet without ever attaining to self-intoxication or self-delusion—I come again upon the fathomless abyss, the silent and melancholy cavern, where dwell 'Die Muetter,' where sleeps that which neither lives nor dies, which has neither movement nor change, nor extension, nor form, and which lasts when all else passes away."

Wonderful sentences! "*Prodiges de la pensee speculative, decrits dans une langue non moins prodigieuse,*" as M. Scherer says of the innumerable passages which describe either this intoxication of the infinite, or the various forms and consequences of that deadening of personality which the abstract processes of thought tend to produce. But it is easy to understand that a man in whom experiences of this kind become habitual is likely to lose his hold upon the normal interests of life. What are politics or literature to such a mind but fragments without real importance—dwarfed reflections of ideal truths for which neither language nor institutions provide any adequate expression! How is it possible to take seriously what is so manifestly relative and temporary as the various existing forms of human activity? Above all, how is it possible to take one's self seriously, to spend one's thought on the petty interests of a petty individuality, when the beatific vision of universal knowledge, of absolute being, has once dawned on the dazzled beholder? The charm and the savor of everything relative and phenomenal is gone. A man may go on talking, teaching, writing—but the spring of personal action is broken; his actions are like the actions of a somnambulist.

No doubt to some extent this mood is familiar to all minds endowed with the true speculative genius. The philosopher has always tended to become unfit for practical life; his unfitness, indeed, is one of the comic motives, so to speak, of literature. But a mood which, in the great majority of thinkers, is intermittent, and is easily kept within bounds by the practical needs, the mere physical instincts of life, was in Amiel almost constant, and the natural impulse of the human animal toward healthy movement and a normal play of function, never very strong in him, was gradually weakened and destroyed by an untoward combination of circumstances. The low health from which he suffered more or less from his boyhood, and then the depressing influences of the social difficulties we have described, made it more and more difficult for the rest of the organism to react against the tyranny of the brain. And as the normal human motives lost their force, what he calls "the Buddhist tendency in me" gathered strength year by year, until, like some strange misgrowth, it had absorbed the whole energies and drained the innermost life-blood of the personality which had developed it. And the result is another soul's tragedy, another story of conflict and failure, which throws fresh light on the mysterious capacities of human nature, and warns us, as the letters of Obermann in their day warned the generation of George Sand, that with the rise of new intellectual perceptions new spiritual dangers come into being, and that across the path of continuous evolution which the modern mind is traversing there lies many a *selva oscura*, many a lonely and desolate tract, in which loss and pain await it. The story of the "Journal Intime" is a story to make us think, to make us anxious; but at the same time, in the case of a nature like Amiel's, there is so much high poetry thrown off from the long process of conflict, the power of vision and of reproduction which the intellect gains at the expense of the rest of the personality is in many respects so real and so splendid, and produces results so stirring often to the heart and imagination of the listener, that in the end we put down the record not so much with a throb of pity as with an impulse of gratitude. The individual error and suffering is almost forgotten; all that we can realize is the enrichment of human feeling, the quickened sense of spiritual reality bequeathed to us by the baffled and solitary thinker whose *via dolorosa* is before us.

The manner in which this intellectual idiosyncrasy we have been describing gradually affected Amiel's life supplies abundant proof of its actuality and sincerity. It is a pitiful story. Amiel might have been saved from despair by love and marriage, by paternity, by strenuous and successful literary production; and this mental habit of his—this tyranny of ideal conceptions, helped by the natural accompaniment of such a tyranny, a critical sense of abnormal acuteness—stood between him and everything healing and restoring. "I am afraid of an imperfect, a faulty synthesis, and I linger in the provisional, from timidity and from loyalty." "As soon as a thing attracts me I turn away from it; or rather, I cannot either be content with the second-best, or discover anything which satisfies my aspiration. The real disgusts me, and I cannot find the ideal." And so one thing after another is put away. Family life attracted him perpetually. "I cannot escape," he writes, "from the ideal of it. A companion, of my life, of my work, of my thoughts, of my hopes; within a common worship—toward the world outside kindness and beneficence; education to undertake; the thousand and one moral relations which develop round the first—all these ideas intoxicate me sometimes." But in vain. "Reality, the present, the irreparable, the necessary, repel and even terrify me. I have too much imagination, conscience, and penetration and not enough character. *The life of thought alone seems to me to have enough elasticity and immensity, to be free enough from the irreparable; practical life makes me afraid.* I am distrustful of myself and of happiness because I know myself. The ideal poisons for me all imperfect possession. And I abhor useless regrets and repentance."

It is the same, at bottom, with his professional work. He protects the intellectual freedom, as it were, of his students with the same jealousy as he protects his own. There shall be no oratorical device, no persuading, no cajoling of the mind this way or that. "A professor is the priest of his subject, and should do the honors of it gravely and with dignity." And so the man who in his private Journal is master of an eloquence and a poetry, capable of illuminating the most difficult and abstract of subjects, becomes in the lecture-room a dry compendium of universal knowledge. "Led by his passion for the whole," says M. Scherer, "Amiel offered his hearers, not so much a series of positive teachings, as an index of subjects, a framework—what the Germans call a *Schematismus*. The skeleton was admirably put together, and excellent of its kind, and lent itself admirably to a certain kind of analysis and demonstration; but it was a skeleton—flesh, body, and life were wanting."

So that as a professor he made no mark. He was conscientiousness itself in whatever he conceived to be his duty. But with all the critical and philosophical power which, as we know from the Journal, he might have lavished on his teaching, had the conditions been other than they were, the study of literature, and the study of philosophy as such, owe him nothing. But for the Journal his years of training and his years of teaching would have left equally little record behind them. "His pupils at Geneva," writes one who was himself among the number, [Footnote: M. Alphonse Rivier, now Professor of International Law at the University of Brussels.] "never learned to appreciate him at his true worth. We did justice no doubt to a knowledge as varied as it was wide, to his vast stores of reading, to that cosmopolitanism of the best kind which he had brought back with him from his travels; we liked him for his indulgence, his kindly wit. But I look back without any sense of pleasure to his lectures."

Many a student, however, has shrunk from the burden and risks of family life, and has found himself incapable of teaching effectively what he knows, and has yet redeemed all other incapacities in the field of literary production. And here indeed we come to the strangest feature in Amiel's career—his literary sterility. That he possessed literary power of the highest order is abundantly proved by the "Journal Intime." Knowledge, insight, eloquence, critical power—all were his. And the impulse to produce, which is the natural, though by no means the invariable, accompaniment of the literary gift, must have been fairly strong in him also. For the "Journal Intime" runs to 17,000 folio pages of MS., and his half dozen volumes of poems, though the actual quantity is not large, represent an amount of labor which would have more than carried him through some serious piece of critical or philosophical work, and so enabled him to content the just expectations of his world. He began to write early, as is proved by the fact that at twenty he was a contributor to the best literary periodical which Geneva possessed. He was a charming correspondent, and in spite of his passion for abstract thought, his intellectual interest, at any rate, in all the activities of the day—politics, religious organizations, literature, art—was of the keenest kind. And yet at the time of his death all that this fine critic and profound thinker had given to the world, after a life entirely spent in the pursuit of letters, was, in the first place, a few volumes of poems which had had no effect except on a small number of sympathetic friends; a few pages of *pensees* intermingled with the poems, and, as we now know, extracted from the Journal; and four or five scattered essays, the length of magazine articles, on Mme. de Stael, Rousseau, the history of the Academy of Geneva, the literature of French-speaking Switzerland, and so on! And more than this, the production, such as it was, had been a production born of effort and difficulty; and the labor squandered on poetical forms, on metrical experiments and intricate problems of translation, as well as the occasional affectations of the prose style, might well have convinced the critical bystander that the mind of which these things were the offspring could have no real importance, no profitable message, for the world.

The whole "Journal Intime" is in some sense Amiel's explanation of these facts. In it he has made full and bitter confession of his weakness, his failure; he has endeavored, with an acuteness of analysis no other hand can rival, to make the reasons of his failure and isolation clear both to himself and others. "To love, to dream, to feel, to learn, to understand—all these are possible to me if only I may be dispensed from willing—I have a sort of primitive horror of ambition, of struggle, of hatred, of all which dissipates the soul and makes it dependent on external things and aims. The joy of becoming once more conscious of myself, of listening to the passage of time and the flow of the universal life, is sometimes enough to make me forget every desire and to quench in me both the wish to produce and the power to execute." It is the result of what he himself calls *"l'eblouissement de l'infini."* He no sooner makes a step toward production, toward action and the realization of himself, than a vague sense of peril overtakes him. The inner life, with its boundless horizons and its indescribable exaltations, seems endangered. Is he not about to place between himself and the forms of speculative truth some barrier of sense and matter—to give up the real for the apparent, the substance for the shadow? One is reminded of Clough's cry under a somewhat similar experience:

"If this pure solace should desert my mind, What were all else? I dare not risk the loss. To the old paths, my soul!"

And in close combination with the speculative sense, with the tendency which carries a man toward the contemplative study of life and nature as a whole, is the critical sense—the tendency which, in the realm of action and concrete performance, carries him, as Amiel expresses it, *"droit au defaut,"* and makes him conscious at once of the weak point, the germ of failure in a project or an action. It is another aspect of the same idiosyncrasy. "The point I have reached seems to be explained by a too restless search for perfection, by the abuse of the critical faculty, and by an unreasonable distrust of first impulses, first thoughts, first words. Confidence and spontaneity of life are drifting out of my reach, and this is why I can no longer act." For abuse of the critical faculty brings with it its natural consequences— timidity of soul, paralysis of the will, complete self-distrust. "To know is enough for me; expression seems to me often a profanity. What I lack is character, will, individuality." "By what mystery," he writes to M. Scherer, "do others expect much from me? whereas I feel myself to be incapable of anything serious or important." *Defiance* and *impuissance* are the words constantly on his lips. "My friends see what I might have been; I see what I am."

And yet the literary instinct remains, and must in some way be satisfied. And so he takes refuge in what he himself calls scales, exercises, *tours de force* in verse-translation of the most laborious and difficult kind, in ingenious *vers d'occasion*, in metrical experiments and other literary trifling, as his friends think it, of the same sort. "I am afraid of greatness. I am not afraid of ingenuity; all my published literary essays are little else than studies, games, exercises, for the purpose of testing myself. I play scales, as it were; I run up and down my instrument. I train my hand and make sure of its capacity and skill. But the work itself remains unachieved. I am always preparing and never accomplishing, and my energy is swallowed up in a kind of barren curiosity."

Not that he surrenders himself to the nature which is stronger than he all at once. His sense of duty rebels, his conscience suffers, and he makes resolution after resolution to shake himself free from the mental tradition which had taken such hold upon him—to write, to produce, to satisfy his friends. In 1861, a year after M. Scherer had left Geneva, Amiel wrote to him, describing his difficulties and his discouragements, and asking, as one may ask an old friend of one's youth, for help and counsel. M. Scherer, much touched by the appeal, answered it plainly and frankly—described the feeling of those who knew him as they watched his life slipping away unmarked by any of the achievements of which his youth had given promise, and pointed out various literary openings in which, if he were to put out his powers, he could not but succeed. To begin with, he urged him to join the *Revue Germanique,* then being started by Charles Dollfus, Renan, Littre, and others. Amiel left the letter for three months unanswered and then wrote a reply which M. Scherer probably received with a sigh of impatience. For, rightly interpreted, it meant that old habits were too strong, and that the momentary impulse had died away. When, a little later, "Les Etrangeres," a collection of verse-translations, came out, it was dedicated to M. Scherer, who did not, however, pretend to give it any very cordial reception. Amiel took his friend's coolness in very good part, calling him his "dear Rhadamanthus." "How little I knew!" cries M. Scherer. "What I regret is to have discovered too late by means of the Journal, the key to a problem which seemed to me hardly serious, and which I now feel to have been tragic. A kind of remorse seizes me that I was not able to understand my friend better, and to soothe his suffering by a sympathy which would have been a mixture of pity and admiration."

Was it that all the while Amiel felt himself sure of his *revanche* that he knew the value of all those sheets of Journal which were slowly accumulating under his hand? Did he say to himself sometimes: "My friends are wrong; my gifts and my knowledge are not lost; I have given expression to them in the only way possible to me, and when I die it will be found that I too, like other men, have performed the task appointed me, and contributed my quota to the human store?" It is clear that very early he began to regard it as possible that portions of the Journal should be published after his death, and, as we have seen, he left certain "literary instructions," dated seven years before his last illness, in which his executors were directed to publish such parts of it as might seem to them to possess any general interest. But it is clear also that the Journal was not, in any sense, written for publication. "These pages," say the Geneva editors, "written *au courant de la plume*—sometimes in the morning, but more often at the end of the day, without any idea of composition or publicity—are marked by the repetition, the *lacunae*, the carelessness, inherent in this kind of monologue. The thoughts and sentiments expressed have no other aim than sincerity of rendering."

And his estimate of the value of the record thus produced was, in general, a low one, especially during the depression and discouragement of his later years. "This Journal of mine," he writes in 1876, "represents the material of a good many volumes; what prodigious waste of time, of thought, of strength! It will be useful to nobody, and even for myself—it has rather helped me to shirk life than to practice it." And again: "Is everything I have produced, taken together—my correspondence, these thousands of Journal pages, my lectures, my articles, my poems, my notes of different kinds—anything better than withered leaves? To whom and to what have I been useful? Will my name survive me a single day, and will it ever mean anything to anybody? A life of no account! When all is added up—nothing!" In passages like these there is no anticipation of any posthumous triumph over the disapproval of his friends and the criticism of his fellow-citizens. The Journal was a relief, the means of satisfying a need of expression which otherwise could find no outlet; "a grief-cheating device," but nothing more. It did not still the sense of remorse for wasted gifts and opportunities which followed poor Amiel through the painful months of his last illness. Like Keats, he passed away, feeling that all was over, and the great game of life lost forever.

It still remains for us to gather up a few facts and impressions of a different kind from those which we have been dwelling on, which may serve to complete and correct the picture we have so far drawn of the author of the Journal. For Amiel is full of contradictions and surprises, which, are indeed one great source of his attractiveness.

Had he only been the thinker, the critic, the idealist we have been describing, he would never have touched our feeling as he now does; what makes him so interesting is that there was in him a *fond* of heredity, a temperament and disposition, which were perpetually reacting against the oppression of the intellect and its accumulations. In his hours of intellectual concentration he freed himself from all trammels of country or society, or even, as he insists, from all sense of personality. But at other times he was the dutiful son of a country which he loved, taking a warm interest in everything Genevese, especially in everything that represented the older life of the town. When it was a question of separating the Genevese state from the church, which had been the center of the national life during three centuries of honorable history, Amiel the philosopher, the cosmopolitan, threw himself ardently on to the side of the opponents of separation, and rejoiced in their victory. A large proportion of his poems deal with national subjects. He was one of the first members of "L'Institut Genevois," founded in 1853, and he took a warm interest in the movement started by M. Eugene Rambert toward 1870, for the improvement of secondary education throughout French-speaking Switzerland. One of his friends dwells with emphasis on his "*sens profond des nationalites, des langues, des villes*"—on his love for local characteristics, for everything deep-rooted in the past, and helping to sustain the present. He is convinced that no state can live and thrive without a certain number of national prejudices, without *a priori* beliefs and traditions. It pleases him to see that there is a force in the Genevese nationality which resists the leveling influences of a crude radicalism; it rejoices him that Geneva "has not yet become a mere copy of anything, and that she is still capable of deciding for herself. Those who say to her, 'Do as they do at New York, at Paris, at Rome, at Berlin,' are still in the minority. The *doctrinaires* who would split her up and destroy her unity waste their breath upon her. She divines the snare laid for her, and turns away. I like this proof of vitality."

His love of traveling never left him. Paris attracted him, as it attracts all who cling to letters, and he gained at one time or another a certain amount of acquaintance with French literary men. In 1852 we find him for a time brought into contact with Thierry, Lamennais, Beranger, Mignet, etc., as well as with Romantics like Alfred de Vigny and Theophile Gautier. There are poems addressed to De Vigny and Gautier in his first published volume of 1854. He revisited Italy and his old haunts and friends in Germany more than once, and in general kept the current of his life fresh and vigorous by his openness to impressions and additions from without.

He was, as we have said, a delightful correspondent, "taking pains with the smallest note," and within a small circle of friends much liked. His was not a nature to be generally appreciated at its true value; the motives which governed his life were too remote from the ordinary motives of human conduct, and his characteristics just those which have always excited the distrust, if not the scorn, of the more practical and vigorous order of minds. Probably, too—especially in his later years—there was a certain amount of self-consciousness and artificiality in his attitude toward the outer world, which was the result partly of the social difficulties we have described, partly of his own sense of difference from his surroundings, and partly again of that timidity of nature, that self-distrust, which is revealed to us in the Journal. So that he was by no means generally popular, and the great success of the Journal is still a mystery to the majority of those who knew him merely as a fellow-citizen and acquaintance. But his friends loved him and believed in him, and the reserved student, whose manners were thought affected in general society, could and did make himself delightful to those who understood him, or those who looked to him for affection. "According to my remembrance of him," writes M. Scherer, "he was bright, sociable, a charming companion. Others who knew him better and longer than I say the same. The mobility of his disposition counteracted his tendency to exaggerations of feeling. In spite of his fits of melancholy, his natural turn of mind was cheerful; up to the end he was young, a child even, amused by mere nothings; and whoever had heard him laugh his hearty student's laugh would have found it difficult to identify him with the author of so many somber pages." M. Rivier, his old pupil, remembers him as "strong and active, still handsome, delightful in conversation, ready to amuse and be amused." Indeed, if the photographs of him are to be trusted, there must have been something specially attractive in the sensitive, expressive face, with its lofty brow, fine eyes, and kindly mouth. It is the face of a poet rather than of a student, and makes one understand certain other little points which his friends lay stress on—for instance, his love for and popularity with children.

In his poems, or at any rate in the earlier ones, this lighter side finds more expression, proportionally, than in the Journal. In the volume called "Grains de Mil," published in 1854, and containing verse written between the ages of eighteen and thirty, there are poems addressed, now to his sister, now to old Genevese friends, and now to famous men of other countries whom he had seen and made friends with in passing, which, read side by side with the "Journal Intime," bring a certain gleam and sparkle into an otherwise somber picture. Amiel was never a master of poetical form; his verse, compared to his prose, is tame and fettered; it never reaches the glow and splendor of expression which mark the finest passages of the Journal. It has ability, thought—beauty even, of a certain kind, but no plastic power, none of the incommunicable magic which a George Eliot seeks for in vain, while it comes unasked, to deck with imperishable charm the commonplace metaphysic and the simpler emotions of a Tennyson or a Burns. Still as Amiel's work, his poetry has an interest for those who are interested in him. Sincerity is written in every line of it. Most of the thoughts and experiences with which one grows familiar in the Journal are repeated in it; the same joys, the same aspirations, the same sorrows are visible throughout it, so that in reading it one is more and more impressed with the force and reality of the inner life which has left behind it so definite an image of itself. And every now and then the poems add a detail, a new impression, which seems by contrast to give fresh value to the fine-spun speculations, the lofty despairs, of the Journal. Take these verses, written at twenty-one, to his younger sister:

"Treize ans! et sur ton front aucun baiser de mere Ne viendra, pauvre enfant, invoquer le bonheur; Treize ans! et dans ce jour mil regard de ton pere Ne fera d'allegresse epanouir ton coeur.

"Orpheline, c'est la le nom dont tu t'appelles, Oiseau ne dans un nid que la foudre a brise; De la couvee, helas! seuls, trois petits, sans ailes Furent lances au vent, loin du reste ecrase.

"Et, semes par l'eclair sur les monts, dans les plaines, Un meme toit encor n'a pu les abriter, Et du foyer natal, malgre leurs plaintes vaines Dieu, peut-etre longtemps, voudra les ecarter.

"Pourtant console-toi! pense, dans tes alarmes, Qu'un double bien te reste, espoir et souvenir; Une main dans le ciel pour essuyer tes larmes; Une main ici-bas, enfant, pour te benir."

The last stanza is especially poor, and in none of them is there much poetical promise. But the pathetic image of a forlorn and orphaned childhood, *"un nid que la foudre a brise,"* which it calls up, and the tone of brotherly affection, linger in one's memory. And through much of the volume of 1863, in the verses to "My Godson," or in the charming poem to Loulou, the little girl who at five years old, daisy in hand, had sworn him eternal friendship over Gretchen's game of *"Er liebt mich—liebt mich nicht,"* one hears the same tender note.

"Merci, prophetique fleurette, Corolle a l'oracle vainqueur, Car voila trois ans, paquerette, Que tu m'ouvris un petit coeur.

"Et depuis trois hivers, ma belle, L'enfant aux grands yeux de velours Maintient son petit coeur fidele, Fidele comme aux premiers jours."

His last poetical volume, "Jour a Jour," published in 1880, is far more uniformly melancholy and didactic in tone than the two earlier collections from which we have been quoting. But though the dominant note is one of pain and austerity, of philosophy touched with emotion, and the general tone more purely introspective, there are many traces in it of the younger Amiel, dear, for very ordinary human reasons, to his sisters and his friends. And, in general, the pathetic interest of the book for all whose sympathy answers to what George Sand calls *"les tragedies que la pensee apercoit et que l'oeil ne voit point"* is very great. Amiel published it a year before his death, and the struggle with failing power which the Journal reveals to us in its saddest and most intimate reality, is here expressed in more reserved and measured form. Faith, doubt, submission, tenderness of feeling, infinite aspiration, moral passion, that straining hope of something beyond, which is the life of the religious soul—they are all here, and the *Dernier Mot* with which the sad little volume ends is poor Amiel's epitaph on himself, his conscious farewell to that more public aspect of his life in which he had suffered much and achieved comparatively so little.

"Nous avons a plaisir complique le bonheur, Et par un ideal frivole et suborneur Attache nos coeurs a la terre; Dupes des faux dehors tenus pour l'important, Mille choses pour nous ont du prix ... et pourtant Une seule etait necessaire.

"Sans fin nous prodiguons calculs, efforts, travaux; Cependant, au milieu des succes, des bravos En nous quelque chose soupire; Multipliant nos pas et nos soins de fourmis, Nous vondrions nous faire une foule d'amis.... Pourtant un seul pouvait suffire.

"Victime des desirs, esclave des regrets, L'homme s'agite, et s'use, et vieillit sans progres Sur sa toile de Penelope; Comme un sage mourant, puissions-nous dire en paix J'ai trop longtemps erre, cherche; je me trompais; Tout est bien, mon Dieu m'enveloppe."

Upon the small remains of Amiel's prose outside the Journal there is no occasion to dwell. The two essays on Madame de Stael and Rousseau contain much fine critical remark, and might find a place perhaps as an appendix to some future edition of the Journal; and some of the "Pensees," published in the latter half of the volume containing the "Grains de Mils," are worthy of preservation. But in general, whatever he himself published was inferior to what might justly have been expected of him, and no one was more conscious of the fact than himself.

The story of his fatal illness, of the weary struggle for health which filled the last seven years of his life, is abundantly told in the Journal—we must not repeat it here. He had never been a strong man, and at fifty-three he received, at his doctor's hands, his *arret de mort*. We are told that what killed him was "heart disease, complicated by disease of the larynx," and that he suffered "much and long." He was buried in the cemetery of Clarens, not far from his great contemporary Alexander Vinet; and the affection of a sculptor friend provided the monument which now marks his resting-place.

We have thus exhausted all the biographical material which is at present available for the description of Amiel's life and relations toward the outside world. It is to be hoped that the friends to whom the charge of his memory has been specially committed may see their way in the future, if not to a formal biography, which is very likely better left unattempted, at least to a volume of Letters, which would complete the "Journal Intime," as Joubert's "Correspondence" completes the "Pensees." There must be ample material for it; and Amiel's letters would probably supply us with more of that literary and critical reflection which his mind produced so freely and so well, as long as there was no question of publication, but which is at present somewhat overweighted in the "Journal Intime."

But whether biography or correspondence is ever forthcoming or not, the Journal remains—and the Journal is the important matter. We shall read the Letters if they appear, as we now read the Poems, for the Journal's sake. The man himself, as poet, teacher, and *litterateur*, produced no appreciable effect on his generation; but the posthumous record of his inner life has stirred the hearts of readers all over Europe, and won him a niche in the House of Fame. What are the reasons for this striking transformation of a man's position — a transformation which, as M. Scherer says, will rank among the curiosities of literary history? In other words, what has given the "Journal Intime" its sudden and unexpected success?

In the first place, no doubt, its poetical quality, its beauty of manner — that fine literary expression in which Amiel has been able to clothe the subtler processes of thought, no less than the secrets of religious feeling, or the aspects of natural scenery. Style is what gives value and currency to thought, and Amiel, in spite of all his Germanisms, has style of the best kind. He possesses in prose that indispensable magic which he lacks in poetry.

His style, indeed, is by no means always in harmony with the central French tradition. Probably a Frenchman will be inclined to apply Sainte-Beuve's remarks on Amiel's elder countryman, Rodolphe Toepffer, to Amiel himself: *"C'est ainsi qu'on ecrit dans les litteratures qui n'ont point de capitale, de quartier general classique, ou d'Academie; c'est ainsi qu'un Allemand, qu'un Americain, ou meme un Anglais, use a son gre de sa langue. En France au contraire, ou il y a une Academie Francaise ... on doit trouver qu'un tel style est une tres-grande nouveaute et le succes qu'il a obtenu un evenement: il a fallu bien des circonstances pour y preparer."* No doubt the preparatory circumstance in Amiel's case has been just that Germanization of the French mind on which M. Taine and M. Bourget dwell with so much emphasis. But, be this as it may, there is no mistaking the enthusiasm with which some of the best living writers of French have hailed these pages — instinct, as one declares, "with a strange and marvelous poetry;" full of phrases *"d'une intense suggestion de beaute;"* according to another. Not that the whole of the Journal flows with the same ease, the same felicity. There are a certain number of passages where Amiel ceases to be the writer, and becomes the technical philosopher; there are others, though not many, into which a certain German heaviness and diffuseness has crept, dulling the edge of the sentences, and retarding the development of the thought. When all deductions have been made, however, Amiel's claim is still first and foremost, the claim of the poet and the artist; of the man whose thought uses at will the harmonies and resources of speech, and who has attained, in words of his own, "to the full and masterly expression of himself."

Then to the poetical beauty of manner which first helped the book to penetrate, *faire sa trouee*, as the French say, we must add its extraordinary psychological interest. Both as poet and as psychologist, Amiel makes another link in a special tradition; he adds another name to the list of those who have won a hearing from their fellows as interpreters of the inner life, as the revealers of man to himself. He is the successor of St. Augustine and Dante; he is the brother of Obermann and Maurice de Guerin. What others have done for the spiritual life of other generations he has done for the spiritual life of this, and the wealth of poetical, scientific, and psychological faculty which he has brought to the analysis of human feeling and human perceptions places him—so far as the present century is concerned—at the head of the small and delicately-gifted class to which he belongs. For beside his spiritual experience Obermann's is superficial, and Maurice de Guerin's a passing trouble, a mere quick outburst of passionate feeling. Amiel indeed has neither the continuous romantic beauty nor the rich descriptive wealth of Senancour. The Dent du Midi, with its untrodden solitude, its primeval silences and its hovering eagles, the Swiss landscape described in the "Fragment on the Ranz des Vaches," the summer moonlight on the Lake of Neufchatel—these various pictures are the work of one of the most finished artists in words that literature has produced. But how true George Sand's criticism is! "*Chez Obermann la sensibilite est active, l'intelligence est paresseuse ou insuffisante.*" He has a certain antique power of making the truisms of life splendid and impressive. No one can write more poetical exercises than he on the old text of *pulvis et umbra sumus*, but beyond this his philosophical power fails him. As soon as he leaves the region of romantic description how wearisome the pages are apt to grow! Instead of a poet, *"un ergoteur Voltairien;"* instead of the explorer of fresh secrets of the heart, a Parisian talking a cheap cynicism! Intellectually, the ground gives way; there is no solidity of knowledge, no range of thought. Above all, the scientific idea in our sense is almost absent; so that while Amiel represents the modern mind at its keenest and best, dealing at will with the vast additions to knowledge which the last fifty years have brought forth, Senancour is still in the eighteenth-century stage, talking like Rousseau of a return to primitive manners, and discussing Christianity in the tone of the "Encyclopedie."

Maurice de Guerin, again, is the inventor of new terms in the language of feeling, a poet as Amiel and Senancour are. His love of nature, the earth-passion which breathes in his letters and journal, has a strange savor, a force and flame which is all his own. Beside his actual sense of community with the visible world, Amiel's love of landscape has a tame, didactic air. The Swiss thinker is too ready to make nature a mere vehicle of moral or philosophical thought; Maurice de Guerin loves her for herself alone, and has found words to describe her influence over him of extraordinary individuality and power. But for the rest the story of his inner life has but small value in the history of thought. His difficulties do not go deep enough; his struggle is intellectually not serious enough—we see in it only a common incident of modern experience poetically told; it throws no light on the genesis and progress of the great forces which are molding and renovating the thought of the present—it tells us nothing for the future.

No—there is much more in the "Journal Intime" than the imagination or the poetical glow which Amiel shares with his immediate predecessors in the art of confession-writing. His book is representative of human experience in its more intimate and personal forms to an extent hardly equaled since Rousseau. For his study of himself is only a means to an end. "What interests me in myself," he declares, "is that I find in my own case a genuine example of human nature, and therefore a specimen of general value." It is the human consciousness of to-day, of the modern world, in its two-fold relation—its relation toward the infinite and the unknowable, and its relation toward the visible universe which conditions it—which is the real subject of the "Journal Intime." There are few elements of our present life which, in a greater or less degree, are not made vocal in these pages. Amiel's intellectual interest is untiring. Philosophy, science, letters, art—he has penetrated the spirit of them all; there is nothing, or almost nothing, within the wide range of modern activities which he has not at one time or other felt the attraction of, and learned in some sense to understand. "Amiel," says M. Renan, "has his defects, but he was certainly one of the strongest speculative heads who, during the period from 1845 to 1880, have reflected on the nature of things." And, although a certain fatal spiritual weakness debarred him to a great extent from the world of practical life, his sympathy with action, whether it was the action of the politician or the social reformer, or merely that steady half-conscious performance of its daily duty which keeps humanity sweet and living, was unfailing. His horizon was not bounded by his own "prison-cell," or by that dream-world which he has described with so much subtle beauty; rather the energies which should have found their natural expression in literary or family life, pent up within the mind itself, excited in it a perpetual eagerness for intellectual discovery, and new powers of sympathy with whatever crossed its field of vision.

So that the thinker, the historian, the critic, will find himself at home with Amiel. The power of organizing his thought, the art of writing a book, *monumentum aere perennius*, was indeed denied him—he laments it bitterly; but, on the other hand, he is receptivity itself, responsive to all the great forces which move the time, catching and reflecting on the mobile mirror of his mind whatever winds are blowing from the hills of thought.

And if the thinker is at home with him, so too are the religious minds, the natures for whom God and duty are the foundation of existence. Here, indeed, we come to the innermost secret of Amiel's charm, the fact which probably goes farther than any other to explain his fascination for a large and growing class of readers. For, while he represents all the intellectual complexities of a time bewildered by the range and number of its own acquisitions, the religious instinct in him is as strong and tenacious as in any of the representative exponents of the life of faith. The intellect is clear and unwavering; but the heart clings to old traditions, and steadies itself on the rock of duty. His Calvinistic training lingers long in him; and what detaches him from the Hegelian school, with which he has much in common, is his own stronger sense of personal need, his preoccupation with the idea of "sin." "He speaks," says M. Renan contemptuously, "of sin, of salvation, of redemption, and conversion, as if these things were realities. He asks me 'What does M. Renan make of sin?' *Eh bien, je crois que je le supprime.*" But it is just because Amiel is profoundly sensitive to the problems of evil and responsibility, and M. Renan dismisses them with this half-tolerant, half-skeptical smile, that M. Renan's "Souvenirs" inform and entertain us, while the "Journal Intime" makes a deep impression on that moral sense which is at the root of individual and national life.

The Journal is full, indeed, of this note of personal religion. Religion, Amiel declares again and again, cannot be replaced by philosophy. The redemption of the intelligence is not the redemption of the heart. The philosopher and critic may succeed in demonstrating that the various definite forms into which the religious thought of man has thrown itself throughout history are not absolute truth, but only the temporary creations of a need which gradually and surely outgrows them all. "The Trinity, the life to come, paradise and hell, may cease to be dogmas and spiritual realities, the form and the letter may vanish away—the question of humanity remains: What is it which saves?" Amiel's answer to the question will recall to a wide English circle the method and spirit of an English teacher, whose dear memory lives to-day in many a heart, and is guiding many an effort in the cause of good—the method and spirit of the late Professor Green of Balliol. In many respects there was a gulf of difference between the two men. The one had all the will and force of personality which the other lacked. But the ultimate creed of both, the way in which both interpret the facts of nature and consciousness, is practically the same. In Amiel's case, we have to gather it through all the variations and inevitable contradictions of a Journal which is the reflection of a life, not the systematic expression of a series of ideas, but the main results are clear enough. Man is saved by love and duty, and by the hope which springs from duty, or rather from the moral facts of consciousness, as a flower springs from the soil. Conscience and the moral progress of the race—these are his points of departure. Faith in the reality of the moral law is what he clings to when his inherited creed has yielded to the pressure of the intellect, and after all the storms of pessimism and necessitarianism have passed over him. The reconciliation of the two certitudes, the two methods, the scientific and the religious, "is to be sought for in that moral law which is also a fact, and every step of which requires for its explanation another cosmos than the cosmos of necessity." "Nature is the virtuality of mind, the soul the fruit of life, and liberty the flower of necessity." Consciousness is the one fixed point in this boundless and bottomless gulf of things, and the soul's inward law, as it has been painfully elaborated by human history, the only revelation of God.

The only but the sufficient revelation! For this first article of a reasonable creed is the key to all else—the clue which leads the mind safely through the labyrinth of doubt into the presence of the Eternal. Without attempting to define the indefinable, the soul rises from the belief in the reality of love and duty to the belief in "a holy will at the root of nature and destiny"—for "if man is capable of conceiving goodness, the general principle of things, which cannot be inferior to man, must be good." And then the religious consciousness seizes on this intellectual deduction, and clothes it in language of the heart, in the tender and beautiful language of faith. "There is but one thing needful—to possess God. All our senses, all our powers of mind and soul, are so many ways of approaching the Divine, so many modes of tasting and adoring God. Religion is not a method; it is a life—a higher and supernatural life, mystical in its root and practical in its fruits; a communion with God, a calm and deep enthusiasm, a love which radiates, a force which acts, a happiness which overflows." And the faith of his youth and his maturity bears the shock of suffering, and supports him through his last hours. He writes a few months before the end: "The animal expires; man surrenders his soul to the author of the soul." ... "We dream alone, we suffer alone, we die alone, we inhabit the last resting-place alone. But there is nothing to prevent us from opening our solitude to God. And so what was an austere monologue becomes dialogue, reluctance becomes docility, renunciation passes into peace, and the sense of painful defeat is lost in the sense of recovered liberty"—"*Tout est bien, mon Dieu m'enveloppe.*"

Nor is this all. It is not only that Amiel's inmost thought and affections are stayed on this conception of "a holy will at the root of nature and destiny"—in a certain very real sense he is a Christian. No one is more sensitive than he to the contribution which Christianity has made to the religious wealth of mankind; no one more penetrated than he with the truth of its essential doctrine "death unto sin and a new birth unto righteousness." "The religion of sin, of repentance and reconciliation," he cries, "the religion of the new birth and of eternal life, is not a religion to be ashamed of." The world has found inspiration and guidance for eighteen centuries in the religious consciousness of Jesus. "The gospel has modified the world and consoled mankind," and so "we may hold aloof from the churches and yet bow ourselves before Jesus. We may be suspicious of the clergy and refuse to have anything to do with catechisms, and yet love the Holy and the Just who came to save and not to curse." And in fact Amiel's whole life and thought are steeped in Christianity. He is the spiritual descendant of one of the intensest and most individual forms of Christian belief, and traces of his religious ancestry are visible in him at every step. Protestantism of the sincerer and nobler kind leaves an indelible impression on the nature which has once surrounded itself to the austere and penetrating influences flowing from the religion of sin and grace; and so far as feeling and temperament are concerned, Amiel retained throughout his life the marks of Calvinism and Geneva.

And yet how clear the intellect remains, through all the anxieties of thought, and in the face of the soul's dearest memories and most passionate needs! Amiel, as soon as his reasoning faculty has once reached its maturity, never deceives himself as to the special claims of the religion which by instinct and inheritance he loves; he makes no compromise with dogma or with miracle. Beyond the religions of the present he sees always the essential religion which lasts when all local forms and marvels have passed away; and as years go on, with more and more clearness of conviction, he learns to regard all special beliefs and systems as "prejudices, useful in practice, but still narrownesses of the mind;" misgrowths of thought, necessary in their time and place, but still of no absolute value, and having no final claim on the thought of man.

And it is just here—in this mixture of the faith which clings and aspires, with the intellectual pliancy which allows the mind to sway freely under the pressure of life and experience, and the deep respect for truth, which will allow nothing to interfere between thought and its appointed tasks—that Amiel's special claim upon us lies. It is this balance of forces in him which makes him so widely representative of the modern mind—of its doubts, its convictions, its hopes. He speaks for the life of to-day as no other single voice has yet spoken for it; in his contradictions, his fears, his despairs, and yet in the constant straining toward the unseen and the ideal which gives a fundamental unity to his inner life, he is the type of a generation universally touched with doubt, and yet as sensitive to the need of faith as any that have gone before it; more widely conscious than its predecessors of the limitations of the human mind, and of the iron pressure of man's physical environment; but at the same time— paradox as it may seem—more conscious of man's greatness, more deeply thrilled by the spectacle of the nobility and beauty interwoven with the universe.

And he plays this part of his so modestly, with so much hesitation, so much doubt of his thought and of himself! He is no preacher, like Emerson and Carlyle, with whom, as poet and idealist, he has so much in common; there is little resemblance between him and the men who speak, as it were, from a height to the crowd beneath, sure always of themselves and what they have to say. And here again he represents the present and foreshadows the future. For the age of the preachers is passing those who speak with authority on the riddles of life and nature as the priests of this or that all-explaining dogma, are becoming less important as knowledge spreads, and the complexity of experience is made evident to a wider range of minds. The force of things is against *the certain people*. Again and again truth escapes from the prisons made for her by mortal hands, and as humanity carries on the endless pursuit she will pay more and more respectful heed to voices like this voice of the lonely Genevese thinker—with its pathetic alterations of hope and fear, and the moral steadfastness which is the inmost note of it—to these meditative lives, which, through all the ebb and flow of thought, and in the dim ways of doubt and suffering, rich in knowledge, and yet rich in faith, grasp in new forms, and proclaim to us in new words,

"The mighty hopes which make us men."

AMIEL'S JOURNAL.

* * * * *

[Where no other name is mentioned, Geneva is to be understood as the author's place of residence.]

BERLIN, July 16. 1848.—There is but one thing needful—to possess God. All our senses, all our powers of mind and soul, all our external resources, are so many ways of approaching the divinity, so many modes of tasting and of adoring God. We must learn to detach ourselves from all that is capable of being lost, to bind ourselves absolutely only to what is absolute and eternal, and to enjoy the rest as a loan, a usufruct.... To adore, to understand, to receive, to feel, to give, to act: there is my law my duty, my happiness, my heaven. Let come what come will—even death. Only be at peace with self, live in the presence of God, in communion with Him, and leave the guidance of existence to those universal powers against whom thou canst do nothing! If death gives me time, so much the better. If its summons is near, so much the better still; if a half-death overtake me, still so much the better, for so the path of success is closed to me only that I may find opening before me the path of heroism, of moral greatness and resignation. Every life has its potentiality of greatness, and as it is impossible to be outside God, the best is consciously to dwell in Him.

BERLIN, July 20, 1848.—It gives liberty and breadth to thought, to learn to judge our own epoch from the point of view of universal history, history from the point of view of geological periods, geology from the point of view of astronomy. When the duration of a man's life or of a people's life appears to us as microscopic as that of a fly and inversely, the life of a gnat as infinite as that of a celestial body, with all its dust of nations, we feel ourselves at once very small and very great, and we are able, as it were, to survey from the height of the spheres our own existence, and the little whirlwinds which agitate our little Europe.

At bottom there is but one subject of study: the forms and metamorphoses of mind. All other subjects may be reduced to that; all other studies bring us back to this study.

GENEVA, April 20, 1849.—It is six years [Footnote: Amiel left Geneva for Paris and Berlin in April, 1848, the preceding year, 1841-

42, having been spent in Italy and Sicily.] to-day since I last left Geneva. How many journeys, how many impressions, observations, thoughts, how many forms of men and things have since then passed before me and in me! The last seven years have been the most important of my life: they have been the novitiate of my intelligence, the initiation of my being into being.

Three snowstorms this afternoon. Poor blossoming plum-trees and peach trees! What a difference from six years ago, when the cherry-trees, adorned in their green spring dress and laden with their bridal flowers, smiled at my departure along the Vaudois fields, and the lilacs of Burgundy threw great gusts of perfume into my face!...

May 3, 1849.—I have never felt any inward assurance of genius, or any presentiment of glory or of happiness. I have never seen myself in imagination great or famous, or even a husband, a father, an influential citizen. This indifference to the future, this absolute self-distrust, are, no doubt, to be taken as signs. What dreams I have are all vague and indefinite; I ought not to live, for I am now scarcely capable of living. Recognize your place; let the living live; and you, gather together your thoughts, leave behind you a legacy of feeling and ideas; you will be most useful so. Renounce yourself, accept the cup given you, with its honey and its gall, as it comes. Bring God down into your heart. Embalm your soul in Him now, make within you a temple for the Holy Spirit, be diligent in good works, make others happier and better.

Put personal ambition away from you, and then you will find consolation in living or in dying, whatever may happen to you.

May 27, 1849.—To be misunderstood even by those whom one loves is the cross and bitterness of life. It is the secret of that sad and melancholy smile on the lips of great men which so few understand; it is the cruelest trial reserved for self-devotion; it is what must have oftenest wrung the heart of the Son of man; and if God could suffer, it would be the wound we should be forever inflicting upon Him. He also—He above all—is the great misunderstood, the least comprehended. Alas! alas! never to tire, never to grow cold; to be patient, sympathetic, tender; to look for the budding flower and the opening heart; to hope always, like God; to love always—this is duty.

June 3, 1849.—Fresh and delicious weather. A long morning walk. Surprised the hawthorn and wild rose-trees in flower. From the fields vague and health-giving scents. The Voirons fringed with dazzling mists, and tints of exquisite softness over the Saleve. Work in the fields, two delightful donkeys, one pulling greedily at a hedge of barberry. Then three little children. I felt a boundless desire to caress and play with them. To be able to enjoy such leisure, these peaceful fields, fine weather, contentment; to have my two sisters with me; to rest my eyes on balmy meadows and blossoming orchards; to listen to the life singing in the grass and on the trees; to be so calmly happy—is it not too much? is it deserved? O let me enjoy it with gratitude. The days of trouble come soon enough and are many enough. I have no presentiment of happiness. All the more let me profit by the present. Come, kind nature, smile and enchant me! Veil from me awhile my own griefs and those of others; let me see only the folds of thy queenly mantle, and hide all miserable and ignoble things from me under thy bounties and splendors!

October 1, 1849.—Yesterday, Sunday, I read through and made extracts from the gospel of St. John. It confirmed me in my belief that about Jesus we must believe no one but Himself, and that what we have to do is to discover the true image of the founder behind all the prismatic reactions through which it comes to us, and which alter it more or less. A ray of heavenly light traversing human life, the message of Christ has been broken into a thousand rainbow colors and carried in a thousand directions. It is the historical task of Christianity to assume with every succeeding age a fresh metamorphosis, and to be forever spiritualizing more and more her understanding of the Christ and of salvation.

I am astounded at the incredible amount of Judaism and formalism which still exists nineteen centuries after the Redeemer's proclamation, "it is the letter which killeth"—after his protest against a dead symbolism. The new religion is so profound that it is not understood even now, and would seem a blasphemy to the greater number of Christians. The person of Christ is the center of it. Redemption, eternal life, divinity, humanity, propitiation, incarnation, judgment, Satan, heaven and hell—all these beliefs have been so materialized and coarsened, that with a strange irony they present to us the spectacle of things having a profound meaning and yet carnally interpreted. Christian boldness and Christian liberty must be reconquered; it is the church which is heretical, the church whose sight is troubled and her heart timid. Whether we will or no, there is an esoteric doctrine, there is a relative revelation; each man enters into God so much as God enters into him, or as Angelus, [Footnote: Angelus Silesius, otherwise Johannes Soheffler, the German seventeenth century hymn-writer, whose tender and mystical verses have been popularized in England by Miss Winkworth's translations in the *Lyra Germanica*.] I think, said, "the eye by which I see God is the same eye by which He sees me."

Christianity, if it is to triumph over pantheism, must absorb it. To our pusillanimous eyes Jesus would have borne the marks of a hateful pantheism, for he confirmed the Biblical phrase "ye are gods," and so would St. Paul, who tells us that we are of "the race of God." Our century wants a new theology—that is to say, a more profound explanation of the nature of Christ and of the light which it flashes upon heaven and upon humanity.

* * * * *

Heroism is the brilliant triumph of the soul over the flesh—that is to say, over fear: fear of poverty, of suffering, of calumny, of sickness, of isolation, and of death. There is no serious piety without heroism. Heroism is the dazzling and glorious concentration of courage.

* * * * *

Duty has the virtue of making us feel the reality of a positive world while at the same time detaching us from it.

* * * * *

December 30, 1850.—The relation of thought to action filled my mind on waking, and I found myself carried toward a bizarre formula, which seems to have something of the night still clinging about it: *Action is but coarsened thought*; thought become concrete, obscure, and unconscious. It seemed to me that our most trifling actions, of eating, walking, and sleeping, were the condensation of a multitude of truths and thoughts, and that the wealth of ideas involved was in direct proportion to the commonness of the action (as our dreams are the more active, the deeper our sleep). We are hemmed round with mystery, and the greatest mysteries are contained in what we see and do every day. In all spontaneity the work of creation is reproduced in analogy. When the spontaneity is unconscious, you have simple action; when it is conscious, intelligent and moral action. At bottom this is nothing more than the proposition of Hegel: ["What is rational is real; and what is real is rational;"] but it had never seemed to me more evident, more palpable. Everything which is, is thought, but not conscious and individual thought. The human intelligence is but the consciousness of being. It is what I have formulated before: Everything is a symbol of a symbol, and a symbol of what? of mind.

... I have just been looking through the complete works of Montesquieu, and cannot yet make plain to myself the impression left on me by this singular style, with its mixture of gravity and affectation, of carelessness and precision, of strength and delicacy; so full of sly intention for all its coldness, expressing at once inquisitiveness and indifference, abrupt, piecemeal, like notes thrown together haphazard, and yet deliberate. I seem to see an intelligence naturally grave and austere donning a dress of wit for convention's sake. The author desires to entertain as much as to teach, the thinker is also a *bel-esprit*, the jurisconsult has a touch of the coxcomb, and a perfumed breath from the temple of Venus has penetrated the tribunal of Minos. Here we have austerity, as the century understood it, in philosophy or religion. In Montesquieu, the art, if there is any, lies not in the words but in the matter. The words run freely and lightly, but the thought is self-conscious.

* * * * *

Each bud flowers but once and each flower has but its minute of perfect beauty; so, in the garden of the soul each feeling has, as it were, its flowering instant, its one and only moment of expansive grace and radiant kingship. Each star passes but once in the night through the meridian over our heads and shines there but an instant; so, in the heaven of the mind each thought touches its zenith but once, and in that moment all its brilliancy and all its greatness culminate. Artist, poet, or thinker, if you want to fix and immortalize your ideas or your feelings, seize them at this precise and fleeting moment, for it is their highest point. Before it, you have but vague outlines or dim presentiments of them. After it you will have only weakened reminiscence or powerless regret; that moment is the moment of your ideal.

Spite is anger which is afraid to show itself, it is an impotent fury conscious of its impotence.

* * * * *

Nothing resembles pride so much as discouragement.

* * * * *

To repel one's cross is to make it heavier.

* * * * *

In the conduct of life, habits count for more than maxims, because habit is a living maxim, becomes flesh and instinct. To reform one's maxims is nothing: it is but to change the title of the book. To learn new habits is everything, for it is to reach the substance of life. Life is but a tissue of habits.

* * * * *

February 17, 1851.—I have been reading, for six or seven hours without stopping the *Pensees* of Joubert. I felt at first a very strong attraction toward the book, and a deep interest in it, but I have already a good deal cooled down. These scattered and fragmentary thoughts, falling upon one without a pause, like drops of light, tire, not my head, but reasoning power. The merits of Joubert consist in the grace of the style, the vivacity or *finesse* of the criticisms, the charm of the metaphors; but he starts many more problems than he solves, he notices and records more than he explains. His philosophy is merely literary and popular; his originality is only in detail and in execution. Altogether, he is a writer of reflections rather than a philosopher, a critic of remarkable gifts, endowed with exquisite sensibility, but, as an intelligence, destitute of the capacity for co-ordination. He wants concentration and continuity. It is not that he has no claims to be considered a philosopher or an artist, but rather that he is both imperfectly, for he thinks and writes marvelously, *on a small scale*. He is an entomologist, a lapidary, a jeweler, a coiner of sentences, of adages, of criticisms, of aphorisms, counsels, problems; and his book, extracted from the accumulations of his journal during fifty years of his life, is a collection of precious stones, of butterflies, coins and engraved gems. The whole, however, is more subtle than strong, more poetical than profound, and leaves upon the reader rather the impression of a great wealth of small curiosities of value, than of a great intellectual existence and a new point of view. The place of Joubert seems to me then, below and very far from the philosophers and the true poets, but honorable among the moralists and the critics. He is one of those men who are superior to their works, and who have themselves the unity which these lack. This first judgment is, besides, indiscriminate and severe. I shall have to modify it later.

February 20th.—I have almost finished these two volumes of *Pensees* and the greater part of the *Correspondance*. This last has especially charmed me; it is remarkable for grace, delicacy, atticism, and precision. The chapters on metaphysics and philosophy are the most insignificant. All that has to do with large views with the whole of things, is very little at Joubert's command; he has no philosophy of history, no speculative intuition. He is the thinker of detail, and his proper field is psychology and matters of taste. In this sphere of the subtleties and delicacies of imagination and feeling, within the circle of personal affectation and preoccupations, of social and educational interests, he abounds in ingenuity and sagacity, in fine criticisms, in exquisite touches. It is like a bee going from flower to flower, a teasing, plundering, wayward zephyr, an Aeolian harp, a ray of furtive light stealing through the leaves. Taken as a whole, there is something impalpable and immaterial about him, which I will not venture to call effeminate, but which is scarcely manly. He wants bone and body: timid, dreamy, and *clairvoyant*, he hovers far above reality. He is rather a soul, a breath, than a man. It is the mind of a woman in the character of a child, so that we feel for him less admiration than tenderness and gratitude.

February 27, 1851.—Read over the first book of *Emile*. I was revolted, contrary to all expectation, for I opened the book with a sort of hunger for style and beauty. I was conscious instead of an impression of heaviness and harshness, of labored, *hammering* emphasis, of something violent, passionate, and obstinate, without serenity, greatness, nobility. Both the qualities and the defects of the book produced in me a sense of lack of good manners, a blaze of talent, but no grace, no distinction, the accent of good company wanting. I understood how it is that Rousseau rouses a particular kind of repugnance, the repugnance of good taste, and I felt the danger to style involved in such a model as well as the danger to thought arising from a truth so alloyed and sophisticated. What there is of true and strong in Rousseau did not escape me, and I still admired him, but his bad sides appeared to me with a clearness relatively new.

(*Same day.*)—The *pensee*-writer is to the philosopher what the *dilettante* is to the artist. He plays with thought, and makes it produce a crowd of pretty things in detail, but he is more anxious about truths than truth, and what is essential in thought, its sequence, its unity, escapes him. He handles his instrument agreeably, but he does not possess it, still less does he create it. He is a gardener and not a geologist; he cultivates the earth only so much as is necessary to make it produce for him flowers and fruits; he does not dig deep enough into it to understand it. In a word, the *pensee*-writer deals with what is superficial and fragmentary. He is the literary, the oratorical, the talking or writing philosopher; whereas the philosopher is the scientific *pensee*-writer. The *pensee*-writers serve to stimulate or to popularize the philosophers. They have thus a double use, besides their charm. They are the pioneers of the army of readers, the doctors of the crowd, the money-changers of thought, which they convert into current coin. The writer of *pensee* is a man of letters, though of a serious type, and therefore he is popular. The philosopher is a specialist, as far as the form of his science goes, though not in substance, and therefore he can never become popular. In France, for one philosopher (Descartes) there have been thirty writers of *pensees*; in Germany, for ten such writers there have been twenty philosophers.

March 25, 1851.—How many illustrious men whom I have known have been already reaped by death, Steffens, Marheineke, Neander, Mendelssohn, Thorwaldsen, Oelenschlaeger, Geijer, Tegner, Oersted, Stuhr, Lachmann; and with us, Sismondi, Toepffer, de Candolle, savants, artists, poets, musicians, historians. [Footnote: Of these Marheineke, Neander, and Lachmann had been lecturing at Berlin during Amiel's residence there. The Danish dramatic poet Oelenschlaeger and the Swedish writer Tegner were among the Scandinavian men of letters with whom he made acquaintance during his tour of Sweden and Denmark in 1845. He probably came across the Swedish historian Geijer on the same occasion. Schelling and Alexander von Humboldt, mentioned a little lower down, were also still holding sway at Berlin when he was a student. There is an interesting description in one of his articles on Berlin, published in the *Bibliotheque Universelle de Geneve*, of a university ceremonial there in or about 1847, and of the effect produced on the student's young imagination by the sight of half the leaders of European research gathered into a single room. He saw Schlosser, the veteran historian, at Heidelberg at the end of 1843.] The old generation is going. What will the new bring us? What shall we ourselves contribute? A few great old men—Schelling, Alexander von Humboldt, Schlosser—still link us with the glorious past. Who is preparing to bear the weight of the future? A shiver seizes us when the ranks grow thin around us, when age is stealing upon us, when we approach the zenith, and when destiny says to us: "Show what is in thee! Now is the moment, now is the hour, else fall back into nothingness! It is thy turn! Give the world thy measure, say thy word, reveal thy nullity or thy capacity. Come forth from the shade! It is no longer a question of promising, thou must perform. The time of apprenticeship is over. Servant, show us what thou hast done with thy talent. Speak now, or be silent forever." This appeal of the conscience is a solemn summons in the life of every man, solemn and awful as the trumpet of the last judgment. It cries, "Art thou ready? Give an account. Give an account of thy years, thy leisure, thy strength, thy studies, thy talent, and thy works. Now and here is the hour of great hearts, the hour of heroism and of genius."

April 6, 1851.—Was there ever any one so vulnerable as I? If I were a father how many griefs and vexations, a child might cause me. As a husband I should have a thousand ways of suffering because my happiness demands a thousand conditions I have a heart too easily reached, a too restless imagination; despair is easy to me, and every sensation reverberates again and again within me. What might be, spoils for me what is. What ought to be consumes me with sadness. So the reality, the present, the irreparable, the necessary, repel and even terrify me. I have too much imagination, conscience and penetration, and not enough character. The life of thought alone seems to me to have enough elasticity and immensity, to be free enough from the irreparable; practical life makes me afraid.

And yet, at the same time it attracts me; I have need of it. Family life, especially, in all its delightfulness, in all its moral depth, appeals to me almost like a duty. Sometimes I cannot escape from the ideal of it. A companion of my life, of my work, of my thoughts, of my hopes; within, a common worship, toward the world outside, kindness and beneficence; educations to undertake, the thousand and one moral relations which develop round the first, all these ideas intoxicate me sometimes. But I put them aside because every hope is, as it were, an egg whence a serpent may issue instead of a dove, because every joy missed is a stab; because every seed confided to destiny contains an ear of grief which the future may develop.

I am distrustful of myself and of happiness because I know myself. The ideal poisons for me all imperfect possession. Everything which compromises the future or destroys my inner liberty, which enslaves me to things or obliges me to be other than I could and ought to be, all which injures my idea of the perfect man, hurts me mortally, degrades and wounds me in mind, even beforehand. I abhor useless regrets and repentances. The fatality of the consequences which follow upon every human act, the leading idea of dramatic art and the most tragic element of life, arrests me more certainly than the arm of the *Commandeur*. I only act with regret, and almost by force.

To be dependent is to me terrible; but to depend upon what is irreparable, arbitrary and unforeseen, and above all to be so dependent by my fault and through my own error, to give up liberty and hope, to slay sleep and happiness, this would be hell!

All that is necessary, providential, in short, *unimputable*, I could bear, I think, with some strength of mind. But responsibility mortally envenoms grief; and as an act is essentially voluntary, therefore I act as little as possible.

Last outbreak of a rebellious and deceitful self-will, craving for repose for satisfaction, for independence! is there not some relic of selfishness in such a disinterestedness, such a fear, such idle susceptibility.

I wish to fulfill my duty, but where is it, what is it? Here inclination comes in again and interprets the oracle. And the ultimate question is this: Does duty consist in obeying one's nature, even the best and most spiritual? or in conquering it?

Life, is it essentially the education of the mind and intelligence, or that of the will? And does will show itself in strength or in resignation? If the aim of life is to teach us renunciation, then welcome sickness, hindrances, sufferings of every kind! But if its aim is to produce the perfect man, then one must watch over one's integrity of mind and body. To court trial is to tempt God. At bottom, the God of justice veils from me the God of love. I tremble instead of trusting.

Whenever conscience speaks with a divided, uncertain, and disputed voice, it is not yet the voice of God. Descend still deeper into yourself, until you hear nothing but a clear and undivided voice, a voice which does away with doubt and brings with it persuasion, light and serenity. Happy, says the apostle, are they who are at peace with themselves, and whose heart condemneth them not in the part they take. This inner identity, this unity of conviction, is all the more difficult the more the mind analyzes, discriminates, and foresees. It is difficult, indeed, for liberty to return to the frank unity of instinct.

Alas! we must then re-climb a thousand times the peaks already scaled, and reconquer the points of view already won, we must *fight the fight*! The human heart, like kings, signs mere truces under a pretence of perpetual peace. The eternal life is eternally to be re-won. Alas, yes! peace itself is a struggle, or rather it is struggle and activity which are the law. We only find rest in effort, as the flame only finds existence in combustion. O Heraclitus! the symbol of happiness is after all the same as that of grief; anxiety and hope, hell and heaven, are equally restless. The altar of Vesta and the sacrifice of Beelzebub burn with the same fire. Ah, yes, there you have life—life double-faced and double-edged. The fire which enlightens is also the fire which consumes; the element of the gods may become that of the accursed.

April 7, 1851.—Read a part of Ruge's [Footnote: Arnold Ruge, born in 1803, died at Brighton in 1880, principal editor of the *Hallische,* afterward the *Deutsche Jahrbuecher* (1838-43), in which Strauss, Bruno Bauer, and Louis Feuerbach wrote. He was a member of the parliament of Frankfort.] volume "*Die Academie*" (1848) where the humanism of the neo-Hegelians in politics, religion, and literature is represented by correspondents or articles (Kuno Fischer, Kollach, etc). They recall the *philosophist* party of the last century, able to dissolve anything by reason and reasoning, but unable to construct anything; for construction rests upon feeling, instinct, and will. One finds them mistaking philosophic consciousness for realizing power, the redemption of the intelligence for the redemption of the heart, that is to say, the part for the whole. These papers make me understand the radical difference between morals and intellectualism. The writers of them wish to supplant religion by philosophy. Man is the principle of their religion, and intellect is the climax of man. Their religion, then, is the religion of intellect. There you have the two worlds: Christianity brings and preaches salvation by the conversion of the will, humanism by the emancipation of the mind. One attacks the heart, the other the brain. Both wish to enable man to reach his ideal. But the ideal differs, if not by its content, at least by the disposition of its content, by the predominance and sovereignty given to this for that inner power. For one, the mind is the organ of the soul; for the other, the soul is an inferior state of the mind; the one wishes to enlighten by making better, the other to make better by enlightening. It is the difference between Socrates and Jesus.

The cardinal question is that of sin. The question of immanence or of dualism is secondary. The trinity, the life to come, paradise and hell, may cease to be dogmas, and spiritual realities, the form and the letter may vanish away, the question of humanity remains: What is it which saves? How can man be led to be truly man? Is the ultimate root of his being responsibility, yes or no? And is doing or knowing the right, acting or thinking, his ultimate end? If science does not produce love it is insufficient. Now all that science gives is the *amor intellectualis* of Spinoza, light without warmth, a resignation which is contemplative and grandiose, but inhuman, because it is scarcely transmissible and remains a privilege, one of the rarest of all. Moral love places the center of the individual in the center of being. It has at least salvation in principle, the germ of eternal life. *To love is virtually to know; to know is not virtually to love;* there you have the relation of these two modes of man. The redemption wrought by science or by intellectual love is then inferior to the redemption wrought by will or by moral love. The first may free a man from himself, it may enfranchise him from egotism. The second drives the *ego* out of itself, makes it active and fruitful. The one is critical, purifying, negative; the other is vivifying, fertilizing, positive. Science, however spiritual and substantial it may be in itself, is still formal relatively to love. Moral force is then the vital point. And this force is only produced by moral force. Like alone acts upon like. Therefore do not amend by reasoning, but by example; approach feeling by feeling; do not hope to excite love except by love. Be what you wish others to become. Let yourself and not your words preach for you.

Philosophy, then, to return to the subject, can never replace religion; revolutionaries are not apostles, although the apostles may have been revolutionaries. To save from the outside to the inside—and by the outside I understand also the intelligence relatively to the will—is an error and danger. The negative part of the humanist's work is good; it will strip Christianity of an outer shell, which has become superfluous; but Ruge and Feuerbach cannot save humanity. She must have her saints and her heroes to complete the work of her philosophers. Science is the power of man, and love his strength;

man *becomes* man only by the intelligence, but he *is* man only by the heart. Knowledge, love, power—there is the complete life.

June 16, 1851.—This evening I walked up and down on the Pont des Bergues, under a clear, moonless heaven delighting in the freshness of the water, streaked with light from the two quays, and glimmering under the twinkling stars. Meeting all these different groups of young people, families, couples and children, who were returning to their homes, to their garrets or their drawing-rooms, singing or talking as they went, I felt a movement of sympathy for all these passers-by; my eyes and ears became those of a poet or a painter; while even one's mere kindly curiosity seems to bring with it a joy in living and in seeing others live.

August 15, 1851.—To know how to be ready, a great thing, a precious gift, and one that implies calculation, grasp and decision. To be always ready a man must be able to cut a knot, for everything cannot be untied; he must know how to disengage what is essential from the detail in which it is enwrapped, for everything cannot be equally considered; in a word, he must be able to simplify his duties, his business, and his life. To know how to be ready, is to know how to start.

It is astonishing how all of us are generally cumbered up with the thousand and one hindrances and duties which are not such, but which nevertheless wind us about with their spider threads and fetter the movement of our wings. It is the lack of order which makes us slaves; the confusion of to-day discounts the freedom of to-morrow.

Confusion is the enemy of all comfort, and confusion is born of procrastination. To know how to be ready we must be able to finish. Nothing is done but what is finished. The things which we leave dragging behind us will start up again later on before us and harass our path. Let each day take thought for what concerns it, liquidate its own affairs and respect the day which is to follow, and then we shall be always ready. To know how to be ready is at bottom to know how to die.

September 2, 1851.—Read the work of Tocqueville (*"De la Democratie en Amerique."*) My impression is as yet a mixed one. A fine book, but I feel in it a little too much imitation of Montesquieu. This abstract, piquant, sententious style, too, is a little dry, over-refined and monotonous. It has too much cleverness and not enough imagination. It makes one think, more than it charms, and though really serious, it seems flippant. His method of splitting up a thought, of illuminating a subject by successive facets, has serious inconveniences. We see the details too clearly, to the detriment of the whole. A multitude of sparks gives but a poor light. Nevertheless, the author is evidently a ripe and penetrating intelligence, who takes a comprehensive view of his subject, while at the same time possessing a power of acute and exhaustive analysis.

September 6th.—Tocqueville's book has on the whole a calming effect upon the mind, but it leaves a certain sense of disgust behind. It makes one realize the necessity of what is happening around us and the inevitableness of the goal prepared for us; but it also makes it plain that the era of *mediocrity* in everything is beginning, and mediocrity freezes all desire. Equality engenders uniformity, and it is by sacrificing what is excellent, remarkable, and extraordinary that we get rid of what is bad. The whole becomes less barbarous, and at the same time more vulgar.

The age of great men is going; the epoch of the ant-hill, of life in multiplicity, is beginning. The century of individualism, if abstract equality triumphs, runs a great risk of seeing no more true individuals. By continual leveling and division of labor, society will become everything and man nothing.

As the floor of valleys is raised by the denudation and washing down of the mountains, what is average will rise at the expense of what is great. The exceptional will disappear. A plateau with fewer and fewer undulations, without contrasts and without oppositions, such will be the aspect of human society. The statistician will register a growing progress, and the moralist a gradual decline: on the one hand, a progress of things; on the other, a decline of souls. The useful will take the place of the beautiful, industry of art, political economy of religion, and arithmetic of poetry. The spleen will become the malady of a leveling age.

Is this indeed the fate reserved for the democratic era? May not the general well-being be purchased too dearly at such a price? The creative force which in the beginning we see forever tending to produce and multiply differences, will it afterward retrace its steps and obliterate them one by one? And equality, which in the dawn of existence is mere inertia, torpor, and death, is it to become at last the natural form of life? Or rather, above the economic and political equality to which the socialist and non-socialist democracy aspires, taking it too often for the term of its efforts, will there not arise a new kingdom of mind, a church of refuge, a republic of souls, in which, far beyond the region of mere right and sordid utility, beauty, devotion, holiness, heroism, enthusiasm, the extraordinary, the infinite, shall have a worship and an abiding city? Utilitarian materialism, barren well-being, the idolatry of the flesh and of the "I," of the temporal and of mammon, are they to be the goal if our efforts, the final recompense promised to the labors of our race? I do not believe it. The ideal of humanity is something different and higher.

But the animal in us must be satisfied first, and we must first banish from among us all suffering which is superfluous and has its origin in social arrangements, before we can return to spiritual goods.

September 7, 1851. (*Aix*).—It is ten o'clock at night. A strange and mystic moonlight, with a fresh breeze and a sky crossed by a few wandering clouds, makes our terrace delightful. These pale and gentle rays shed from the zenith a subdued and penetrating peace; it is like the calm joy or the pensive smile of experience, combined with a certain stoic strength. The stars shine, the leaves tremble in the silver light. Not a sound in all the landscape; great gulfs of shadow under the green alleys and at the corners of the steps. Everything is secret, solemn, mysterious.

O night hours, hours of silence and solitude! with you are grace and melancholy; you sadden and you console. You speak to us of all that has passed away, and of all that must still die, but you say to us, "courage!" and you promise us rest.

November 9, 1851. (Sunday).—At the church of St. Gervais, a second sermon from Adolphe Monod, less grandiose perhaps but almost more original, and to me more edifying than that of last Sunday. The subject was St. Paul or the active life, his former one having been St. John or the inner life, of the Christian. I felt the golden spell of eloquence: I found myself hanging on the lips of the orator, fascinated by his boldness, his grace, his energy, and his art, his sincerity, and his talent; and it was borne in upon me that for some men difficulties are a source of inspiration, so that what would make others stumble is for them the occasion of their highest triumphs. He made St. Paul *cry* during an hour and a half; he made an old nurse of him, he hunted up his old cloak, his prescriptions of water and wine to Timothy, the canvas that he mended, his friend Tychicus, in short, all that could raise a smile; and from it he drew the most unfailing pathos, the most austere and penetrating lessons. He made the whole St. Paul, martyr, apostle and man, his grief, his charities, his tenderness, live again before us, and this with a grandeur, an unction, a warmth of reality, such as I had never seen equaled.

How stirring is such an apotheosis of pain in our century of comfort, when shepherds and sheep alike sink benumbed in Capuan languors, such an apotheosis of ardent charity in a time of coldness and indifference toward souls, such an apotheosis of a *human*, natural, inbred Christianity, in an age, when some put it, so to speak, above man, and others below man! Finally, as a peroration, he dwelt upon the necessity for a new people, for a stronger generation, if the world is to be saved from the tempests which threaten it. "People of God, awake! Sow in tears, that ye may reap in triumph!" What a study is such a sermon! I felt all the extraordinary literary skill of it, while my eyes were still dim with tears. Diction, composition, similes, all is instructive and precious to remember. I was astonished, shaken, taken hold of.

November 18, 1851.—The energetic subjectivity, which has faith in itself, which does not fear to be something particular and definite without any consciousness or shame of its subjective illusion, is unknown to me. I am, so far as the intellectual order is concerned, essentially objective, and my distinctive speciality, is to be able to place myself in all points of view, to see through all eyes, to emancipate myself, that is to say, from the individual prison. Hence aptitude for theory and irresolution in practice; hence critical talent and difficulty in spontaneous production. Hence, also, a continuous uncertainty of conviction and opinion, so long as my aptitude remained mere instinct; but now that it is conscious and possesses itself, it is able to conclude and affirm in its turn, so that, after having brought disquiet, it now brings peace. It says: "There is no repose for the mind except in the absolute; for feeling, except in the infinite; for the soul, except in the divine." Nothing finite is true, is interesting, or worthy to fix my attention. All that is particular is exclusive, and all that is exclusive, repels me. There is nothing non-exclusive but the All; my end is communion with Being through the whole of Being. Then, in the light of the absolute, every idea becomes worth studying; in that of the infinite, every existence worth respecting; in that of the divine, every creature worth loving.

December 2, 1851.—Let mystery have its place in you; do not be always turning up your whole soil with the plowshare of self-examination, but leave a little fallow corner in your heart ready for any seed the winds may bring, and reserve a nook of shadow for the passing bird; keep a place in your heart for the unexpected guests, an altar for the unknown God. Then if a bird sing among your branches, do not be too eager to tame it. If you are conscious of something new—thought or feeling, wakening in the depths of your being—do not be in a hurry to let in light upon it, to look at it; let the springing germ have the protection of being forgotten, hedge it round with quiet, and do not break in upon its darkness; let it take shape and grow, and not a word of your happiness to any one! Sacred work of nature as it is, all conception should be enwrapped by the triple veil of modesty, silence and night.

* * * * *

Kindness is the principle of tact, and respect for others the first condition of *savoir-vivre*.

* * * * *

He who is silent is forgotten; he who abstains is taken at his word; he who does not advance, falls back; he who stops is overwhelmed, distanced, crushed; he who ceases to grow greater becomes smaller; he who leaves off, gives up; the stationary condition is the beginning of the end—it is the terrible symptom which precedes death. To live, is to achieve a perpetual triumph; it is to assert one's self against destruction, against sickness, against the annulling and dispersion of one's physical and moral being. It is to will without ceasing, or rather to refresh one's will day by day.

* * * * *

It is not history which teaches conscience to be honest; it is the conscience which educates history. Fact is corrupting, it is we who correct it by the persistence of our ideal. The soul moralizes the past in order not to be demoralized by it. Like the alchemists of the middle ages, she finds in the crucible of experience only the gold that she herself has poured into it.

* * * * *

February 1, 1852. (Sunday).—Passed the afternoon in reading the *Monologues* of Schleiermacher. This little book made an impression on me almost as deep as it did twelve years ago, when I read it for the first time. It replunged me into the inner world, to which I return with joy whenever I may have forsaken it. I was able besides, to measure my progress since then by the transparency of all the thoughts to me, and by the freedom with which I entered into and judged the point of view.

It is great, powerful, profound, but there is still pride in it, and even selfishness. For the center of the universe is still the self, the great *Ich* of Fichte. The tameless liberty, the divine dignity of the individual spirit, expanding till it admits neither any limit nor anything foreign to itself, and conscious of a strength instinct with creative force, such is the point of view of the *Monologues*.

The inner life in its enfranchisement from time, in its double end, the realization of the species and of the individuality, in its proud dominion over all hostile circumstances, in its prophetic certainty of the future, in its immortal youth, such is their theme. Through them we are enabled to enter into a life of monumental interest, wholly original and beyond the influence of anything exterior, an astonishing example of the autonomy of the *ego*, an imposing type of character, Zeno and Fichte in one. But still the motive power of this life is not religious; it is rather moral and philosophic. I see in it not so much a magnificent model to imitate as a precious subject of study. This ideal of a liberty, absolute, indefeasible, inviolable, respecting itself above all, disdaining the visible and the universe, and developing itself after its own laws alone, is also the ideal of Emerson, the stoic of a young America. According to it, man finds his joy in himself, and, safe in the inaccessible sanctuary, of his personal consciousness, becomes almost a god. [Footnote: Compare Clough's lines:

"Where are the great, whom thou would'st wish to praise thee? Where are the pure, whom thou would'st choose to love thee? Where are the brave, to stand supreme above thee? Whose high commands would cheer, whose chidings raise thee? Seek, seeker, in thyself; submit to find In the stones, bread, and life in the blank mind."]

He is himself principle, motive, and end of his own destiny; he is himself, and that is enough for him. This superb triumph of life is not far from being a sort of impiety, or at least a displacement of adoration. By the mere fact that it does away with humility, such a superhuman point of view becomes dangerous; it is the very temptation to which the first man succumbed, that of becoming his own master by becoming like unto the Elohim. Here then the heroism of the philosopher approaches temerity, and the *Monologues* are therefore open to three reproaches: Ontologically, the position of man in the spiritual universe is wrongly indicated; the individual soul, not being unique and not springing from itself, can it be conceived without God? Psychologically, the force of spontaneity in the *ego* is allowed a dominion too exclusive of any other. As a fact, it is not everything in man. Morally, evil is scarcely named, and conflict, the condition of true peace, is left out of count. So that the peace described in the *Monologues* is neither a conquest by man nor a grace from heaven; it is rather a stroke of good fortune.

February 2d.—Still the *Monologues*. Critically I defended myself enough against them yesterday; I may abandon myself now, without scruple and without danger, to the admiration and the sympathy with which they inspire me. This life so proudly independent, this sovereign conception of human dignity, this actual possession of the universe and the infinite, this perfect emancipation from all which passes, this calm sense of strength and superiority, this invincible energy of will, this infallible clearness of self-vision, this autocracy of the consciousness which is its own master, all these decisive marks of a royal personality of a nature Olympian, profound, complete, harmonious, penetrate the mind with joy and heart with gratitude. What a life! what a man! These glimpses into the inner regions of a great soul do one good. Contact of this kind strengthens, restores, refreshes. Courage returns as we gaze; when we see what has been, we doubt no more that it can be again. At the sight of a *man* we too say to ourselves, let us also be men.

March 3, 1852.—Opinion has its value and even its power: to have it against us is painful when we are among friends, and harmful in the case of the outer world. We should neither flatter opinion nor court it; but it is better, if we can help it, not to throw it on to a false scent. The first error is a meanness; the second an imprudence. We should be ashamed of the one; we may regret the other. Look to yourself; you are much given to this last fault, and it has already done you great harm. Be ready to bend your pride; abase yourself even so far as to show yourself ready and clever like others. This world of skillful egotisms and active ambitions, this world of men, in which one must deceive by smiles, conduct, and silence as much as by actual words, a world revolting to the proud and upright soul, it is our business to learn to live in it! Success is required in it: succeed. Only force is recognized there: be strong. Opinion seeks to impose her law upon all, instead of setting her at defiance, it would be better to struggle with her and conquer.... I understand the indignation of contempt, and the wish to crush, roused irresistibly by all that creeps, all that is tortuous, oblique, ignoble.... But I cannot maintain such a mood, which is a mood of vengeance, for long. This world is a world of men, and these men are our brothers. We must not banish from us the divine breath, we must love. Evil must be conquered by good; and before all things one must keep a pure conscience. Prudence may be preached from this point of view too. "Be ye simple as the dove and prudent as the serpent," are the words of Jesus. Be careful of your reputation, not through vanity, but that you may not harm your life's work, and out of love for truth. There is still something of self-seeking in the refined disinterestedness which will not justify itself, that it may feel itself superior to opinion. It requires ability, to make what we seem agree with what we are, and humility, to feel that we are no great things.

There, thanks to this journal, my excitement has passed away. I have just read the last book of it through again, and the morning has passed by. On the way I have been conscious of a certain amount of monotony. It does not signify! These pages are not written to be read; they are written for my own consolation and warning. They are landmarks in my past; and some of the landmarks are funeral crosses, stone pyramids, withered stalks grown green again, white pebbles, coins—all of them helpful toward finding one's way again through the Elysian fields of the soul. The pilgrim has marked his stages in it; he is able to trace by it his thoughts, his tears, his joys. This is my traveling diary: if some passages from it may be useful to others, and if sometimes even I have communicated such passages to the public, these thousand pages as a whole are only of value to me and to those who, after me, may take some interest in the itinerary of an obscurely conditioned soul, far from the world's noise and fame. These sheets will be monotonous when my life is so; they will repeat themselves when feelings repeat themselves; truth at any rate will be always there, and truth is their only muse, their only pretext, their only duty.

April 2, 1852.—What a lovely walk! Sky clear, sun rising, all the tints bright, all the outlines sharp, save for the soft and misty infinite of the lake. A pinch of white frost, powdered the fields, lending a metallic relief to the hedges of green box, and to the whole landscape, still without leaves, an air of health and vigor, of youth and freshness. "Bathe, O disciple, thy thirsty soul in the dew of the dawn!" says Faust, to us, and he is right. The morning air breathes a new and laughing energy into veins and marrow. If every day is a repetition of life, every dawn gives signs as it were a new contract with existence. At dawn everything is fresh, light, simple, as it is for children. At dawn spiritual truth, like the atmosphere, is more transparent, and our organs, like the young leaves, drink in the light more eagerly, breathe in more ether, and less of things earthly. If night and the starry sky speak to the meditative soul of God, of eternity and the infinite, the dawn is the time for projects, for resolutions, for the birth of action. While the silence and the "sad serenity of the azure vault," incline the soul to self-recollection, the vigor and gayety of nature spread into the heart and make it eager for life and living. Spring is upon us. Primroses and violets have already hailed her coming. Rash blooms are showing on the peach trees; the swollen buds of the pear trees and the lilacs point to the blossoming that is to be; the honeysuckles are already green.

April 26, 1852.—This evening a feeling of emptiness took possession of me; and the solemn ideas of duty, the future, solitude, pressed themselves upon me. I gave myself to meditation, a very necessary defense against the dispersion and distraction brought about by the day's work and its detail. Read a part of Krause's book *"Urbild der Menschheit"* [Footnote: Christian Frederick Krause, died 1832, Hegel's younger contemporary, and the author of a system which he called *panentheism*—Amiel alludes to it later on.] which answered marvelously to my thought and my need. This philosopher has always a beneficent effect upon me; his sweet religious serenity gains upon me and invades me. He inspires me with a sense of peace and infinity.

Still I miss something, common worship, a positive religion, shared with other people. Ah! when will the church to which I belong in heart rise into being? I cannot like Scherer, content myself with being in the right all alone. I must have a less solitary Christianity. My religious needs are not satisfied any more than my social needs, or my needs of affection. Generally I am able to forget them and lull them to sleep. But at times they wake up with a sort of painful bitterness ... I waver between languor and *ennui*, between frittering myself away on the infinitely little, and longing after what is unknown and distant. It is like the situation which French novelists are so fond of, the story of a *vie de province*; only the province is all that is not the country of the soul, every place where the heart feels itself strange, dissatisfied, restless and thirsty. Alas! well understood, this place is the earth, this country of one's dreams is heaven, and this suffering is the eternal homesickness, the thirst for happiness.

"In der Beschraenkung zeigt sich erst der Meister," says Goethe. *Male resignation*, this also is the motto of those who are masters of the art of life; "manly," that is to say, courageous, active, resolute, persevering, "resignation," that is to say, self-sacrifice, renunciation, limitation. Energy in resignation, there lies the wisdom of the sons of earth, the only serenity possible in this life of struggle and of combat. In it is the peace of martyrdom, in it too the promise of triumph.

April 28, 1852. (Lancy.) [Footnote: A village near Geneva.]—Once more I feel the spring languor creeping over me, the spring air about me. This morning the poetry of the scene, the song of the birds, the tranquil sunlight, the breeze blowing over the fresh green fields, all rose into and filled my heart. Now all is silent. O silence, thou art terrible! terrible as that calm of the ocean which lets the eye penetrate the fathomless abysses below. Thou showest us in ourselves depths which make us giddy, inextinguishable needs, treasures of suffering. Welcome tempests! at least they blur and trouble the surface of these waters with their terrible secrets. Welcome the passion blasts which stir the wares of the soul, and so veil from us its bottomless gulfs! In all of us, children of dust, sons of time, eternity inspires an involuntary anguish, and the infinite, a mysterious terror. We seem to be entering a kingdom of the dead. Poor heart, thy craving is for life, for love, for illusions! And thou art right after all, for life is sacred.

In these moments of *tete-a-tete* with the infinite, how different life looks! How all that usually occupies and excites us becomes suddenly puerile, frivolous and vain. We seem to ourselves mere puppets, marionettes, strutting seriously through a fantastic show, and mistaking gewgaws for things of great price. At such moments, how everything becomes transformed, how everything changes! Berkeley and Fichte seem right, Emerson too; the world is but an allegory; the idea is more real than the fact; fairy tales, legends, are as true as natural history, and even more true, for they are emblems of greater transparency. The only substance properly so called is the soul. What is all the rest? Mere shadow, pretext, figure, symbol, or dream. Consciousness alone is immortal, positive, perfectly real. The world is but a firework, a sublime phantasmagoria, destined to cheer and form the soul. Consciousness is a universe, and its sun is love....

Already I am falling back into the objective life of thought. It delivers me from—shall I say? no, it deprives me of the intimate life of feeling. Reflection solves reverie and burns her delicate wings. This is why science does not make men, but merely entities and abstractions. Ah, let us feel and live and beware of too much analysis! Let us put spontaneity, *naivete*, before reflection, experience before study; let us make life itself our study. Shall I then never have the heart of a woman to rest upon? a son in whom to live again, a little world where I may see flowering and blooming all that is stifled in me? I shrink and draw back, for fear of breaking my dream. I have staked so much on this card that I dare not play it. Let me dream again....

Do no violence to yourself, respect in yourself the oscillations of feeling. They are your life and your nature; One wiser than you ordained them. Do not abandon yourself altogether either to instinct or to will. Instinct is a siren, will a despot. Be neither the slave of your impulses and sensations of the moment, nor of an abstract and general plan; be open to what life brings from within and without, and welcome the unforeseen; but give to your life unity, and bring the unforeseen within the lines of your plan. Let what is natural in you raise itself to the level of the spiritual, and let the spiritual become once more natural. Thus will your development be harmonious, and the peace of heaven will shine upon your brow; always on condition that your peace is made, and that you have climbed your Calvary.

Afternoon—Shall I ever enjoy again those marvelous reveries of past days, as, for instance, once, when I was still quite a youth, in the early dawn, sitting among the ruins of the castle of Faucigny; another time in the mountains above Lavey, under the midday sun, lying under a tree and visited by three butterflies; and again another night on the sandy shore of the North Sea, stretched full length upon the beach, my eyes wandering over the Milky Way? Will they ever return to me, those grandiose, immortal, cosmogonic dreams, in which one seems to carry the world in one's breast, to touch the stars, to possess the infinite? Divine moments, hours of ecstasy, when thought flies from world to world, penetrates the great enigma, breathes with a respiration large, tranquil, and profound, like that of the ocean, and hovers serene and boundless like the blue heaven! Visits from the muse, Urania, who traces around the foreheads of those she loves the phosphorescent nimbus of contemplative power, and who pours into their hearts the tranquil intoxication, if not the authority of genius, moments of irresistible intuition in which a man feels himself great like the universe and calm like a god! From the celestial spheres down to the shell or the moss, the whole of creation is then submitted to our gaze, lives in our breast, and accomplishes in us its eternal work with the regularity of destiny and the passionate ardor of love. What hours, what memories! The traces which remain to us of them are enough to fill us with respect and enthusiasm, as though they had been visits of the Holy Spirit. And then, to fall back again from these heights with their boundless horizons into the muddy ruts of triviality! what a fall! Poor Moses! Thou too sawest undulating in the distance the ravishing hills of the promised land, and it was thy fate nevertheless to lay thy weary bones in a grave dug in the desert! Which of us has not his promised land, his day of ecstasy and his death in exile? What a pale counterfeit is real life of the life we see in glimpses, and how these flaming lightnings of our prophetic youth make the twilight of our dull monotonous manhood more dark and dreary!

April 29 (Lancy).—This morning the air was calm, the sky slightly veiled. I went out into the garden to see what progress the spring was making. I strolled from the irises to the lilacs, round the flower-beds, and in the shrubberies. Delightful surprise! at the corner of the walk, half hidden under a thick clump of shrubs, a small leaved *chorchorus* had flowered during the night. Gay and fresh as a bunch of bridal flowers, the little shrub glittered before me in all the attraction of its opening beauty. What springlike innocence, what soft and modest loveliness, there was in these white corollas, opening gently to the sun, like thoughts which smile upon us at waking, and perched upon their young leaves of virginal green like bees upon the wing! Mother of marvels, mysterious and tender nature, why do we not live more in thee? The poetical *flaneurs* of Toepffer, his Charles and Jules, the friends and passionate lovers of thy secret graces, the dazzled and ravished beholders of thy beauties, rose up in my memory, at once a reproach and a lesson. A modest garden and a country rectory, the narrow horizon of a garret, contain for those who know how to look and to wait more instruction than a library, even than that of *Mon oncle*. [Footnote: The allusions in this passage are to Toepffer's best known books—"La Presbytere" and "La Bibliotheque de mon Oncle," that airy chronicle of a hundred romantic or vivacious nothings which has the young student Jules for its center.] Yes, we are too busy, too encumbered, too much occupied, too active! We read too much! The one thing needful is to throw off all one's load of cares, of preoccupations, of pedantry, and to become again young, simple, child-like, living happily and gratefully in the present hour. We must know how to put occupation aside, which does not mean that we must be idle. In an inaction which is meditative and attentive the wrinkles of the soul are smoothed away, and the soul itself spreads, unfolds, and springs afresh, and, like the trodden grass of the roadside or the bruised leaf of a plant, repairs its injuries, becomes new, spontaneous, true, and original. Reverie, like the rain of night, restores color and force to thoughts which have been blanched and wearied by the heat of the day. With gentle fertilizing power it awakens within us a thousand sleeping germs, and as though in play, gathers round us materials for the future, and images for the use of talent. *Reverie is the Sunday of thought*; and who knows which is the more important and fruitful for man, the laborious tension of the week, or the life-giving repose of the Sabbath? The *flanerie* so exquisitely glorified and sung by Toepffer is not only delicious, but useful. It is like a bath which gives vigor and suppleness to the whole being, to the mind as to the body; it is the sign and festival of liberty, a joyous and wholesome banquet, the banquet of the butterfly wandering from flower to flower over the hills and in the fields. And remember, the soul too is a butterfly.

May 2, 1852. (Sunday) Lancy.—This morning read the epistle of St. James, the exegetical volume of Cellerier [Footnote: Jacob-Elysee Cellerier, professor of theology at the Academy of Geneva, and son of the pastor of Satigny mentioned in Madame de Stael's "L'Allemagne."] on this epistle, and a great deal of Pascal, after having first of all passed more than an hour in the garden with the children. I made them closely examine the flowers, the shrubs, the grasshoppers, the snails, in order to practice them in observation, in wonder, in kindness.

How enormously important are these first conversations of childhood! I felt it this morning with a sort of religious terror. Innocence and childhood are sacred. The sower who casts in the seed, the father or mother casting in the fruitful word are accomplishing a pontifical act and ought to perform it with religious awe, with prayer and gravity, for they are laboring at the kingdom of God. All seed-sowing is a mysterious thing, whether the seed fall into the earth or into souls. Man is a husbandman; his whole work rightly understood is to develop life, to sow it everywhere. Such is the mission of humanity, and of this divine mission the great instrument is speech. We forget too often that language is both a seed-sowing and a revelation. The influence of a word in season, is it not incalculable? What a mystery is speech! But we are blind to it, because we are carnal and earthy. We see the stones and the trees by the road, the furniture of our houses, all that is palpable and material. We have no eyes for the invisible phalanxes of ideas which people the air and hover incessantly around each one of us.

Every life is a profession of faith, and exercises an inevitable and silent propaganda. As far as lies in its power, it tends to transform the universe and humanity into its own image. Thus we have all a cure of souls. Every man is the center of perpetual radiation like a luminous body; he is, as it were, a beacon which entices a ship upon the rocks if it does not guide it into port. Every man is a priest, even involuntarily; his conduct is an unspoken sermon, which is forever preaching to others; but there are priests of Baal, of Moloch, and of all the false gods. Such is the high importance of example. Thence comes the terrible responsibility which weighs upon us all. An evil example is a spiritual poison: it is the proclamation of a sacrilegious faith, of an impure God. Sin would be only an evil for him who commits it, were it not a crime toward the weak brethren, whom it corrupts. Therefore, it has been said: "It were better for a man not to have been born than to offend one of these little ones."

May 6, 1852.—It is women who, like mountain flowers, mark with most characteristic precision the gradation of social zones. The hierarchy of classes is plainly visible among them; it is blurred in the other sex. With women this hierarchy has the average regularity of nature; among men we see it broken by the incalculable varieties of human freedom. The reason is that the man on the whole, makes himself by his own activity, and that the woman, is, on the whole, made by her situation; that the one modifies and shapes circumstance by his own energy, while the gentleness of the other is dominated by and reflects circumstance; so that woman, so to speak, inclines to be species, and man to be individual.

Thus, which is curious, women are at once the sex which is most constant and most variable. Most constant from the moral point of view, most variable from the social. A confraternity in the first case, a hierarchy in the second. All degrees of culture and all conditions of society are clearly marked in their outward appearance, their manners and their tastes; but the inward fraternity is traceable in their feelings, their instincts, and their desires. The feminine sex represents at the same time natural and historical inequality; it maintains the unity of the species and marks off the categories of society, it brings together and divides, it gathers and separates, it makes castes and breaks through them, according as it interprets its twofold *role* in the one sense or the other. At bottom, woman's mission is essentially conservative, but she is a conservative without discrimination. On the one side, she maintains God's work in man, all that is lasting, noble, and truly human, in the race, poetry, religion, virtue, tenderness. On the other, she maintains the results of circumstance, all that is passing, local, and artificial in society; that is to say, customs, absurdities, prejudices, littlenesses. She surrounds with the same respectful and tenacious faith the serious and the frivolous, the good and the bad. Well, what then? Isolate if you can, the fire from its smoke. It is a divine law that you are tracing, and therefore good. The woman preserves; she is tradition as the man is progress. And if there is no family and no humanity without the two sexes, without these two forces there is no history.

May 14, 1852. (Lancy.)—Yesterday I was full of the philosophy of joy, of youth, of the spring, which smiles and the roses which intoxicate; I preached the doctrine of strength, and I forgot that, tried and afflicted like the two friends with whom I was walking, I should probably have reasoned and felt as they did.

Our systems, it has been said, are the expression of our character, or the theory of our situation, that is to say, we like to think of what has been given as having been acquired, we take our nature for our own work, and our lot in life for our own conquest, an illusion born of vanity and also of the craving for liberty. We are unwilling to be the product of circumstances, or the mere expansion of an inner germ. And yet we have received everything, and the part which is really ours, is small indeed, for it is mostly made up of negation, resistance, faults. We receive everything, both life and happiness; but the *manner* in which we receive, this is what is still ours. Let us then, receive trustfully without shame or anxiety. Let us humbly accept from God even our own nature, and treat it charitably, firmly, intelligently. Not that we are called upon to accept the evil and the disease in us, but let us accept *ourselves* in spite of the evil and the disease. And let us never be afraid of innocent joy; God is good, and what He does is well done; resign yourself to everything, even to happiness; ask for the spirit of sacrifice, of detachment, of renunciation, and above all, for the spirit of joy and gratitude, that genuine and religious optimism which sees in God a father, and asks no pardon for His benefits. We must dare to be happy, and dare to confess it, regarding ourselves always as the depositaries, not as the authors of our own joy.

* * * * *

... This evening I saw the first glow-worm of the season in the turf beside the little winding road which descends from Lancy toward the town. It was crawling furtively under the grass, like a timid thought or a dawning talent.

June 17, 1852.—Every despotism has a specially keen and hostile instinct for whatever keeps up human dignity, and independence. And it is curious to see scientific and realist teaching used everywhere as a means of stifling all freedom of investigation as addressed to moral questions under a dead weight of facts. Materialism is the auxiliary doctrine of every tyranny, whether of the one or of the masses. To crush what is spiritual, moral, human so to speak, in man, by specializing him; to form mere wheels of the great social machine, instead of perfect individuals; to make society and not conscience the center of life, to enslave the soul to things, to depersonalize man, this is the dominant drift of our epoch. Everywhere you may see a tendency to substitute the laws of dead matter (number, mass) for the laws of the moral nature (persuasion, adhesion, faith) equality, the principle of mediocrity, becoming a dogma; unity aimed at through uniformity; numbers doing duty for argument; negative liberty, which has no law *in itself*, and recognizes no limit except in force, everywhere taking the place of positive liberty, which means action guided by an inner law and curbed by a moral authority. Socialism *versus* individualism: this is how Vinet put the dilemma. I should say rather that it is only the eternal antagonism between letter and spirit, between form and matter, between the outward and the inward, appearance and reality, which is always present in every conception and in all ideas.

Materialism coarsens and petrifies everything; makes everything vulgar and every truth false. And there is a religious and political materialism which spoils all that it touches, liberty, equality, individuality. So that there are two ways of understanding democracy....

What is threatened to-day is moral liberty, conscience, respect for the soul, the very nobility of man. To defend the soul, its interests, its rights, its dignity, is the most pressing duty for whoever sees the danger. What the writer, the teacher, the pastor, the philosopher, has to do, is to defend humanity in man. Man! the true man, the ideal man! Such should be their motto, their rallying cry. War to all that debases, diminishes, hinders, and degrades him; protection for all that fortifies, ennobles, and raises him. The test of every religious, political, or educational system, is the man which it forms. If a system injures the intelligence it is bad. If it injures the character it is vicious. If it injures the conscience it is criminal.

August 12, 1852. (Lancy.)—Each sphere of being tends toward a higher sphere, and has already revelations and presentiments of it. The ideal under all its forms is the anticipation and the prophetic vision of that existence, higher than his own, toward which every being perpetually aspires. And this higher and more dignified existence is more inward in character, that is to say, more spiritual. Just as volcanoes reveal to us the secrets of the interior of the globe, so enthusiasm and ecstasy are the passing explosions of this inner world of the soul; and human life is but the preparation and the means of approach to this spiritual life. The degrees of initiation are innumerable. Watch, then, disciple of life, watch and labor toward the development of the angel within thee! For the divine Odyssey is but a series of more and more ethereal metamorphoses, in which each form, the result of what goes before, is the condition of those which follow. The divine life is a series of successive deaths, in which the mind throws off its imperfections and its symbols, and yields to the growing attraction of the ineffable center of gravitation, the sun of intelligence and love. Created spirits in the accomplishment of their destinies tend, so to speak, to form constellations and milky ways within the empyrean of the divinity; in becoming gods, they surround the throne of the sovereign with a sparkling court. In their greatness lies their homage. The divinity with which they are invested is the noblest glory of God. God is the father of spirits, and the constitution of the eternal kingdom rests on the vassalship of love.

September 27, 1852. (Lancy.)—To-day I complete my thirty-first year....

The most beautiful poem there is, is life—life which discerns its own story in the making, in which inspiration and self-consciousness go together and help each other, life which knows itself to be the world in little, a repetition in miniature of the divine universal poem. Yes, be man; that is to say, be nature, be spirit, be the image of God, be what is greatest, most beautiful, most lofty in all the spheres of being, be infinite will and idea, a reproduction of the great whole. And be everything while being nothing, effacing thyself, letting God enter into thee as the air enters an empty space, reducing the *ego* to the mere vessel which contains the divine essence. Be humble, devout, silent, that so thou mayest hear within the depths of thyself the subtle and profound voice; be spiritual and pure, that so thou mayest have communion with the pure spirit. Withdraw thyself often into the sanctuary of thy inmost consciousness; become once more point and atom, that so thou mayest free thyself from space, time, matter, temptation, dispersion, that thou mayest escape thy very organs themselves and thine own life. That is to say, die often, and examine thyself in the presence of this death, as a preparation for the last death. He who can without shuddering confront blindness, deafness, paralysis, disease, betrayal, poverty; he who can without terror appear before the sovereign justice, he alone can call himself prepared for partial or total death. How far am I from anything of the sort, how far is my heart from any such stoicism! But at least we can try to detach ourselves from all that can be taken away from us, to accept everything as a loan and a gift, and to cling only to the imperishable—this at any rate we can attempt. To believe in a good and fatherly God, who educates us, who tempers the wind to the shorn lamb, who punishes only when he must, and takes away only with regret; this thought, or rather this conviction, gives courage and security. Oh, what need we have of love, of tenderness, of affection, of kindness, and how vulnerable we are, we the sons of God, we, immortal and sovereign beings! Strong as the universe or feeble as the worm, according as we represent God or only ourselves, as we lean upon infinite being, or as we stand alone.

The point of view of religion, of a religion at once active and moral, spiritual and profound, alone gives to life all the dignity and all the energy of which it is capable. Religion makes invulnerable and invincible. Earth can only be conquered in the name of heaven. All good things are given over and above to him who desires but righteousness. To be disinterested is to be strong, and the world is at the feet of him whom it cannot tempt. Why? Because spirit is lord of matter, and the world belongs to God. "Be of good cheer," saith a heavenly voice, "I have overcome the world."

Lord, lend thy strength to those who are weak in the flesh, but willing in the spirit!

October 31, 1852. (Lancy.)—Walked for half an hour in the garden. A fine rain was falling, and the landscape was that of autumn. The sky was hung with various shades of gray, and mists hovered about the distant mountains, a melancholy nature. The leaves were falling on all sides like the last illusions of youth under the tears of irremediable grief. A brood of chattering birds were chasing each other through the Shrubberies, and playing games among the branches, like a knot of hiding schoolboys. The ground strewn with leaves, brown, yellow, and reddish; the trees half-stripped, some more, some less, and decked in ragged splendors of dark-red, scarlet, and yellow; the reddening shrubs and plantations; a few flowers still lingering behind, roses, nasturtiums, dahlias, shedding their petals round them; the bare fields, the thinned hedges; and the fir, the only green thing left, vigorous and stoical, like eternal youth braving decay; all these innumerable and marvelous symbols which forms colors, plants, and living beings, the earth and the sky, yield at all times to the eye which has learned to look for them, charmed and enthralled me. I wielded a poetic wand, and had but to touch a phenomenon to make it render up to me its moral significance. Every landscape is, as it were, a state of the soul, and whoever penetrates into both is astonished to find how much likeness there is in each detail. True poetry is truer than science, because it is synthetic, and seizes at once what the combination of all the sciences is able at most to attain as a final result. The soul of nature is divined by the poet; the man of science, only serves to accumulate materials for its demonstration.

November 6, 1852.—I am capable of all the passions, for I bear them all within me. Like a tamer of wild beasts, I keep them caged and lassoed, but I sometimes hear them growling. I have stifled more than one nascent love. Why? Because with that prophetic certainty which belongs to moral intuition, I felt it lacking in true life, and less durable than myself. I choked it down in the name of the supreme affection to come. The loves of sense, of imagination, of sentiment, I have seen through and rejected them all; I sought the love which springs from the central profundities of being. And I still believe in it. I will have none of those passions of straw which dazzle, burn up, and wither; I invoke, I await, and I hope for the love which is great, pure and earnest, which lives and works in all the fibres and through all the powers of the soul. And even if I go lonely to the end, I would rather my hope and my dream died with me, than that my soul should content itself with any meaner union.

November 8, 1852.—Responsibility is my invisible nightmare. To suffer through one's own fault is a torment worthy of the lost, for so grief is envenomed by ridicule, and the worst ridicule of all, that which springs from shame of one's self. I have only force and energy wherewith to meet evils coming from outside; but an irreparable evil brought about by myself, a renunciation for life of my liberty, my peace of mind, the very thought of it is maddening—I expiate my privilege indeed. My privilege is to be spectator of my life drama, to be fully conscious of the tragi-comedy of my own destiny, and, more than that, to be in the secret of the tragi-comic itself, that is to say, to be unable to take my illusions seriously, to see myself, so to speak, from the theater on the stage, or to be like a man looking from beyond the tomb into existence. I feel myself forced to feign a particular interest in my individual part, while all the time I am living in the confidence of the poet who is playing with all these agents which seem so important, and knows all that they are ignorant of. It is a strange position, and one which becomes painful as soon as grief obliges me to betake myself once more to my own little *role*, binding me closely to it, and warning me that I am going too far in imagining myself, because of my conversations with the poet, dispensed from taking up again my modest part of valet in the piece. Shakespeare must have experienced this feeling often, and Hamlet, I think, must express it somewhere. It is a *Doppelgaengerei*, quite German in character, and which explains the disgust with reality and the repugnance to public life, so common among the thinkers of Germany. There is, as it were, a degradation a gnostic fall, in thus folding one's wings and going back again into the vulgar shell of one's own individuality. Without grief, which is the string of this venturesome kite, man would soar too quickly and too high, and the chosen souls would be lost for the race, like balloons which, save for gravitation, would never return from the empyrean.

How, then, is one to recover courage enough for action? By striving to restore in one's self something of that unconsciousness, spontaneity, instinct, which reconciles us to earth and makes man useful and relatively happy.

By believing more practically in the providence which pardons and allows of reparation.

By accepting our human condition in a more simple and childlike spirit, fearing trouble less, calculating less, hoping more. For we decrease our responsibility, if we decrease our clearness of vision, and fear lessens with the lessening of responsibility.

By extracting a richer experience out of our losses and lessons.

November 9, 1852.—A few pages of the *Chrestomathie Francaise* and Vinet's remarkable letter at the head of the volume, have given me one or two delightful hours. As a thinker, as a Christian, and as a man, Vinet occupies a typical place. His philosophy, his theology, his esthetics, in short, his work, will be, or has been already surpassed at all points. His was a great soul and a fine talent. But neither were well enough served by circumstances. We see in him a personality worthy of all veneration, a man of singular goodness and a writer of distinction, but not quite a great man, nor yet a great writer. Profundity and purity, these are what he possesses in a high degree, but not greatness, properly speaking. For that, he is a little too subtle and analytical, too ingenious and fine-spun; his thought is overladen with detail, and has not enough flow, eloquence, imagination, warmth, and largeness. Essentially and constantly meditative, he has not strength enough left to deal with what is outside him. The casuistries of conscience and of language, eternal self-suspicion, and self-examination, his talent lies in these things, and is limited by them. Vinet wants passion, abundance, *entrainement*, and therefore popularity. The individualism which is his title to glory is also the cause of his weakness.

We find in him always the solitary and the ascetic. His thought is, as it were, perpetually at church; it is perpetually devising trials and penances for itself. Hence the air of scruple and anxiety which characterizes it even in its bolder flights. Moral energy, balanced by a disquieting delicacy of fibre; a fine organization marred, so to speak, by low health, such is the impression it makes upon us. Is it reproach or praise to say of Vinet's mind that it seems to one a force perpetually reacting upon itself? A warmer and more self-forgetful manner; more muscles, as it were, around the nerves, more circles of intellectual and historical life around the individual circle, these are what Vinet, of all writers perhaps the one who makes us *think* most, is still lacking in. Less *reflexivity* and more plasticity, the eye more on the object, would raise the style of Vinet, so rich in substance, so nervous, so full of ideas, and variety, into a grand style. Vinet, to sum up, is conscience personified, as man and as writer. Happy the literature and the society which is able to count at one time two or three like him, if not equal to him!

November 10, 1852.—How much have we not to learn from the Greeks, those immortal ancestors of ours! And how much better they solved their problem than we have solved ours. Their ideal man is not ours, but they understood infinitely better than we how to reverence, cultivate and ennoble the man whom they knew. In a thousand respects we are still barbarians beside them, as Beranger said to me with a sigh in 1843: barbarians in education, in eloquence, in public life, in poetry, in matters of art, etc. We must have millions of men in order to produce a few elect spirits: a thousand was enough in Greece. If the measure of a civilization is to be the number of perfected men that it produces, we are still far from this model people. The slaves are no longer below us, but they are among us. Barbarism is no longer at our frontiers; it lives side by side with us. We carry within us much greater things than they, but we ourselves are smaller. It is a strange result. Objective civilization produced great men while making no conscious effort toward such a result; subjective civilization produces a miserable and imperfect race, contrary to its mission and its earnest desire. The world grows more majestic but man diminishes. Why is this?

We have too much barbarian blood in our veins, and we lack measure, harmony and grace. Christianity, in breaking man up into outer and inner, the world into earth and heaven, hell and paradise, has decomposed the human unity, in order, it is true, to reconstruct it more profoundly and more truly. But Christianity has not yet digested this powerful leaven. She has not yet conquered the true humanity; she is still living under the antimony of sin and grace, of here below and there above. She has not penetrated into the whole heart of Jesus. She is still in the *narthex* of penitence; she is not reconciled, and even the churches still wear the livery of service, and have none of the joy of the daughters of God, baptized of the Holy Spirit.

Then, again, there is our excessive division of labor; our bad and foolish education which does not develop the whole man; and the problem of poverty. We have abolished slavery, but without having solved the question of labor. In law there are no more slaves, in fact, there are many. And while the majority of men are not free, the free man, in the true sense of the term can neither be conceived nor realized. Here are enough causes for our inferiority.

November 12, 1852.—St. Martin's summer is still lingering, and the days all begin in mist. I ran for a quarter of an hour round the garden to get some warmth and suppleness. Nothing could be lovelier than the last rosebuds, or than the delicate gaufred edges of the strawberry leaves embroidered with hoar-frost, while above them Arachne's delicate webs hung swaying in the green branches of the pines, little ball-rooms for the fairies carpeted with powdered pearls and kept in place by a thousand dewy strands hanging from above like the chains of a lamp and supporting them from below like the anchors of a vessel. These little airy edifices had all the fantastic lightness of the elf-world and all the vaporous freshness of dawn. They recalled to me the poetry of the north, wafting to me a breath from Caledonia or Iceland or Sweden, Frithiof and the Edda, Ossian and the Hebrides. All that world of cold and mist, of genius and of reverie, where warmth comes not from the sun but from the heart where man is more noticeable than nature—that chaste and vigorous world in which will plays a greater part than sensation and thought has more power than instinct—in short the whole romantic cycle of German and northern poetry, awoke little by little in my memory and laid claim upon my sympathy. It is a poetry of bracing quality, and acts upon one like a moral tonic. Strange charm of imagination! A twig of pine wood and a few spider-webs are enough to make countries, epochs, and nations live again before her.

December 26, 1852. (Sunday.)—If I reject many portions of our theology and of our church system, it is that I may the better reach the Christ himself. My philosophy allows me this. It does not state the dilemma as one of religion or philosophy, but as one of religion accepted or experienced, understood or not understood. For me philosophy is a manner of apprehending things, a mode of perception of reality. It does not create nature, man or God, but it finds them and seeks to understand them. Philosophy is consciousness taking account of itself with all that it contains. Now consciousness may contain a new life—the facts of regeneration and of salvation, that is to say, Christian experience. The understanding of the Christian consciousness is an integral part of philosophy, as the Christian consciousness is a leading form of religious consciousness, and religious consciousness an essential form of consciousness.

* * * * *

An error is the more dangerous in proportion to the degree of truth which it contains.

Look twice, if what you want is a just conception; look once, if what you want is a sense of beauty.

* * * * *

A man only understands what is akin to something already existing in himself.

* * * * *

Common sense is the measure of the possible; it is composed of experience and prevision; it is calculation applied to life.

* * * * *

The wealth of each mind is proportioned to the number and to the precision of its categories and its points of view.

* * * * *

To feel himself freer than his neighbor is the reward of the critic.

Modesty (*pudeur*) is always the sign and safeguard of a mystery. It is explained by its contrary—profanation. Shyness or modesty is, in truth, the half-conscious sense of a secret of nature or of the soul too intimately individual to be given or surrendered. It is *exchanged*. To surrender what is most profound and mysterious in one's being and personality at any price less than that of absolute reciprocity is profanation.

January 6, 1853.—Self-government with tenderness—here you have the condition of all authority over children. The child must discover in us no passion, no weakness of which he can make use; he must feel himself powerless to deceive or to trouble us; then he will recognize in us his natural superiors, and he will attach a special value to our kindness, because he will respect it. The child who can rouse in us anger, or impatience, or excitement, feels himself stronger than we, and a child only respects strength. The mother should consider herself as her child's sun, a changeless and ever radiant world, whither the small restless creature, quick at tears and laughter, light, fickle, passionate, full of storms, may come for fresh stores of light, warmth, and electricity, of calm and of courage. The mother represents goodness, providence, law; that is to say, the divinity, under that form of it which is accessible to childhood. If she is herself passionate, she will inculcate on her child a capricious and despotic God, or even several discordant gods. The religion of a child depends on what its mother and its father are, and not on what they say. The inner and unconscious ideal which guides their life is precisely what touches the child; their words, their remonstrances, their punishments, their bursts of feeling even, are for him merely thunder and comedy; what they worship, this it is which his instinct divines and reflects.

The child sees what we are, behind what we wish to be. Hence his reputation as a physiognomist. He extends his power as far as he can with each of us; he is the most subtle of diplomatists. Unconsciously he passes under the influence of each person about him, and reflects it while transforming it after his own nature. He is a magnifying mirror. This is why the first principle of education is: train yourself; and the first rule to follow if you wish to possess yourself of a child's will is: master your own.

February 5, 1853 (seven o'clock in the morning).—I am always astonished at the difference between one's inward mood of the evening and that of the morning. The passions which are dominant in the evening, in the morning leave the field free for the contemplative part of the soul. Our whole being, irritated and overstrung by the nervous excitement of the day, arrives in the evening at the culminating point of its human vitality; the same being, tranquilized by the calm of sleep, is in the morning nearer heaven. We should weigh a resolution in the two balances, and examine an idea under the two lights, if we wish to minimize the chances of error by taking the average of our daily oscillations. Our inner life describes regular curves, barometical curves, as it were, independent of the accidental disturbances which the storms of sentiment and passion may raise in us. Every soul has its climate, or rather, is a climate; it has, so to speak, its own meteorology in the general meteorology of the soul. Psychology, therefore, cannot be complete so long as the physiology of our planet is itself incomplete—that science to which we give nowadays the insufficient name of physics of the globe.

I became conscious this morning that what appears to us impossible is often an impossibility altogether subjective. Our mind, under the action of the passions, produces by a strange mirage gigantic obstacles, mountains or abysses, which stop us short. Breathe upon the passion and the phantasmagoria will vanish. This power of mirage, by which we are able to delude and fascinate ourselves, is a moral phenomenon worthy of attentive study. We make for ourselves, in truth, our own spiritual world monsters, chimeras, angels, we make objective what ferments in us. All is marvelous for the poet; all is divine for the saint; all is great for the hero; all is wretched, miserable, ugly, and bad for the base and sordid soul. The bad man creates around him a pandemonium, the artist, an Olympus, the elect soul, a paradise, which each of them sees for himself alone. We are all visionaries, and what we see is our soul in things. We reward ourselves and punish ourselves without knowing it, so that all appears to change when we change.

The soul is essentially active, and the activity of which we are conscious is but a part of our activity, and voluntary activity is but a part of our conscious activity. Here we have the basis of a whole psychology and system of morals. Man reproducing the world, surrounding himself with a nature which is the objective rendering of his spiritual nature, rewarding and punishing himself; the universe identical with the divine nature, and the nature of the perfect spirit only becoming understood according to the measure of our perfection; intuition the recompense of inward purity; science as the result of goodness; in short, a new phenomenology more complete and more moral, in which the total soul of things becomes spirit. This shall perhaps be my subject for my summer lectures. How much is contained in it! the whole domain of inner education, all that is mysterious in our life, the relation of nature to spirit, of God and all other beings to man, the repetition in miniature of the cosmogony, mythology, theology, and history of the universe, the evolution of mind, in a word the problem of problems into which I have often plunged but from which finite things, details, minutiae, have turned me back a thousand times. I return to the brink of the great abyss with the clear perception that here lies the problem of science, that to sound it is a duty, that God hides Himself only in light and love, that He calls upon us to become spirits, to possess ourselves and to possess Him in the measure of our strength and that it is our incredulity, our spiritual cowardice, which is our infirmity and weakness.

Dante, gazing into the three worlds with their divers heavens, saw under the form of an image what I would fain seize under a purer form. But he was a poet, and I shall only be a philosopher. The poet makes himself understood by human generations and by the crowd; the philosopher addresses himself only to a few rare minds. The day has broken. It brings with it dispersion of thought in action. I feel myself de-magnetized, pure clairvoyance gives place to study, and the ethereal depth of the heaven of contemplation vanishes before the glitter of finite things. Is it to be regretted? No. But it proves that the hours most apt for philosophical thought are those which precede the dawn.

February 10, 1853.—This afternoon I made an excursion to the Salève with my particular friends, Charles Heim, Edmond Scherer, Elie Lecoultre, and Ernest Naville. The conversation was of the most interesting kind, and prevented us from noticing the deep mud which hindered our walking. It was especially Scherer, Naville, and I who kept it alive. Liberty in God, the essence of Christianity, new publications in philosophy, these were our three subjects of conversation. The principle result for me was an excellent exercise in dialectic and in argumentation with solid champions. If I learned nothing, many of my ideas gained new confirmation, and I was able to penetrate more deeply into the minds of my friends. I am much nearer to Scherer than to Naville, but from him also I am in some degree separated.

It is a striking fact, not unlike the changing of swords in "Hamlet," that the abstract minds, those which move from ideas to facts, are always fighting on behalf of concrete reality; while the concrete minds, which move from facts to ideas, are generally the champions of abstract notions. Each pretends to that over which he has least power; each aims instinctively at what he himself lacks. It is an unconscious protest against the incompleteness of each separate nature. We all tend toward that which we possess least of, and our point of arrival is essentially different from our point of departure. The promised land is the land where one is not. The most intellectual of natures adopts an ethical theory of mind; the most moral of natures has an intellectual theory of morals. This reflection was brought home to me in the course of our three or four hours' discussion. Nothing is more hidden from us than the illusion which lives with us day by day, and our greatest illusion is to believe that we are what we think ourselves to be.

The mathematical intelligence and the historical intelligence (the two classes of intelligences) can never understand each other. When they succeed in doing so as to words, they differ as to the things which the words mean. At the bottom of every discussion of detail between them reappears the problem of the origin of ideas. If the problem is not present to them, there is confusion; if it is present to them, there is separation. They only agree as to the goal—truth; but never as to the road, the method, and the criterion.

Heim represented the impartiality of consciousness, Naville the morality of consciousness, Lecoultre the religion of consciousness, Scherer the intelligence of consciousness, and I the consciousness of consciousness. A common ground, but differing individualities. *Discrimen ingeniorum.*

What charmed me most in this long discussion was the sense of mental freedom which it awakened in me. To be able to set in motion the greatest subjects of thought without any sense of fatigue, to be greater than the world, to play with one's strength, this is what makes the well-being of intelligence, the Olympic festival of thought. *Habere, non haberi.* There is an equal happiness in the sense of reciprocal confidence, of friendship, and esteem in the midst of conflict; like athletes, we embrace each other before and after the combat, and the combat is but a deploying of the forces of free and equal men.

March 20, 1853.—I sat up alone; two or three times I paid a visit to the children's room. It seemed to me, young mothers, that I understood you! sleep is the mystery of life; there is a profound charm in this darkness broken by the tranquil light of the night-lamp, and in this silence measured by the rhythmic breathings of two young sleeping creatures. It was brought home to me that I was looking on at a marvelous operation of nature, and I watched it in no profane spirit. I sat silently listening, a moved and hushed spectator of this poetry of the cradle, this ancient and ever new benediction of the family, this symbol of creation, sleeping under the wing of God, of our consciousness withdrawing into the shade that it may rest from the burden of thought, and of the tomb, that divine bed, where the soul in its turn rests from life. To sleep is to strain and purify our emotions, to deposit the mud of life, to calm the fever of the soul, to return into the bosom of maternal nature, thence to re-issue, healed and strong. Sleep is a sort of innocence and purification. Blessed be He who gave it to the poor sons of men as the sure and faithful companion of life, our daily healer and consoler.

April 27, 1853.—This evening I read the treatise by Nicole so much admired by Mme. de Sevigne: "*Des moyens de conserver la paix avec les hommes.*" Wisdom so gentle and so insinuating, so shrewd, piercing, and yet humble, which divines so well the hidden thoughts and secrets of the heart, and brings them all into the sacred bondage of love to God and man, how good and delightful a thing it is! Everything in it is smooth, even well put together, well thought out, but no display, no tinsel, no worldly ornaments of style. The moralist forgets himself and in us appeals only to the conscience. He becomes a confessor, a friend, a counsellor.

May 11, 1853.—Psychology, poetry, philosophy, history, and science, I have swept rapidly to-day on the wings of the invisible hippogriff through all these spheres of thought. But the general impression has been one of tumult and anguish, temptation and disquiet.

I love to plunge deep into the ocean of life; but it is not without losing sometimes all sense of the axis and the pole, without losing myself and feeling the consciousness of my own nature and vocation growing faint and wavering. The whirlwind of the wandering Jew carries me away, tears me from my little familiar enclosure, and makes me behold all the empires of men. In my voluntary abandonment to the generality, the universal, the infinite, my particular *ego* evaporates like a drop of water in a furnace; it only condenses itself anew at the return of cold, after enthusiasm has died out and the sense of reality has returned. Alternate expansion and condensation, abandonment and recovery of self, the conquest of the world to be pursued on the one side, the deepening of consciousness on the other—such is the play of the inner life, the march of the microcosmic mind, the marriage of the individual soul with the universal soul, the finite with the infinite, whence springs the intellectual progress of man. Other betrothals unite the soul to God, the religious consciousness with the divine; these belong to the history of the will. And what precedes will is feeling, preceded itself by instinct. Man is only what he becomes—profound truth; but he becomes only what he is, truth still more profound. What am I? Terrible question! Problem of predestination, of birth, of liberty, there lies the abyss. And yet one must plunge into it, and I have done so. The prelude of Bach I heard this evening predisposed me to it; it paints the soul tormented and appealing and finally seizing upon God, and possessing itself of peace and the infinite with an all-prevailing fervor and passion.

May 14, 1853.—Third quartet concert. It was short. Variations for piano and violin by Beethoven, and two quartets, not more. The quartets were perfectly clear and easy to understand. One was by Mozart and the other by Beethoven, so that I could compare the two masters. Their individuality seemed to become plain to me: Mozart—grace, liberty, certainty, freedom, and precision of style, and exquisite and aristocratic beauty, serenity of soul, the health and talent of the master, both on a level with his genius; Beethoven—more pathetic, more passionate, more torn with feeling, more intricate, more profound, less perfect, more the slave of his genius, more carried away by his fancy or his passion, more moving, and more sublime than Mozart. Mozart refreshes you, like the "Dialogues" of Plato; he respects you, reveals to you your strength, gives you freedom and balance. Beethoven seizes upon you; he is more tragic and oratorical, while Mozart is more disinterested and poetical. Mozart is more Greek, and Beethoven more Christian. One is serene, the other serious. The first is stronger than destiny, because he takes life less profoundly; the second is less strong, because he has dared to measure himself against deeper sorrows. His talent is not always equal to his genius, and pathos is his dominant feature, as perfection is that of Mozart. In Mozart the balance of the whole is perfect, and art triumphs; in Beethoven feeling governs everything and emotion troubles his art in proportion as it deepens it.

July 26, 1853.—Why do I find it easier and more satisfactory, as a writer of verse, to compose in the short metres than in the long and serious ones? Why, in general, am I better fitted for what is difficult than for what is easy? Always for the same reason. I cannot bring myself to move freely, to show myself without a veil, to act on my own account and act seriously, to believe in and assert myself, whereas a piece of badinage which diverts attention from myself to the thing in hand, from the feeling to the skill of the writer, puts me at my ease. It is timidity which is at the bottom of it. There is another reason, too—I am afraid of greatness, I am not afraid of ingenuity, and distrustful as I am both of my gift and my instrument, I like to reassure myself by an elaborate practice of execution. All my published literary essays, therefore, are little else than studies, games, exercises for the purpose of testing myself. I play scales, as it were; I run up and down my instrument, I train my hand and make sure of its capacity and skill. But the work itself remains unachieved. My effort expires, and satisfied with the *power* to act I never arrive at the will to act. I am always preparing and never accomplishing, and my energy is swallowed up in a kind of barren curiosity. Timidity, then, and curiosity—these are the two obstacles which bar against me a literary career. Nor must procrastination be forgotten. I am always reserving for the future what is great, serious, and important, and meanwhile, I am eager to exhaust what is pretty and trifling. Sure of my devotion to things that are vast and profound, I am always lingering in their contraries lest I should neglect them. Serious at bottom, I am frivolous in appearance. A lover of thought, I seem to care above all, for expression; I keep the substance for myself, and reserve the form for others. So that the net result of my timidity is that I never treat the public seriously, and that I only show myself to it in what is amusing, enigmatical, or capricious; the result of my curiosity is that everything tempts me, the shell as well as the mountain, and that I lose myself in endless research; while the habit of procrastination keeps me forever at preliminaries and antecedents, and production itself is never even begun.

But if that is the fact, the fact might be different. I understand myself, but I do not approve myself.

August 1, 1853.—I have just finished Pelletan's book, "Profession de foi du dix-neuvieme Siecle." It is a fine book Only one thing is wanting to it—the idea of evil. It is a kind of supplement to the theory of Condorcet—indefinite perfectibility, man essentially good, *life*, which is a physiological notion, dominating virtue, duty, and holiness, in short, a non-ethical conception of history, liberty identified with nature, the natural man taken for the whole man. The aspirations which such a book represents are generous and poetical, but in the first place dangerous, since they lead to an absolute confidence in instinct; and in the second, credulous and unpractical, for they set before us a mere dream man, and throw a veil over both present and past reality. The book is at once the plea justificatory of progress, conceived as fatal and irresistible, and an enthusiastic hymn to the triumph of humanity. It is earnest, but morally superficial; poetical, but fanciful and untrue. It confounds the progress of the race with the progress of the individual, the progress of civilization with the advance of the inner life. Why? Because its criterion is quantitative, that is to say, purely exterior (having regard to the wealth of life), and not qualitative (the goodness of life).

Always the same tendency to take the appearance for the thing, the form for the substance, the law for the essence, always the same absence of moral personality, the same obtuseness of conscience, which has never recognized sin present in the will, which places evil outside of man, moralizes from outside, and transforms to its own liking the whole lesson of history! What is at fault is the philosophic superficiality of France, which she owes to her fatal notion of religion, itself due to a life fashioned by Catholicism and by absolute monarchy.

Catholic thought cannot conceive of personality as supreme and conscious of itself. Its boldness and its weakness come from one and the same cause—from an absence of the sense of responsibility, from that vassal state of conscience which knows only slavery or anarchy, which proclaims but does not obey the law, because the law is outside it, not within it. Another illusion is that of Quinet and Michelet, who imagine it possible to come out of Catholicism without entering into any other positive form of religion, and whose idea is to fight Catholicism by philosophy, a philosophy which is, after all, Catholic at bottom, since it springs from anti-Catholic reaction. The mind and the conscience, which have been formed by Catholicism, are powerless to rise to any other form of religion. From Catholicism, as from Epicureanism there is no return.

October 11, 1853.—My third day at Turin, is now over. I have been able to penetrate farther than ever before into the special genius of this town and people. I have felt it live, have realized it little by little, as my intuition became more distinct. That is what I care for most: to seize the soul of things, the soul of a nation; to live the objective life, the life outside self; to find my way into a new moral country. I long to assume the citizenship of this unknown world, to enrich myself with this fresh form of existence, to feel it from within, to link myself to it, and to reproduce it sympathetically; this is the end and the reward of my efforts. To-day the problem grew clear to me as I stood on the terrace of the military hospital, in full view of the Alps, the weather fresh and clear in spite of a stormy sky. Such an intuition after all is nothing out a synthesis wrought by instinct, a synthesis to which everything—streets, houses, landscape, accent, dialect, physiognomies, history, and habits contribute their share. I might call it the ideal integration of a people or its reduction to the generating point, or an entering into its consciousness. This generating point explains everything else, art, religion, history, politics, manners; and without it nothing can be explained. The ancients realized their consciousness in the national God. Modern nationalities, more complicated and less artistic, are more difficult to decipher. What one seeks for in them is the daemon, the fatum, the inner genius, the mission, the primitive disposition, both what there is desire for and what there is power for, the force in them and its limitations.

A pure and life-giving freshness of thought and of the spiritual life seemed to play about me, borne on the breeze descending from the Alps. I breathed an atmosphere of spiritual freedom, and I hailed with emotion and rapture the mountains whence was wafted to me this feeling of strength and purity. A thousand sensations, thoughts, and analogies crowded upon me. History, too, the history of the sub-Alpine countries, from the Ligurians to Hannibal, from Hannibal to Charlemagne, from Charlemagne to Napoleon, passed through my mind. All the possible points of view, were, so to speak, piled upon each other, and one caught glimpses of some eccentrically across others. I was enjoying and I was learning. Sight passed into vision without a trace of hallucination, and the landscape was my guide, my Virgil.

All this made me very sensible of the difference between me and the majority of travelers, all of whom have a special object, and content themselves with one thing or with several, while I desire all or nothing, and am forever straining toward the total, whether of all possible objects, or of all the elements present in the reality. In other words, what I desire is the sum of all desires, and what I seek to know is the sum of all different kinds of knowledge. Always the complete, the absolute; the *teres atque rotundum*, sphericity, non-resignation.

October 27, 1853.—I thank Thee, my God, for the hour that I have just passed in Thy presence. Thy will was clear to me; I measured my faults, counted my griefs, and felt Thy goodness toward me. I realized my own nothingness, Thou gavest me Thy peace. In bitterness there is sweetness; in affliction, joy; in submission, strength; in the God who punishes, the God who loves. To lose one's life that one may gain it, to offer it that one may receive it, to possess nothing that one may conquer all, to renounce self that God may give Himself to us, how impossible a problem, and how sublime a reality! No one truly knows happiness who has not suffered, and the redeemed are happier than the elect.

(Same day.)—The divine miracle *par excellence* consists surely in the apotheosis of grief, the transfiguration of evil by good. The work of creation finds its consummation, and the eternal will of the infinite mercy finds its fulfillment only in the restoration of the free creature to God and of an evil world to goodness, through love. Every soul in which conversion has taken place is a symbol of the history of the world. To be happy, to possess eternal life, to be in God, to be saved, all these are the same. All alike mean the solution of the problem, the aim of existence. And happiness is cumulative, as misery may be. An eternal growth is an unchangeable peace, an ever profounder depth of apprehension, a possession constantly more intense and more spiritual of the joy of heaven—this is happiness. Happiness has no limits, because God has neither bottom nor bounds, and because happiness is nothing but the conquest of God through love.

The center of life is neither in thought nor in feeling, nor in will, nor even in consciousness, so far as it thinks, feels, or wishes. For moral truth may have been penetrated and possessed in all these ways, and escape us still. Deeper even than consciousness there is our being itself, our very substance, our nature. Only those truths which have entered into this last region, which have become ourselves, become spontaneous and involuntary, instinctive and unconscious, are really our life—that is to say something more than our property. So long as we are able to distinguish any space whatever between the truth and us we remain outside it. The thought, the feeling, the desire, the consciousness of life, are not yet quite life. But peace and repose can nowhere be found except in life, and in eternal life and the eternal life is the divine life, is God. To become divine is then the aim of life: then only can truth be said to be ours beyond the possibility of loss, because it is no longer outside us, nor even in us, but we are it, and it is we; we ourselves are a truth, a will, a work of God. Liberty has become nature; the creature is one with its creator—one through love. It is what it ought to be; its education is finished, and its final happiness begins. The sun of time declines and the light of eternal blessedness arises.

Our fleshly hearts may call this mysticism. It is the mysticism of Jesus: "I am one with my Father; ye shall be one with me. We will be one with you."

Do not despise your situation; in it you must act, suffer, and conquer. From every point on earth we are equally near to heaven and to the infinite.

There are two states or conditions of pride. The first is one of self-approval, the second one of self-contempt. Pride is seen probably at its purest in the last.

* * * * *

It is by teaching that we teach ourselves, by relating that we observe, by affirming that we examine, by showing that we look, by writing that we think, by pumping that we draw water into the well.

* * * * *

February 1, 1854.—A walk. The atmosphere incredibly pure, a warm caressing gentleness in the sunshine—joy in one's whole being. Seated motionless upon a bench on the Tranchees, beside the slopes clothed with moss and tapestried with green, I passed some intense delicious moments, allowing great elastic waves of music, wafted to me from a military band on the terrace of St. Antoine, to surge and bound through me. Every way I was happy, as idler, as painter, as poet. Forgotten impressions of childhood and youth came back to me—all those indescribable effects wrought by color, shadow, sunlight, green hedges, and songs of birds, upon the soul just opening to poetry. I became again young, wondering, and simple, as candor and ignorance are simple. I abandoned myself to life and to nature, and they cradled me with an infinite gentleness. To open one's heart in purity to this ever pure nature, to allow this immortal life of things to penetrate into one's soul, is at the same time to listen to the voice of God. Sensation may be a prayer, and self-abandonment an act of devotion.

February 18, 1854.—Everything tends to become fixed, solidified, and crystallized in this French tongue of ours, which seeks form and not substance, the result and not its formation, what is seen rather than what is thought, the outside rather than the inside.

We like the accomplished end and not the pursuit of the end, the goal and not the road, in short, ideas ready-made and bread ready-baked, the reverse of Lessing's principle. What we look for above all are conclusions. This clearness of the "ready-made" is a superficial clearness—physical, outward, solar clearness, so to speak, but in the absence of a sense for origin and genesis it is the clearness of the incomprehensible, the clearness of opacity, the clearness of the obscure. We are always trifling on the surface. Our temper is formal—that is to say, frivolous and material, or rather artistic and not philosophical. For what it seeks is the figure, the fashion and manner of things, not their deepest life, their soul, their secret.

March 16, 1854. (From Veevay to Geneva.)—What message had this lake for me, with its sad serenity, its soft and even tranquility, in which was mirrored the cold monotonous pallor of mountains and clouds? That disenchanted disillusioned life may still be traversed by duty, lit by a memory of heaven. I was visited by a clear and profound intuition of the flight of things, of the fatality of all life, of the melancholy which is below the surface of all existence, but also of that deepest depth which subsists forever beneath the fleeting wave.

December 17, 1854.—When we are doing nothing in particular, it is then that we are living through all our being; and when we cease to add to our growth it is only that we may ripen and possess ourselves. Will is suspended, but nature and time are always active and if our life is no longer our work, the work goes on none the less. With us, without us, or in spite of us, our existence travels through its appointed phases, our invisible Psyche weaves the silk of its chrysalis, our destiny fulfills itself, and all the hours of life work together toward that flowering time which we call death. This activity, then, is inevitable and fatal; sleep and idleness do not interrupt it, but it may become free and moral, a joy instead of a terror.

Nothing is more characteristic of a man than the manner in which he behaves toward fools.

It costs us a great deal of trouble not to be of the same opinion as our self-love, and not to be ready to believe in the good taste of those who believe in our merits.

Does not true humility consist in accepting one's infirmity as a trial, and one's evil disposition as a cross, in sacrificing all one's pretensions and ambitions, even those of conscience? True humility is contentment.

* * * * *

A man only understands that of which he has already the beginnings in himself.

Let us be true: this is the highest maxim of art and of life, the secret of eloquence and of virtue, and of all moral authority.

* * * * *

March 28, 1855.—Not a blade of grass but has a story to tell, not a heart but has its romance, not a life which does not hide a secret which is either its thorn or its spur. Everywhere grief, hope, comedy, tragedy; even under the petrifaction of old age, as in the twisted forms of fossils, we may discover the agitations and tortures of youth. This thought is the magic wand of poets and of preachers: it strips the scales from our fleshly eyes, and gives us a clear view into human life; it opens to the ear a world of unknown melodies, and makes us understand the thousand languages of nature. Thwarted love makes a man a polyglot, and grief transforms him into a diviner and a sorcerer.

April 16, 1855.—I realized this morning the prodigious effect of climate on one's state of mind. I was Italian or Spanish. In this blue and limpid air, and under this southern sun, the very walls smile at you. All the chestnut trees were en fete; with their glistening buds shining like little flames at the curved ends of the branches, they were the candelabra of the spring decking the festival of eternal nature. How young everything was, how kindly, how gracious! the moist freshness of the grass, the transparent shadows in the courtyards, the strength of the old cathedral towers, the white edges of the roads. I felt myself a child; the sap of life mounted again into my veins as it does in plants. How sweet a thing is a little simple enjoyment! And now, a brass band which has stopped in the street makes my heart leap as it did at eighteen. Thanks be to God; there have been so many weeks and months when I thought myself an old man. Come poetry, nature, youth, and love, knead my life again with your fairy hands; weave round me once more your immortal spells; sing your siren melodies, make me drink of the cup of immortality, lead me back to the Olympus of the soul. Or rather, no paganism! God of joy and of grief, do with me what Thou wilt; grief is good, and joy is good also. Thou art leading me now through joy. I take it from Thy hands, and I give Thee thanks for it.

April 17, 1855.—The weather is still incredibly brilliant, warm, and clear. The day is full of the singing of birds, the night is full of stars, nature has become all kindness, and it is a kindness clothed upon with splendor.

For nearly two hours have I been lost in the contemplation of this magnificent spectacle. I felt myself in the temple of the infinite, in the presence of the worlds, God's guest in this vast nature. The stars wandering in the pale ether drew me far away from earth. What peace beyond the power of words, what dews of life eternal, they shed on the adoring soul! I felt the earth floating like a boat in this blue ocean. Such deep and tranquil delight nourishes the whole man, it purifies and ennobles. I surrendered myself, I was all gratitude and docility.

April 21, 1855.—I have been reading a great deal: ethnography, comparative anatomy, cosmical systems. I have traversed the universe from the deepest depths of the empyrean to the peristaltic movements of the atoms in the elementary cell. I have felt myself expanding in the infinite, and enfranchised in spirit from the bounds of time and space, able to trace back the whole boundless creation to a point without dimensions, and seeing the vast multitude of suns, of milky ways, of stars, and nebulae, all existent in the point.

And on all sides stretched mysteries, marvels and prodigies, without limit, without number, and without end. I felt the unfathomable thought of which the universe is the symbol live and burn within me; I touched, proved, tasted, embraced my nothingness and my immensity; I kissed the hem of the garments of God, and gave Him thanks for being Spirit and for being life. Such moments are glimpses of the divine. They make one conscious of one's immortality; they bring home to one that an eternity is not too much for the study of the thoughts and works of the eternal; they awaken in us an adoring ecstasy and the ardent humility of love.

May 23, 1855.—Every hurtful passion draws us to it, as an abyss does, by a kind of vertigo. Feebleness of will brings about weakness of head, and the abyss in spite of its horror, comes to fascinate us, as though it were a place of refuge. Terrible danger! For this abyss is within us; this gulf, open like the vast jaws of an infernal serpent bent on devouring us, is in the depth of our own being, and our liberty floats over this void, which is always seeking to swallow it up. Our only talisman lies in that concentration of moral force which we call conscience, that small inextinguishable flame of which the light is duty and the warmth love. This little flame should be the star of our life; it alone can guide our trembling ark across the tumult of the great waters; it alone can enable us to escape the temptations of the sea, the storms and the monsters which are the offspring of night and the deluge. Faith in God, in a holy, merciful, fatherly God, is the divine ray which kindles this flame.

How deeply I feel the profound and terrible poetry of all these primitive terrors from which have issued the various theogonies of the world, and how it all grows clear to me, and becomes a symbol of the one great unchanging thought, the thought of God about the universe! How present and sensible to my inner sense is the unity of everything! It seems to me that I am able to pierce to the sublime motive which, in all the infinite spheres of existence, and through all the modes of space and time, every created form reproduces and sings within the bond of an eternal harmony. From the infernal shades I feel myself mounting toward the regions of light; my flight across chaos finds its rest in paradise. Heaven, hell, the world, are within us. Man is the great abyss.

July 27, 1855.—So life passes away, tossed like a boat by the waves up and down, hither and thither, drenched by the spray, stained by the foam, now thrown upon the bank, now drawn back again according to the endless caprice of the water. Such, at least, is the life of the heart and the passions, the life which Spinoza and the stoics reprove, and which is the exact opposite of that serene and contemplative life, always equable like the starlight, in which man lives at peace, and sees everything tinder its eternal aspect; the opposite also of the life of conscience, in which God alone speaks, and all self-will surrenders itself to His will made manifest.

I pass from one to another of these three existences, which are equally known to me; but this very mobility deprives me of the advantages of each. For my heart is worn with scruples, the soul in me cannot crush the needs of the heart, and the conscience is troubled and no longer knows how to distinguish, in the chaos of contradictory inclinations, the voice of duty or the will of God. The want of simple faith, the indecision which springs from distrust of self, tend to make all my personal life a matter of doubt and uncertainty. I am afraid of the subjective life, and recoil from every enterprise, demand, or promise which may oblige me to realize myself; I feel a terror of action, and am only at ease in the impersonal, disinterested, and objective life of thought. The reason seems to be timidity, and the timidity springs from the excessive development of the reflective power which has almost destroyed in me all spontaneity, impulse, and instinct, and therefore all boldness and confidence. Whenever I am forced to act, I see cause for error and repentance everywhere, everywhere hidden threats and masked vexations. From a child I have been liable to the disease of irony, and that it may not be altogether crushed by destiny, my nature seems to have armed itself with a caution strong enough to prevail against any of life's blandishments. It is just this strength which is my weakness. I have a horror of being duped, above all, duped by myself, and I would rather cut myself off from all life's joys than deceive or be deceived. Humiliation, then, is the sorrow which I fear the most, and therefore it would seem as if pride were the deepest rooted of my faults.

This may be logical, but it is not the truth: it seems to me that it is really distrust, incurable doubt of the future, a sense of the justice but not of the goodness of God—in short, unbelief, which is my misfortune and my sin. Every act is a hostage delivered over to avenging destiny—there is the instinctive belief which chills and freezes; every act is a pledge confided to a fatherly providence, there is the belief which calms.

Pain seems to me a punishment and not a mercy: this is why I have a secret horror of it. And as I feel myself vulnerable at all points, and everywhere accessible to pain, I prefer to remain motionless, like a timid child, who, left alone in his father's laboratory, dares not touch anything for fear of springs; explosions, and catastrophes, which may burst from every corner at the least movement of his inexperienced hands. I have trust in God directly and as revealed in nature, but I have a deep distrust of all free and evil agents. I feel or foresee evil, moral and physical, as the consequence of every error, fault, or sin, and I am ashamed of pain.

At bottom, is it not a mere boundless self-love, the purism of perfection, an incapacity to accept our human condition, a tacit protest against the order of the world, which lies at the root of my inertia? It means *all or nothing*, a vast ambition made inactive by disgust, a yearning that cannot be uttered for the ideal, joined with an offended dignity and a wounded pride which will have nothing to say to what they consider beneath them. It springs from the ironical temper which refuses to take either self or reality seriously, because it is forever comparing both with the dimly-seen infinite of its dreams. It is a state of mental reservation in which one lends one's self to circumstances for form's sake, but refuses to recognize them in one's heart because one cannot see the necessity or the divine order in them. I am disinterested because I am indifferent; I have nothing to say against what is, and yet I am never satisfied. I am too weak to conquer, and yet I will not be Conquered—it is the isolation of the disenchanted soul, which has put even hope away from it.

But even this is a trial laid upon one. Its providential purpose is no doubt to lead one to that true renunciation of which charity is the sign and symbol. It is when one expects nothing more for one's self that one is able to love. To do good to men because we love them, to use every talent we have so as to please the Father from whom we hold it for His service, there is no other way of reaching and curing this deep discontent with life which hides itself under an appearance of indifference.

September 4, 1855.—In the government of the soul the parliamentary form succeeds the monarchical. Good sense, conscience, desire, reason, the present and the past, the old man and the new, prudence and generosity, take up their parable in turn; the reign of argument begins; chaos replaces order, and darkness light. Simple will represents the autocratic *regime*, interminable discussion the deliberate regime of the soul. The one is preferable from the theoretical point of view, the other from the practical. Knowledge and action are their two respective advantages.

But the best of all would be to be able to realize three powers in the soul. Besides the man of counsel we want the man of action and the man of judgment. In me, reflection comes to no useful end, because it is forever returning upon itself, disputing and debating. I am wanting in both the general who commands and the judge who decides.

Analysis is dangerous if it overrules the synthetic faculty; reflection is to be feared if it destroys our power of intuition, and inquiry is fatal if it supplants faith. Decomposition becomes deadly when it surpasses in strength the combining and constructive energies of life, and the *separate* action of the powers of the soul tends to mere disintegration and destruction as soon as it becomes impossible to bring them to bear as *one* undivided force. When the sovereign abdicates anarchy begins.

It is just here that my danger lies. Unity of life, of force, of action, of expression, is becoming impossible to me; I am legion, division, analysis, and reflection; the passion for dialectic, for fine distinctions, absorbs and weakens me. The point which I have reached seems to be explained by a too restless search for perfection, by the abuse of the critical faculty, and by an unreasonable distrust of first impulses, first thoughts, first words. Unity and simplicity of being, confidence, and spontaneity of life, are drifting out of my reach, and this is why I can no longer act.

Give up, then, this trying to know all, to embrace all. Learn to limit yourself, to content yourself with some definite thing, and some definite work; dare to be what you are, and learn to resign with a good grace all that you are not, and to believe in your own individuality. Self-distrust is destroying you; trust, surrender, abandon yourself; "believe and thou shalt be healed." Unbelief is death, and depression and self-satire are alike unbelief.

* * * * *

From the point of view of happiness, the problem of life is insoluble, for it is our highest aspirations which prevent us from being happy. From the point of view of duty, there is the same difficulty, for the fulfillment of duty brings peace, not happiness. It is divine love, the love of the holiest, the possession of God by faith, which solves the difficulty; for if sacrifice has itself become a joy, a lasting, growing and imperishable joy—the soul is then secure of an all-sufficient and unfailing nourishment.

* * * * *

January 21, 1856.—Yesterday seems to me as far off as though it were last year. My memory holds nothing more of the past than its general plan, just as my eye perceives nothing more in the starry heaven. It is no more possible for me to recover one of my days from the depths of memory than if it were a glass of water poured into a lake; it is not so much a lost thing as a thing melted and fused; the individual has returned into the whole. The divisions of time are categories which have no power to mold my life, and leave no more lasting impression than lines traced by a stick in water. My life, my individuality, are fluid, there is nothing for it but to resign one's self.

April 9, 1856.—How true it is that our destinies are decided by nothings and that a small imprudence helped by some insignificant accident, as an acorn is fertilized by a drop of rain, may raise the trees on which perhaps we and others shall be crucified. What happens is quite different from that we planned; we planned a blessing and there springs from it a curse. How many times the serpent of fatality, or rather the law of life, the force of things, intertwining itself with some very simple facts, cannot be cut away by any effort, and the logic of situations and characters leads inevitably to a dreaded *denouement*. It is the fatal spell of destiny, which obliges us to feed our grief from our own hand, to prolong the existence of our vulture, to throw into the furnace of our punishment and expiation, our powers, our qualities, our very virtues, one by one, and so forces us to recognize our nothingness, our dependence and the implacable majesty of law. Faith in a providence softens punishment but does not do away with it. The wheels of the divine chariot crush us first of all that justice may be satisfied and an example given to men, and then a hand is stretched out to us to raise us up, or at least to reconcile us with the love hidden under the justice. Pardon cannot precede repentance and repentance only begins with humility. And so long as any fault whatever appears trifling to us, so long as we see, not so much the culpability of as the excuses for imprudence or negligence, so long, in short, as Job murmurs and as providence is thought to be too severe, so long as there is any inner protestation against fate, or doubt as to the perfect justice of God, there is not yet entire humility or true repentance. It is when we accept the expiation that it can be spared us; it is when we submit sincerely that grace can be granted to us. Only when grief finds its work done can God dispense us from it. Trial then only stops when it is useless: that is why it scarcely ever stops. Faith in the justice and love of the Father is the best and indeed the only support under the sufferings of this life. The foundation of all of our pains is unbelief; we doubt whether what happens to us ought to happen to us; we think ourselves wiser than providence, because to avoid fatalism we believe in accident. Liberty in submission—what a problem! And yet that is what we must always come back to.

May 7, 1856.—I have been reading Rosenkrantz's "History of Poetry" [Footnote: "Geschichte der Poesie," by Rosenkrantz, the pupil and biographer of Hegel] all day: it touches upon all the great names of Spain, Portugal, and France, as far as Louis XV. It is a good thing to take these rapid surveys; the shifting point of view gives a perpetual freshness to the subject and to the ideas presented, a literary experience which is always pleasant and bracing. For one of my temperament, this philosophic and morphological mode of embracing and expounding literary history has a strong attraction. But it is the antipodes of the French method of proceeding, which takes, as it were, only the peaks of the subject, links them together by theoretical figures and triangulations, and then assumes these lines to represent the genuine face of the country. The real process of formation of a general opinion, of a public taste, of an established *genre*, cannot be laid bare by an abstract method, which suppresses the period of growth in favor of the final fruit, which prefers clearness of outline to fullness of statement, and sacrifices the preparation to the result, the multitude to the chosen type. This French method, however, is eminently characteristic, and it is linked by invisible ties to their respect for custom and fashion, to the Catholic and dualist instinct which admits two truths, two contradictory worlds, and accepts quite naturally what is magical, incomprehensible, and arbitrary in God, the king, or language. It is the philosophy of accident become habit, instinct, nature and belief, it is the religion of caprice.

By one of those eternal contrasts which redress the balance of things, the romance peoples, who excel in the practical matters of life, care nothing for the philosophy of it; while the Germans, who know very little about the practice of life, are masters of its theory. Every living being seeks instinctively to complete itself; this is the secret law according to which that nation whose sense of life is fullest and keenest, drifts most readily toward a mathematical rigidity of theory. Matter and form are the eternal oppositions, and the mathematical intellects are often attracted by the facts of life, just as the sensuous minds are often drawn toward the study of abstract law. Thus strangely enough, what we think we are is just what we are not: what we desire to be is what suits us least; our theories condemn us, and our practice gives the lie to our theories. And the contradiction is an advantage, for it is the source of conflict, of movement, and therefore a condition of progress. Every life is an inward struggle, every struggle supposes two contrary forces; nothing real is simple, and whatever thinks itself simple is in reality the farthest from simplicity. Therefore it would seem that every state is a moment in a series; every being a compromise between contraries. In concrete dialectic we have the key which opens to us the understanding of beings in the series of beings, of states in the series of moments; and it is in dynamics that we have the explanation of equilibrium. Every situation is an *equilibrium* of forces; every life is a *struggle* between opposing forces working within the limits of a certain equilibrium.

These two principles have been often clear to me, but I have never applied them widely or rigorously enough.

July 1, 1856.—A man and still more a woman, always betrays something of his or her nationality. The women of Russia, for instance, like the lakes and rivers of their native country, seem to be subject to sudden and prolonged fits of torpor. In their movement, undulating and caressing like that of water, there is always a threat of unforeseen frost. The high latitude, the difficulty of life, the inflexibility of their autocratic *regime*, the heavy and mournful sky, the inexorable climate, all these harsh fatalities have left their mark upon the Muscovite race. A certain somber obstinacy, a kind of primitive ferocity, a foundation of savage harshness which, under the influence of circumstances, might become implacable and pitiless; a cold strength, an indomitable power of resolution which would rather wreck the whole world than yield, the indestructible instinct of the barbarian tribe, perceptible in the half-civilized nation, all these traits are visible to an attentive eye, even in the harmless extravagances and caprices of a young woman of this powerful race. Even in their *badinage* they betray something of that fierce and rigid nationality which burns its own towns and [as Napoleon said] keeps battalions of dead soldiers on their feet.

What terrible rulers the Russians would be if ever they should spread the night of their rule over the countries of the south! They would bring us a polar despotism, tyranny such as the world has never known, silent as darkness, rigid as ice, insensible as bronze, decked with an outer amiability and glittering with the cold brilliancy of snow, a slavery without compensation or relief. Probably, however, they will gradually lose both the virtues and the defects of their semi-barbarism. The centuries as they pass will ripen these sons of the north, and they will enter into the concert of peoples in some other capacity than as a menace or a dissonance. They have only to transform their hardiness into strength, their cunning into grace, their Muscovitism into humanity, to win love instead of inspiring aversion or fear.

July 3, 1856.—The German admires form, but he has no genius for it. He is the opposite of the Greek; he has critical instinct, aspiration, and desire, but no serene command of beauty. The south, more artistic, more self-satisfied, more capable of execution, rests idly in the sense of its own power to achieve. On one side you have ideas, on the other side, talent. The realm of Germany is beyond the clouds; that of the southern peoples is on this earth. The Germanic race thinks and feels; the southerners feel and express; the Anglo-Saxons will and do. To know, to feel, to act, there you have the trio of Germany, Italy, England. France formulates, speaks, decides, and laughs. Thought, talent, will, speech; or, in other words science, art, action, proselytism. So the parts of the quartet are assigned.

July 21, 1856.—*Mit sack und pack* here I am back again in my town rooms. I have said good-bye to my friends and my country joys, to verdure, flowers, and happiness. Why did I leave them after all? The reason I gave myself was that I was anxious about my poor uncle, who is ill. But at bottom are there not other reasons? Yes, several. There is the fear of making myself a burden upon the two or three families of friends who show me incessant kindness, for which I can make no return. There are my books, which call me back. There is the wish to keep faith with myself. But all that would be nothing, I think, without another instinct, the instinct of the wandering Jew, which snatches from me the cup I have but just raised to my lips, which forbids me any prolonged enjoyment, and cries "go forward! Let there be no falling asleep, no stopping, no attaching yourself to this or that!" This restless feeling is not the need of change. It is rather the fear of what I love, the mistrust of what charms me, the unrest of happiness. What a *bizarre* tendency, and what a strange nature! not to be able to enjoy anything simply, naively, without scruple, to feel a force upon one impelling one to leave the table, for fear the meal should come to an end. Contradiction and mystery! not to use, for fear of abusing; to think one's self obliged to go, not because one has had enough, but because one has stayed awhile. I am indeed always the same; the being who wanders when he need not, the voluntary exile, the eternal traveler, the man incapable of repose, who, driven on by an inward voice, builds nowhere, buys and labors nowhere, but passes, looks, camps, and goes. And is there not another reason for all this restlessness, in a certain sense of void? of incessant pursuit of something wanting? of longing for a truer peace and a more entire satisfaction? Neighbors, friends, relations, I love them all; and so long as these affections are active, they leave in me no room for a sense of want. But yet they do not *fill* my heart; and that is why they have no power to fix it. I am always waiting for the woman and the work which shall be capable of taking entire possession of my soul, and of becoming my end and aim.

"Promenant par tout sejour Le deuil que tu celes, Psyche-papillon, un jour Puisses-tu trouver l'amour Et perdre tes ailes!"

I have not given away my heart: hence this restlessness of spirit. I will not let it be taken captive by that which cannot fill and satisfy it; hence this instinct of pitiless detachment from all that charms me without permanently binding me; so that it seems as if my love of movement, which looks so like inconstancy, was at bottom only a perpetual search, a hope, a desire, and a care, the malady of the ideal.

... Life indeed must always be a compromise between common sense and the ideal, the one abating nothing of its demands, the other accommodating itself to what is practicable and real. But marriage by common sense! arrived at by a bargain! Can it be anything but a profanation? On the other, hand, is that not a vicious ideal which hinders life from completing itself, and destroys the family in germ? Is there not too much of pride in my ideal, pride which will not accept the common destiny?...

Noon.—I have been dreaming—my head in my hand. About what? About happiness. I have as it were, been asleep on the fatherly breast of God. His will be done!

August 3, 1856.—A delightful Sunday afternoon at Pressy. Returned late, under a great sky magnificently starred, with summer lightning playing from a point behind the Jura. Drunk with poetry, and overwhelmed by sensation after sensation, I came back slowly, blessing the God of life, and plunged in the joy of the infinite. One thing only I lacked, a soul with whom to share it all—for emotion and enthusiasm overflowed like water from a full cup. The Milky Way, the great black poplars, the ripple of the waves, the shooting stars, distant songs, the lamp-lit town, all spoke to me in the language of poetry. I felt myself almost a poet. The wrinkles of science disappeared under the magic breath of admiration; the old elasticity of soul, trustful, free, and living was mine once more. I was once more young, capable of self-abandonment and of love. All my barrenness had disappeared; the heavenly dew had fertilized the dead and gnarled stick; it began to be green and flower again. My God, how wretched should we be without beauty! But with it, everything is born afresh in us; the senses, the heart, imagination, reason, will, come together like the dead bones of the prophet, and become one single and self-same energy. What is happiness if it is not this plentitude of existence, this close union with the universal and divine life? I have been happy a whole half day, and I have been brooding over my joy, steeping myself in it to the very depths of consciousness.

October 22, 1856.—We must learn to look upon life as an apprenticeship to a progressive renunciation, a perpetual diminution in our pretensions, our hopes, our powers, and our liberty. The circle grows narrower and narrower; we began with being eager to learn everything, to see everything, to tame and conquer everything, and in all directions we reach our limit—*non plus ultra*. Fortune, glory, love, power, health, happiness, long life, all these blessings which have been possessed by other men seem at first promised and accessible to us, and then we have to put the dream away from us, to withdraw one personal claim after another to make ourselves small and humble, to submit to feel ourselves limited, feeble, dependent, ignorant and poor, and to throw ourselves upon God for all, recognizing our own worthlessness, and that we have no right to anything. It is in this nothingness that we recover something of life— the divine spark is there at the bottom of it. Resignation comes to us, and, in believing love, we reconquer the true greatness.

October 27, 1856.—In all the chief matters of life we are alone, and our true history is scarcely ever deciphered by others. The chief part of the drama is a monologue, rather an intimate debate between God, our conscience, and ourselves. Tears, griefs, depressions, disappointments, irritations, good and evil thoughts, decisions, uncertainties, deliberations, all these belong to our secret, and are almost all incommunicable and intransmissible, even when we try to speak of them, and even when we write them down. What is most precious in us never shows itself, never finds an issue even in the closest intimacy. Only a part of it reaches our consciousness, it scarcely enters into action except in prayer, and is perhaps only perceived by God, for our past rapidly becomes strange to us. Our monad may be influenced by other monads, but none the less does it remain impenetrable to them in its essence; and we ourselves, when all is said, remain outside our own mystery. The center of our consciousness is unconscious, as the kernel of the sun is dark. All that we are, desire, do, and know, is more or less superficial, and below the rays and lightnings of our periphery there remains the darkness of unfathomable substance.

I was then well-advised when, in my theory of the inner man, I placed at the foundation of the self, after the seven spheres which the self contains had been successively disengaged, a lowest depth of darkness, the abyss of the un-revealed, the virtual pledge of an infinite future, the obscure self, the pure subjectivity which is incapable of realizing itself in mind, conscience, or reason, in the soul, the heart, the imagination, or the life of the senses, and which makes for itself attributes and conditions out of all these forms of its own life.

But the obscure only exists that it may cease to exist. In it lies the opportunity of all victory and all progress. Whether it call itself fatality, death, night, or matter, it is the pedestal of life, of light, of liberty, and the spirit. For it represents *resistance*—that is to say, the fulcrum of all activity, the occasion for its development and its triumph.

December 17, 1856.—This evening was the second quartet concert. It stirred me much more than the first; the music chosen was loftier and stronger. It was the quartet in D minor of Mozart, and the quartet in C major of Beethoven, separated by a Spohr concerto. This last, vivid, and brilliant as a whole, has fire in the allegro, feeling in the adagio, and elegance in the *finale*, but it is the product of one fine gift in a mediocre personality. With the two others you are at once in contact with genius; you are admitted to the secrets of two great souls. Mozart stands for inward liberty, Beethoven for the power of enthusiasm. The one sets us free, the other ravishes us out of ourselves. I do not think I ever felt more distinctly than to-day, or with more intensity, the difference between these two masters. Their two personalities became transparent to me, and I seemed to read them to their depths.

The work of Mozart, penetrated as it is with mind and thought, represents a solved problem, a balance struck between aspiration and executive capacity, the sovereignty of a grace which is always mistress of itself, marvelous harmony and perfect unity. His quartet describes a day in one of those Attic souls who pre-figure on earth the serenity of Elysium. The first scene is a pleasant conversation, like that of Socrates on the banks of the Ilissus; its chief mark is an exquisite urbanity. The second scene is deeply pathetic. A cloud has risen in the blue of this Greek heaven. A storm, such as life inevitably brings with it, even in the case of great souls who love and esteem each other, has come to trouble the original harmony. What is the cause of it—a misunderstanding, apiece of neglect? Impossible to say, but it breaks out notwithstanding. The andante is a scene of reproach and complaint, but as between immortals. What loftiness in complaint, what dignity, what feeling, what noble sweetness in reproach! The voice trembles and grows graver, but remains affectionate and dignified. Then, the storm has passed, the sun has come back, the explanation has taken place, peace is re-established. The third scene paints the brightness of reconciliation. Love, in its restored confidence, and as though in sly self-testing, permits itself even gentle mocking and friendly *badinage*. And the *finale* brings us back to that tempered gaiety and happy serenity, that supreme freedom, flower of the inner life, which is the leading motive of the whole composition.

In Beethoven's on the other hand, a spirit of tragic irony paints for you the mad tumult of existence as it dances forever above the threatening abyss of the infinite. No more unity, no more satisfaction, no more serenity! We are spectators of the eternal duel between the great forces, that of the abyss which absorbs all finite things, and that of life which defends and asserts itself, expands, and enjoys. The first bars break the seals and open the caverns of the great deep. The struggle begins. It is long. Life is born, and disports itself gay and careless as the butterfly which flutters above a precipice. Then it expands the realm of its conquests, and chants its successes. It founds a kingdom, it constructs a system of nature. But the typhon rises from the yawning gulf, and the Titans beat upon the gates of the new empire. A battle of giants begins. You hear the tumultuous efforts of the powers of chaos. Life triumphs at last, but the victory is not final, and through all the intoxication of it there is a certain note of terror and bewilderment. The soul of Beethoven was a tormented soul. The passion and the awe of the infinite seemed to toss it to and fro from heaven to hell, Hence its vastness. Which is the greater, Mozart or Beethoven? Idle question! The one is more perfect, the other more colossal. The first gives you the peace of perfect art, beauty, at first sight. The second gives you sublimity, terror, pity, a beauty of second impression. The one gives that for which the other rouses a desire. Mozart has the classic purity of light and the blue ocean; Beethoven the romantic grandeur which belongs to the storms of air and sea, and while the soul of Mozart seems to dwell on the ethereal peaks of Olympus, that of Beethoven climbs shuddering the storm-beaten sides of a Sinai. Blessed be they both! Each represents a moment of the ideal life, each does us good. Our love is due to both.

* * * * *

To judge is to see clearly, to care for what is just and therefore to be impartial, more exactly, to be disinterested, more exactly still, to be impersonal.

* * * * *

To do easily what is difficult for others is the mark of talent. To do what is impossible for talent is the mark of genius.

* * * * *

Our duty is to be useful, not according to our desires but according to our powers.

* * * * *

If nationality is consent, the state is compulsion.

* * * * *

Self-interest is but the survival of the animal in us. Humanity only begins for man with self-surrender.

* * * * *

The man who insists upon seeing with perfect clearness before he decides, never decides. Accept life, and you must accept regret.

* * * * *

Without passion man is a mere latent force and possibility, like the flint which awaits the shock of the iron before it can give forth its spark.

February 3, 1857.—The phantasmagoria of the soul cradles and soothes me as though I were an Indian yoghi, and everything, even my own life, becomes to me smoke, shadow, vapor, and illusion. I hold so lightly to all phenomena that they end by passing over me like gleams over a landscape, and are gone without leaving any impression. Thought is a kind of opium; it can intoxicate us, while still broad awake; it can make transparent the mountains and everything that exists. It is by love only that one keeps hold upon reality, that one recovers one's proper self, that one becomes again will, force, and individuality. Love could do everything with me; by myself and for myself I prefer to be nothing....

I have the imagination of regret and not that of hope. My clear-sightedness is retrospective, and the result with me of disinterestedness and prudence is that I attach myself to what I have no chance of obtaining....

May 27, 1857. (Vandoeuvres. [Footnote: Also a village in the neighborhood of Geneva.])—We are going down to Geneva to hear the "Tannhaeuser" of Richard Wagner performed at the theater by the German troup now passing through. Wagner's is a powerful mind endowed with strong poetical sensitiveness. His work is even more poetical than musical. The suppression of the lyrical element, and therefore of melody, is with him a systematic *parti pris*. No more duos or trios; monologue and the *aria* are alike done away with. There remains only declamation, the recitative, and the choruses. In order to avoid the conventional in singing, Wagner falls into another convention—that of not singing at all. He subordinates the voice to articulate speech, and for fear lest the muse should take flight he clips her wings. So that his works are rather symphonic dramas than operas. The voice is brought down to the rank of an instrument, put on a level with the violins, the hautboys, and the drums, and treated instrumentally. Man is deposed from his superior position, and the center of gravity of the work passes into the baton of the conductor. It is music depersonalized, neo-Hegelian music—music multiple instead of individual. If this is so, it is indeed the music of the future, the music of the socialist democracy replacing the art which is aristocratic, heroic, or subjective.

The overture pleased me even less than at the first hearing: it is like nature before man appeared. Everything in it is enormous, savage, elementary, like the murmur of forests and the roar of animals. It is forbidding and obscure, because man, that is to say, mind, the key of the enigma, personality, the spectator, is wanting to it.

The idea of the piece is grand. It is nothing less than the struggle of passion and pure love, of flesh and spirit, of the animal and the angel in man. The music is always expressive, the choruses very beautiful, the orchestration skillful, but the whole is fatiguing and excessive, too full, too laborious. When all is said, it lacks gayety, ease, naturalness and vivacity—it has no smile, no wings. Poetically one is fascinated, but one's musical enjoyment is hesitating, often doubtful, and one recalls nothing but the general impression—Wagner's music represents the abdication of the self, and the emancipation of all the forces once under its rule. It is a falling back into Spinozism—the triumph of fatality. This music has its root and its fulcrum in two tendencies of the epoch, materialism and socialism—each of them ignoring the true value of the human personality, and drowning it in the totality of nature or of society.

June 17, 1857. (Vandoeuvres).—I have just followed Maine de Biran from his twenty-eighth to his forty-eighth year by means of his journal, and a crowd of thoughts have besieged me. Let me disengage those which concern myself. In this eternal self-chronicler and observer I seem to see myself reflected with all my faults, indecision, discouragement, over-dependence on sympathy, difficulty of finishing, with my habit of watching myself feel and live, with my growing incapacity for practical action, with my aptitude for psychological study. But I have also discovered some differences which cheer and console me. This nature is, as it were, only one of the men which exist in me. It is one of my departments. It is not the whole of my territory, the whole of my inner kingdom. Intellectually, I am more objective and more constructive; my horizon is vaster; I have seen much more of men, things, countries, peoples and books; I have a greater mass of experiences—in a word, I feel that I have more culture, greater wealth, range, and freedom of mind, in spite of my wants, my limits, and my weaknesses. Why does Maine de Biran make *will* the whole of man? Perhaps because he had too little will. A man esteems most highly what he himself lacks, and exaggerates what he longs to possess. Another incapable of thought, and meditation, would have made self-consciousness the supreme thing. Only the totality of things has an objective value. As soon as one isolates a part from the whole, as soon as one chooses, the choice is involuntarily and instinctively dictated by subjective inclinations which obey one or other of the two opposing laws, the attraction of similars or the affinity of contraries.

Five o'clock.—The morning has passed like a dream. I went on with the journal of Maine de Biran down to the end of 1817. After dinner I passed my time with the birds in the open air, wandering in the shady walks which wind along under Pressy. The sun was brilliant and the air clear. The midday orchestra of nature was at its best. Against the humming background made by a thousand invisible insects there rose the delicate caprices and improvisations of the nightingale singing from the ash-trees, or of the hedge-sparrows and the chaffinches in their nests. The hedges are hung with wild roses, the scent of the acacia still perfumes the paths; the light down of the poplar seeds floated in the air like a kind of warm, fair-weather snow. I felt myself as gay as a butterfly. On coming in I read the three first books of that poem "Corinne," which I have not seen since I was a youth. Now as I read it again, I look at it across interposing memories; the romantic interest of it seems to me to have vanished, but not the poetical, pathetic, or moral interest.

June 18th.—I have just been spending three hours in the orchard under the shade of the hedge, combining the spectacle of a beautiful morning with reading and taking a turn between each chapter. Now the sky is again covered with its white veil of cloud, and I have come up with Biran, whose "Pensee" I have just finished, and Corinne, whom I have followed with Oswald in their excursions among the monuments of the eternal city. Nothing is so melancholy and wearisome as this journal of Maine de Biran. This unchanging monotony of perpetual reflection has an enervating and depressing effect upon one. Here, then, is the life of a distinguished man seen in its most intimate aspects! It is one long repetition, in which the only change is an almost imperceptible displacement of center in the writer's manner of viewing himself. This thinker takes thirty years to move from the Epicurean quietude to the quietism of Fenelon, and this only speculatively, for his practical life remains the same, and all his anthropological discovery consists in returning to the theory of the three lives, lower, human, and higher, which is in Pascal and in Aristotle. And this is what they call a philosopher in France! Beside the great philosophers, how poor and narrow seems such an intellectual life! It is the journey of an ant, bounded by the limits of a field; of a mole, who spends his days in the construction of a mole-hill. How narrow and stifling the swallow who flies across the whole Old World, and whose sphere of life embraces Africa and Europe, would find the circle with which the mole and the ant are content! This volume of Biran produces in me a sort of asphyxia; as I assimilate it, it seems to paralyze me; I am chained to it by some spell of secret sympathy. I pity, and I am afraid of my pity, for I feel how near I am to the same evils and the same faults....

Ernest Naville's introductory essay is full of interest, written in a serious and noble style; but it is almost as sad as it is ripe and mature. What displeases me in it a little is its exaggeration of the merits of Biran. For the rest, the small critical impatience which the volume has stirred in me will be gone by to-morrow. Maine de Biran is an important link in the French literary tradition. It is from him that our Swiss critics descend, Naville father and son, Secretan. He is the source of our best contemporary psychology, for Stapfer, Royer-Collard, and Cousin called him their master, and Ampere, his junior by nine years, was his friend.

July 25, 1857. (Vandoeuvres).—At ten o'clock this evening, under a starlit sky, a group of rustics under the windows of the salon employed themselves in shouting disagreeable songs. Why is it that this tuneless shrieking of false notes and scoffing words delights these people? Why is it that this ostentatious parade of ugliness, this jarring vulgarity and grimacing is their way of finding expression and expansion in the great solitary and tranquil night?

Why? Because of a sad and secret instinct. Because of the need they have of realizing themselves as individuals, of asserting themselves exclusively, egotistically, idolatrously—opposing the self in them to everything else, placing it in harsh contrast with the nature which enwraps us, with the poetry which raises us above ourselves, with the harmony which binds us to others, with the adoration which carries us toward God. No, no, no! Myself only, and that is enough! Myself by negation, by ugliness, by grimace and irony! Myself, in my caprice, in my independence, in my irresponsible sovereignty; myself, set free by laughter, free as the demons are, and exulting in my freedom; I, master of myself, invincible and self-sufficient, living for this one time yet by and for myself! This is what seems to me at the bottom of this merry-making. One hears in it an echo of Satan, the temptation to make self the center of all things, to be like an Elohim, the worst and last revolt of man. It means also, perhaps, some rapid perception of what is absolute in personality, some rough exaltation of the subject, the individual, who thus claims, by abasing them, the rights of subjective existence. If so, it is the caricature of our most precious privilege, the parody of our apotheosis, a vulgarizing of our highest greatness. Shout away, then, drunkards! Your ignoble concert, with all its repulsive vulgarity, still reveals to us, without knowing it, something of the majesty of life and the sovereign power of the soul.

September 15, 1857.—I have just finished Sismondi's journal and correspondence. Sismondi is essentially the honest man, conscientious, upright, respectable, the friend of the public good and the devoted upholder of a great cause, the amelioration of the common lot of men. Character and heart are the dominant elements in his individuality, and cordiality is the salient feature of his nature. Sismondi's is a most encouraging example. With average faculties, very little imagination, not much taste, not much talent, without subtlety of feeling, without great elevation or width or profundity of mind, he yet succeeded in achieving a career which was almost illustrious, and he has left behind him some sixty volumes, well-known and well spoken of. How was this? His love for men on the one side, and his passion for work on the other, are the two factors in his fame. In political economy, in literary or political history, in personal action, Sismondi showed no genius—scarcely talent; but in all he did there was solidity, loyalty, good sense and integrity. The poetical, artistic and philosophic sense is deficient in him, but he attracts and interests us by his moral sense. We see in him the sincere writer, a man of excellent heart, a good citizen and warm friend, worthy and honest in the widest sense of terms, not brilliant, but inspiring trust and confidence by his character, his principles and his virtues. More than this, he is the best type of good Genevese liberalism, republican but not democratic, Protestant but not Calvinist, human but not socialist, progressive but without any sympathy with violence. He was a conservative without either egotism or hypocrisy, a patriot without narrowness. In his theories he was governed by experience and observation, and in his practice by general ideas. A laborious philanthropist, the past and the present were to him but fields of study, from which useful lessons might be gleaned. Positive and reasonable in temper, his mind was set upon a high average well-being for human society, and his efforts were directed toward founding such a social science as might most readily promote it.

September 24, 1857.—In the course of much thought yesterday about "Atala" and "Rene," Chateaubriand became clear to me. I saw in him a great artist but not a great man, immense talent but a still vaster pride—a nature at once devoured with ambition and unable to find anything to love or admire in the world except itself—indefatigable in labor and capable of everything except of true devotion, self-sacrifice and faith. Jealous of all success, he was always on the opposition side, that he might be the better able to disavow all services received, and to hold aloof from any other glory but his own. Legitimist under the empire, a parliamentarian tinder the legitimist *regime*, republican under the constitutional monarchy, defending Christianity when France was philosophical, and taking a distaste for religion as soon as it became once more a serious power, the secret of these endless contradictions in him was simply the desire to reign alone like the sun—a devouring thirst for applause, an incurable and insatiable vanity, which, with the true, fierce instinct of tyranny, would endure no brother near the throne. A man of magnificent imagination but of poor character, of indisputable power, but cursed with a cold egotism and an incurable barrenness of feeling, which made it impossible for him to tolerate about him anybody but slaves or adorers. A tormented soul and miserable life, when all is said, under its aureole of glory and its crown of laurels!

Essentially jealous and choleric, Chateaubriand from the beginning was inspired by mistrust, by the passion for contradicting, for crushing and conquering. This motive may always be traced in him. Rousseau seems to me his point of departure, the man who suggested to him by contrast and opposition all his replies and attacks, Rousseau is revolutionary: Chateaubriand therefore writes his "Essay on Revolutions." Rousseau is republican and Protestant; Chateaubriand will be royalist and Catholic. Rousseau is *bourgeois*; Chateaubriand will glorify nothing but noble birth, honor, chivalry and deeds of arms. Rousseau conquered nature for French letters, above all the nature of the mountains and of the Swiss and Savoy, and lakes. He pleaded for her against civilization. Chateaubriand will take possession of a new and colossal nature, of the ocean, of America; but he will make his savages speak the language of Louis XIV., he will bow Atala before a Catholic missionary, and sanctify passions born on the banks of the Mississippi by the solemnities of Catholic ceremonial. Rousseau was the apologist of reverie; Chateaubriand will build the monument of it in order to break it in Rene. Rousseau preaches Deism with all his eloquence in the "Vicaire Savoyard;" Chateaubriand surrounds the Roman creed with all the garlands of his poetry in the "Genie du Christianisme." Rousseau appeals to natural law and pleads for the future of nations; Chateaubriand will only sing the glories of the past, the ashes of history and the noble ruins of empires. Always a role to be filled, cleverness to be displayed, a *parti-pris* to be upheld and fame to be won—his theme, one of imagination, his faith one to order, but sincerity, loyalty, candor, seldom or never! Always a real indifference simulating a passion for truth; always an imperious thirst for glory instead of devotion to the good; always the ambitious artist, never the citizen, the believer, the man. Chateaubriand posed all his life as the wearied Colossus, smiling pitifully upon a pygmy world, and contemptuously affecting to desire nothing from it, though at the same time wishing it to be believed that he could if he pleased possess himself of everything by mere force of genius. He is the type of an untoward race, and the father of a disagreeable lineage.

But to return to the two episodes. "Rene" seems to me very superior to "Atala.'" Both the stories show a talent of the first rank, but of the two the beauty of "Atala" is of the more transitory kind. The attempt to render in the style of Versailles the loves of a Natchez and a Seminole, and to describe the manners of the adorers of the Manitous in the tone of Catholic sentiment, was an attempt too violent to succeed. But the work is a *tour de force* of style, and it was only by the polished classicism of the form, that the romantic matter of the sentiments and the descriptions could have been imported into the colorless literature of the empire. "Atala" is already old-fashioned and theatrical in all the parts which are not descriptive or European—that is to say, throughout all the sentimental savagery.

"Rene" is infinitely more durable. Its theme, which is the malady of a whole generation—distaste for life brought about by idle reverie and the ravages of a vague and unmeasured ambition—is true to reality. Without knowing or wishing it, Chateaubriand has been sincere, for Rene is himself. This little sketch is in every respect a masterpiece. It is not, like "Atala," spoilt artistically by intentions alien to the subject, by being made the means of expression of a particular tendency. Instead of taking a passion for Rene, indeed, future generations will scorn and wonder at him; instead of a hero they will see in him a pathological case; but the work itself, like the Sphinx, will endure. A work of art will bear all kinds of interpretations; each in turn finds a basis in it, while the work itself, because it represents an idea, and therefore partakes of the richness and complexity which belong to ideas, suffices for all and survives all. A portrait proves whatever one asks of it. Even in its forms of style, in the disdainful generality of the terms in which the story is told, in the terseness of the sentences, in the sequence of the images and of the pictures, traced with classic purity and marvelous vigor, "Rene" maintains its monumental character. Carved, as it were, in material of the present century, with the tools of classical art, "Rene" is the immortal cameo of Chateaubriand.

We are never more discontented with others than when we are discontented with ourselves. The consciousness of wrong-doing makes us irritable, and our heart in its cunning quarrels with what is outside it, in order that it may deafen the clamor within.

* * * * *

The faculty of intellectual metamorphosis is the first and indispensable faculty of the critic; without it he is not apt at understanding other minds, and ought, therefore, if he love truth, to hold his peace. The conscientious critic must first criticise himself; what we do not understand we have not the right to judge.

* * * * *

June 14, 1858.—Sadness and anxiety seem to be increasing upon me. Like cattle in a burning stable, I cling to what consumes me, to the solitary life which does me so much harm. I let myself be devoured by inward suffering....

Yesterday, however, I struggled against this fatal tendency. I went out into the country, and the children's caresses restored to me something of serenity and calm. After we had dined out of doors all three sang some songs and school hymns, which were delightful to listen to. The spring fairy had been scattering flowers over the fields with lavish hands; it was a little glimpse of paradise. It is true, indeed, that the serpent too was not far off. Yesterday there was a robbery close by the house, and death had visited another neighbor. Sin and death lurk around every Eden, and sometimes within it. Hence the tragic beauty, the melancholy poetry of human destiny. Flowers, shade, a fine view, a sunset sky, joy, grace, feeling, abundance and serenity, tenderness and song—here you have the element of beauty: the dangers of the present and the treacheries of the future, here is the element of pathos. The fashion of this world passeth away. Unless we have laid hold upon eternity, unless we take the religious view of life, these bright, fleeting days can only be a subject for terror. Happiness should be a prayer—and grief also. Faith in the moral order, in the protecting fatherhood of God, appeared to me in all its serious sweetness.

"Pense, aime, agis et souffre en Dieu C'est la grande science."

July 18, 1858.—To-day I have been deeply moved by the *nostalgia* of happiness and by the appeals of memory. My old self, the dreams which used to haunt me in Germany, passionate impulses, high aspirations, all revived in me at once with unexpected force. The dread lest I should have missed my destiny and stifled my true nature, lest I should have buried myself alive, passed through me like a shudder. Thirst for the unknown, passionate love of life, the yearning for the blue vaults of the infinite and the strange worlds of the ineffable, and that sad ecstasy which the ideal wakens in its beholders—all these carried me away in a whirlwind of feeling that I cannot describe. Was it a warning, a punishment, a temptation? Was it a secret protest, or a violent act of rebellion on the part of a nature which is unsatisfied?—the last agony of happiness and of a hope that will not die?

What raised all this storm? Nothing but a book—the first number of the *"Revue Germanique."* The articles of Dollfus, Renan, Littre, Montegut, Taillandier, by recalling to me some old and favorite subjects, made me forget ten wasted years, and carried me back to my university life. I was tempted to throw off my Genevese garb and to set off, stick in hand, for any country that might offer—stripped and poor, but still young, enthusiastic, and alive, full of ardor and of faith.

... I have been dreaming alone since ten o'clock at the window, while the stars twinkled among the clouds, and the lights of the neighbors disappeared one by one in the houses round. Dreaming of what? Of the meaning of this tragic comedy which we call life. Alas! alas! I was as melancholy as the preacher. A hundred years seemed to me a dream, life a breath, and everything a nothing. What tortures of mind and soul, and all that we may die in a few minutes! What should interest us, and why?

"Le temps n'est rien pour l'ame, enfant, ta vie est pleine, Et ce jour vaut cent ans, s'il te fait trouver Dieu."

To make an object for myself, to hope, to struggle, seems to me more and more impossible and amazing. At twenty I was the embodiment of curiosity, elasticity and spiritual ubiquity; at thirty-seven I have not a will, a desire, or a talent left; the fireworks of my youth have left nothing but a handful of ashes behind them.

December 13, 1858.—Consider yourself a refractory pupil for whom you are responsible as mentor and tutor. To sanctify sinful nature, by bringing it gradually under the control of the angel within us, by the help of a holy God, is really the whole of Christian pedagogy and of religious morals. Our work—my work—consists in taming, subduing, evangelizing and *angelizing* the evil self; and in restoring harmony with the good self. Salvation lies in abandoning the evil self in principle and in taking refuge with the other, the divine self, in accepting with courage and prayer the task of living with one's own demon, and making it into a less and less rebellious instrument of good. The Abel in us must labor for the salvation of the Cain. To undertake it is to be converted, and this conversion must be repeated day by day. Abel only redeems and touches Cain by exercising him constantly in good works. To do right is in one sense an act of violence; it is suffering, expiation, a cross, for it means the conquest and enslavement of self. In another sense it is the apprenticeship to heavenly things, sweet and secret joy, contentment and peace. Sanctification implies perpetual martyrdom, but it is a martyrdom which glorifies. A crown of thorns is the sad eternal symbol of the life of the saints. The best measure of the profundity of any religious doctrine is given by its conception of sin and the cure of sin.

A duty is no sooner divined than from that very moment it becomes binding upon us.

* * * * *

Latent genius is but a presumption. Everything that can be, is bound to come into being, and what never comes into being is nothing.

July 14, 1859.—I have just read "Faust" again. Alas, every year I am fascinated afresh by this somber figure, this restless life. It is the type of suffering toward which I myself gravitate, and I am always finding in the poem words which strike straight to my heart. Immortal, malign, accursed type! Specter of my own conscience, ghost of my own torment, image of the ceaseless struggle of the soul which has not yet found its true aliment, its peace, its faith—art thou not the typical example of a life which feeds upon itself, because it has not found its God, and which, in its wandering flight across the worlds, carries within it, like a comet, an inextinguishable flame of desire, and an agony of incurable disillusion? I also am reduced to nothingness, and I shiver on the brink of the great empty abysses of my inner being, stifled by longing for the unknown, consumed with the thirst for the infinite, prostrate before the ineffable. I also am torn sometimes by this blind passion for life, these desperate struggles for happiness, though more often I am a prey to complete exhaustion and taciturn despair. What is the reason of it all? Doubt—doubt of one's self, of thought, of men, and of life—doubt which enervates the will and weakens all our powers, which makes us forget God and neglect prayer and duty—that restless and corrosive doubt which makes existence impossible and meets all hope with satire.

July 17, 1859.—Always and everywhere salvation is torture, deliverance means death, and peace lies in sacrifice. If we would win our pardon, we must kiss the fiery crucifix. Life is a series of agonies, a Calvary, which we can only climb on bruised and aching knees. We seek distractions; we wander away; we deafen and stupefy ourselves that we may escape the test; we turn away oar eyes from the *via dolorosa*; and yet there is no help for it—we must come back to it in the end. What we have to recognize is that each of us carries within himself his own executioner—his demon, his hell, in his sin; that his sin is his idol, and that this idol, which seduces the desire of his heart, is his curse.

Die unto sin! This great saying of Christianity remains still the highest theoretical solution of the inner life. Only in it is there any peace of conscience; and without this peace there is no peace....

I have just read seven chapters of the gospel. Nothing calms me so much. To do one's duty in love and obedience, to do what is right— these are the ideas which remain with one. To live in God and to do his work—this is religion, salvation, life eternal; this is both the effect and the sign of love and of the Holy Spirit; this is the new man announced by Jesus, and the new life into which we enter by the second birth. To be born again is to renounce the old life, sin, and the natural man, and to take to one's self another principle of life. It is to exist for God with another self, another will, another love.

August 9, 1859.—Nature is forgetful: the world is almost more so. However little the individual may lend himself to it, oblivion soon covers him like a shroud. This rapid and inexorable expansion of the universal life, which covers, overflows, and swallows up all individual being, which effaces our existence and annuls all memory of us, fills me with unbearable melancholy. To be born, to struggle, to disappear—there is the whole ephemeral drama of human life. Except in a few hearts, and not even always in one, our memory passes like a ripple on the water, or a breeze in the air. If nothing in us is immortal, what a small thing is life. Like a dream which trembles and dies at the first glimmer of dawn, all my past, all my present, dissolve in me, and fall away from my consciousness at the moment when it returns upon itself. I feel myself then stripped and empty, like a convalescent who remembers nothing. My travels, my reading, my studies, my projects, my hopes, have faded from my mind. It is a singular state. All my faculties drop away from me like a cloak that one takes off, like the chrysalis case of a larva. I feel myself returning into a more elementary form. I behold my own unclothing; I forget, still more than I am forgotten; I pass gently into the grave while still living, and I feel, as it were, the indescribable peace of annihilation, and the dim quiet of the Nirvana. I am conscious of the river of time passing before and in me, of the impalpable shadows of life gliding past me, but nothing breaks the cateleptic tranquillity which enwraps me.

I come to understand the Buddhist trance of the Soufis, the kief of the Turk, the "ecstasy" of the orientals, and yet I am conscious all the time that the pleasure of it is deadly, that, like the use of opium or of hasheesh, it is a kind of slow suicide, inferior in all respects to the joys of action, to the sweetness of love, to the beauty of enthusiasm, to the sacred savor of accomplished duty. November 28, 1859.—This evening I heard the first lecture of Ernest Naville [Footnote: The well-known Genevese preacher and writer, Ernest Naville, the son of a Genevese pastor, was born in 1816, became professor at the Academy of Geneva in 1844, lost his post after the revolution of 1846, and, except for a short interval in 1860, has since then held no official position. His courses of theological lectures, delivered at intervals from 1859 onward, were an extraordinary success. They were at first confined to men only, and an audience of two thousand persons sometimes assembled to hear them. To literature he is mainly known as the editor of Maine de Biran's Journal.] on "The Eternal Life." It was admirably sure in touch, true, clear, and noble throughout. He proved that, whether we would or no, we were bound to face the question of another life. Beauty of character, force of expression, depth of thought, were all equally visible in this extemporized address, which was as closely reasoned as a book, and can scarcely be disentangled from the quotations of which it was full. The great room of the Casino was full to the doors, and one saw a fairly large number of white heads.

December 13, 1859.—Fifth lecture on "The Eternal Life" ("The Proof of the Gospel by the Supernatural.") The same talent and great eloquence; but the orator does not understand that the supernatural must either be historically proved, or, supposing it cannot be proved, that it must renounce all pretensions to overstep the domain of faith and to encroach upon that of history and science. He quotes Strauss, Renan, Scherer, but he touches only the letter of them, not the spirit. Everywhere one sees the Cartesian dualism and a striking want of the genetic, historical, and critical sense. The idea of a living evolution has not penetrated into the consciousness of the orator. With every intention of dealing with things as they are, he remains, in spite of himself, subjective and oratorical. There is the inconvenience of handling a matter polemically instead of in the spirit of the student. Naville's moral sense is too strong for his discernment and prevents him from seeing what he does not wish to see. In his metaphysic, will is placed above intelligence, and in his personality the character is superior to the understanding, as one might logically expect. And the consequence is, that he may prop up what is tottering, but he makes no conquests; he may help to preserve existing truths and beliefs, but he is destitute of initiative or vivifying power. He is a moralizing but not a suggestive or stimulating influence. A popularizer, apologist and orator of the greatest merit, he is a schoolman at bottom; his arguments are of the same type as those of the twelfth century, and he defends Protestantism in the same way in which Catholicism has been commonly defended. The best way of demonstrating the insufficiency of this point of view is to show by history how incompletely it has been superseded. The chimera of a simple and absolute truth is wholly Catholic and anti-historic. The mind of Naville is mathematical and his objects moral. His strength lies in *mathematicizing* morals. As soon as it becomes a question of development, metamorphosis, organization—as soon as he is brought into contact with the mobile world of actual life, especially of the spiritual life, he has no longer anything serviceable to say. Language is for him a system of fixed signs; a man, a people, a book, are so many geometrical figures of which we have only to discover the properties.

December 15th.—Naville's sixth lecture, an admirable one, because it did nothing more than expound the Christian doctrine of eternal life. As an extempore performance—marvelously exact, finished, clear and noble, marked by a strong and disciplined eloquence. There was not a single reservation to make in the name of criticism, history or philosophy. It was all beautiful, noble, true and pure. It seems to me that Naville has improved in the art of speech during these latter years. He has always had a kind of dignified and didactic beauty, but he has now added to it the contagious cordiality and warmth of feeling which complete the orator; he moves the whole man, beginning with the intellect but finishing with the heart. He is now very near to the true virile eloquence, and possesses one species of it indeed very nearly in perfection. He has arrived at the complete command of the resources of his own nature, at an adequate and masterly expression of himself. Such expression is the joy and glory of the oratorical artist as of every other. Naville is rapidly becoming a model in the art of premeditated and self-controlled eloquence.

There is another kind of eloquence—that which seems inspired, which finds, discovers, and illuminates by bounds and flashes, which is born in the sight of the audience and transports it. Such is not Naville's kind. Is it better worth having? I do not know.

* * * * *

Every real need is stilled, and every vice is stimulated by satisfaction.

* * * * *

Obstinacy is will asserting itself without being able to justify itself. It is persistence without a plausible motive. It is the tenacity of self-love substituted for the tenacity of reason or conscience.

It is not what he has, nor even what he does, which directly expresses the worth of a man, but what he is.

* * * * *

What comfort, what strength, what economy there is in *order*—material order, intellectual order, moral order. To know where one is going and what one wishes—this is order; to keep one's word and one's engagements—again order; to have everything ready under one's hand, to be able to dispose of all one's forces, and to have all one's means of whatever kind under command—still order; to discipline one's habits, one's effort, one's wishes; to organize one's life, to distribute one's time, to take the measure of one's duties and make one's rights respected; to employ one's capital and resources, one's talent and one's chances profitably—all this belongs to and is included in the word *order*. Order means light and peace, inward liberty and free command over one's self; order is power. Aesthetic and moral beauty consist, the first in a true perception of order, and the second in submission to it, and in the realization of it, by, in, and around one's self. Order is man's greatest need and his true well-being.

April 17, 1860.—The cloud has lifted; I am better. I have been able to take my usual walk on the Treille; all the buds were opening and the young shoots were green on all the branches. The rippling of clear water, the merriment of birds, the young freshness of plants, and the noisy play of children, produce a strange effect upon an invalid. Or rather it was strange to me to be looking at such things with the eyes of a sick and dying man; it was my first introduction to a new phase of experience. There is a deep sadness in it. One feels one's self cut off from nature—outside her communion as it were. She is strength and joy and eternal health. "Room for the living," she cries to us; "do not come to darken my blue sky with your miseries; each has his turn: begone!" But to strengthen our own courage, we must say to ourselves, No; it is good for the world to see suffering and weakness; the sight adds zest to the joy of the happy and the careless, and is rich in warning for all who think. Life has been lent to us, and we owe it to our traveling companions to let them see what use we make of it to the end. We must show our brethren both how to live and how to die. These first summonses of illness have besides a divine value; they give us glimpses behind the scenes of life; they teach us something of its awful reality and its inevitable end. They teach us sympathy. They warn us to redeem the time while it is yet day. They awaken in us gratitude for the blessings which are still ours, and humility for the gifts which are in us. So that, evils though they seem, they are really an appeal to us from on high, a touch of God's fatherly scourge.

How frail a thing is health, and what a thin envelope protects our life against being swallowed up from without, or disorganized from within! A breath, and the boat springs a leak or founders; a nothing, and all is endangered; a passing cloud, and all is darkness! Life is indeed a flower which a morning withers and the beat of a passing wing breaks down; it is the widow's lamp, which the slightest blast of air extinguishes. In order to realize the poetry which clings to morning roses, one needs to have just escaped from the claws of that vulture which we call illness. The foundation and the heightening of all things is the graveyard. The only certainty in this world of vain agitations and endless anxieties, is the certainty of death, and that which is the foretaste and small change of death—pain.

As long as we turn our eyes away from this implacable reality, the tragedy of life remains hidden from us. As soon as we look at it face to face, the true proportions of everything reappear, and existence becomes solemn again. It is made clear to us that we have been frivolous and petulant, intractable and forgetful, and that we have been wrong.

We must die and give an account of our life: here in all its simplicity is the teaching of sickness! "Do with all diligence what you have to do; reconcile yourself with the law of the universe; think of your duty; prepare yourself for departure:" such is the cry of conscience and of reason.

May 3, 1860.—Edgar Quinet has attempted everything: he has aimed at nothing but the greatest things; he is rich in ideas, a master of splendid imagery, serious, enthusiastic, courageous, a noble writer. How is it, then, that he has not more reputation? Because he is too pure; because he is too uniformly ecstatic, fantastic, inspired—a mood which soon palls on Frenchmen. Because he is too single-minded, candid, theoretical, and speculative, too ready to believe in the power of words and of ideas, too expansive and confiding; while at the same time he is lacking in the qualities which amuse clever people—in sarcasm, irony, cunning and *finesse*. He is an idealist reveling in color: a Platonist brandishing the *thyrsus* of the Menads. At bottom his is a mind of no particular country. It is in vain that he satirizes Germany and abuses England; he does not make himself any more of a Frenchman by doing so. It is a northern intellect wedded to a southern imagination, but the marriage has not been a happy one. He has the disease of chronic magniloquence, of inveterate sublimity; abstractions for him become personified and colossal beings, which act or speak in colossal fashion; he is intoxicated with the infinite. But one feels all the time that his creations are only individual monologues; he cannot escape from the bounds of a subjective lyrism. Ideas, passions, anger, hopes, complaints—he himself is present in them all. We never have the delight of escaping from his magic circle, of seeing truth as it is, of entering into relation with the phenomena and the beings of whom he speaks, with the reality of things. This imprisonment of the author within his personality looks like conceit. But on the contrary, it is because the heart is generous that the mind is egotistical. It is because Quinet thinks himself so much of a Frenchman that he is it so little. These ironical compensations of destiny are very familiar to me: I have often observed them. Man is nothing but contradiction:

the less he knows it the more dupe he is. In consequence of his small capacity for seeing things as they are, Quinet has neither much accuracy nor much balance of mind. He recalls Victor Hugo, with much less artistic power but more historical sense. His principal gift is a great command of imagery and symbolism. He seems to me a Goerres [Footnote: Joseph Goerres, a German mystic and disciple of Schelling. He published, among other works, "Mythengeschichte der Asiatischen Welt," and "Christliche Mystik."] transplanted to Franche Comte, a sort of supernumerary prophet, with whom his nation hardly knows what to do, seeing that she loves neither enigmas nor ecstasy nor inflation of language, and that the intoxication of the tripod bores her.

The real excellence of Quinet seems to me to lie in his historical works ("Marnix," "L'Italie," "Les Roumains"), and especially in his studies of nationalities. He was born, to understand these souls, at once more vast and more sublime than individual souls.

(*Later*).—I have been translating into verse that page of Goethe's "Faust" in which is contained his pantheistic confession of faith. The translation is not bad, I think. But what a difference between the two languages in the matter of precision! It is like the difference between stump and graving-tool—the one showing the effort, the other noting the result of the act; the one making you feel all that is merely dreamed or vague, formless or vacant, the other determining, fixing, giving shape even to the indefinite; the one representing the cause, the force, the limbo whence things issue, the other the things themselves. German has the obscure depth of the infinite, French the clear brightness of the finite.

May 5, 1860.—To grow old is more difficult than to die, because to renounce a good once and for all, costs less than to renew the sacrifice day by day and in detail. To bear with one's own decay, to accept one's own lessening capacity, is a harder and rarer virtue than to face death.

* * * * *

There is a halo round tragic and premature death; there is but a long sadness in declining strength. But look closer: so studied, a resigned and religious old age will often move us more than the heroic ardor of young years. The maturity of the soul is worth more than the first brilliance of its faculties, or the plentitude of its strength, and the eternal in us can but profit from all the ravages made by time. There is comfort in this thought.

May 22, 1860.—There is in me a secret incapacity for expressing my true feeling, for saying what pleases others, for bearing witness to the present—a reserve which I have often noticed in myself with vexation. My heart never dares to speak seriously, either because it is ashamed of being thought to flatter, or afraid lest it should not find exactly the right expression. I am always trifling with the present moment. Feeling in me is retrospective. My refractory nature is slow to recognize the solemnity of the hour in which I actually stand. An ironical instinct, born of timidity, makes me pass lightly over what I have on pretence of waiting for some other thing at some other time. Fear of being carried away, and distrust of myself pursue me even in moments of emotion; by a sort of invincible pride, I can never persuade myself to say to any particular instant: "Stay! decide for me; be a supreme moment! stand out from the monotonous depths of eternity and mark a unique experience in my life!" I trifle, even with happiness, out of distrust of the future.

May 27, 1860. (Sunday).—I heard this morning a sermon on the Holy Spirit—good but insufficient. Why was I not edified? Because there was no unction. Why was there no unction? Because Christianity from this rationalistic point of view is a Christianity of *dignity*, not of humility. Penitence, the struggles of weakness, austerity, find no place in it. The law is effaced, holiness and mysticism evaporate; the specifically Christian accent is wanting. My impression is always the same—faith is made a dull poor thing by these attempts to reduce it to simple moral psychology. I am oppressed by a feeling of inappropriateness and *malaise* at the sight of philosophy in the pulpit. "They have taken away my Saviour, and I know not where they have laid him;" so the simple folk have a right to say, and I repeat it with them. Thus, while some shock me by their sacerdotal dogmatism, others repel me by their rationalizing laicism. It seems to me that good preaching ought to combine, as Schleiermacher did, perfect moral humility with energetic independence of thought, a profound sense of sin with respect for criticism and a passion for truth.

* * * * *

The free being who abandons the conduct of himself, yields himself to Satan; in the moral world there is no ground without a master, and the waste lands belong to the Evil One.

The poetry of childhood consists in simulating and forestalling the future, just as the poetry of mature life consists often in going backward to some golden age. Poetry is always in the distance. The whole art of moral government lies in gaining a directing and shaping hold over the poetical ideals of an age.

January 9, 1861.—I have just come from the inaugural lecture of Victor Cherbuliez in a state of bewildered admiration. As a lecture it was exquisite: if it was a recitation of prepared matter, it was admirable; if an extempore performance, it was amazing. In the face of superiority and perfection, says Schiller, we have but one resource—to love them, which is what I have done. I had the pleasure, mingled with a little surprise, of feeling in myself no sort of jealousy toward this young conqueror.

March 15th.—This last lecture in Victor Cherbuliez's course on "Chivalry," which is just over, showed the same magical power over his subject as that with which he began the series two months ago. It was a triumph and a harvest of laurels. Cervantes, Ignatius Loyola, and the heritage of chivalry—that is to say, individualism, honor, the poetry of the present and the poetry of contrasts, modern liberty and progress—have been the subjects of this lecture.

The general impression left upon me all along has been one of admiration for the union in him of extraordinary skill in execution with admirable cultivation of mind. With what freedom of spirit he uses and wields his vast erudition, and what capacity for close attention he must have to be able to carry the weight of a whole improvised speech with the same ease as though it were a single sentence! I do not know if I am partial, but I find no occasion for anything but praise in this young wizard and his lectures. The fact is, that in my opinion we have now one more first rate mind, one more master of language among us. This course, with the "Causeries Atheniennes," seems to me to establish Victor Cherbuliez's position at Geneva.

March 17, 1861.—This afternoon a homicidal languor seized hold upon me—disgust, weariness of life, mortal sadness. I wandered out into the churchyard, hoping to find quiet and peace there, and so to reconcile myself with duty. Vain dream! The place of rest itself had become inhospitable. Workmen were stripping and carrying away the turf, the trees were dry, the wind cold, the sky gray—something arid, irreverent, and prosaic dishonored the resting-place of the dead. I was struck with something wanting in our national feeling—respect for the dead, the poetry of the tomb, the piety of memory. Our churches are too little open; our churchyards too much. The result in both cases is the same. The tortured and trembling heart which seeks, outside the scene of its daily miseries, to find some place where it may pray in peace, or pour out its grief before God, or meditate in the presence of eternal things, with us has nowhere to go. Our church ignores these wants of the soul instead of divining and meeting them. She shows very little compassionate care for her children, very little wise consideration for the more delicate griefs, and no intuition of the deeper mysteries of tenderness, no religious suavity. Under a pretext of spirituality we are always checking legitimate aspirations. We have lost the mystical sense; and what is religion without mysticism? A rose without perfume.

The words *repentance* and *sanctification* are always on our lips. But *adoration* and *consolation* are also two essential elements in religion, and we ought perhaps to make more room for them than we do.

April 28, 1861.—In the same way as a dream transforms according to its nature, the incidents of sleep, so the soul converts into psychical phenomena the ill-defined impressions of the organism. An uncomfortable attitude becomes nightmare; an atmosphere charged with storm becomes moral torment. Not mechanically and by direct causality; but imagination and conscience engender, according to their own nature, analogous effects; they translate into their own language, and cast into their own mold, whatever reaches them from outside. Thus dreams may be helpful to medicine and to divination, and states of weather may stir up and set free within the soul vague and hidden evils. The suggestions and solicitations which act upon life come from outside, but life produces nothing but itself after all. Originality consists in rapid and clear reaction against these outside influences, in giving to them our individual stamp. To think is to withdraw, as it were, into one's impression—to make it clear to one's self, and then to put it forth in the shape of a personal judgment. In this also consists self-deliverance, self-enfranchisement, self-conquest. All that comes from outside is a question to which we owe an answer—a pressure to be met by counter-pressure, if we are to remain free and living agents. The development of our unconscious nature follows the astronomical laws of Ptolemy; everything in it is change—cycle, epi-cycle, and metamorphosis.

Every man then possesses in himself the analogies and rudiments of all things, of all beings, and of all forms of life. He who knows how to divine the small beginnings, the germs and symptoms of things, can retrace in himself the universal mechanism, and divine by intuition the series which he himself will not finish, such as vegetable and animal existences, human passions and crises, the diseases of the soul and those of the body. The mind which is subtle and powerful may penetrate all these potentialities, and make every point flash out the world which it contains. This is to be conscious of and to possess the general life, this is to enter into the divine sanctuary of contemplation.

September 12, 1861.—In me an intellect which would fain forget itself in things, is contradicted by a heart which yearns to live in human beings. The uniting link of the two contradictions is the tendency toward self-abandonment, toward ceasing to will and exist for one's self, toward laying down one's own personality, and losing —dissolving—one's self in love and contemplation. What I lack above all things is character, will, individuality. But, as always happens, the appearance is exactly the contrary of the reality, and my outward life the reverse of my true and deepest aspiration. I whose whole being—heart and intellect—thirsts to absorb itself in reality, in its neighbor man, in nature and in God, I, whom solitude devours and destroys, I shut myself up in solitude and seem to delight only in myself and to be sufficient for myself. Pride and delicacy of soul, timidity of heart, have made me thus do violence to all my instincts and invert the natural order of my life. It is not astonishing that I should be unintelligible to others. In fact I have always avoided what attracted me, and turned my back upon the point where secretly I desired to be.

"Deux instincts sont en moi: vertige et deraison; J'ai l'effroi du bonheur et la soif du poison."

It is the Nemesis which dogs the steps of life, the secret instinct and power of death in us, which labors continually for the destruction of all that seeks to be, to take form, to exist; it is the passion for destruction, the tendency toward suicide, identifying itself with the instinct of self-preservation. This antipathy toward all that does one good, all that nourishes and heals, is it not a mere variation of the antipathy to moral light and regenerative truth? Does not sin also create a thirst for death, a growing passion for what does harm? Discouragement has been my sin. Discouragement is an act of unbelief. Growing weakness has been the consequence of it; the principle of death in me and the influence of the Prince of Darkness have waxed stronger together. My will in abdicating has yielded up the scepter to instinct; and as the corruption of the best results in what is worst, love of the ideal, tenderness, unworldliness, have led me to a state in which I shrink from hope and crave for annihilation. Action is my cross.

October 11, 1861. (*Heidelberg*).—After eleven days journey, here I am under the roof of my friends, in their hospitable house on the banks of the Neckar, with its garden climbing up the side of the Heiligenberg.... Blazing sun; my room is flooded with light and warmth. Sitting opposite the Geisberg, I write to the murmur of the Neckar, which rolls its green waves, flecked with silver, exactly beneath the balcony on which my room opens. A great barge coming from Heilbron passes silently under my eyes, while the wheels of a cart which I cannot see are dimly heard on the road which skirts the river. Distant voices of children, of cocks, of chirping sparrows, the clock of the Church of the Holy Spirit, which chimes the hour, serve to gauge, without troubling, the general tranquility of the scene. One feels the hours gently slipping by, and time, instead of flying, seems to hover. A peace beyond words steals into my heart, an impression of morning grace, of fresh country poetry which brings back the sense of youth, and has the true German savor.... Two decked barges carrying red flags, each with a train of flat boats filled with coal, are going up the river and making their way under the arch of the great stone bridge. I stand at the window and see a whole perspective of boats sailing in both directions; the Neckar is as animated as the street of some great capital; and already on the slope of the wooded mountain, streaked by the smoke-wreaths of the town, the castle throws its shadow like a vast drapery, and traces the outlines of its battlements and turrets. Higher up, in front of me, rises the dark profile of the Molkenkur; higher still, in relief against the dazzling east, I can distinguish the misty forms of the two towers of the Kaiserstuhl and the Trutzheinrich.

But enough of landscape. My host, Dr. George Weber, tells me that his manual of history is translated into Polish, Dutch, Spanish, Italian, and French, and that of his great "Universal History"—three volumes are already published. What astonishing power of work, what prodigious tenacity, what solidity! *O deutscher Fleiss*!

November 25, 1861.—To understand a drama requires the same mental operation as to understand an existence, a biography, a man. It is a putting back of the bird into the egg, of the plant into its seed, a reconstitution of the whole genesis of the being in question. Art is simply the bringing into relief of the obscure thought of nature; a simplification of the lines, a falling into place of groups otherwise invisible. The fire of inspiration brings out, as it were, designs traced beforehand in sympathetic ink. The mysterious grows clear, the confused plain; what is complicated becomes simple—what is accidental, necessary.

In short, art reveals nature by interpreting its intentions and formulating its desires. Every ideal is the key of a long enigma. The great artist is the simplifier.

Every man is a tamer of wild beasts, and these wild beasts are his passions. To draw their teeth and claws, to muzzle and tame them, to turn them into servants and domestic animals, fuming, perhaps, but submissive—in this consists personal education.

February 3, 1862.—Self-criticism is the corrosive of all oratorical or literary spontaneity. The thirst to know turned upon the self is punished, like the curiosity of Psyche, by the flight of the thing desired. Force should remain a mystery to itself; as soon as it tries to penetrate its own secret it vanishes away. The hen with the golden eggs becomes unfruitful as soon as she tries to find out why her eggs are golden. The consciousness of consciousness is the term and end of analysis. True, but analysis pushed to extremity devours itself, like the Egyptian serpent. We must give it some external matter to crush and dissolve if we wish to prevent its destruction by its action upon itself. "We are, and ought to be, obscure to ourselves," said Goethe, "turned outward, and working upon the world which surrounds us." Outward radiation constitutes health; a too continuous concentration upon what is within brings us back to vacuity and blank. It is better that life should dilate and extend itself in ever-widening circles, than that it should be perpetually diminished and compressed by solitary contraction. Warmth tends to make a globe out of an atom; cold, to reduce a globe to the dimensions of an atom. Analysis has been to me self-annulling, self-destroying.

April 23, 1862. (*Mornex sur Saleve*).—I was awakened by the twittering of the birds at a quarter to five, and saw, as I threw open my windows, the yellowing crescent of the moon looking in upon me, while the east was just faintly whitening. An hour later it was delicious out of doors. The anemones were still closed, the appletrees in full flower:

"Ces beaux pommiers, coverts de leurs fleurs etoileens, Neige odorante du printemps."

The view was exquisite, and nature, in full festival, spread freshness and joy around her. I breakfasted, read the paper, and here I am. The ladies of the *pension* are still under the horizon. I pity them for the loss of two or three delightful hours.

Eleven o'clock.—Preludes, scales, piano-exercises going on under my feet. In the garden children's voices. I have just finished Rosenkrantz on "Hegel's Logic," and have run through a few articles in the Reviews.... The limitation of the French mind consists in the insufficiency of its spiritual alphabet, which does not allow it to translate the Greek, German, or Spanish mind without changing the accent. The hospitality of French manners is not completed by a real hospitality of thought.... My nature is just the opposite. I am individual in the presence of men, objective in the presence of things. I attach myself to the object, and absorb myself in it; I detach myself from subjects [*i.e.*. persons], and hold myself on my guard against them. I feel myself different from the mass of men, and akin to the great whole of nature. My way of asserting myself is in cherishing this sense of sympathetic unity with life, which I yearn to understand, and in repudiating the tyranny of commonplace. All that is imitative and artificial inspires me with a secret repulsion, while the smallest true and spontaneous existence (plant, animal, child) draws and attracts me. I feel myself in community of spirit with the Goethes, the Hegels, the Schleiermachers, the Leibnitzes, opposed as they are among themselves; while the French mathematicians, philosophers, or rhetoricians, in spite of their high qualities, leave me cold, because there is in them no sense of the whole, the sum of things [Footnote: The following passage from Sainte-Beuve may be taken as a kind of answer by anticipation to this accusation, which Amiel brings more than once in the course of the Journal:

"Toute nation livree a elle-meme et a son propre genie se fait une critique litteraire qui y est conforme. La France en son beau temps a eu la sienne, qui ne ressemble ni a celle de l'Allemagne ni a celle de ses autres voisins—un peu plus superficielle, dira-t-on—je ne le crois pas: mais plus vive, moins chargee d'erudition, moins theorique et systematique, plus confiante au sentiment immediat du gout. *Un peu de chaque chose et rien de l'ensemble, a la Francaise*: telle etait la devise de Montaigne et telle est aussi la devise de la critique francaise. Nous ne sommes pas *synthetiques*, comme diraient les Allemands; le mot meme n'est pas francaise. L'imagination de detail nous suffit. Montaigne, La Fontaine Madame de Sevigne, sont volontiers nos livres de chevet."

The French critic then goes on to give a rapid sketch of the authors and the books, "qui ont peu a peu forme comme notre rhetorique." French criticism of the old characteristic kind rests ultimately upon the minute and delicate knowledge of a few Greek and Latin classics. Arnauld, Boileau, Fenelon, Rollin, Racine *fils*, Voltaire, La Harpe, Marmontel, Delille, Fontanes, and Chateaubriand in one aspect, are the typical names of this tradition, the creators and maintainers of this common literary *fonds*, this "sorte de circulation courante a l'usage des gens instruits. J'avoue ma faiblesse: nous sommes devenus bien plus forts dans la dissertation erudite, mais j'aurais un eternel regret pour cette moyenne et plus libre habitude litteraire qui laissait a l'imagination tout son espace et a l'esprit tout son jeu; qui formait une atmosphere saine et facile ou le talent respirait et se mouvait a son gre: cette atmosphere-la, je ne la trouve plus, et je la regrette." —(*Chateaubriand et son Groupe Litteraire*, vol. i. p. 311.)

The following *pensee* of La Bruyere applies to the second half of Amiel's criticism of the French mind: "If you wish to travel in the Inferno or the Paradiso you must take other guides," etc.

"Un homme ne Chretien et Francois se trouve contraint dans la satyre; les grands sujets lui sont defendus, il les entame quelquefois, et se detourne ensuite sur de petites choses qu'il releve par la beaute de son genie et de son style."—*Les Caracteres*, etc., "*Des Ouvrages del'Esprit.*"]—because they have no *grasp* of reality in its fullness, and therefore either cramp and limit me or awaken my distrust. The French lack that intuitive faculty to which the living unity of things is revealed, they have very little sense of what is sacred, very little penetration into the mysteries of being. What they excel in is the construction of special sciences; the art of writing a book, style, courtesy, grace, literary models, perfection and urbanity; the spirit of order, the art of teaching, discipline, elegance, truth of detail, power of arrangement; the desire and the gift for proselytism, the vigor necessary for practical conclusions. But if you wish to travel in the "Inferno" or the "Paradiso" you must take other guides. Their home is on the earth, in the region of the finite, the changing, the historical, and the diverse. Their logic never goes beyond the category of mechanism nor their metaphysic beyond dualism. When they undertake anything else they are doing violence to themselves.

April 24th. (*Noon*).—All around me profound peace, the silence of the mountains in spite of a full house and a neighboring village. No sound is to be heard but the murmur of the flies. There is something very striking in this calm. The middle of the day is like the middle of the night. Life seems suspended just when it is most intense. These are the moments in which one hears the infinite and perceives the ineffable. Victor Hugo, in his "Contemplations," has been carrying me from world to world, and since then his contradictions have reminded me of the convinced Christian with whom I was talking yesterday in a house near by.... The same sunlight floods both the book and nature, the doubting poet and the believing preacher, as well as the mobile dreamer, who, in the midst of all these various existences, allows himself to be swayed by every passing breath, and delights, stretched along the car of his balloon, in floating aimlessly through all the sounds and shallows of the ether, and in realizing within himself all the harmonies and dissonances of the soul, of feeling, and of thought. Idleness and contemplation! Slumber of the will, lapses of the vital force, indolence of the whole being—how well I know you! To love, to dream, to feel, to learn, to understand—all these are possible to me if only I may be relieved from willing. It is my tendency, my instinct, my fault, my sin. I have a sort of primitive horror of ambition, of struggle, of hatred, of all which dissipates the soul and makes it dependent upon external things and aims. The joy of becoming once more conscious of myself, of listening to the passage of time and the flow of the universal life, is sometimes enough to make me forget every desire, and to quench in me both the wish to produce and the power to execute. Intellectual Epicureanism is always threatening to overpower me. I can only combat it by the idea of duty; it is as the poet has said:

"Ceux qui vivent, ce sont ceux qui luttent; ce sont Ceux dont un dessein ferme emplit l'ame et le front, Ceux qui d'un haut destin gravissent l'apre cime, Ceux qui marchent pensifs, epris d'un but sublime, Ayant devant les yeux sans cesse, nuit et jour, Ou quelque saint labeur ou quelque grand amour!"

[Footnote: Victor Hugo, "Les Chatiments."]

Five o'clock.—In the afternoon our little society met in general talk upon the terrace. Some amount of familiarity and friendliness begins to show itself in our relations to each other. I read over again with emotion some passages of "Jocelyn." How admirable it is!

"Il se fit de sa vie une plus male idee: Sa douleur d'un seul trait ne l'avait pas videe; Mais, adorant de Dieu le severe dessein, Il sut la porter pleine et pure dans son sein, Et ne se hatant pas de la repandre toute, Sa resignation l'epancha goutte a goutte, Selon la circonstance et le besoin d'autrui, Pour tout vivifier sur terre autour de lui."

[Footnote: Epilogue of "Jocelyn."]

The true poetry is that which raises you, as this does, toward heaven, and fills you with divine emotion; which sings of love and death, of hope and sacrifice, and awakens the sense of the infinite. "Jocelyn" always stirs in me impulses of tenderness which it would be hateful to me to see profaned by satire. As a tragedy of feeling, it has no parallel in French, for purity, except "Paul et Virginie," and I think that I prefer "Jocelyn." To be just, one ought to read them side by side.

Six o'clock.—One more day is drawing to its close. With the exception of Mont Blanc, all the mountains have already lost their color. The evening chill succeeds the heat of the afternoon. The sense of the implacable flight of things, of the resistless passage of the hours, seizes upon me afresh and oppresses me.

"Nature au front serein, comme vous oubliez!"

In vain we cry with the poet, "O time, suspend thy flight!"... And what days, after all, would we keep and hold? Not only the happy days, but the lost days! The first have left at least a memory behind them, the others nothing but a regret which is almost a remorse....

Eleven o'clock.—A gust of wind. A few clouds in the sky. The nightingale is silent. On the other hand, the cricket and the river are still singing.

August 9, 1862.—Life, which seeks its own continuance, tends to repair itself without our help. It mends its spider's webs when they have been torn; it re-establishes in us the conditions of health, and itself heals the injuries inflicted upon it; it binds the bandage again upon our eyes, brings back hope into our hearts, breathes health once more into our organs, and regilds the dream of our imagination. But for this, experience would have hopelessly withered and faded us long before the time, and the youth would be older than the centenarian. The wise part of us, then, is that which is unconscious of itself; and what is most reasonable in man are those elements in him which do not reason. Instinct, nature, a divine, an impersonal activity, heal in us the wounds made by our own follies; the invisible *genius* of our life is never tired of providing material for the prodigalities of the self. The essential, maternal basis of our conscious life, is therefore that unconscious life which we perceive no more than the outer hemisphere of the moon perceives the earth, while all the time indissolubly and eternally bound to it. It is our [Greek: antichoon], to speak with Pythagoras.

November 7, 1862.—How malign, infectious, and unwholesome is the eternal smile of that indifferent criticism, that attitude of ironical contemplation, which corrodes and demolishes everything, that mocking pitiless temper, which holds itself aloof from every personal duty and every vulnerable affection, and cares only to understand without committing itself to action! Criticism become a habit, a fashion, and a system, means the destruction of moral energy, of faith, and of all spiritual force. One of my tendencies leads me in this direction, but I recoil before its results when I come across more emphatic types of it than myself. And at least I cannot reproach myself with having ever attempted to destroy the moral force of others; my reverence for life forbade it, and my self-distrust has taken from me even the temptation to it.

This kind of temper is very dangerous among us, for it flatters all the worst instincts of men—indiscipline, irreverence, selfish individualism—and it ends in social atomism. Minds inclined to mere negation are only harmless in great political organisms, which go without them and in spite of them. The multiplication of them among ourselves will bring about the ruin of our little countries, for small states only live by faith and will. Woe to the society where negation rules, for life is an affirmation; and a society, a country, a nation, is a living whole capable of death. No nationality is possible without prejudices, for public spirit and national tradition are but webs woven out of innumerable beliefs which have been acquired, admitted, and continued without formal proof and without discussion. To act, we must believe; to believe, we must make up our minds, affirm, decide, and in reality prejudge the question. He who will only act upon a full scientific certitude is unfit for practical life. But we are made for action, and we cannot escape from duty. Let us not, then, condemn prejudice so long as we have nothing but doubt to put in its place, or laugh at those whom we should be incapable of consoling! This, at least, is my point of view.

* * * * *

Beyond the element which is common to all men there is an element which separates them. This element may be religion, country, language, education. But all these being supposed common, there still remains something which serves as a line of demarcation—namely, the ideal. To have an ideal or to have none, to have this ideal or that—this is what digs gulfs between men, even between those who live in the same family circle, under the same roof or in the same room. You must love with the same love, think with the same thought as some one else, if you are to escape solitude.

Mutual respect implies discretion and reserve even in love itself; it means preserving as much liberty as possible to those whose life we share. We must distrust our instinct of intervention, for the desire to make one's own will prevail is often disguised under the mask of solicitude.

How many times we become hypocrites simply by remaining the same outwardly and toward others, when we know that inwardly and to ourselves we are different. It is not hypocrisy in the strict sense, for we borrow no other personality than our own; still, it is a kind of deception. The deception humiliates us, and the humiliation is a chastisement which the mask inflicts upon the face, which our past inflicts upon our present. Such humiliation is good for us; for it produces shame, and shame gives birth to repentance. Thus in an upright soul good springs out of evil, and it falls only to rise again.

* * * * *

January 8, 1863.—This evening I read through the "Cid" and "Rodogune." My impression is still a mixed and confused one. There is much disenchantment in my admiration, and a good deal of reserve in my enthusiasm. What displeases me in this dramatic art, is the mechanical abstraction of the characters, and the scolding, shrewish tone of the interlocutors. I had a vague impression of listening to gigantic marionettes, perorating through a trumpet, with the emphasis of Spaniards. There is power in it, but we have before us heroic idols rather than human beings. The element of artificiality, of strained pomposity and affectation, which is the plague of classical tragedy, is everywhere apparent, and one hears, as it were, the cords and pulleys of these majestic *colossi* creaking and groaning. I much prefer Racine and Shakespeare; the one from the point of view of aesthetic sensation, the other from that of psychological sensation. The southern theater can never free itself from masks. Comic masks are bearable, but in the case of tragic heroes, the abstract type, the mask, make one impatient. I can laugh with personages of tin and pasteboard: I can only weep with the living, or what resembles them. Abstraction turns easily to caricature; it is apt to engender mere shadows on the wall, mere ghosts and puppets. It is psychology of the first degree—elementary psychology—just as the colored pictures of Germany are elementary painting. And yet with all this, you have a double-distilled and often sophistical refinement: just as savages are by no means simple. The fine side of it all is the manly vigor, the bold frankness of ideas, words, and sentiments. Why is it that we find so large an element of factitious grandeur, mingled with true grandeur, in this drama of 1640, from which the whole dramatic development of monarchical France was to spring? Genius is there, but it is hemmed round by a conventional civilization, and, strive as he may, no man wears a wig with impunity.

January 13, 1863.—To-day it has been the turn of "Polyeucte" and "La Morte de Pompee." Whatever one's objections may be, there is something grandiose in the style of Corneille which reconciles you at last even to his stiff, emphatic manner, and his over-ingenious rhetoric. But it is the dramatic *genre* which is false. His heroes are roles rather than men. They pose as magnanimity, virtue, glory, instead of realizing them before us. They are always *en scene*, studied by others, or by themselves. With them glory—that is to say, the life of ceremony and of affairs, and the opinion of the public—replaces nature—becomes nature. They never speak except *ore rotundo*, in *cothurnus*, or sometimes on stilts. And what consummate advocates they all are! The French drama is an oratorical tournament, a long suit between opposing parties, on a day which is to end with the death of somebody, and where all the personages represented are in haste to speak before the hour of silence strikes. Elsewhere, speech serves to make action intelligible; in French tragedy action is but a decent motive for speech. It is the procedure calculated to extract the finest possible speeches from the persons who are engaged in the action, and who represent different perceptions of it at different moments and from different points of view. Love and nature, duty and desire, and a dozen other moral antitheses, are the limbs moved by the wire of the dramatist, who makes them fall into all the tragic attitudes. What is really curious and amusing is that the people of all others the most vivacious, gay, and intelligent, should have always understood the grand style in this pompous, pedantic fashion. But it was inevitable.

April 8, 1863.—I have been turning over the 3,500 pages of "Les Miserables," trying to understand the guiding idea of this vast composition. The fundamental idea of "Les Miserables" seems to be this. Society engenders certain frightful evils—prostitution, vagabondage, rogues, thieves, convicts, war, revolutionary clubs and barricades. She ought to impress this fact on her mind, and not treat all those who come in contact with her law as mere monsters. The task before us is to humanize law and opinion, to raise the fallen as well as the vanquished, to create a social redemption. How is this to be done? By enlightening vice and lawlessness, and so diminishing the sum of them, and by bringing to bear upon the guilty the healing influence of pardon. At bottom is it not a Christianization of society, this extension of charity from the sinner to the condemned criminal, this application to our present life of what the church applies more readily to the other? Struggle to restore a human soul to order and to righteousness by patience and by love, instead of crushing it by your inflexible vindictiveness, your savage justice! Such is the cry of the book. It is great and noble, but it is a little optimistic and Rousseau-like. According to it the individual is always innocent and society always responsible, and the ideal before us for the twentieth century is a sort of democratic age of gold, a universal republic from which war, capital punishment, and pauperism will have disappeared. It is the religion and the city of progress; in a word, the Utopia of the eighteenth century revived on a great scale. There is a great deal of generosity in it, mixed with not a little fanciful extravagance. The fancifulness consists chiefly in a superficial notion of evil. The author ignores or pretends to forget the instinct of perversity, the love of evil for evil's sake, which is contained in the human heart.

The great and salutary idea of the book, is that honesty before the law is a cruel hypocrisy, in so far as it arrogates to itself the right of dividing society according to its own standard into elect and reprobates, and thus confounds the relative with the absolute. The leading passage is that in which Javert, thrown off the rails, upsets the whole moral system of the strict Javert, half spy, half priest—of the irreproachable police-officer. In this chapter the writer shows us social charity illuminating and transforming a harsh and unrighteous justice. Suppression of the social hell, that is to say, of all irreparable stains, of all social outlawries for which there is neither end nor hope—it is an essentially religious idea.

The erudition, the talent, the brilliancy of execution, shown in the book are astonishing, bewildering almost. Its faults are to be found in the enormous length allowed to digressions and episodical dissertations, in the exaggeration of all the combinations and all the theses, and, finally, in something strained, spasmodic, and violent in the style, which is very different from the style of natural eloquence or of essential truth. Effect is the misfortune of Victor Hugo, because he makes it the center of his aesthetic system; and hence exaggeration, monotony of emphasis, theatricality of manner, a tendency to force and over-drive. A powerful artist, but one with whom you never forget the artist; and a dangerous model, for the master himself is already grazing the rock of burlesque, and passes from the sublime to the repulsive, from lack of power to produce one harmonious impression of beauty. It is natural enough that he should detest Racine.

But what astonishing philological and literary power has Victor Hugo! He is master of all the dialects contained in our language, dialects of the courts of law, of the stock-exchange, of war, and of the sea, of philosophy and the convict-gang, the dialects of trade and of archaeology, of the antiquarian and the scavenger. All the bric-a-brac of history and of manners, so to speak, all the curiosities of soil, and subsoil, are known and familiar to him. He seems to have turned his Paris over and over, and to know it body and soul as one knows the contents of one's pocket. What a prodigious memory and what a lurid imagination! He is at once a visionary and yet master of his dreams; he summons up and handles at will the hallucinations of opium or of hasheesh, without ever becoming their dupe; he makes of madness one of his tame animals, and bestrides, with equal coolness, Pegasus or Nightmare, the Hippogriff or the Chimera. As a psychological phenomenon he is of the deepest interest. Victor Hugo draws in sulphuric acid, he lights his pictures with electric light. He deafens, blinds, and bewilders his reader rather than he charms or persuades him. Strength carried to such a point as this is a fascination; without seeming to take you captive, it makes you its prisoner; it does not enchant you, but it holds you spellbound. His ideal is the extraordinary, the gigantic, the overwhelming, the incommensurable. His most characteristic words are *immense, colossal, enormous, huge, monstrous*. He finds a way of making even child-nature extravagant and bizarre. The only thing which seems impossible to him is to be natural. In short, his passion is grandeur, his fault is excess; his distinguishing mark is a kind of Titanic power with strange dissonances of puerility in its magnificence. Where he is weakest is, in measure, taste, and sense of humor: he fails in *esprit*, in the subtlest sense of the word. Victor Hugo is a gallicized Spaniard, or rather he unites all the extremes of south and north, the Scandinavian and the African. Gaul has less part in him than any other country. And yet, by a caprice of destiny, he is one of the literary geniuses of France in the nineteenth century! His resources are inexhaustible, and age seems to have no power over him. What an infinite store of words, forms, and ideas he carries about with him, and what a pile of works he has left behind him to mark his passage! His eruptions are like those of a volcano; and, fabulous workman that he is, he goes on forever raising, destroying, crushing, and rebuilding a world of his own creation, and a world rather Hindoo than Hellenic.

He amazes me: and yet I prefer those men of genius who awaken in me the sense of truth, and who increase the sum of one's inner liberty. In Hugo one feels the effort of the laboring Cyclops; give me rather the sonorous bow of Apollo, and the tranquil brow of the Olympian Jove. His type is that of the Satyr in the "Legende des Siecles," who crushes Olympus, a type midway between the ugliness of the faun and the overpowering sublimity of the great Pan.

May 23, 1863.—Dull, cloudy, misty weather; it rained in the night and yet the air is heavy. This somber reverie of earth and sky has a sacredness of its own, but it fills the spectator with a vague and stupefying *ennui*. Light brings life: darkness may bring thought, but a dull daylight, the uncertain glimmer of a leaden sky, merely make one restless and weary. These indecisive and chaotic states of nature are ugly, like all amorphous things, like smeared colors, or bats, or the viscous polyps of the sea. The source of all attractiveness is to be found in character, in sharpness of outline, in individualization. All that is confused and indistinct, without form, or sex, or accent, is antagonistic to beauty; for the mind's first need is light; light means order, and order means, in the first place, the distinction of the parts, in the second, their regular action. Beauty is based on reason.

August 7, 1863.—A walk after supper, a sky sparkling with stars, the Milky Way magnificent. Alas! all the same my heart is heavy. At bottom I am always brought up against an incurable distrust of myself and of life, which toward my neighbor has become indulgence, but for myself has led to a *regime* of absolute abstention. All or nothing! This is my inborn disposition, my primitive stuff, my "old man." And yet if some one will but give me a little love, will but penetrate a little into my inner feeling, I am happy and ask for scarcely anything else. A child's caresses, a friend's talk, are enough to make me gay and expansive. So then I aspire to the infinite, and yet a very little contents me; everything disturbs me and the least thing calms me. I have often surprised in my self the wish for death, and yet my ambitions for happiness scarcely go beyond those of the bird: wings! sun! a nest! I persist in solitude because of a taste for it, so people think. No, it is from distaste, disgust, from shame at my own need of others, shame at confessing it, a fear of passing into bondage if I do confess it.

September 2, 1863.—How shall I find a name for that subtle feeling which seized hold upon me this morning in the twilight of waking? It was a reminiscence, charming indeed, but nameless, vague, and featureless, like the figure of a woman seen for an instant by a sick man in the uncertainty of delirium, and across the shadows of his darkened room. I had a distinct sense of a form which I had seen somewhere, and which had moved and charmed me once, and then had fallen back with time into the catacombs of oblivion. But all the rest was confused: place, occasion, and the figure itself, for I saw neither the face nor its expression. The whole was like a fluttering veil under which the enigma—the secret of happiness—might have been hidden. And I was awake enough to be sure that it was not a dream.

In impressions like these we recognize the last trace of things which are sinking out of sight and call within us, of memories which are perishing. It is like a shimmering marsh-light falling upon some vague outline of which one scarcely knows whether it represents a pain or a pleasure—a gleam upon a grave. How strange! One might almost call such things the ghosts of the soul, reflections of past happiness, the *manes* of our dead emotions. If, as the Talmud, I think, says, every feeling of love gives birth involuntarily to an invisible genius or spirit which yearns to complete its existence, and these glimmering phantoms, which have never taken to themselves form and reality, are still wandering in the limbo of the soul, what is there to astonish us in the strange apparitions which sometimes come to visit our pillow? At any rate, the fact remains that I was not able to force the phantom to tell me its name, nor to give any shape or distinctness to my reminiscence.

What a melancholy aspect life may wear to us when we are floating down the current of such dreamy thoughts as these! It seems like some vast nocturnal shipwreck in which a hundred loving voices are clamoring for help, while the pitiless mounting wave is silencing all the cries one by one, before we have been able, in this darkness of death, to press a hand or give the farewell kiss. Prom such a point of view destiny looks harsh, savage, and cruel, and the tragedy of life rises like a rock in the midst of the dull waters of daily triviality. It is impossible not to be serious under the weight of indefinable anxiety produced in us by such a spectacle. The surface of things may be smiling or commonplace, but the depths below are austere and terrible. As soon as we touch upon eternal things, upon the destiny of the soul, upon truth or duty, upon the secrets of life and death, we become grave whether we will or no.

Love at its highest point—love sublime, unique, invincible—leads us straight to the brink of the great abyss, for it speaks to us directly of the infinite and of eternity. It is eminently religious; it may even become religion. When all around a man is wavering and changing, when everything is growing dark and featureless to him in the far distance of an unknown future, when the world seems but a fiction or a fairy tale, and the universe a chimera, when the whole edifice of ideas vanishes in smoke, and all realities are penetrated with doubt, what is the fixed point which may still be his? The faithful heart of a woman! There he may rest his head; there he will find strength to live, strength to believe, and, if need be, strength to die in peace with a benediction on his lips. Who knows if love and its beatitude, clear manifestation as it is of the universal harmony of things, is not the best demonstration of a fatherly and understanding God, just as it is the shortest road by which to reach him? Love is a faith, and one faith leads to another. And this faith is happiness, light and force. Only by it does a man enter into the series of the living, the awakened, the happy, the redeemed—of those true men who know the value of existence and who labor for the glory of God and of the truth. Till then we are but babblers and chatterers, spendthrifts of our time, our faculties and our gifts, without aim, without real joy—weak, infirm, and useless beings, of no account in the scheme of things. Perhaps it is through love that I shall find my way back to faith, to religion, to energy, to concentration. It seems to me, at least, that if I could but find my work-fellow and my destined companion, all the rest would be added unto me, as though to confound my unbelief and make me blush for my despair. Believe, then, in a fatherly Providence, and dare to love!

November 25, 1863.—Prayer is the essential weapon of all religions. He who can no longer pray because he doubts whether there is a being to whom prayer ascends and from whom blessing descends, he indeed is cruelly solitary and prodigiously impoverished. And you, what do you believe about it? At this moment I should find it very difficult to say. All my positive beliefs are in the crucible ready for any kind of metamorphosis. Truth above all, even when it upsets and overwhelms us! But what I believe is that the highest idea we can conceive of the principle of things will be the truest, and that the truest truth is that which makes man the most wholly good, wisest, greatest, and happiest.

My creed is in transition. Yet I still believe in God, and the immortality of the soul. I believe in holiness, truth, beauty; I believe in the redemption of the soul by faith in forgiveness. I believe in love, devotion, honor. I believe in duty and the moral conscience. I believe even in prayer. I believe in the fundamental intuitions of the human race, and in the great affirmations of the inspired of all ages. I believe that our higher nature is our truer nature.

Can one get a theology and a theodicy out of this? Probably, but just now I do not see it distinctly. It is so long since I have ceased to think about my own metaphysic, and since I have lived in the thoughts of others, that I am ready even to ask myself whether the crystallization of my beliefs is necessary. Yes, for preaching and acting; less for studying, contemplating and learning.

December 4, 1863.—The whole secret of remaining young in spite of years, and even of gray hairs, is to cherish enthusiasm in one's self by poetry, by contemplation, by charity—that is, in fewer words, by the maintenance of harmony in the soul. When everything is in its right place within us, we ourselves are in equilibrium with the whole work of God. Deep and grave enthusiasm for the eternal beauty and the eternal order, reason touched with emotion and a serene tenderness of heart—these surely are the foundations of wisdom.

Wisdom! how inexhaustible a theme! A sort of peaceful aureole surrounds and illumines this thought, in which are summed up all the treasures of moral experience, and which is the ripest fruit of a well-spent life. Wisdom never grows old, for she is the expression of order itself—that is, of the Eternal. Only the wise man draws from life, and from every stage of it, its true savor, because only he feels the beauty, the dignity, and the value of life. The flowers of youth may fade, but the summer, the autumn, and even the winter of human existence, have their majestic grandeur, which the wise man recognizes and glorifies. To see all things in God; to make of one's own life a journey toward the ideal; to live with gratitude, with devoutness, with gentleness and courage; this was the splendid aim of Marcus Aurelius. And if you add to it the humility which kneels, and the charity which gives, you have the whole wisdom of the children of God, the immortal joy which is the heritage of the true Christian. But what a false Christianity is that which slanders wisdom and seeks to do without it! In such a case I am on the side of wisdom, which is, as it were, justice done to God, even in this life. The relegation of life to some distant future, and the separation of the holy man from the virtuous man, are the signs of a false religious conception. This error is, in some degree, that of the whole Middle Age, and belongs, perhaps, to the essence of Catholicism. But the true Christianity must purge itself from so disastrous a mistake. The eternal life is not the future life; it is life in harmony with the true order of things—life in God. We must learn to look upon time as a movement of eternity, as an undulation in the ocean of being. To live, so as to keep this consciousness of ours in perpetual relation with the eternal, is to be wise; to live, so as to personify and embody the eternal, is to be religious.

The modern leveler, after having done away with conventional inequalities, with arbitrary privilege and historical injustice, goes still farther, and rebels against the inequalities of merit, capacity, and virtue. Beginning with a just principle, he develops it into an unjust one. Inequality may be as true and as just as equality: it depends upon what you mean by it. But this is precisely what nobody cares to find out. All passions dread the light, and the modern zeal for equality is a disguised hatred which tries to pass itself off as love.

Liberty, equality—bad principles! The only true principle for humanity is justice, and justice toward the feeble becomes necessarily protection or kindness.

April 2, 1864.—To-day April has been displaying her showery caprices. We have had floods of sunshine followed by deluges of rain, alternate tears and smiles from the petulant sky, gusts of wind and storms. The weather is like a spoiled child whose wishes and expression change twenty times in an hour. It is a blessing for the plants, and means an influx of life through all the veins of the spring. The circle of mountains which bounds the valley is covered with white from top to toe, but two hours of sunshine would melt the snow away. The snow itself is but a new caprice, a simple stage decoration ready to disappear at the signal of the scene-shifter.

How sensible I am to the restless change which rules the world. To appear, and to vanish—there is the biography of all individuals, whatever may be the length of the cycle of existence which they describe, and the drama of the universe is nothing more. All life is the shadow of a smoke-wreath, a gesture in the empty air, a hieroglyph traced for an instant in the sand, and effaced a moment afterward by a breath of wind, an air-bubble expanding and vanishing on the surface of the great river of being—an appearance, a vanity, a nothing. But this nothing is, however, the symbol of the universal being, and this passing bubble is the epitome of the history of the world.

The man who has, however imperceptibly, helped in the work of the universe, has lived; the man who has been conscious, in however small a degree, of the cosmical movement, has lived also. The plain man serves the world by his action and as a wheel in the machine; the thinker serves it by his intellect, and as a light upon its path. The man of meditative soul, who raises and comforts and sustains his traveling companions, mortal and fugitive like himself, plays a nobler part still, for he unites the other two utilities. Action, thought, speech, are the three modes of human life. The artisan, the savant, and the orator, are all three God's workmen. To do, to discover, to teach—these three things are all labor, all good, all necessary. Will-o'-the-wisps that we are, we may yet leave a trace behind us; meteors that we are, we may yet prolong our perishable being in the memory of men, or at least in the contexture of after events. Everything disappears, but nothing is lost, and the civilization or city of man is but an immense spiritual pyramid, built up out of the work of all that has ever lived under the forms of moral being, just as our calcareous mountains are made of the debris of myriads of nameless creatures who have lived under the forms of microscopic animal life.

April 5, 1864.—I have been reading "Prince Vitale" for the second time, and have been lost in admiration of it. What wealth of color, facts, ideas—what learning, what fine-edged satire, what *esprit*, science, and talent, and what an irreproachable finish of style—so limpid, and yet so profound! It is not heartfelt and it is not spontaneous, but all other kinds of merit, culture, and cleverness the author possesses. It would be impossible to be more penetrating, more subtle, and less fettered in mind, than this wizard of language, with his irony and his chameleon-like variety. Victor Cherbuliez, like the sphinx, is able to play all lyres, and takes his profit from them all, with a Goethe-like serenity. It seems as if passion, grief, and error had no hold on this impassive soul. The key of his thought is to be looked for in Hegel's "Phenomenology of Mind," remolded by Greek and French influences.

His faith, if he has one, is that of Strauss-Humanism. But he is perfectly master of himself and of his utterances, and will take good care never to preach anything prematurely.

What is there quite at the bottom of this deep spring?

In any case a mind as free as any can possibly be from stupidity and prejudice. One might almost say that Cherbuliez knows all that he wishes to know, without the trouble of learning it. He is a calm Mephistopheles, with perfect manners, grace, variety, and an exquisite urbanity; and Mephisto is a clever jeweler; and this jeweler is a subtle musician; and this fine singer and storyteller, with his amber-like delicacy and brilliancy, is making mock of us all the while. He takes a malicious pleasure in withdrawing his own personality from scrutiny and divination, while he himself divines everything, and he likes to make us feel that although he holds in his hand the secret of the universe, he will only unfold his prize at his own time, and if it pleases him. Victor Cherbuliez is a little like Proudhon and plays with paradoxes, to shock the *bourgeois*. Thus he amuses himself with running down Luther and the Reformation in favor of the Renaissance. Of the troubles of conscience he seems to know nothing. His supreme tribunal is reason. At bottom he is Hegelian and intellectualist. But it is a splendid organization. Only sometimes he must be antipathetic to those men of duty who make renunciation, sacrifice, and humility the measure of individual worth.

July, 1864.—Among the Alps I become a child again, with all the follies and *naivete* of childhood. Shaking off the weight of years, the trappings of office, and all the tiresome and ridiculous caution with which one lives, I plunge into the full tide of pleasure, and amuse myself sans facon, as it comes. In this careless light-hearted mood, my ordinary formulas and habits fall away from me so completely that I feel myself no longer either townsman, or professor, or savant, or bachelor, and I remember no more of my past than if it were a dream. It is like a bath in Lethe.

It makes me really believe that the smallest illness would destroy my memory, and wipe out all my previous existence, when I see with what ease I become a stranger to myself, and fall back once more into the condition of a blank sheet, a *tabula rasa*. Life wears such a dream-aspect to me that I can throw myself without any difficulty into the situation of the dying, before whose eyes all this tumult of images and forms fades into nothingness. I have the inconsistency of a fluid, a vapor, a cloud, and all is easily unmade or transformed in me; everything passes and is effaced like the waves which follow each other on the sea. When I say all, I mean all that is arbitrary, indifferent, partial, or intellectual in the combinations of one's life. For I feel that the things of the soul, our immortal aspirations, our deepest affections, are not drawn into this chaotic whirlwind of impressions. It is the finite things which are mortal and fugitive. Every man feels it OH his deathbed. I feel it during the whole of life; that is the only difference between me and others. Excepting only love, thought, and liberty, almost everything is now a matter of indifference to me, and those objects which excite the desires of most men, rouse in me little more than curiosity. What does it mean— detachment of soul, disinterestedness, weakness, or wisdom?

September 19, 1864.—I have been living for two hours with a noble soul—with Eugenie de Guerin, the pious heroine of fraternal love. How many thoughts, feelings, griefs, in this journal of six years! How it makes one dream, think and live! It produces a certain homesick impression on me, a little like that of certain forgotten melodies whereof the accent touches the heart, one knows not why.

It is as though far-off paths came back to me, glimpses of youth, a confused murmur of voices, echoes from my past. Purity, melancholy, piety, a thousand memories of a past existence, forms fantastic and intangible, like the fleeting shadows of a dream at waking, began to circle round the astonished reader.

September 20, 1864.—Read Eugenie de Guerin's volume again right and left with a growing sense of attraction. Everything is heart, force, impulse, in these pages which have the power of sincerity and a brilliance of suffused poetry. A great and strong soul, a clear mind, distinction, elevation, the freedom of unconscious talent, reserve and depth—nothing is wanting for this Sevigne of the fields, who has to hold herself in with both hands lest she should write verse, so strong in her is the artistic impulse.

October 16, 1864.—I have just read a part of Eugenie de Guerin's journal over again. It charmed me a little less than the first time. The nature seemed to me as beautiful, but the life of Eugenie was too empty, and the circle of ideas which occupied her, too narrow.

It is touching and wonderful to see how little space is enough for thought to spread its wings in, but this perpetual motion within the four walls of a cell ends none the less by becoming wearisome to minds which are accustomed to embrace more objects in their field of vision. Instead of a garden, the world; instead of a library, the whole of literature; instead of three or four faces, a whole people and all history—this is what the virile, the philosophic temper demands. Men must have more air, more room, mere horizon, more positive knowledge, and they end by suffocating in this little cage where Eugenie lives and moves, though the breath of heaven blows into it and the radiance of the stars shines down upon it.

October 27, 1864. (*Promenade de la Treille*).—The air this morning was so perfectly clear and lucid that one might have distinguished a figure on the Vouache. [Footnote: The Vouache is the hill which bounds the horizon of Geneva to the south-west.] This level and brilliant sun had set fire to the whole range of autumn colors; amber, saffron, gold, sulphur, yellow ochre, orange, red, copper-color, aquamarine, amaranth, shone resplendent on the leaves which were still hanging from the boughs or had already fallen beneath the trees. It was delicious. The martial step of our two battalions going out to their drilling-ground, the sparkle of the guns, the song of the bugles, the sharp distinctness of the house outlines, still moist with the morning dew, the transparent coolness of all the shadows—every detail in the scene was instinct with a keen and wholesome gayety.

There are two forms of autumn: there is the misty and dreamy autumn, there is the vivid and brilliant autumn: almost the difference between the two sexes. The very word autumn is both masculine and feminine. Has not every season, in some fashion, its two sexes? Has it not its minor and its major key, its two sides of light and shadow, gentleness and force? Perhaps. All that is perfect is double; each face has two profiles, each coin two sides. The scarlet autumn stands for vigorous activity: the gray autumn for meditative feeling. The one is expansive and overflowing; the other still and withdrawn. Yesterday our thoughts were with the dead. To-day we are celebrating the vintage.

November 16, 1864.—Heard of the death of—. Will and intelligence lasted till there was an effusion on the brain which stopped everything.

A bubble of air in the blood, a drop of water in the brain, and a man is out of gear, his machine falls to pieces, his thought vanishes, the world disappears from him like a dream at morning. On what a spider thread is hung our individual existence! Fragility, appearance, nothingness. If it were for our powers of self-detraction and forgetfulness, all the fairy world which surrounds and draws us would seem to us but a broken spectre in the darkness, an empty appearance, a fleeting hallucination. Appeared—disappeared—there is the whole history of a man, or of a world, or of an infusoria.

Time is the supreme illusion. It is but the inner prism by which we decompose being and life, the mode under which we perceive successively what is simultaneous in idea. The eye does not see a sphere all at once although the sphere exists all at once. Either the sphere must turn before the eye which is looking at it, or the eye must go round the sphere. In the first case it is the world which unrolls, or seems to unroll in time; in the second case it is our thought which successively analyzes and recomposes. For the supreme intelligence there is no time; what will be, is. Time and space are fragments of the infinite for the use of finite creatures. God permits them, that he may not be alone. They are the mode under which creatures are possible and conceivable. Let us add that they are also the Jacob's ladder of innumerable steps by which the creation reascends to its Creator, participates in being, tastes of life, perceives the absolute, and can adore the fathomless mystery of the infinite divinity. That is the other side of the question. Our life is nothing, it is true, but our life is divine. A breath of nature annihilates us, but we surpass nature in penetrating far beyond her vast phantasmagoria to the changeless and the eternal. To escape by the ecstasy of inward vision from the whirlwind of time, to see one's self *sub specie eterni* is the word of command of all the great religions of the higher races; and this psychological possibility is the foundation of all great hopes. The soul may be immortal because she is fitted to rise toward that which is neither born nor dies, toward that which exists substantially, necessarily, invariably, that is to say toward God.

To know how to suggest is the great art of teaching. To attain it we must be able to guess what will interest; we must learn to read the childish soul as we might a piece of music. Then, by simply changing the key, we keep up the attraction and vary the song.

The germs of all things are in every heart, and the greatest criminals as well as the greatest heroes are but different modes of ourselves. Only evil grows of itself, while for goodness we want effort and courage.

Melancholy is at the bottom of everything, just as at the end of all rivers is the sea. Can it be otherwise in a world where nothing lasts, where all that we have loved or shall love must die? Is death, then, the secret of life? The gloom of an eternal mourning enwraps, more or less closely, every serious and thoughtful soul, as night enwraps the universe.

A man takes to "piety" from a thousand different reasons—from imitation or from eccentricity, from bravado or from reverence, from shame of the past or from terror of the future, from weakness and from pride, for pleasure's sake or for punishment's sake, in order to be able to judge, or in order to escape being judged, and for a thousand other reasons; but he only becomes truly religious for religion's sake.

January 11, 1865.—It is pleasant to feel nobly—that is to say, to live above the lowlands of vulgarity. Manufacturing Americanism and Caesarian democracy tend equally to the multiplying of crowds, governed by appetite, applauding charlatanism, vowed to the worship of mammon and of pleasure, and adoring no other God than force. What poor samples of mankind they are who make up this growing majority! Oh, let us remain faithful to the altars of the ideal! It is possible that the spiritualists may become the stoics of a new epoch of Caesarian rule. Materialistic naturalism has the wind in its sails, and a general moral deterioration is preparing. NO matter, so long as the salt does not lose its savor, and so long as the friends of the higher life maintain the fire of Vesta. The wood itself may choke the flame, but if the flame persists, the fire will only be the more splendid in the end. The great democratic deluge will not after all be able to effect what the invasion of the barbarians was powerless to bring about; it will not drown altogether the results of the higher culture; but we must resign ourselves to the fact that it tends in the beginning to deform and vulgarize everything. It is clear that aesthetic delicacy, elegance, distinction, and nobleness—that atticism, urbanity, whatever is suave and exquisite, fine and subtle—all that makes the charm of the higher kinds of literature and of aristocratic cultivation—vanishes simultaneously with the society which corresponds to it. If, as Pascal, [Footnote: The saying of Pascal's alluded to is in the *Pensees*, Art. xi. No. 10: "A mesure qu'on a plus d'esprit on trouve qu'il y a plus d'hommes originaux. Les gens du commun ne trouvent pas de difference entre les hommes."] I think, says, the more one develops, the more difference one observes between man and man, then we cannot say that the democratic instinct tends to mental development, since it tends to make a man believe that the pretensions have only to be the same to make the merits equal also.

March 20, 1865.—I have just heard of fresh cases of insubordination among the students. Our youth become less and less docile, and seem to take for their motto, "Our master is our enemy." The boy insists upon having the privileges of the young man, and the young man tries to keep those of the *gamin*. At bottom all this is the natural consequence of our system of leveling democracy. As soon as difference of quality is, in politics, officially equal to zero, the authority of age, of knowledge, and of function disappears.

The only counterpoise of pure equality is military discipline. In military uniform, in the police court, in prison, or on the execution ground, there is no reply possible. But is it not curious that the *regime* of individual right should lead to nothing but respect for brute strength? Jacobinism brings with it Caesarism; the rule of the tongue leads to the rule of the sword. Democracy and liberty are not one but two. A republic supposes a high state of morals, but no such state of morals is possible without the habit of respect; and there is no respect without humility. Now the pretension that every man has the necessary qualities of a citizen, simply because he was born twenty-one years ago, is as much as to say that labor, merit, virtue, character, and experience are to count for nothing; and we destroy humility when we proclaim that a man becomes the equal of all other men, by the mere mechanical and vegetative process of natural growth. Such a claim annihilates even the respect for age; for as the elector of twenty-one is worth as much as the elector of fifty, the boy of nineteen has no serious reason to believe himself in any way the inferior of his elder by one or two years. Thus the fiction on which the political order of democracy is based ends in something altogether opposed to that which democracy desires: its aim was to increase the whole sum of liberty; but the result is to diminish it for all.

The modern state is founded on the philosophy of atomism. Nationality, public spirit, tradition, national manners, disappear like so many hollow and worn-out entities; nothing remains to create movement but the action of molecular force and of dead weight. In such a theory liberty is identified with caprice, and the collective reason and age-long tradition of an old society are nothing more than soap-bubbles which the smallest urchin may shiver with a snap of the fingers.

Does this mean that I am an opponent of democracy? Not at all. Fiction for fiction, it is the least harmful. But it is well not to confound its promises with realities. The fiction consists in the postulate of all democratic government, that the great majority of the electors in a state are enlightened, free, honest, and patriotic—whereas such a postulate is a mere chimera. The majority in any state is necessarily composed of the most ignorant, the poorest, and the least capable; the state is therefore at the mercy of accident and passion, and it always ends by succumbing at one time or another to the rash conditions which have been made for its existence. A man who condemns himself to live upon the tight-rope must inevitably fall; one has no need to be a prophet to foresee such a result.

"[Greek: Aridton men udor]," said Pindar; the best thing in the world is wisdom, and, in default of wisdom, science. States, churches, society itself, may fall to pieces; science alone has nothing to fear—until at least society once more falls a prey to barbarism. Unfortunately this triumph of barbarism is not impossible. The victory of the socialist Utopia, or the horrors of a religious war, reserve for us perhaps even this lamentable experience.

April 3, 1865.—What doctor possesses such curative resources as those latent in a spark of happiness or a single ray of hope? The mainspring of life is in the heart. Joy is the vital air of the soul, and grief is a kind of asthma complicated by atony. Our dependence upon surrounding circumstances increases with our own physical weakness, and on the other hand, in health there is liberty. Health is the first of all liberties, and happiness gives us the energy which is the basis of health. To make any one happy, then, is strictly to augment his store of being, to double the intensity of his life, to reveal him to himself, to ennoble him and transfigure him. Happiness does away with ugliness, and even makes the beauty of beauty. The man who doubts it, can never have watched the first gleams of tenderness dawning in the clear eyes of one who loves; sunrise itself is a lesser marvel. In paradise, then, everybody will be beautiful. For, as the righteous soul is naturally beautiful, as the spiritual body is but the *visibility* of the soul, its impalpable and angelic form, and as happiness beautifies all that it penetrates or even touches, ugliness will have no more place in the universe, and will disappear with grief, sin, and death.

To the materialist philosopher the beautiful is a mere accident, and therefore rare. To the spiritualist philosopher the beautiful is the rule, the law, the universal foundation of things, to which every form returns as soon as the force of accident is withdrawn. Why are we ugly? Because we are not in the angelic state, because we are evil, morose, and unhappy.

Heroism, ecstasy, prayer, love, enthusiasm, weave a halo round the brow, for they are a setting free of the soul, which through them gains force to make its envelope transparent and shine through upon all around it. Beauty is, then, a phenomenon belonging to the spiritualization of matter. It is a momentary transfiguration of the privileged object or being—a token fallen from heaven to earth in order to remind us of the ideal world. To study it, is to Platonize almost inevitably. As a powerful electric current can render metals luminous, and reveal their essence by the color of their flame, so intense life and supreme joy can make the most simple mortal dazzlingly beautiful. Man, therefore, is never more truly man than in these divine states.

The ideal, after all, is truer than the real: for the ideal is the eternal element in perishable things: it is their type, their sum, their *raison d'etre*, their formula in the book of the Creator, and therefore at once the most exact and the most condensed expression of them.

April 11, 1865.—I have been measuring and making a trial of the new gray plaid which is to take the place of my old mountain shawl. The old servant which has been my companion for ten years, and which recalls to me so many poetical and delightful memories, pleases me better than its brilliant successor, even though this last has been a present from a friendly hand. But can anything take the place of the past, and have not even the inanimate witnesses of our life voice and language for us? Glion, Villars, Albisbrunnen, the Righi, the Chamossaire, and a hundred other places, have left something of themselves behind them in the meshes of this woolen stuff which makes a part of my most intimate history. The shawl, besides, is the only *chivalrous* article of dress which is still left to the modern traveler, the only thing about him which may be useful to others than himself, and by means of which he may still do his *devoir* to fair women! How many times mine has served them for a cushion, a cloak, a shelter, on the damp grass of the Alps, on seats of hard rock, or in the sudden cool of the pinewood, during the walks, the rests, the readings, and the chats of mountain life! How many kindly smiles it has won for me! Even its blemishes are dear to me, for each darn and tear has its story, each scar is an armorial bearing. This tear was made by a hazel tree under Jaman—that by the buckle of a strap on the Frohnalp—that, again, by a bramble at Charnex; and each time fairy needles have repaired the injury.

"Mon vieux manteau, que je vous remercie Car c'est a vous que je dois ces plaisirs!"

And has it not been to me a friend in suffering, a companion in good and evil fortune? It reminds me of that centaur's tunic which could not be torn off without carrying away the flesh and blood of its wearer. I am unwilling to give it up; whatever gratitude for the past, and whatever piety toward my vanished youth is in me, seem to forbid it. The warp of this rag is woven out of Alpine joys, and its woof out of human affections. It also says to me in its own way:

"Pauvre bouquet, fleurs aujourd'hui fanees!"

And the appeal is one of those which move the heart, although profane ears neither hear it nor understand it.

What a stab there is in those words, *thou hast been*! when the sense of them becomes absolutely clear to us. One feels one's self sinking gradually into one's grave, and the past tense sounds the knell of our illusions as to ourselves. What is past is past: gray hairs will never become black curls again; the forces, the gifts, the attractions of youth, have vanished with our young days.

"Plus d'amour; partant plus de joie."

How hard it is to grow old, when we have missed our life, when we have neither the crown of completed manhood nor of fatherhood! How sad it is to feel the mind declining before it has done its work, and the body growing weaker before it has seen itself renewed in those who might close our eyes and honor our name! The tragic solemnity of existence strikes us with terrible force, on that morning when we wake to find the mournful word *too late* ringing in our ears! "Too late, the sand is turned, the hour is past! Thy harvest is unreaped—too late! Thou hast been dreaming, forgetting, sleeping—so much the worse! Every man rewards or punishes himself. To whom or of whom wouldst thou complain?"—Alas!

April 21, 1865. (*Mornex*).—A morning of intoxicating beauty, fresh as the feelings of sixteen, and crowned with flowers like a bride. The poetry of youth, of innocence, and of love, overflowed my soul. Even to the light mist hovering over the bosom of the plain—image of that tender modesty which veils the features and shrouds in mystery the inmost thoughts of the maiden—everything that I saw delighted my eyes and spoke to my imagination. It was a sacred, a nuptial day! and the matin bells ringing in some distant village harmonized marvelously with the hymn of nature. "Pray," they said, "and love! Adore a fatherly and beneficent God." They recalled to me the accent of Haydn; there was in them and in the landscape a childlike joyousness, a naive gratitude, a radiant heavenly joy innocent of pain and sin, like the sacred, simple-hearted ravishment of Eve on the first day of her awakening in the new world. How good a thing is feeling, admiration! It is the bread of angels, the eternal food of cherubim and seraphim.

I have not yet felt the air so pure, so life-giving, so ethereal, during the five days that I have been here. To breathe is a beatitude. One understands the delights of a bird's existence—that emancipation from all encumbering weight—that luminous and empyrean life, floating in blue space, and passing from one horizon to another with a stroke of the wing. One must have a great deal of air below one before one can be conscious of such inner freedom as this, such lightness of the whole being. Every element has its poetry, but the poetry of air is liberty. Enough; to your work, dreamer!

May 30, 1865.—All snakes fascinate their prey, and pure wickedness seems to inherit the power of fascination granted to the serpent. It stupefies and bewilders the simple heart, which sees it without understanding it, which touches it without being able to believe in it, and which sinks engulfed in the problem of it, like Empedocles in Etna. *Non possum capere te, cape me*, says the Aristotelian motto. Every diminutive of Beelzebub is an abyss, each demoniacal act is a gulf of darkness. Natural cruelty, inborn perfidy and falseness, even in animals, cast lurid gleams, as it were, into that fathomless pit of Satanic perversity which is a moral reality.

Nevertheless behind this thought there rises another which tells me that sophistry is at the bottom of human wickedness, that the majority of monsters like to justify themselves in their own eyes, and that the first attribute of the Evil One is to be the father of lies. Before crime is committed conscience must be corrupted, and every bad man who succeeds in reaching a high point of wickedness begins with this. It is all very well to say that hatred is murder; the man who hates is determined to see nothing in it but an act of moral hygiene. It is to do himself good that he does evil, just as a mad dog bites to get rid of his thirst.

To injure others while at the same time knowingly injuring one's self is a step farther; evil then becomes a frenzy, which, in its turn, sharpens into a cold ferocity.

Whenever a man, under the influence of such a diabolical passion, surrenders himself to these instincts of the wild or venomous beast he must seem to the angels a madman—a lunatic, who kindles his own Gehenna that he may consume the world in it, or as much of it as his devilish desires can lay hold upon. Wickedness is forever beginning a new spiral which penetrates deeper still into the abysses of abomination, for the circles of hell have this property—that they have no end. It seems as though divine perfection were an infinite of the first degree, but as though diabolical perfection were an infinite of unknown power. But no; for if so, evil would be the true God, and hell would swallow up creation. According to the Persian and the Christian faiths, good is to conquer evil, and perhaps even Satan himself will be restored to grace—which is as much as to say that the divine order will be everywhere re-established. Love will be more potent than hatred; God will save his glory, and his glory is in his goodness. But it is very true that all gratuitous wickedness troubles the soul, because it seems to make the great lines of the moral order tremble within us by the sudden withdrawal of the curtain which hides from us the action of those dark corrosive forces which have ranged themselves in battle against the divine plan.

June 26, 1865.—One may guess the why and wherefore of a tear and yet find it too subtle to give any account of. A tear may be the poetical *resume* of so many simultaneous impressions, the quintessence of so many opposing thoughts! It is like a drop of one of those precious elixirs of the East which contain the life of twenty plants fused into a single aroma. Sometimes it is the mere overflow of the soul, the running over of the cup of reverie. All that one cannot or will not say, all that one refuses to confess even to one's self—confused desires, secret trouble, suppressed grief, smothered conflict, voiceless regret, the emotions we have struggled against, the pain we have sought to hide, our superstitious fears, our vague sufferings, our restless presentiments, our unrealized dreams, the wounds inflicted upon our ideal, the dissatisfied languor, the vain hopes, the multitude of small indiscernible ills which accumulate slowly in a corner of the heart like water dropping noiselessly from the roof of a cavern—all these mysterious movements of the inner life end in an instant of emotion, and the emotion concentrates itself in a tear just visible on the edge of the eyelid.

For the rest, tears express joy as well as sadness. They are the symbol of the powerlessness of the soul to restrain its emotion and to remain mistress of itself. Speech implies analysis; when we are overcome by sensation or by feeling analysis ceases, and with it speech and liberty. Our only resource, after silence and stupor, is the language of action—pantomime. Any oppressive weight of thought carries us back to a stage anterior to humanity, to a gesture, a cry, a sob, and at last to swooning and collapse; that is to say, incapable of bearing the excessive strain of sensation as men, we fall back successively to the stage of mere animate being, and then to that of the vegetable. Dante swoons at every turn in his journey through hell, and nothing paints better the violence of his emotions and the ardor of his piety.

... And intense joy? It also withdraws into itself and is silent. To speak is to disperse and scatter. Words isolate and localize life in a single point; they touch only the circumference of being; they analyze, they treat one thing at a time. Thus they decentralize emotion, and chill it in doing so. The heart would fain brood over its feeling, cherishing and protecting it. Its happiness is silent and meditative; it listens to its own beating and feeds religiously upon itself.

August 8, 1865. (*Gryon sur Bex*).—Splendid moonlight without a cloud. The night is solemn and majestic. The regiment of giants sleeps while the stars keep sentinel. In the vast shadow of the valley glimmer a few scattered roofs, while the torrent, organ-like, swells its eternal note in the depths of this mountain cathedral which has the heavens for roof.

A last look at this blue night and boundless landscape. Jupiter is just setting on the counterscarp of the Dent du Midi. Prom the starry vault descends an invisible snow-shower of dreams, calling us to a pure sleep. Nothing of voluptuous or enervating in this nature. All is strong, austere and pure. Good night to all the world!—to the unfortunate and to the happy. Rest and refreshment, renewal and hope; a day is dead—*vive le lendemain!* Midnight is striking. Another step made toward the tomb.

August 13, 1865.—I have just read through again the letter of J. J. Rousseau to Archbishop Beaumont with a little less admiration than I felt for it—was it ten or twelve years ago? This emphasis, this precision, which never tires of itself, tires the reader in the long run. The intensity of the style produces on one the impression of a treatise on mathematics. One feels the need of relaxation after it in something easy, natural, and gay. The language of Rousseau demands an amount of labor which makes one long for recreation and relief.

But how many writers and how many books descend from our Rousseau! On my way I noticed the points of departure of Chateaubriand, Lamennais, Proudhon. Proudhon, for instance, modeled the plan of his great work, "De la Justice dang l'Eglise et dans la Revolution," upon the letter of Rousseau to Beaumont; his three volumes are a string of letters to an archbishop; eloquence, daring, and elocution are all fused in a kind of *persiflage*, which is the foundation of the whole.

How many men we may find in one man, how many styles in a great writer! Rousseau, for instance, has created a number of different *genres*. Imagination transforms him, and he is able to play the most varied parts with credit, among them even that of the pure logician. But as the imagination is his intellectual axis—his master faculty—he is, as it were, in all his works only half sincere, only half in earnest. We feel that his talent has laid him the wager of Carneades; it will lose no cause, however bad, as soon as the point of honor Is engaged. It is indeed the temptation of all talent to subordinate things to itself and not itself to things; to conquer for the sake of conquest, and to put self-love in the place of conscience. Talent is glad enough, no doubt, to triumph in a good cause; but it easily becomes a free lance, content, whatever the cause, so long as victory follows its banner. I do not know even whether success in a weak and bad cause is not the most flattering for talent, which then divides the honors of its triumph with nothing and no one.

Paradox is the delight of clever people and the joy of talent. It is so pleasant to pit one's self against the world, and to overbear mere commonplace good sense and vulgar platitudes! Talent and love of truth are then not identical; their tendencies and their paths are different. In order to make talent obey when its instinct is rather to command, a vigilant moral sense and great energy of character are needed. The Greeks—those artists of the spoken or written word— were artificial by the time of Ulysses, sophists by the time of Pericles, cunning, rhetorical, and versed in all the arts of the courtier down to the end of the lower empire. From the talent of the nation sprang its vices.

For a man to make his mark, like Rousseau by polemics, is to condemn himself to perpetual exaggeration and conflict. Such a man expiates his celebrity by a double bitterness; he is never altogether true, and he is never able to recover the free disposal of himself. To pick a quarrel with the world is attractive, but dangerous.

J. J. Rousseau is an ancestor in all things. It was he who founded traveling on foot before Toepffer, reverie before "Rene," literary botany before George Sand, the worship of nature before Bernardin de S. Pierre, the democratic theory before the Revolution of 1789, political discussion and theological discussion before Mirabeau and Renan, the science of teaching before Pestalozzi, and Alpine description before De Saussure. He made music the fashion, and created the taste for confessions to the public. He formed a new

French style—the close, chastened, passionate, interwoven style we know so well. Nothing indeed of Rousseau has been lost, and nobody has had more influence than he upon the French Revolution, for he was the demigod of it, and stands between Neckar and Napoleon. Nobody, again, has had more than he upon the nineteenth century, for Byron, Chateaubriand, Madame de Stael, and George Sand all descend from him.

And yet, with these extraordinary talents, he was an extremely unhappy man—why? Because he always allowed himself to be mastered by his imagination and his sensations; because he had no judgment in deciding, no self-control in acting. Regret indeed on this score would be hardly reasonable, for a calm, judicious, orderly Rousseau would never have made so great an impression. He came into collision with his time: hence his eloquence and his misfortunes. His naive confidence in life and himself ended in jealous misanthropy and hypochondria.

What a contrast to Goethe or Voltaire, and how differently they understood the practical wisdom of life and the management of literary gifts! They were the able men—Rousseau is a visionary. They knew mankind as it is—he always represented it to himself either whiter or blacker than it is; and having begun by taking life the wrong way, he ended in madness. In the talent of Rousseau there is always something unwholesome, uncertain, stormy, and sophistical, which destroys the confidence of the reader; and the reason is no doubt that we feel passion to have been the governing force in him as a writer: passion stirred his imagination, and ruled supreme over his reason.

* * * * *

Our systems, perhaps, are nothing more than an unconscious apology for our faults—a gigantic scaffolding whose object is to hide from us our favorite sin.

* * * * *

The unfinished is nothing.

* * * * *

Great men are the true men, the men in whom nature has succeeded. They are not extraordinary—they are in the true order. It is the other species of men who are not what they ought to be.

January 7, 1866.—Our life is but a soap-bubble hanging from a reed; it is formed, expands to its full size, clothes itself with the loveliest colors of the prism, and even escapes at moments from the law of gravitation; but soon the black speck appears in it, and the globe of emerald and gold vanishes into space, leaving behind it nothing but a simple drop of turbid water. All the poets have made this comparison, it is so striking and so true. To appear, to shine, to disappear; to be born, to suffer, and to die; is it not the whole sum of life, for a butterfly, for a nation, for a star?

Time is but the measure of the difficulty of a conception. Pure thought has scarcely any need of time, since it perceives the two ends of an idea almost at the same moment. The thought of a planet can only be worked out by nature with labor and effort, but supreme intelligence sums up the whole in an instant. Time is then the successive dispersion of being, just as speech is the successive analysis of an intuition or of an act of will. In itself it is relative and negative, and disappears within the absolute being. God is outside time because he thinks all thought at once; Nature is within time, because she is only speech—the discursive unfolding of each thought contained within the infinite thought. But nature exhausts herself in this impossible task, for the analysis of the infinite is a contradiction. With limitless duration, boundless space, and number without end, Nature does at least what she can to translate into visible form the wealth of the creative formula. By the vastness of the abysses into which she penetrates, in the effort—the unsuccessful effort—to house and contain the eternal thought, we may measure the greatness of the divine mind. For as soon as this mind goes out of itself and seeks to explain itself, the effort at utterance heaps universe upon universe, during myriads of centuries, and still it is not expressed, and the great harangue must go on for ever and ever.

The East prefers immobility as the form of the Infinite: the West, movement. It is because the West is infected by the passion for details, and sets proud store by individual worth. Like a child upon whom a hundred thousand francs have been bestowed, he thinks she is multiplying her fortune by counting it out in pieces of twenty sous, or five centimes. Her passion for progress is in great part the product of an infatuation, which consists in forgetting the goal to be aimed at, and absorbing herself in the pride and delight of each tiny step, one after the other. Child that she is, she is even capable of confounding change with improvement—beginning over again, with growth in perfectness.

At the bottom of the modern man there is always a great thirst for self-forgetfulness, self-distraction; he has a secret horror of all which makes him feel his own littleness; the eternal, the infinite, perfection, therefore scare and terrify him. He wishes to approve himself, to admire and congratulate himself; and therefore he turns away from all those problems and abysses which might recall to him his own nothingness. This is what makes the real pettiness of so many of our great minds, and accounts for the lack of personal dignity among us—civilized parrots that we are—as compared with the Arab of the desert; or explains the growing frivolity of our masses, more and more educated, no doubt, but also more and more superficial in all their conceptions of happiness.

Here, then, is the service which Christianity—the oriental element in our culture—renders to us Westerns. It checks and counterbalances our natural tendency toward the passing, the finite, and the changeable, by fixing the mind upon the contemplation of eternal things, and by Platonizing our affections, which otherwise would have too little outlook upon the ideal world. Christianity leads us back from dispersion to concentration, from worldliness to self-recollection. It restores to our souls, fevered with a thousand sordid desires, nobleness, gravity, and calm. Just as sleep is a bath of refreshing for our actual life, so religion is a bath of refreshing for our immortal being. What is sacred has a purifying virtue; religious emotion crowns the brow with an aureole, and thrills the heart with an ineffable joy.

I think that the adversaries of religion as such deceive themselves as to the needs of the western man, and that the modern world will lose its balance as soon as it has passed over altogether to the crude doctrine of progress. We have always need of the infinite, the eternal, the absolute; and since science contents itself with what is relative, it necessarily leaves a void, which it is good for man to fill with contemplation, worship, and adoration. "Religion," said Bacon, "is the spice which is meant to keep life from corruption," and this is especially true to-day of religion taken in the Platonist and oriental sense. A capacity for self-recollection—for withdrawal from the outward to the inward—is in fact the condition of all noble and useful activity.

This return, indeed, to what is serious, divine, and sacred, is becoming more and more difficult, because of the growth of critical anxiety within the church itself, the increasing worldliness of religious preaching, and the universal agitation and disquiet of society. But such a return is more and more necessary. Without it there is no inner life, and the inner life is the only means whereby we may oppose a profitable resistance to circumstance. If the sailor did not carry with him his own temperature he could not go from the pole to the equator, and remain himself in spite of all. The man who has no refuge in himself, who lives, so to speak, in his front rooms, in the outer whirlwind of things and opinions, is not properly a personality at all; he is not distinct, free, original, a cause—in a word, *some one*. He is one of a crowd, a taxpayer, an elector, an anonymity, but not a man. He helps to make up the mass—to fill up the number of human consumers or producers; but he interests nobody but the economist and the statistician, who take the heap of sand as a whole into consideration, without troubling themselves about the uninteresting uniformity of the individual grains. The crowd counts only as a massive elementary force—why? because its constituent parts are individually insignificant: they are all like each other, and we add them up like the molecules of water in a river, gauging them by the fathom instead of appreciating them as individuals. Such men are reckoned and weighed merely as so many bodies: they have never been individualized by conscience, after the manner of souls.

He who floats with the current, who does not guide himself according to higher principles, who has no ideal, no convictions—such a man is a mere article of the world's furniture—a thing moved, instead of a living and moving being—an echo, not a voice. The man who has no inner life is the slave of his surroundings, as the barometer is the obedient servant of the air at rest, and the weathercock the humble servant of the air in motion.

January 21, 1866.—This evening after supper I did not know whither to betake my solitary self. I was hungry for conversation, society, exchange of ideas. It occurred to me to go and see our friends, the ——s; they were at supper. Afterward we went into the *salon*: mother and daughter sat down to the piano and sang a duet by Boieldieu. The ivory keys of the old grand piano, which the mother had played on before her marriage, and which has followed and translated into music the varying fortunes of the family, were a little loose and jingling; but the poetry of the past sang in this faithful old servant, which had been a friend in trouble, a companion in vigils, and the echo of a lifetime of duty, affection, piety and virtue. I was more moved than I can say. It was like a scene of Dickens, and I felt a rush of sympathy, untouched either by egotism or by melancholy.

Twenty-five years! It seems to me a dream as far as I am concerned, and I can scarcely believe my eyes, or this inanimate witness to so many lustres passed away. How strange a thing *to have lived*, and to feel myself so far from a past which yet is so present to me! One does not know whether one is sleeping or waking. Time is but the space between our memories; as soon as we cease to perceive this space, time has disappeared. The whole life of an old man may appear to him no longer than an hour, or less still; and as soon as time is but a moment to us, we have entered upon eternity. Life is but the dream of a shadow; I felt it anew this evening with strange intensity.

January 29, 1866. (*Nine o'clock in the morning*).—The gray curtain of mist has spread itself again over the town; everything is dark and dull. The bells are ringing in the distance for some festival; with this exception everything is calm and silent. Except for the crackling of the fire, no noise disturbs my solitude in this modest home, the shelter of my thoughts and of my work, where the man of middle age carries on the life of his student-youth without the zest of youth, and the sedentary professor repeats day by day the habits which he formed as a traveler.

What is it which makes the charm of this existence outwardly so barren and empty? Liberty! What does the absence of comfort and of all else that is wanting to these rooms matter to me? These things are indifferent to me. I find under this roof light, quiet, shelter. I am near to a sister and her children, whom I love; my material life is assured—that ought to be enough for a bachelor.... Am I not, besides, a creature of habit? more attached to the *ennuis* I know, than in love with pleasures unknown to me. I am, then, free and not unhappy. Then I am well off here, and I should be ungrateful to complain. Nor do I. It is only the heart which sighs and seeks for something more and better. The heart is an insatiable glutton, as we all know—and for the rest, who is without yearnings? It is our destiny here below. Only some go through torments and troubles in order to satisfy themselves, and all without success; others foresee the inevitable result, and by a timely resignation save themselves a barren and fruitless effort. Since we cannot be happy, why give ourselves so much trouble? It is best to limit one's self to what is strictly necessary, to live austerely and by rule, to content one's self with a little, and to attach no value to anything but peace of conscience and a sense of duty done.

It is true that this itself is no small ambition, and that it only lands us in another impossibility. No—the simplest course is to submit one's self wholly and altogether to God. Everything else, as saith the preacher, is but vanity and vexation of spirit.

It is a long while now since this has been plain to me, and since this religious renunciation has been sweet and familiar to me. It is the outward distractions of life, the examples of the world, and the irresistible influence exerted upon us by the current of things which make us forget the wisdom we have acquired and the principles we have adopted. That is why life is such weariness! This eternal beginning over again is tedious, even to repulsion. It would be so good to go to sleep when we have gathered the fruit of experience, when we are no longer in opposition to the supreme will, when we have broken loose from self, when we are at peace with all men. Instead of this, the old round of temptations, disputes, *ennuis*, and forgettings, has to be faced again and again, and we fall back into prose, into commonness, into vulgarity. How melancholy, how humiliating! The poets are wise in withdrawing their heroes more quickly from the strife, and in not dragging them after victory along the common rut of barren days. "Whom the gods love die young," said the proverb of antiquity.

Yes, but it is our secret self-love which is set upon this favor from on high; such may be our desire, but such is not the will of God. We are to be exercised, humbled, tried, and tormented to the end. It is our patience which is the touchstone of our virtue. To bear with life even when illusion and hope are gone; to accept this position of perpetual war, while at the same time loving only peace; to stay patiently in the world, even when it repels us as a place of low company, and seems to us a mere arena of bad passions; to remain faithful to one's own faith without breaking with the followers of the false gods; to make no attempt to escape from the human hospital, long-suffering and patient as Job upon his dung hill—this is duty. When life ceases to be a promise it does not cease to be a task; its true name even is trial.

April 2, 1866. (*Mornex*).—The snow is melting and a damp fog is spread over everything. The asphalt gallery which runs along the *salon* is a sheet of quivering water starred incessantly by the hurrying drops falling from the sky. It seems as if one could touch the horizon with one's hand, and the miles of country which were yesterday visible are all hidden under a thick gray curtain.

This imprisonment transports me to Shetland, to Spitzbergen, to Norway, to the Ossianic countries of mist, where man, thrown back upon himself, feels his heart beat more quickly and his thought expand more freely—so long, at least, as he is not frozen and congealed by cold. Fog has certainly a poetry of its own—a grace, a dreamy charm. It does for the daylight what a lamp does for us at night; it turns the mind toward meditation; it throws the soul back on itself. The sun, as it were, sheds us abroad in nature, scatters and disperses us; mist draws us together and concentrates us—it is cordial, homely, charged with feeling. The poetry of the sun has something of the epic in it; that of fog and mist is elegaic and religious. Pantheism is the child of light; mist engenders faith in near protectors. When the great world is shut off from us, the house becomes itself a small universe. Shrouded in perpetual mist, men love each other better; for the only reality then is the family, and, within the family, the heart; and the greatest thoughts come from the heart—so says the moralist.

April 6, 1866.—The novel by Miss Mulock, "John Halifax, Gentleman," is a bolder book than it seems, for it attacks in the English way the social problem of equality. And the solution reached is that every one may become a gentleman, even though he may be born in the gutter. In its way the story protests against conventional superiorities, and shows that true nobility consists in character, in personal merit, in moral distinction, in elevation of feeling and of language, in dignity of life, and in self-respect. This is better than Jacobinism, and the opposite of the mere brutal passion for equality. Instead of dragging everybody down, the author simply proclaims the right of every one to rise. A man may be born rich and noble—he is not born a gentleman. This word is the Shibboleth of England; it divides her into two halves, and civilized society into two castes. Among gentlemen—courtesy, equality, and politeness; toward those below—contempt, disdain, coldness and indifference. It is the old separation between the *ingenui* and all others; between the [Greek: eleutheroi] and the [Greek: banauphoi], the continuation of the feudal division between the gentry and the *roturiers*.

What, then, is a gentleman? Apparently he is the free man, the man who is stronger than things, and believes in personality as superior to all the accessory attributes of fortune, such as rank and power, and as constituting what is essential, real, and intrinsically valuable in the individual. Tell me what you are, and I will tell you what you are worth. "God and my Right;" there is the only motto he believes in. Such an ideal is happily opposed to that vulgar ideal which is equally English, the ideal of wealth, with its formula, "*How much* is he worth?" In a country where poverty is a crime, it is good to be able to say that a nabob need not as such be a gentleman. The mercantile ideal and the chivalrous ideal counterbalance each other; and if the one produces the ugliness of English society and its brutal side, the other serves as a compensation.

The gentleman, then, is the man who is master of himself, who respects himself, and makes others respect him. The essence of gentlemanliness is self-rule, the sovereignty of the soul. It means a character which possesses itself, a force which governs itself, a liberty which affirms and regulates itself, according to the type of true dignity. Such an ideal is closely akin to the Roman type of *dignitas cum auctoritate*. It is more moral than intellectual, and is particularly suited to England, which is pre-eminently the country of will. But from self-respect a thousand other things are derived—such as the care of a man's person, of his language, of his manners; watchfulness over his body and over his soul; dominion over his instincts and his passions; the effort to be self-sufficient; the pride which will accept no favor; carefulness not to expose himself to any humiliation or mortification, and to maintain himself independent of any human caprice; the constant protection of his honor and of his self-respect. Such a condition of sovereignty, insomuch as it is only easy to the man who is well-born, well-bred, and rich, was naturally long identified with birth, rank, and above all with property. The idea "gentleman" is, then, derived from feudality; it is, as it were, a milder version of the seigneur.

In order to lay himself open to no reproach, a gentleman will keep himself irreproachable; in order to be treated with consideration, he will always be careful himself to observe distances, to apportion respect, and to observe all the gradations of conventional politeness, according to rank, age, and situation. Hence it follows that he will be imperturbably cautious in the presence of a stranger, whose name and worth are unknown to him, and to whom he might perhaps show too much or too little courtesy. He ignores and avoids him; if he is approached, he turns away, if he is addressed, he answers shortly and with *hauteur*. His politeness is not human and general, but individual and relative to persons. This is why every Englishman contains two different men—one turned toward the world, and another. The first, the outer man, is a citadel, a cold and angular wall; the other, the inner man, is a sensible, affectionate, cordial, and loving creature. Such a type is only formed in a moral climate full of icicles, where, in the face of an indifferent world, the hearth alone is hospitable.

So that an analysis of the national type of gentlemen reveals to us the nature and the history of the nation, as the fruit reveals the tree.

April 7, 1866.—If philosophy is the art of understanding, it is evident that it must begin by saturating itself with facts and realities, and that premature abstraction kills it, just as the abuse of fasting destroys the body at the age of growth. Besides, we only understand that which is already within us. To understand is to possess the thing understood, first by sympathy and then by intelligence. Instead, then, of first dismembering and dissecting the object to be conceived, we should begin by laying hold of it in its *ensemble*, then in its formation, last of all in its parts. The procedure is the same, whether we study a watch or a plant, a work of art or a character. We must study, respect, and question what we want to know, instead of massacring it. We must assimilate ourselves to things and surrender ourselves to them; we must open our minds with docility to their influence, and steep ourselves in their spirit and their distinctive form, before we offer violence to them by dissecting them.

April 14, 1866.—Panic, confusion, *sauve qui peut* on the Bourse at Paris. In our epoch of individualism, and of "each man for himself and God for all," the movements of the public funds are all that now represent to us the beat of the common heart. The solidarity of interests which they imply counterbalances the separateness of modern affections, and the obligatory sympathy they impose upon us recalls to one a little the patriotism which bore the forced taxes of old days. We feel ourselves bound up with and compromised in all the world's affairs, and we must interest ourselves whether we will or no in the terrible machine whose wheels may crush us at any moment. Credit produces a restless society, trembling perpetually for the security of its artificial basis. Sometimes society may forget for awhile that it is dancing upon a volcano, but the least rumor of war recalls the fact to it inexorably. Card-houses are easily ruined.

All this anxiety is intolerable to those humble little investors who, having no wish to be rich, ask only to be able to go about their work in peace. But no; tyrant that it is, the world cries to us, "Peace, peace—there is no peace: whether you will or no you shall suffer and tremble with me!" To accept humanity, as one does nature, and to resign one's self to the will of an individual, as one does to destiny, is not easy. We bow to the government of God, but we turn against the despot. No man likes to share in the shipwreck of a vessel in which he has been embarked by violence, and which has been steered contrary to his wish and his opinion. And yet such is perpetually the case in life. We all of us pay for the faults of the few.

Human solidarity is a fact more evident and more certain than personal responsibility, and even than individual liberty. Our dependence has it over our independence; for we are only independent in will and desire, while we are dependent upon our health, upon nature and society; in short, upon everything in us and without us. Our liberty is confined to one single point. We may protest against all these oppressive and fatal powers; we may say, Crush me—you will never win my consent! We may, by an exercise of will, throw ourselves into opposition to necessity, and refuse it homage and obedience. In that consists our moral liberty. But except for that, we belong, body and goods, to the world. We are its playthings, as the dust is the plaything of the wind, or the dead leaf of the floods. God at least respects our dignity, but the world rolls us contemptuously along in its merciless waves, in order to make it plain that we are its thing and its chattel.

All theories of the nullity of the individual, all pantheistic and materialist conceptions, are now but so much forcing of an open door, so much slaying of the slain. As soon as we cease to glorify this imperceptible point of conscience, and to uphold the value of it, the individual becomes naturally a mere atom in the human mass, which is but an atom in the planetary mass, which is a mere nothing in the universe. The individual is then but a nothing of the third power, with a capacity for measuring its nothingness! Thought leads to resignation. Self-doubt leads to passivity, and passivity to servitude. From this a voluntary submission is the only escape, that is to say, a state of dependence religiously accepted, a vindication of ourselves as free beings, bowed before duty only. Duty thus becomes our principle of action, our source of energy, the guarantee of our partial independence of the world, the condition of our dignity, the sign of our nobility. The world can neither make me will nor make me will my duty; here I am my own and only master, and treat with it as sovereign with sovereign. It holds my body in its clutches; but my soul escapes and braves it. My thought and my love, my faith and my hope, are beyond its reach. My true being, the essence of my nature, myself, remain inviolate and inaccessible to the world's attacks. In this respect we are greater than the universe, which has mass and not will; we become once more independent even in relation to the human mass, which also can destroy nothing more than our happiness, just as the mass of the universe can destroy nothing more than our body. Submission, then, is not defeat; on the contrary, it is strength.

April 28, 1866.—I have just read the *proces-verbal* of the Conference of Pastors held on the 15th and 16th of April at Paris. The question of the supernatural has split the church of France in two. The liberals insist upon individual right; the orthodox upon the notion of a church. And it is true indeed that a church is an affirmation, that it subsists by the positive element in it, by definite belief; the pure critical element dissolves it. Protestantism is a combination of two factors—the authority of the Scriptures and free inquiry; as soon as one of these factors is threatened or disappears, Protestantism disappears; a new form of Christianity succeeds it, as, for example, the church of the Brothers of the Holy Ghost, or that of Christian Theism. As far as I am concerned, I see nothing objectionable in such a result, but I think the friends of the Protestant church are logical in their refusal to abandon the apostle's creed, and the individualists are illogical in imagining that they can keep Protestantism and do away with authority.

It is a question of method which separates the two camps. I am fundamentally separated from both. As I understand it, Christianity is above all religions, and religion is not a method, it is a life, a higher and supernatural life, mystical in its root and practical in its fruits, a communion with God, a calm and deep enthusiasm, a love which radiates, a force which acts, a happiness which overflows. Religion, in short, is a state of the soul. These quarrels as to method have their value, but it is a secondary value; they will never console a heart or edify a conscience. This is why I feel so little interest in these ecclesiastical struggles. Whether the one party or the other gain the majority and the victory, what is essential is in no way profited, for dogma, criticism, the church, are not religion; and it is religion, the sense of a divine life, which matters. "Seek ye first the kingdom of God and his righteousness, and all these things shall be added unto you." The most holy is the most Christian; this will always be the criterion which is least deceptive. "By this ye shall know my disciples, if they have love one to another."

As is the worth of the individual, so is the worth of his religion. Popular instinct and philosophic reason are at one on this point. Be good and pious, patient and heroic, faithful and devoted, humble and charitable; the catechism which has taught you these things is beyond the reach of blame. By religion we live in God; but all these quarrels lead to nothing but life with men or with cassocks. There is therefore no equivalence between the two points of view.

Perfection as an end—a noble example for sustenance on the way—the divine proved by its own excellence, is not this the whole of Christianity? God manifest in all men, is not this its true goal and consummation?

September 20, 1866.—My old friends are, I am afraid, disappointed in me; they think that I do nothing, that I have deceived their expectations and their hopes. I, too, am disappointed. All that would restore my self-respect and give me a right to be proud of myself, seems to me unattainable and impossible, and I fall back upon trivialities, gay talk, distractions. I am always equally lacking in hope, in faith, in resolution. The only difference is that my weakness takes sometimes the form of despairing melancholy and sometimes that of a cheerful quietism. And yet I read, I talk, I teach, I write, but to no effect; it is as though I were walking in my sleep. The Buddhist tendency in me blunts the faculty of free self-government and weakens the power of action; self-distrust kills all desire, and reduces me again and again to a fundamental skepticism. I care for nothing but the serious and the real, and I can take neither myself nor my circumstances seriously. I hold my own personality, my own aptitudes, my own aspirations, too cheap. I am forever making light of myself in the name of all that is beautiful and admirable. In a word, I bear within me a perpetual self-detractor, and this is what takes all spring out of my life. I have been passing the evening with Charles Heim, who, in his sincerity, has never paid me any literary compliment. As I love and respect him, he is forgiven. Self-love has nothing to do with it—and yet it would be sweet to be praised by so upright a friend! It is depressing to feel one's self silently disapproved of; I will try to satisfy him, and to think of a book which may please both him and Scherer.

October 6, 1866.—I have just picked up on the stairs a little yellowish cat, ugly and pitiable. Now, curled up in a chair at my side, he seems perfectly happy, and as if he wanted nothing more. Far from being wild, nothing will induce him to leave me, and he has followed me from room to room all day. I have nothing at all that is eatable in the house, but what I have I give him—that is to say, a look and a caress—and that seems to be enough for him, at least for the moment. Small animals, small children, young lives—they are all the same as far as the need of protection and of gentleness is concerned.... People have sometimes said to me that weak and feeble creatures are happy with me. Perhaps such a fact has to do with some special gift or beneficent force which flows from one when one is in the sympathetic state. I have often a direct perception of such a force; but I am no ways proud of it, nor do I look upon it as anything belonging to me, but simply as a natural gift. It seems to me sometimes as though I could woo the birds to build in my beard as they do in the headgear of some cathedral saint! After all, this is the natural state and the true relation of man toward all inferior creatures. If man was what he ought to be he would be adored by the animals, of whom he is too often the capricious and sanguinary tyrant. The legend of Saint Francis of Assisi is not so legendary as we think; and it is not so certain that it was the wild beasts who attacked man first.... But to exaggerate nothing, let us leave on one side the beasts of prey, the carnivora, and those that live by rapine and slaughter. How many other species are there, by thousands and tens of thousands, who ask peace from us and with whom we persist in waging a brutal war? Our race is by far the most destructive, the most hurtful, and the most formidable, of all the species of the planet. It has even invented for its own use the right of the strongest—a divine right which quiets its conscience in the face of the conquered and the oppressed; we have outlawed all that lives except ourselves. Revolting and manifest abuse; notorious and contemptible breach of the law of justice! The bad faith and hypocrisy of it are renewed on a small scale by all successful usurpers. We are always making God our accomplice, that so we may legalize our own iniquities. Every successful massacre is consecrated by a Te Deum, and the clergy have never been wanting in benedictions for any victorious enormity. So that what, in the beginning, was the relation of man to the animal becomes that of people to people and man to man.

If so, we have before us an expiation too seldom noticed but altogether just. All crime must be expiated, and slavery is the repetition among men of the sufferings brutally imposed by man upon other living beings; it is the theory bearing its fruits. The right of man over the animal seems to me to cease with the need of defense and of subsistence. So that all unnecessary murder and torture are cowardice and even crime. The animal renders a service of utility; man in return owes it a need of protection and of kindness. In a word, the animal has claims on man, and the man has duties to the animal. Buddhism, no doubt, exaggerates this truth, but the Westerns leave it out of count altogether. A day will come, however, when our standard will be higher, our humanity more exacting, than it is to-day. *Homo homini lupus*, said Hobbes: the time will come when man will be humane even for the wolf—*homo lupo homo*.

December 30, 1866.—Skepticism pure and simple as the only safeguard of intellectual independence—such is the point of view of almost all our young men of talent. Absolute freedom from credulity seems to them the glory of man. My impression has always been that this excessive detachment of the individual from all received prejudices and opinions in reality does the work of tyranny. This evening, in listening to the conversation of some of our most cultivated men, I thought of the Renaissance, of the Ptolemies, of the reign of Louis XV., of all those times in which the exultant anarchy of the intellect has had despotic government for its correlative, and, on the other hand, of England, of Holland, of the United States, countries in which political liberty is bought at the price of necessary prejudices and *a priori* opinions.

That society may hold together at all, we must have a principle of cohesion—that is to say, a common belief, principles recognized and undisputed, a series of practical axioms and institutions which are not at the mercy of every caprice of public opinion. By treating everything as if it were an open question, we endanger everything.

Doubt is the accomplice of tyranny. "If a people will not believe it must obey," said Tocqueville. All liberty implies dependence, and has its conditions; this is what negative and quarrelsome minds are apt to forget. They think they can do away with religion; they do not know that religion is indestructible, and that the question is simply, Which will you have? Voltaire plays the game of Loyola, and *vice versa*. Between these two there is no peace, nor can there be any for the society which has once thrown itself into the dilemma. The only solution lies in a free religion, a religion of free choice and free adhesion.

December 23, 1866.—It is raining over the whole sky—as far at least as I can see from my high point of observation. All is gray from the Saleve to the Jura, and from the pavement to the clouds; everything that one sees or touches is gray; color, life, and gayety are dead— each living thing seems to lie hidden in its own particular shell. What are the birds doing in such weather as this? We who have food and shelter, fire on the hearth, books around us, portfolios of engravings close at hand, a nestful of dreams in the heart, and a whirlwind of thoughts ready to rise from the ink-bottle—we find nature ugly and *triste*, and turn away our eyes from it; but you, poor sparrows, what can you be doing? Bearing and hoping and waiting? After all, is not this the task of each one of us?

I have just been reading over a volume of this Journal, and feel a little ashamed of the languid complaining tone of so much of it. These pages reproduce me very imperfectly, and there are many things in me of which I find no trace in them. I suppose it is because, in the first place, sadness takes up the pen more readily than joy; and in the next, because I depend so much upon surrounding circumstances. When there is no call upon me, and nothing to put me to the test, I fall back into melancholy; and so the practical man, the cheerful man, the literary man, does not appear in these pages. The portrait is lacking in proportion and breadth; it is one-sided, and wants a center; it has, as it were, been painted from too near.

The true reason why we know ourselves so little lies in the difficulty we find in standing at a proper distance from ourselves, in taking up the right point of view, so that the details may help rather than hide the general effect. We must learn to look at ourselves socially and historically if we wish to have an exact idea of our relative worth, and to look at our life as a whole, or at least as one complete period of life, if we wish to know what we are and what we are not. The ant which crawls to and fro over a face, the fly perched upon the forehead of a maiden, touch them indeed, but do not see them, for they never embrace the whole at a glance.

Is it wonderful that misunderstandings should play so great a part in the world, when one sees how difficult it is to produce a faithful portrait of a person whom one has been studying for more than twenty years? Still, the effort has not been altogether lost; its reward has been the sharpening of one's perceptions of the outer world. If I have any special power of appreciating different shades of mind, I owe it no doubt to the analysis I have so perpetually and unsuccessfully practiced on myself. In fact, I have always regarded myself as matter for study, and what has interested me most in myself has been the pleasure of having under my hand a man, a person, in whom, as an authentic specimen of human nature, I could follow, without importunity or indiscretion, all the metamorphoses, the secret thoughts, the heart-beats, and the temptations of humanity. My attention has been drawn to myself impersonally and philosophically. One uses what one has, and one must shape one's arrow out of one's own wood.

To arrive at a faithful portrait, succession must be converted into simultaneousness, plurality into unity, and all the changing phenomena must be traced back to their essence. There are ten men in me, according to time, place, surrounding, and occasion; and in their restless diversity I am forever escaping myself. Therefore, whatever I may reveal of my past, of my Journal, or of myself, is of no use to him who is without the poetic intuition, and cannot recompose me as a whole, with or in spite of the elements which I confide to him.

I feel myself a chameleon, a kaleidoscope, a Proteus; changeable in every way, open to every kind of polarization; fluid, virtual, and therefore latent—latent even in manifestation, and absent even in presentation. I am a spectator, so to speak, of the molecular whirlwind which men call individual life; I am conscious of an incessant metamorphosis, an irresistible movement of existence, which is going on within me. I am sensible of the flight, the revival, the modification, of all the atoms of my being, all the particles of my river, all the radiations of my special force.

This phenomenology of myself serves both as the magic lantern of my own destiny, and as a window opened upon the mystery of the world. I am, or rather, my sensible consciousness is concentrated upon this ideal standing-point, this invisible threshold, as it were, whence one hears the impetuous passage of time, rushing and foaming as it flows out into the changeless ocean of eternity. After all the bewildering distractions of life, after having drowned myself in a multiplicity of trifles and in the caprices of this fugitive existence, yet without ever attaining to self-intoxication or self-delusion, I come again upon the fathomless abyss, the silent and melancholy cavern where dwell *"Die Muetter,"* [Footnote: *"Die Muetter"*—an allusion to a strange and enigmatical, but very effective conception in "Faust" (Part II. Act I. Scene v.) *Die Muetter* are the prototypes, the abstract forms, the generative ideas, of things. "Sie sehn dich nicht, denn Schemen sehn sie nur." Goethe borrowed the term from a passage of Plutarch's, but he has made the idea half Platonic, half legendary. Amiel, however, seems rather to have in his mind Faust's speech in Scene vii. than the speech of Mephistopheles in Scene v:

"In eurem Namen, Muetter, die ihr thront Im Graenzenlosen, ewig einsam wohnt, Und doch gesellig! Euer haupt umschweben Des Lebens Bilder, regsam, ohne Leben."]

where sleeps that which neither lives nor dies, that which has neither movement, nor change, nor extension, nor form, and which lasts when all else passes away.

"Dans l'eternel azur de l'insondable espace S'enveloppe de paix notre globe agitee: Homme, enveloppe ainsi tes jours, reve qui passe, Du calme firmament de ton eternite."

(H. P. AMIEL, *Penseroso*.)

Geneva, January 11, 1867.

"Eheu fugaces, Postume, Postume, Labuntar anni...."

I hear the drops of my life falling distinctly one by one into the devouring abyss of eternity. I feel my days flying before the pursuit of death. All that remains to me of weeks, or months, or years, in which I may drink in the light of the sun, seems to me no more than a single night, a summer night, which scarcely counts, because it will so soon be at an end.

Death! Silence! Eternity! What mysteries, what names of terror to the being who longs for happiness, immortality, perfection! Where shall I be to-morrow—in a little while—when the breath of life has forsaken me? Where will those be whom I love? Whither are we all going? The eternal problems rise before us in their implacable solemnity. Mystery on all sides! And faith the only star in this darkness and uncertainty!

No matter!—so long as the world is the work of eternal goodness, and so long as conscience has not deceived us. To give happiness and to do good, there is our only law, our anchor of salvation, our beacon light, our reason for existing. All religions may crumble away; so long as this survives we have still an ideal, and life is worth living.

Nothing can lessen the dignity and value of humanity

Was einmal war, in allem Glanz und Schein, Es regt sich dort; denn es will ewig sein. Und ihr vertheilt es, allgewaltige Maechte, Zum Zelt des Tages, zum Gewoelb' der Naechte.

so long as the religion of love, of unselfishness and devotion endures; and none can destroy the altars of this faith for us so long as we feel ourselves still capable of love.

April 15,1867—(*Seven* A. M.).—Rain storms in the night—the weather is showing its April caprice. From the window one sees a gray and melancholy sky, and roofs glistering with rain. The spring is at its work. Yes, and the implacable flight of time is driving us toward the grave. Well—each has his turn!

"Allez, allez, o jeunes filles, Cueillir des bleuets dans les bles!"

I am overpowered with melancholy, languor, lassitude. A longing for the last great sleep has taken possession of me, combated, however, by a thirst for sacrifice—sacrifice heroic and long-sustained. Are not both simply ways of escape from one's self? "Sleep, or self-surrender, that I may die to self!"—such is the cry of the heart. Poor heart!

April 17, 1867.—Awake, thou that sleepest, and rise from the dead.

What needs perpetually refreshing and renewing in me is my store of courage. By nature I am so easily disgusted with life, I fall a prey so readily to despair and pessimism.

"The happy man, as this century is able to produce him," according to Madame — —, is a *Weltmuede*, one who keeps a brave face before the world, and distracts himself as best he can from dwelling upon the thought which is hidden at his heart—a thought which has in it the sadness of death—the thought of the irreparable. The outward peace of such a man is but despair well masked; his gayety is the carelessness of a heart which has lost all its illusions, and has learned to acquiesce in an indefinite putting off of happiness. His wisdom is really acclimatization to sacrifice, his gentleness should be taken to mean privation patiently borne rather than resignation. In a word, he submits to an existence in which he feels no joy, and he cannot hide from himself that all the alleviations with which it is strewn cannot satisfy the soul. The thirst for the infinite is never appeased. God is wanting.

To win true peace, a man needs to feel himself directed, pardoned, and sustained by a supreme power, to feel himself in the right road, at the point where God would have him be—in order with God and the universe. This faith gives strength and calm. I have not got it. All that is, seems to me arbitrary and fortuitous. It may as well not be, as be. Nothing in my own circumstances seems to me providential. All appears to me left to my own responsibility, and it is this thought which disgusts me with the government of my own life. I longed to give myself up wholly to some great love, some noble end; I would willingly have lived and died for the ideal—that is to say, for a holy cause. But once the impossibility of this made clear to me, I have never since taken a serious interest in anything, and have, as it were, but amused myself with a destiny of which I was no longer the dupe.

Sybarite and dreamer, will you go on like this to the end—forever tossed backward and forward between duty and happiness, incapable of choice, of action? Is not life the test of our moral force, and all these inward waverings, are they not temptations of the soul?

September 6, 1867, *Weissenstein*. [Footnote: Weissenstein is a high point in the Jura, above Soleure.] (*Ten o'clock in the morning*).—A marvelous view of blinding and bewildering beauty. Above a milky sea of cloud, flooded with morning light, the rolling waves of which are beating up against the base of the wooded steeps of the Weissenstein, the vast circle of the Alps soars to a sublime height. The eastern side of the horizon is drowned in the splendors of the rising mists; but from the Toedi westward, the whole chain floats pure and clear between the milky plain and the pale blue sky. The giant assembly is sitting in council above the valleys and the lakes still submerged in vapor. The Clariden, the Spannoerter, the Titlis, then the Bernese *colossi* from the Wetterhorn to the Diablerets, then the peaks of Vaud, Valais, and Fribourg, and beyond these high chains the two kings of the Alps, Mont Blanc, of a pale pink, and the bluish point of Monte Rosa, peering out through a cleft in the Doldenhorn—such is the composition of the great snowy amphitheatre. The outline of the horizon takes all possible forms: needles, ridges, battlements, pyramids, obelisks, teeth, fangs, pincers, horns, cupolas; the mountain profile sinks, rises again, twists and sharpens itself in a thousand ways, but always so as to maintain an angular and serrated line. Only the inferior and secondary groups of mountains show any large curves or sweeping undulations of form. The Alps are more than an upheaval; they are a tearing and gashing of the earth's surface. Their granite peaks bite into the sky instead of caressing it. The Jura, on the contrary, spreads its broad back complacently under the blue dome of air.

Eleven o'clock.—The sea of vapor has risen and attacked the mountains, which for a long time overlooked it like so many huge reefs. For awhile it surged in vain over the lower slopes of the Alps. Then rolling back upon itself, it made a more successful onslaught upon the Jura, and now we are enveloped in its moving waves. The milky sea has become one vast cloud, which has swallowed up the plain and the mountains, observatory and observer. Within this cloud one may hear the sheep-bells ringing, and see the sunlight darting hither and thither. Strange and fanciful sight!

The Hanoverian pianist has gone; the family from Colmar has gone; a young girl and her brother have arrived. The girl is very pretty, and particularly dainty and elegant in all her ways; she seems to touch things only with the tips of her fingers; one compares her to an ermine, a gazelle. But at the same time she has no interests, does not know how to admire, and thinks of herself more than of anything else. This perhaps is a drawback inseparable from a beauty and a figure which attract all eyes. She is, besides, a townswoman to the core, and feels herself out of place in this great nature, which probably seems to her barbarous and ill-bred. At any rate she does not let it interfere with her in any way, and parades herself on the mountains with her little bonnet and her scarcely perceptible sunshade, as though she were on the boulevard. She belongs to that class of tourists so amusingly drawn by Toepffer. Character: *naive* conceit. Country: France. Standard of life: fashion. Some cleverness but no sense of reality, no understanding of nature, no consciousness of the manifold diversities of the world and of the right of life to be what it is, and to follow its own way and not ours.

This ridiculous element in her is connected with the same national prejudice which holds France to be the center point of the world, and leads Frenchmen to neglect geography and languages. The ordinary French townsman is really deliciously stupid in spite of all his natural cleverness, for he understands nothing but himself. His pole, his axis, his center, his all is Paris—or even less—Parisian manners, the taste of the day, fashion. Thanks to this organized fetishism, we have millions of copies of one single original pattern; a whole people moving together like bobbins in the same machine, or the legs of a single *corps d'armee*. The result is wonderful but wearisome; wonderful in point of material strength, wearisome psychologically. A hundred thousand sheep are not more instructive than one sheep, but they furnish a hundred thousand times more wool, meat, and manure. This is all, you may say, that the shepherd—that is, the master—requires. Very well, but one can only maintain breeding-farms or monarchies on these principles. For a republic you must have men: it cannot get on without individualities.

Noon.—An exquisite effect. A great herd of cattle are running across the meadows under my window, which is just illuminated by a furtive ray of sunshine. The picture has a ghostly suddenness and brilliancy; it pierces the mists which close upon it, like the slide of a magic lantern.

What a pity I must leave this place now that everything is so bright!

* * * * *

The calm sea says more to the thoughtful soul than the same sea in storm and tumult. But we need the understanding of eternal things and the sentiment of the infinite to be able to feel this. The divine state *par excellence* is that of silence and repose, because all speech and all action are in themselves limited and fugitive. Napoleon with his arms crossed over his breast is more expressive than the furious Hercules beating the air with his athlete's fists. People of passionate temperament never understand this. They are only sensitive to the energy of succession; they know nothing of the energy of condensation. They can only be impressed by acts and effects, by noise and effort. They have no instinct of contemplation, no sense of the pure cause, the fixed source of all movement, the principle of all effects, the center of all light, which does not need to spend itself in order to be sure of its own wealth, nor to throw itself into violent motion to be certain of its own power. The art of passion is sure to please, but it is not the highest art; it is true, indeed, that under the rule of democracy, the serener and calmer forms of art become more and more difficult; the turbulent herd no longer knows the gods.

* * * * *

Minds accustomed to analysis never allow objections more than a half-value, because they appreciate the variable and relative elements which enter in.

＊＊＊＊

A well-governed mind learns in time to find pleasure in nothing but the true and the just.

January 10, 1868. (*Eleven* P. M.).—We have had a philosophical meeting at the house of Edouard Claparede. [Footnote: Edouard Claparede, a Genevese naturalist, born 1832, died 1871.] The question on the order of the day was the nature of sensation. Claparede pronounced for the absolute subjectivity of all experience—in other words, for pure idealism—which is amusing, from a naturalist. According to him the *ego* alone exists, and the universe is but a projection of the *ego*, a phantasmagoria which we ourselves create without suspecting it, believing all the time that we are lookers-on. It is our nouemenon which objectifies itself as phenomenon. The *ego*, according to him, is a radiating force which, modified without knowing what it is that modifies it, imagines it, by virtue of the principle of causality—that is to say, produces the great illusion of the objective world in order so to explain itself. Our waking life, therefore, is but a more connected dream. The self is an unknown which gives birth to an infinite number of unknowns, by a fatality of its nature. Science is summed up in the consciousness that nothing exists but consciousness. In other words, the intelligent issues from the unintelligible in order to return to it, or rather the ego explains itself by the hypothesis of the *non-ego*, while in reality it is but a dream, dreaming itself. We might say with Scarron:

"Et je vis l'ombre d'un esprit Qui tracait l'ombre d'um systeme Avec l'ombre de l'ombre meme."

This abolition of nature by natural science is logical, and it was, in fact, Schelling's starting-point. From the standpoint of physiology, nature is but a necessary illusion, a constitutional hallucination. We only escape from this bewitchment by the moral activity of the *ego*, which feels itself a cause and a free cause, and which by its responsibility breaks the spell and issues from the enchanted circle of Maia.

Maia! Is she indeed the true goddess? Hindoo wisdom long ago regarded the world as the dream of Brahma. Must we hold with Fichte that it is the individual dream of each individual *ego*? Every fool would then be a cosmogonic poet producing the firework of the universe under the dome of the infinite. But why then give ourselves such gratuitous trouble to learn? In our dreams, at least, nightmare excepted, we endow ourselves with complete ubiquity, liberty and omniscience. Are we then less ingenious and inventive awake than asleep?

January 25, 1868.—It is when the outer man begins to decay that it becomes vitally important to us to believe in immortality, and to feel with the apostle that the inner man is renewed from day to day. But for those who doubt it and have no hope of it? For them the remainder of life can only be the compulsory dismemberment of their small empire, the gradual dismantling of their being by inexorable destiny. How hard it is to bear—this long-drawn death, of which the stages are melancholy and the end inevitable! It is easy to see why it was that stoicism maintained the right of suicide. What is my real faith? Has the universal, or at any rate the very general and common doubt of science, invaded me in my turn? I have defended the cause of the immortality of the soul against those who questioned it, and yet when I have reduced them to silence, I have scarcely known whether at bottom I was not after all on their side. I try to do without hope; but it is possible that I have no longer the strength for it, and that, like other men, I must be sustained and consoled by a belief, by the belief in pardon and immortality—that is to say, by religious belief of the Christian type. Reason and thought grow tired, like muscles and nerves. They must have their sleep, and this sleep is the relapse into the tradition of childhood, into the common hope. It takes so much effort to maintain one's self in an exceptional point of view, that one falls back into prejudice by pure exhaustion, just as the man who stands indefinitely always ends by sinking to the ground and reassuming the horizontal position.

What is to become of us when everything leaves us—health, joy, affections, the freshness of sensation, memory, capacity for work—when the sun seems to us to have lost its warmth, and life is stripped of all its charm? What is to become of us without hope? Must we either harden or forget? There is but one answer—keep close to duty. Never mind the future, if only you have peace of conscience, if you feel yourself reconciled, and in harmony with the order of things. Be what you ought to be; the rest is God's affair. It is for him to know what is best, to take care of his own glory, to ensure the happiness of what depends on him, whether by another life or by annihilation. And supposing that there were no good and holy God, nothing but universal being, the law of the all, an ideal without hypostasis or reality, duty would still be the key of the enigma, the pole-star of a wandering humanity.

"Fais ce que dois, advienne que pourra."

January 26, 1868.—Blessed be childhood, which brings down something of heaven into the midst of our rough earthliness. These eighty thousand daily births, of which statistics tell us, represent as it were an effusion of innocence and freshness, struggling not only against the death of the race, but against human corruption, and the universal gangrene of sin. All the good and wholesome feeling which is intertwined with childhood and the cradle is one of the secrets of the providential government of the world. Suppress this life-giving dew, and human society would be scorched and devastated by selfish passion. Supposing that humanity had been composed of a thousand millions of immortal beings, whose number could neither increase nor diminish, where should we be, and what should we be! A thousand times more learned, no doubt, but a thousand times more evil. There would have been a vast accumulation of science, but all the virtues engendered by suffering and devotion—that is to say, by the family and society—would have no existence. And for this there would be no compensation.

Blessed be childhood for the good that it does, and for the good which it brings about carelessly and unconsciously by simply making us love it and letting itself be loved. What little of paradise we see still on earth is due to its presence among us. Without fatherhood, without motherhood, I think that love itself would not be enough to prevent men from devouring each other—men, that is to say, such as human passions have made them. The angels have no need of birth and death as foundations for their life, because their life is heavenly.

February 16, 1868.—I have been finishing About's "Mainfroy (Les Mariages de Province)." What subtlety, what cleverness, what *verve*, what *aplomb*! About is a master of epithet, of quick, light-winged satire. For all his cavalier freedom of manner, his work is conceived at bottom in a spirit of the subtlest irony, and his detachment of mind is so great that he is able to make sport of everything, to mock at others and himself, while all the time amusing himself extremely with his own ideas and inventions. This is indeed the characteristic mark, the common signature, so to speak, of *esprit* like his.

Irrepressible mischief, indefatigable elasticity, a power of luminous mockery, delight in the perpetual discharge of innumerable arrows from an inexhaustible quiver, the unquenchable laughter of some little earth-born demon, perpetual gayety, and a radiant force of epigram—there are all these in the true humorist. *Stulti sunt innumerabiles,* said Erasmus, the patron of all these dainty mockers. Folly, conceit, foppery, silliness, affectation, hypocrisy, attitudinizing and pedantry of all shades, and in all forms, everything that poses, prances, bridles, struts, bedizens, and plumes itself, everything that takes itself seriously and tries to impose itself on mankind—all this is the natural prey of the satirist, so many targets ready for his arrows, so many victims offered to his attack. And we all know how rich the world is in prey of this kind! An alderman's feast of folly is served up to him in perpetuity; the spectacle of society offers him an endless *noce de Gamache.* [Footnote: *Noce de Gamache*—"repas tres somptueux."—Littre. The allusion, of course, is to Don Quixote, Part II. chap. xx.—"Donde se cuentan las bodas de Bamacho el rico, con el suceso de Basilio el pobre."] With what glee he raids through his domains, and what signs of destruction and massacre mark the path of the sportsman! His hand is infallible like his glance. The spirit of sarcasm lives and thrives in the midst of universal wreck; its balls are enchanted and itself invulnerable, and it braves retaliations and reprisals because itself is a mere flash, a bodiless and magical nothing.

Clever men will recognize and tolerate nothing but cleverness; every authority rouses their ridicule, every superstition amuses them, every convention moves them to contradiction. Only force finds favor in their eyes, and they have no toleration for anything that is not purely natural and spontaneous. And yet ten clever men are not worth one man of talent, nor ten men of talent worth one man of genius. And in the individual, feeling is more than cleverness, reason is worth as much as feeling, and conscience has it over reason. If, then, the clever man is not *mockable,* he may at least be neither loved, nor considered, nor esteemed. He may make himself feared, it is true, and force others to respect his independence; but this negative advantage, which is the result of a negative superiority, brings no happiness with it. Cleverness is serviceable for everything, sufficient for nothing.

March 8, 1868.—Madame——kept me to have tea with three young friends of hers—three sisters, I think. The two youngest are extremely pretty, the dark one as pretty as the blonde. Their fresh faces, radiant with the bloom of youth, were a perpetual delight to the eye. This electric force of beauty has a beneficent effect upon the man of letters; it acts as a real restorative. Sensitive, impressionable, absorbent as I am, the neighborhood of health, of beauty, of intelligence and of goodness, exercises a powerful influence upon my whole being; and in the same way I am troubled and affected just as easily by the presence near me of troubled lives or diseased souls. Madame —— said of me that I must be "superlatively feminine" in all my perceptions. This ready sympathy and sensitiveness is the reason of it. If I had but desired it ever so little, I should have had the magical clairvoyance of the somnambulist, and could have reproduced in myself a number of strange phenomena. I know it, but I have always been on my guard against it, whether from indifference or from prudence. When I think of the intuitions of every kind which have come to me since my youth, it seems to me that I have lived a multitude of lives. Every characteristic individuality shapes itself ideally in me, or rather molds me for the moment into its own image; and I have only to turn my attention upon myself at such a time to be able to understand a new mode of being, a new phase of human nature. In this way I have been, turn by turn, mathematician, musician, *savant*, monk, child, or mother. In these states of universal sympathy I have even seemed to myself sometimes to enter into the condition of the animal or the plant, and even of an individual animal, of a given plant. This faculty of ascending and descending metamorphosis, this power of simplifying or of adding to one's individuality, has sometimes astounded my friends, even the most subtle of them. It has to do no doubt with the extreme facility which I have for impersonal and objective thought, and this again accounts for the difficulty which I feel in realizing my own individuality, in being simply one man having his proper number and ticket. To withdraw within my own individual limits has always seemed to me a strange, arbitrary, and conventional process. I seem to myself to be a mere conjuror's apparatus, an instrument of vision and perception, a person without personality, a subject without any determined individuality—an instance, to speak technically, of pure "determinability" and "formability," and therefore I can only resign myself with difficulty to play the purely arbitrary part of a private citizen, inscribed upon the roll of a particular town or a particular country. In action I feel myself out of place; my true *milieu* is contemplation. Pure virtuality and perfect equilibrium—in these I am most at home. There I feel myself free, disinterested, and sovereign. Is it a call or a temptation?

It represents perhaps the oscillation between the two geniuses, the Greek and the Roman, the eastern and the western, the ancient and the Christian, or the struggle between the two ideals, that of liberty and that of holiness. Liberty raises us to the gods; holiness prostrates us on the ground. Action limits us; whereas in the state of contemplation we are endlessly expansive. Will localizes us; thought universalizes us. My soul wavers between half a dozen antagonistic general conceptions, because it is responsive to all the great instincts of human nature, and its aspiration is to the absolute, which is only to be reached through a succession of contraries. It has taken me a great deal of time to understand myself, and I frequently find myself beginning over again the study of the oft-solved problem, so difficult is it for us to maintain any fixed point within us. I love everything, and detest one thing only—the hopeless imprisonment of my being within a single arbitrary form, even were it chosen by myself. Liberty for the inner man is then the strongest of my passions—perhaps my only passion. Is such a passion lawful? It has been my habit to think so, but intermittently, by fits and starts. I am not perfectly sure of it.

March 17, 1868.—Women wish to be loved without a why or a wherefore; not because they are pretty, or good, or well bred, or graceful, or intelligent, but because they are themselves. All analysis seems to them to imply a loss of consideration, a subordination of their personality to something which dominates and measures it. They will have none of it; and their instinct is just. As soon as we can give a reason for a feeling we are no longer under the spell of it; we appreciate, we weigh, we are free, at least in principle. Love must always remain a fascination, a witchery, if the empire of woman is to endure. Once the mystery gone, the power goes with it. Love must always seem to us indivisible, insoluble, superior to all analysis, if it is to preserve that appearance of infinity, of something supernatural and miraculous, which makes its chief beauty. The majority of beings despise what they understand, and bow only before the inexplicable. The feminine triumph *par excellence* is to convict of obscurity that virile intelligence which makes so much pretense to enlightenment. And when a woman inspires love, it is then especially that she enjoys this proud triumph. I admit that her exultation has its grounds. Still, it seems to me that love—true and profound love—should be a source of light and calm, a religion and a revelation, in which there is no place left for the lower victories of vanity. Great souls care only for what is great, and to the spirit which hovers in the sight of the Infinite, any sort of artifice seems a disgraceful puerility.

March 19, 1868.—What we call little things are merely the causes of great things; they are the beginning, the embryo, and it is the point of departure which, generally speaking, decides the whole future of an existence. One single black speck may be the beginning of a gangrene, of a storm, of a revolution. From one insignificant misunderstanding hatred and separation may finally issue. An enormous avalanche begins by the displacement of one atom, and the conflagration of a town by the fall of a match. Almost everything comes from almost nothing, one might think. It is only the first crystallization which is the affair of mind; the ultimate aggregation is the affair of mass, of attraction, of acquired momentum, of mechanical acceleration. History, like nature, illustrates for us the application of the law of inertia and agglomeration which is put lightly in the proverb, "Nothing succeeds like success." Find the right point at starting; strike straight, begin well; everything depends on it. Or more simply still, provide yourself with good luck—for accident plays a vast part in human affairs. Those who have succeeded most in this world (Napoleon or Bismarck) confess it; calculation is not without its uses, but chance makes mock of calculation, and the result of a planned combination is in no wise proportional to its merit. From the supernatural point of view people say: "This chance, as you call it, is, in reality, the action of providence. Man may give himself what trouble he will—God leads him all the same." Only, unfortunately, this supposed intervention as often as not ends in the defeat of zeal, virtue, and devotion, and the success of crime, stupidity, and selfishness. Poor, sorely-tried Faith! She has but one way out of the difficulty—the word Mystery! It is in the origins of things that the great secret of destiny lies hidden, although the breathless sequence of after events has often many surprises for us too. So that at first sight history seems to us accident and confusion; looked at for the second time, it seems to us logical and necessary; looked at for the third time, it appears to us a mixture of necessity and liberty; on the fourth examination we scarcely know what to think of it, for if force is the source of right, and chance the origin of force, we come back to our first explanation, only with a heavier heart than when we began.

Is Democritus right after all? Is chance the foundation of everything, all laws being but the imaginations of our reason, which, itself born of accident, has a certain power of self-deception and of inventing laws which it believes to be real and objective, just as a man who dreams of a meal thinks that he is eating, while in reality there is neither table, nor food, nor guest nor nourishment? Everything goes on as if there were order and reason and logic in the world, while in reality everything is fortuitous, accidental, and apparent. The universe is but the kaleidoscope which turns within the mind of the so-called thinking being, who is himself a curiosity without a cause, an accident conscious of the great accident around him, and who amuses himself with it so long as the phenomenon of his vision lasts. Science is a lucid madness occupied in tabulating its own necessary hallucinations. The philosopher laughs, for he alone escapes being duped, while he sees other men the victims of persistent illusion. He is like some mischievous spectator of a ball who has cleverly taken all the strings from the violins, and yet sees musicians and dancers moving and pirouetting before him as though the music were still going on. Such an experience would delight him as proving that the universal St. Vitus' dance is also nothing but an aberration of the inner consciousness, and that the philosopher is in the right of it as against the general credulity. Is it not even enough simply to shut one's ears in a ballroom, to believe one's self in a madhouse?

The multitude of religions on the earth must have very much the same effect upon the man who has killed the religious idea in himself. But it is a dangerous attempt, this repudiation of the common law of the race—this claim to be in the right, as against all the world.

It is not often that the philosophic scoffers forget themselves for others. Why should they? Self-devotion is a serious thing, and seriousness would be inconsistent with their role of mockery. To be unselfish we must love; to love we must believe in the reality of what we love; we must know how to suffer, how to forget ourselves, how to yield ourselves up—in a word, how to be serious. A spirit of incessant mockery means absolute isolation; it is the sign of a thoroughgoing egotism. If we wish to do good to men we must pity and not despise them. We must learn to say of them, not "What fools!" but "What unfortunates!" The pessimist or the nihilist seems to me less cold and icy than the mocking atheist. He reminds me of the somber words of "Ahasverus:"

"Vous qui manquez de charite, Tremblez a mon supplice etrange: Ce n'est point sa divinite, C'est l'humanite que Dieu venge!"

Amiel's Journal

[Footnote: The quotation is from Quinet's "Ahasverus" (first published 1833), that strange *Welt-gedicht*, which the author himself described as "l'histoire du monde, de Dieu dans le monde, et enfin du doute dans le monde," and which, with Faust, probably suggested the unfinished but in many ways brilliant performance of the young Spaniard, Espronceda—*El Diablo Mundo*.]

It is better to be lost than to be saved all alone; and it is a wrong to one's kind to wish to be wise without making others share our wisdom. It is, besides, an illusion to suppose that such a privilege is possible, when everything proves the solidarity of individuals, and when no one can think at all except by means of the general store of thought, accumulated and refined by centuries of cultivation and experience. Absolute individualism is an absurdity. A man may be isolated in his own particular and temporary *milieu*, but every one of our thoughts or feelings finds, has found, and will find, its echo in humanity. Such an echo is immense and far-resounding in the case of those representative men who have been adopted by great fractions of humanity as guides, revealers, and reformers; but it exists for everybody. Every sincere utterance of the soul, every testimony faithfully borne to a personal conviction, is of use to some one and some thing, even when you know it not, and when your mouth is stopped by violence, or the noose tightens round your neck. A word spoken to some one preserves an indestructible influence, just as any movement whatever may be metamorphosed, but not undone. Here, then, is a reason for not mocking, for not being silent, for affirming, for acting. We must have faith in truth; we must seek the true and spread it abroad; we must love men and serve them.

April 9, 1868.—I have been spending three hours over Lotze's big volume ("Geschichte der Aesthetikin Deutschland"). It begins attractively, but the attraction wanes, and by the end I was very tired of it. Why? Because the noise of a mill-wheel sends one to sleep, and these pages without paragraphs, these interminable chapters, and this incessant, dialectical clatter, affect me as though I were listening to a word-mill. I end by yawning like any simple non-philosophical mortal in the face of all this heaviness and pedantry. Erudition, and even thought, are not everything. An occasional touch of esprit, a little sharpness of phrase, a little vivacity, imagination, and grace, would spoil neither. Do these pedantic books leave a single image or formula, a single new or striking fact behind them in the memory, when one puts them down? No; nothing but confusion and fatigue.

Oh for clearness, terseness, brevity! Diderot, Voltaire, and even Galiani!

A short article by Sainte-Beuve, Scherer, Renan, Victor Cherbuliez, gives one more pleasure, and makes one think and reflect more, than a thousand of these heavy German pages, stuffed to the brim, and showing rather the work itself than its results. The Germans gather fuel for the pile: it is the French who kindle it. For heaven's sake, spare me your lucubrations; give me facts or ideas. Keep your vats, your must, your dregs, in the background. What I ask is wine—wine which will sparkle in the glass, and stimulate intelligence instead of weighing it down.

April 11, 1868. (*Mornex sur Saleve*).—I left town in a great storm of wind, which was raising clouds of dust along the suburban roads, and two hours later I found myself safely installed among the mountains, just like last year. I think of staying a week here.... The sounds of the village are wafted to my open window, barkings of distant dogs, voices of women at the fountain, the songs of birds in the lower orchards. The green carpet of the plain is dappled by passing shadows thrown upon it by the clouds; the landscape has the charm of delicate tint and a sort of languid grace. Already I am full of a sense of well-being, I am tasting the joys of that contemplative state in which the soul, issuing from itself, becomes as it were the soul of a country or a landscape, and feels living within it a multitude of lives. Here is no more resistance, negation, blame; everything is affirmative; I feel myself in harmony with nature and with surroundings, of which I seem to myself the expression. The heart opens to the immensity of things. This is what I love! *Nam mihires, non me rebus submittere conor.* April 12, 1868. (*Easter Day*), *Mornex Eight* A. M.—The day has opened solemnly and religiously. There is a tinkling of bells from the valley: even the fields seem to be breathing forth a canticle of praise. Humanity must have a worship, and, all things considered, is not the Christian worship the best among those which have existed on a large scale? The religion of sin, of repentance, and reconciliation—the religion of the new birth and of eternal life—is not a religion to be ashamed of. In spite of all the aberrations of fanaticism, all the superstitions of formalism, all the ugly superstructures of hypocrisy, all the fantastic puerilities of theology, the gospel has modified the world and consoled mankind. Christian humanity is not much better than pagan humanity, but it would be much worse without a religion, and without this religion. Every religion proposes an ideal and a model; the Christian ideal is sublime, and its model of a divine beauty. We may hold aloof from the churches, and yet bow ourselves before Jesus. We may be suspicious of the clergy, and refuse to have anything to do with catechisms, and yet love the Holy and the Just, who came to save and not to curse. Jesus will always supply us with the best criticism of Christianity, and when Christianity has passed away the religion of Jesus will in all probability survive. After Jesus as God we shall come back to faith in the God of Jesus.

Five o'clock P. M.—I have been for a long walk through Cezargues, Eseri, and the Yves woods, returning by the Pont du Loup. The weather was cold and gray. A great popular merrymaking of some sort, with its multitude of blouses, and its drums and fifes, has been going on riotously for an hour under my window. The crowd has sung a number of songs, drinking songs, ballads, romances, but all more or less heavy and ugly. The muse has never touched our country people, and the Swiss race is not graceful even in its gayety. A bear in high spirits—this is what one thinks of. The poetry it produces, too, is desperately vulgar and commonplace. Why? In the first place, because, in spite of the pretenses of our democratic philosophies, the classes whose backs are bent with manual labor are aesthetically inferior to the others. In the next place, because our old rustic peasant poetry is dead, and the peasant, when he tries to share the music or the poetry of the cultivated classes, only succeeds in caricaturing it, and not in copying it. Democracy, by laying it down that there is but one class for all men, has in fact done a wrong to everything that is not first-rate. As we can no longer without offense judge men according to a certain recognized order, we can only compare them to the best that exists, and then they naturally seem to us more mediocre, more ugly, more deformed than before. If the passion for equality potentially raises the average, it *really* degrades nineteen-twentieths of individuals below their former place. There is a progress in the domain of law and a falling back in the domain of art. And meanwhile the artists see multiplying before them their *bete-noire*, the *bourgeois*, the Philistine, the presumptuous ignoramus, the quack who plays at science, and the feather-brain who thinks himself the equal of the intelligent.

"Commonness will prevail," as De Candolle said in speaking of the graminaceous plants. The era of equality means the triumph of mediocrity. It is disappointing, but inevitable; for it is one of time's revenges. Humanity, after having organized itself on the basis of the dissimilarity of individuals, is now organizing itself on the basis of their similarity, and the one exclusive principle is about as true as the other. Art no doubt will lose, but justice will gain. Is not universal leveling-down the law of nature, and when all has been leveled will not all have been destroyed? So that the world is striving with all its force for the destruction of what it has itself brought forth. Life is the blind pursuit of its own negation; as has been said of the wicked, nature also works for her own disappointment, she labors at what she hates, she weaves her own shroud, and piles up the stones of her own tomb. God may well forgive us, for "we know not what to do."

Just as the sum of force is always identical in the material universe, and presents a spectacle not of diminution nor of augmentation but simply of constant metamorphosis, so it is not impossible that the sum of good is in reality always the same, and that therefore all progress on one side is compensated inversely on another side. If this were so we ought never to say that period or a people is absolutely and as a whole superior to another time or another people, but only that there is superiority in certain points. The great difference between man and man would, on these principles, consist in the art of transforming vitality into spirituality, and latent power into useful energy. The same difference would hold good between nation and nation, so that the object of the simultaneous or successive competition of mankind in history would be the extraction of the maximum of humanity from a given amount of animality. Education, morals, and politics would be only variations of the same art, the art of living—that is to say, of disengaging the pure form and subtlest essence of our individual being.

April 26, 1868. (*Sunday, Mid-day*).—A gloomy morning. On all sides a depressing outlook, and within, disgust with self.

Ten P.M.—Visits and a walk. I have spent the evening alone. Many things to-day have taught me lessons of wisdom. I have seen the hawthorns covering themselves with blossom, and the whole valley springing up afresh under the breath of the spring. I have been the spectator of faults of conduct on the part of old men who will not grow old, and whose heart is in rebellion against the natural law. I have watched the working of marriage in its frivolous and commonplace forms, and listened to trivial preaching. I have been a witness of griefs without hope, of loneliness that claimed one's pity. I have listened to pleasantries on the subject of madness, and to the merry songs of the birds. And everything has had the same message for me: "Place yourself once more in harmony with the universal law; accept the will of God; make a religious use of life; work while it is yet day; be at once serious and cheerful; know how to repeat with the apostle, 'I have learned in whatsoever state I am therewith to be content.'"

August 26, 1868.—After all the storms of feeling within and the organic disturbances without, which during these latter months have pinned me so closely to my own individual existence, shall I ever be able to reascend into the region of pure intelligence, to enter again upon the disinterested and impersonal life, to recover my old indifference toward subjective miseries, and regain a purely scientific and contemplative state of mind? Shall I ever succeed in forgetting all the needs which bind me to earth and to humanity? Shall I ever become pure spirit? Alas! I cannot persuade myself to believe it possible for an instant. I see infirmity and weakness close upon me, I feel I cannot do without affection, and I know that I have no ambition, and that my faculties are declining. I remember that I am forty-seven years old, and that all my brood of youthful hopes has flown away. So that there is no deceiving myself as to the fate which awaits me: increasing loneliness, mortification of spirit, long-continued regret, melancholy neither to be consoled nor confessed, a mournful old age, a slow decay, a death in the desert!

Terrible dilemma! Whatever is still possible to me has lost its savor, while all that I could still desire escapes me, and will always escape me. Every impulse ends in weariness and disappointment. Discouragement, depression, weakness, apathy; there is the dismal series which must be forever begun and re-begun, while we are still rolling up the Sisyphean rock of life. Is it not simpler and shorter to plunge head-foremost into the gulf?

No, rebel as we may, there is but one solution—to submit to the general order, to accept, to resign ourselves, and to do still what we can. It is our self-will, our aspirations, our dreams, that must be sacrificed. We must give up the hope of happiness once for all! Immolation of the self—death to self—this is the only suicide which is either useful or permitted. In my present mood of indifference and disinterestedness, there is some secret ill-humor, some wounded pride, a little rancor; there is selfishness in short, since a premature claim for rest is implied in it. Absolute disinterestedness is only reached in that perfect humility which tramples the self under foot for the glory of God.

I have no more strength left, I wish for nothing; but that is not what is wanted. I must wish what God wishes; I must pass from indifference to sacrifice, and from sacrifice to self-devotion. The cup which I would fain put away from me is the misery of living, the shame of existing and suffering as a common creature who has missed his vocation; it is the bitter and increasing humiliation of declining power, of growing old under the weight of one's own disapproval, and the disappointment of one's friends! "Wilt thou be healed?" was the text of last Sunday's sermon. "Come to me, all ye who are weary and heavy-laden, and I will give you rest." "And if our heart condemn us, God is greater than our heart."

August 27, 1868.—To-day I took up the "Penseroso" [Footnote: "Il Penseroso," poesies-maximes par H. F. Amiel: Geneve, 1858. This little book, which contains one hundred and thirty-three maxims, several of which are quoted in the *Journal Intime*, is prefaced by a motto translated from Shelley—"Ce n'est pas la science qui nous manque, a nous modernes; nous l'avons surabondamment.... Mais ce que nous avons absorbe nous absorbe.... Ce qui nous manque c'est la poesie de la vie."] again. I have often violated its maxims and forgotten its lessons. Still, this volume is a true son of my soul, and breathes the true spirit of the inner life. Whenever I wish to revive my consciousness of my own tradition, it is pleasant to me to read over this little gnomic collection which has had such scant justice done to it, and which, were it another's, I should often quote. I like to feel that in it I have attained to that relative truth which may be defined as consistency with self, the harmony of appearance with reality, of thought with expression—in other words, sincerity, ingenuousness, inwardness. It is personal experience in the strictest sense of the word.

September 21, 1868. (*Villars*).—A lovely autumn effect. Everything was veiled in gloom this morning, and a gray mist of rain floated between us and the whole circle of mountains. Now the strip of blue sky which made its appearance at first behind the distant peaks has grown larger, has mounted to the zenith, and the dome of heaven, swept almost clear of cloud, sends streaming down upon us the pale rays of a convalescent sun. The day now promises kindly, and all is well that ends well.

Thus after a season of tears a sober and softened joy may return to us. Say to yourself that you are entering upon the autumn of your life; that the graces of spring and the splendors of summer are irrevocably gone, but that autumn too has its beauties. The autumn weather is often darkened by rain, cloud, and mist, but the air is still soft, and the sun still delights the eyes, and touches the yellowing leaves caressingly; it is the time for fruit, for harvest, for the vintage, the moment for making provision for the winter. Here the herds of milch-cows have already come down to the level of the *chalet*, and next week they will be lower than we are. This living barometer is a warning to us that the time has come to say farewell to the mountains. There is nothing to gain, and everything to lose, by despising the example of nature, and making arbitrary rules of life for one's self. Our liberty, wisely understood, is but a voluntary obedience to the universal laws of life. My life has reached its month of September. May I recognize it in time, and suit thought and action to the fact!

November 13, 1868.—I am reading part of two books by Charles Secretan [Footnote: Charles Secretan, a Lausanne professor, the friend of Vinet, born 1819. He published "Lecons sur la Philosophie de Leibnitz," "Philosophie de la Liberte," "La Raison et le Christianisme," etc.] "Recherches sur la Methode," 1857; "Precis elementaire de Philosophie," 1868. The philosophy of Secretan is the philosophy of Christianity, considered as the one true religion. Subordination of nature to intelligence, of intelligence to will, and of will to dogmatic faith —such is its general framework. Unfortunately there are no signs of critical, or comparative, or historical study in it, and as an apologetic—in which satire is curiously mingled with glorification of the religion of love—it leaves upon one an impression of *parti pris*. A philosophy of religion, apart from the comparative science of religions, and apart also from a disinterested and general philosophy of history, must always be more or less arbitrary and factitious. It is only pseudo-scientific, this reduction of human life to three spheres—industry, law, and religion. The author seems to me to possess a vigorous and profound mind, rather than a free mind. Not only is he dogmatic, but he dogmatizes in favor of a given religion, to which his whole allegiance is pledged. Besides, Christianity being an X which each church defines in its own way, the author takes the same liberty, and defines the X in his way; so that he is at once too free and not free enough; too free in respect to historical Christianity, not free enough in respect to Christianity as a particular church. He does not satisfy the believing Anglican, Lutheran, Reformed Churchman, or Catholic; and he does not satisfy the freethinker. This Schellingian type of speculation, which consists in logically deducing a particular religion—that is to say, in making philosophy the servant of Christian theology—is a legacy from the Middle Ages.

After belief comes judgment; but a believer is not a judge. A fish lives in the ocean, but it cannot see all around it; it cannot take a view of the whole; therefore it cannot judge what the ocean is. In order to understand Christianity we must put it in its historical place, in its proper framework; we must regard it as a part of the religious development of humanity, and so judge it, not from a Christian point of view, but from a human point of view, *sine ira nec studio*.

December 16, 1868.—I am in the most painful state of anxiety as to my poor kind friend, Charles Heim.... Since the 30th of November I have had no letter from the dear invalid, who then said his last farewell to me. How long these two weeks have seemed to me—and how keenly I have realized that strong craving which many feel for the last words, the last looks, of those they love! Such words and looks are a kind of testament. They have a solemn and sacred character which is not merely an effect of our imagination. For that which is on the brink of death already participates to some extent in eternity. A dying man seems to speak to us from beyond the tomb; what he says has the effect upon us of a sentence, an oracle, an injunction; we look upon him as one endowed with second sight. Serious and solemn words come naturally to the man who feels life escaping him, and the grave opening before him. The depths of his nature are then revealed; the divine within him need no longer hide itself. Oh, do not let us wait to be just or pitiful or demonstrative toward those we love until they or we are struck down by illness or threatened with death! Life is short and we have never too much time for gladdening the hearts of those who are traveling the dark journey with us. Oh, be swift to love, make haste to be kind!

December 26, 1868.—My dear friend died this morning at Hyeres. A beautiful soul has returned to heaven. So he has ceased to suffer! Is he happy now?

* * * * *

If men are always more or less deceived on the subject of women, it is because they forget that they and women do not speak altogether the same language, and that words have not the same weight or the same meaning for them, especially in questions of feeling. Whether from shyness or precaution or artifice, a woman never speaks out her whole thought, and moreover what she herself knows of it is but a part of what it really is. Complete frankness seems to be impossible to her, and complete self-knowledge seems to be forbidden her. If she is a sphinx to us, it is because she is a riddle of doubtful meaning even to herself. She has no need of perfidy, for she is mystery itself. A woman is something fugitive, irrational, indeterminable, illogical, and contradictory. A great deal of forbearance ought to be shown her, and a good deal of prudence exercised with regard to her, for she may bring about innumerable evils without knowing It. Capable of all kinds of devotion, and of all kinds of treason, "*monstre incomprehensible*," raised to the second power, she is at once the delight and the terror of man.

* * * * *

The more a man loves, the more he suffers. The sum of possible grief for each soul is in proportion to its degree of perfection.

* * * * *

He who is too much afraid of being duped has lost the power of being magnanimous.

* * * * *

Doubt of the reality of love ends by making us doubt everything. The final result of all deceptions and disappointments is atheism, which may not always yield up its name and secret, but which lurks, a masked specter, within the depths of thought, as the last supreme explainer. "Man is what his love is," and follows the fortunes of his love.

* * * * *

The beautiful souls of the world have an art of saintly alchemy, by which bitterness is converted into kindness, the gall of human experience into gentleness, ingratitude into benefits, insults into pardon. And the transformation ought to become so easy and habitual that the lookers-on may think it spontaneous, and nobody give us credit for it.

January 27, 1869.—What, then, is the service rendered to the world by Christianity? The proclamation of "good news." And what is this "good news?" The pardon of sin. The God of holiness loving the world and reconciling it to himself by Jesus, in order to establish the kingdom of God, the city of souls, the life of heaven upon earth—here you have the whole of it; but in this is a revolution. "Love ye one another, as I have loved you;" "Be ye one with me, as I am one with the Father:" for this is life eternal, here is perfection, salvation, joy. Faith in the fatherly love of God, who punishes and pardons for our good, and who desires not the death of the sinner, but his conversion and his life—here is the motive power of the redeemed.

What we call Christianity is a vast ocean, into which flow a number of spiritual currents of distant and various origin; certain religions, that is to say, of Asia and of Europe, the great ideas of Greek wisdom, and especially those of Platonism. Neither its doctrine nor its morality, as they have been historically developed, are new or spontaneous. What is essential and original in it is the practical demonstration that the human and the divine nature may co-exist, may become fused into one sublime flame; that holiness and pity, justice and mercy, may meet together and become one, in man and in God. What is specific in Christianity is Jesus—the religious consciousness of Jesus. The sacred sense of his absolute union with God through perfect love and self-surrender, this profound, invincible, and tranquil faith of his, has become a religion; the faith of Jesus has become the faith of millions and millions of men. From this torch has sprung a vast conflagration. And such has been the brilliancy and the radiance both of revealer and revelation, that the astonished world has forgotten its justice in its admiration, and has referred to one single benefactor the whole of those benefits which are its heritage from the past.

The conversion of ecclesiastical and confessional Christianity into historical Christianity is the work of biblical science. The conversion of historical Christianity into philosophical Christianity is an attempt which is to some extent an illusion, since faith cannot be entirely resolved into science. The transference, however, of Christianity from the region of history to the region of psychology is the great craving of our time. What we are trying to arrive at is the *eternal gospel*. But before we can reach it, the comparative history and philosophy of religions must assign to Christianity its true place, and must judge it. The religion, too, which Jesus professed must be disentangled from the religion which has taken Jesus for its object.

And when at last we are able to point out the state of consciousness which is the primitive cell, the principle of the eternal gospel, we shall have reached our goal, for in it is the *punctum saliens* of pure religion.

Perhaps the extraordinary will take the place of the supernatural, and the great geniuses of the world will come to be regarded as the messengers of God in history, as the providential revealers through whom the spirit of God works upon the human mass. What is perishing is not the admirable and the adorable; it is simply the arbitrary, the accidental, the miraculous. Just as the poor illuminations of a village *fete*, or the tapers of a procession, are put out by the great marvel of the sun, so the small local miracles, with their meanness and doubtfulness, will sink into insignificance beside the law of the world of spirits, the incomparable spectacle of human history, led by that all-powerful Dramaturgus whom we call God. *Utinam!*

March 1, 1869.—Impartiality and objectivity are as rare as justice, of which they are but two special forms. Self-interest is an inexhaustible source of convenient illusions. The number of beings who wish to see truly is extraordinarily small. What governs men is the fear of truth, unless truth is useful to them, which is as much as to say that self-interest is the principle of the common philosophy or that truth is made for us but not we for truth. As this fact is humiliating, the majority of people will neither recognize nor admit it. And thus a prejudice of self-love protects all the prejudices of the understanding, which are themselves the result of a stratagem of the *ego*. Humanity has always slain or persecuted those who have disturbed this selfish repose of hers. She only improves in spite of herself. The only progress which she desires is an increase of enjoyments. All advances in justice, in morality, in holiness, have been imposed upon or forced from her by some noble violence. Sacrifice, which is the passion of great souls, has never been the law of societies. It is too often by employing one vice against another— for example, vanity against cupidity, greed against idleness—that the great agitators have broken through routine. In a word, the human world is almost entirely directed by the law of nature, and the law of the spirit, which is the leaven of its coarse paste, has but rarely succeeded in raising it into generous expansion.

From the point of view of the ideal, humanity is *triste* and ugly. But if we compare it with its probable origins, we see that the human race has not altogether wasted its time. Hence there are three possible views of history: the view of the pessimist, who starts from the ideal; the view of the optimist, who compares the past with the present; and the view of the hero-worshiper, who sees that all progress whatever has cost oceans of blood and tears.

European hypocrisy veils its face before the voluntary suicide of those Indian fanatics who throw themselves under the wheels of their goddess' triumphal car. And yet these sacrifices are but the symbol of what goes on in Europe as elsewhere, of that offering of their life which is made by the martyrs of all great causes. We may even say that the fierce and sanguinary goddess is humanity itself, which is only spurred to progress by remorse, and repents only when the measure of its crimes runs over. The fanatics who sacrifice themselves are an eternal protest against the universal selfishness. We have only overthrown those idols which are tangible and visible, but perpetual sacrifice still exists everywhere, and everywhere the *elite* of each generation suffers for the salvation of the multitude. It is the austere, bitter, and mysterious law of solidarity. Perdition and redemption in and through each other is the destiny of men.

March 18, 1869 (*Thursday*).—Whenever I come back from a walk outside the town I am disgusted and repelled by this cell of mine. Out of doors, sunshine, birds, spring, beauty, and life; in here, ugliness, piles of paper, melancholy, and death. And yet my walk was one of the saddest possible. I wandered along the Rhone and the Arve, and all the memories of the past, all the disappointments of the present and all the anxieties of the future laid siege to my heart like a whirlwind of phantoms. I took account of my faults, and they ranged themselves in battle against me. The vulture of regret gnawed at my heart, and the sense of the irreparable choked me like the iron collar of the pillory. It seemed to me that I had failed in the task of life, and that now life was failing me. Ah! how terrible spring is to the lonely! All the needs which had been lulled to sleep start into life again, all the sorrows which had disappeared are reborn, and the old man which had been gagged and conquered rises once more and makes his groans heard. It is as though all the old wounds opened and bewailed themselves afresh. Just when one had ceased to think, when one had succeeded in deadening feeling by work or by amusement, all of a sudden the heart, solitary captive that it is, sends a cry from its prison depths, a cry which shakes to its foundations the whole surrounding edifice.

Even supposing that one had freed one's self from all other fatalities, there is still one yoke left from which it is impossible to escape—that of Time. I have succeeded in avoiding all other servitudes, but I had reckoned without the last—the servitude of age. Age comes, and its weight is equal to that of all other oppressions taken together. Man, under his mortal aspect, is but a species of ephemera.

As I looked at the banks of the Rhone, which have seen the river flowing past them some ten or twenty thousand years, or at the trees forming the avenue of the cemetery, which, for two centuries, have been the witnesses of so many funeral processions; as I recognized the walls, the dykes, the paths, which saw me playing as a child, and watched other children running over that grassy plain of Plain Palais which bore my own childish steps—I had the sharpest sense of the emptiness of life and the flight of things. I felt the shadow of the upas tree darkening over me. I gazed into the great implacable abyss in which are swallowed up all those phantoms which call themselves living beings. I saw that the living are but apparitions hovering for a moment over the earth, made out of the ashes of the dead, and swiftly re-absorbed by eternal night, as the will-o'-the-wisp sinks into the marsh. The nothingness of our joys, the emptiness of our existence, and the futility of our ambitions, filled me with a quiet disgust. From regret to disenchantment I floated on to Buddhism, to universal weariness. Ah, the hope of a blessed immortality would be better worth having!

With what different eyes one looks at life at ten, at twenty, at thirty, at sixty! Those who live alone are specially conscious of this psychological metamorphosis. Another thing, too, astonishes them; it is the universal conspiracy which exists for hiding the sadness of the world, for making men forget suffering, sickness, and death, for smothering the wails and sobs which issue from every house, for painting and beautifying the hideous face of reality. Is it out of tenderness for childhood and youth, or is it simply from fear, that we are thus careful to veil the sinister truth? Or is it from a sense of equity? and does life contain as much good as evil—perhaps more? However it may be, men feed themselves rather upon illusion than upon truth. Each one unwinds his own special reel of hope, and as soon as he has come to the end of it he sits him down to die, and lets his sons and his grandsons begin the same experience over again. We all pursue happiness, and happiness escapes the pursuit of all.

The only *viaticum* which can help us in the journey of life is that furnished by a great duty and some serious affections. And even affections die, or at least their objects are mortal; a friend, a wife, a child, a country, a church, may precede us in the tomb; duty alone lasts as long as we.

This maxim exorcises the spirits of revolt, of anger, discouragement, vengeance, indignation, and ambition, which rise one after another to tempt and trouble the heart, swelling with the sap of the spring. O all ye saints of the East, of antiquity, of Christianity, phalanx of heroes! Ye too drank deep of weariness and agony of soul, but ye triumphed over both. Ye who have come forth victors from the strife, shelter us under your palms, fortify us by your example!

April 6, 1869.—Magnificent weather. The Alps are dazzling under their silver haze. Sensations of all kinds have been crowding upon me; the delights of a walk under the rising sun, the charms of a wonderful view, longing for travel, and thirst for joy, hunger for work, for emotion, for life, dreams of happiness and of love. A passionate wish to live, to feel, to express, stirred the depths of my heart. It was a sudden re-awakening of youth, a flash of poetry, a renewing of the soul, a fresh growth of the wings of desire—I was overpowered by a host of conquering, vagabond, adventurous aspirations. I forgot my age, my obligations, my duties, my vexations, and youth leaped within me as though life were beginning again. It was as though something explosive had caught fire, and one's soul were scattered to the four winds; in such a mood one would fain devour the whole world, experience everything, see everything. Faust's ambition enters into one, universal desire—a horror of one's own prison cell. One throws off one's hair shirt, and one would fain gather the whole of nature into one's arms and heart. O ye passions, a ray of sunshine is enough to rekindle you all! The cold black mountain is a volcano once more, and melts its snowy crown with one single gust of flaming breath. It is the spring which brings about these sudden and improbable resurrections, the spring which, sending a thrill and tumult of life through all that lives, is the parent of impetuous desires, of overpowering inclinations, of unforeseen and inextinguishable outbursts of passion. It breaks through the rigid bark of the trees, and rends the mask on the face of asceticism; it makes the monk tremble in the shadow of his convent, the maiden behind the curtains of her room, the child sitting on his school bench, the old man bowed under his rheumatism.

Amiel's Journal

"O Hymen, Hymenae!"

April 24, 1869.—Is Nemesis indeed more real than Providence, the jealous God more true than the good God? grief more certain than joy? darkness more secure of victory than light? Is it pessimism or optimism which is nearest the truth, and which—Leibnitz or Schopenhauer—has best understood the universe? Is it the healthy man or the sick man who sees best to the bottom of things? which is in the right?

Ah! the problem of grief and evil is and will be always the greatest enigma of being, only second to the existence of being itself. The common faith of humanity has assumed the victory of good over evil. But if good consists not in the result of victory, but in victory itself, then good implies an incessant and infinite contest, interminable struggle, and a success forever threatened. And if this is life, is not Buddha right in regarding life as synonymous with evil since it means perpetual restlessness and endless war? Repose according to the Buddhist is only to be found in annihilation. The art of self-annihilation, of escaping the world's vast machinery of suffering, and the misery of renewed existence—the art of reaching Nirvana, is to him the supreme art, the only means of deliverance. The Christian says to God: Deliver us from evil. The Buddhist adds: And to that end deliver us from finite existence, give us back to nothingness! The first believes that when he is enfranchised from the body he will enter upon eternal happiness; the second believes that individuality is the obstacle to all repose, and he longs for the dissolution of the soul itself. The dread of the first is the paradise of the second.

One thing only is necessary—the committal of the soul to God. Look that thou thyself art in order, and leave to God the task of unraveling the skein of the world and of destiny. What do annihilation or immortality matter? What is to be, will be. And what will be, will be for the best. Faith in good—perhaps the individual wants nothing more for his passage through life. Only he must have taken sides with Socrates, Plato, Aristotle, and Zeno, against materialism, against the religion of accident and pessimism. Perhaps also he must make up his mind against the Buddhist nihilism, because a man's system of conduct is diametrically opposite according as he labors to increase his life or to lessen it, according as he aims at cultivating his faculties or at systematically deadening them.

To employ one's individual efforts for the increase of good in the world—this modest ideal is enough for us. To help forward the victory of good has been the common aim of saints and sages. *Socii Dei sumus* was the word of Seneca, who had it from Cleanthus.

April 30, 1869.—I have just finished Vacherot's [Footnote: Etienne Vacherot, a French philosophical writer, who owed his first successes in life to the friendship of Cousin, and was later brought very much into notice by his controversy with the Abbe Gratry, by the prosecution brought against him in consequence of his book, "La Democratie" (1859), and by his rejection at the hands of the Academy of Moral and Political Sciences in 1865, for the same kind of reasons which had brought about the exclusion of Littre in the preceding year. In 1868, however, he became a member of the Institute in succession to Cousin. A Liberal of the old school, he has separated himself from the republicans since the war, and has made himself felt as a severe critic of republican blunders in the *Revue des deux Mondes. La Religion*, which discusses the psychological origins of the religious sense, was published in 1868.] book "La Religion," 1869, and it has set me thinking. I have a feeling that his notion of religion is not rigorous and exact, and that therefore his logic is subject to correction. If religion is a psychological stage, anterior to that of reason, it is clear that it will disappear in man, but if, on the contrary, it is a mode of the inner life, it may and must last, as long as the need of feeling, and alongside the need of thinking. The question is between theism and non-theism. If God is only the category of the ideal, religion will vanish, of course, like the illusions of youth. But if Universal Being can be felt and loved at the same time as conceived, the philosopher may be a religious man just as he may be an artist, an orator, or a citizen. He may attach himself to a worship or ritual without derogation. I myself incline to this solution. To me religion is life before God and in God.

And even if God were defined as the universal life, so long as this life is positive and not negative, the soul penetrated with the sense of the infinite is in the religious state. Religion differs from philosophy as the simple and spontaneous self differs from the reflecting self, as synthetic intuition differs from intellectual analysis. We are initiated into the religious state by a sense of voluntary dependence on, and joyful submission to the principle of order and of goodness. Religious emotion makes man conscious of himself; he finds his own place within the infinite unity, and it is this perception which is sacred.

But in spite of these reservations I am much impressed by the book, which is a fine piece of work, ripe and serious in all respects.

May 13, 1869.—A break in the clouds, and through the blue interstices a bright sun throws flickering and uncertain rays. Storms, smiles, whims, anger, tears—it is May, and nature is in its feminine phase! She pleases our fancy, stirs our heart, and wears out our reason by the endless succession of her caprices and the unexpected violence of her whims.

This recalls to me the 213th verse of the second book of the Laws of Manou. "It is in the nature of the feminine sex to seek here below to corrupt men, and therefore wise men never abandon themselves to the seductions of women." The same code, however, says: "Wherever women are honored the gods are satisfied." And again: "In every family where the husband takes pleasure in his wife, and the wife in her husband, happiness is ensured." And again: "One mother is more venerable than a thousand fathers." But knowing what stormy and irrational elements there are in this fragile and delightful creature, Manou concludes: "At no age ought a woman to be allowed to govern herself as she pleases."

Up to the present day, in several contemporary and neighboring codes, a woman is a minor all her life. Why? Because of her dependence upon nature, and of her subjection to passions which are the diminutives of madness; in other words, because the soul of a woman has something obscure and mysterious in it, which lends itself to all superstitions and weakens the energies of man. To man belong law, justice, science, and philosophy, all that is disinterested, universal, and rational. Women, on the contrary, introduce into everything favor, exception, and personal prejudice. As soon as a man, a people, a literature, an epoch, become feminine in type, they sink in the scale of things. As soon as a woman quits the state of subordination in which her merits have free play, we see a rapid increase in her natural defects. Complete equality with man makes her quarrelsome; a position of supremacy makes her tyrannical. To honor her and to govern her will be for a long time yet the best solution. When education has formed strong, noble, and serious women in whom conscience and reason hold sway over the effervescence of fancy and sentimentality, then we shall be able not only to honor woman, but to make a serious end of gaining her consent and adhesion. Then she will be truly an equal, a work-fellow, a companion. At present she is so only in theory. The moderns are at work upon the problem, and have not solved it yet.

June 15, 1869.—The great defect of liberal Christianity [Footnote: At this period the controversy between the orthodox party and "Liberal Christianity" was at its height, both in Geneva and throughout Switzerland.] is that its conception of holiness is a frivolous one, or, what comes to the same thing, its conception of sin is a superficial one. The defects of the baser sort of political liberalism recur in liberal Christianity; it is only half serious, and its theology is too much mixed with worldliness. The sincerely pious folk look upon the liberals as persons whose talk is rather profane, and who offend religious feelings by making sacred subjects a theme for rhetorical display. They shock the *convenances* of sentiment, and affront the delicacy of conscience by the indiscreet familiarities they take with the great mysteries of the inner life. They seem to be mere clever special pleaders, religious rhetoricians like the Greek sophists, rather than guides in the narrow road which leads to salvation.

It is not to the clever folk, nor even to the scientific folk, that the empire over souls belongs, but to those who impress us as having conquered nature by grace, passed through the burning bush, and as speaking, not the language of human wisdom, but that of the divine will. In religious matters it is holiness which gives authority; it is love, or the power of devotion and sacrifice, which goes to the heart, which moves and persuades.

What all religious, poetical, pure, and tender souls are least able to pardon is the diminution or degradation of their ideal. We must never rouse an ideal against us; our business is to point men to another ideal, purer, higher, more spiritual than the old, and so to raise behind a lofty summit one more lofty still. In this way no one is despoiled; we gain men's confidence, while at the same time forcing them to think, and enabling those minds which are already tending toward change to perceive new objects and goals for thought. Only that which is replaced is destroyed, and an ideal is only replaced by satisfying the conditions of the old with some advantages over.

Let the liberal Protestants offer us a spectacle of Christian virtue of a holier, intenser, and more intimate kind than before; let us see it active in their persons and in their influence, and they will have furnished the proof demanded by the Master; the tree will be judged by its fruits.

Amiel's Journal

* * * * *

June 22, 1869 (*Nine* A. M).—Gray and lowering weather. A fly lies dead of cold on the page of my book, in full summer! What is life? I said to myself, as I looked at the tiny dead creature. It is a loan, as movement is. The universal life is a sum total, of which the units are visible here, there, and everywhere, just as an electric wheel throws off sparks along its whole surface. Life passes through us; we do not possess it. Hirn admits three ultimate principles: [Footnote: Gustave-Adolphe Hirn, a French physicist, born near Colmar, 1815, became a corresponding member of the Academy of Sciences in 1867. The book of his to which Amiel refers is no doubt *Consequences philosophiques at metaphysiques de la thermodynamique, Analyse elementaire de l'univers* (1869).] the atom, the force, the soul; the force which acts upon atoms, the soul which acts upon force. Probably he distinguishes between anonymous souls and personal souls. Then my fly would be an anonymous soul.

(*Same day*).—The national churches are all up in arms against so-called Liberal Christianity; Basle and Zurich began the fight, and now Geneva has entered the lists too. Gradually it is becoming plain that historical Protestantism has no longer a *raison d'etre* between pure liberty and pure authority. It is, in fact, a provisional stage, founded on the worship of the Bible—that is to say, on the idea of a written revelation, and of a book divinely inspired, and therefore authoritative. When once this thesis has been relegated to the rank of a fiction Protestantism crumbles away. There is nothing for it but to retire up on natural religion, or the religion of the moral consciousness. M.M. Reville, Conquerel, Fontanes, Buisson, [Footnote: The name of M. Albert Reville, the French Protestant theologian, is more or less familiar in England, especially since his delivery of the Hibbert lectures in 1884. Athanase Coquerel, born 1820, died 1876, the well-known champion of liberal ideas in the French Protestant Church, was suspended from his pastoral functions by the Consistory of Paris, on account of his review of M. Renan's "Vie de Jesus" in 1864. Ferdinand-Edouard Buisson, a liberal Protestant, originally a professor at Lausanne, was raised to the important function of Director of Primary Instruction by M. Ferry in 1879. He was denounced by Bishop Dupanloup, in the National Assembly of 1871, as the author of certain liberal pamphlets on the dangers connected with Scripture-teaching in schools, and, for the time, lost his employment under the Ministry of Education.] accept this logical outcome. They are the advance-guard of Protestantism and the laggards of free thought.

Their mistake is not seeing that all institutions rest upon a legal fiction, and that every living thing involves a logical absurdity. It may be logical to demand a church based on free examination and absolute sincerity; but to realize it is a different matter. A church lives by what is positive, and this positive element necessarily limits investigation. People confound the right of the individual, which is to be free, with the duty of the institution, which is to be something. They take the principle of science to be the same as the principle of the church, which is a mistake. They will not see that religion is different from philosophy, and that the one seeks union by faith, while the other upholds the solitary independence of thought. That the bread should be good it must have leaven; but the leaven is not the bread. Liberty is the means whereby we arrive at an enlightened faith—granted; but an assembly of people agreeing only upon this criterion and this method could not possibly found a church, for they might differ completely as to the results of the method. Suppose a newspaper the writers of which were of all possible parties—it would no doubt be a curiosity in journalism, but it would have no opinions, no faith, no creed. A drawing-room filled with refined people, carrying on polite discussion, is not a church, and a dispute, however courteous, is not worship. It is a mere confusion of kinds.

July 13, 1869.—Lamennais, Heine—the one the victim of a mistaken vocation, the other of a tormenting craving to astonish and mystify his kind. The first was wanting in common sense; the second was wanting in seriousness. The Frenchman was violent, arbitrary, domineering; the German was a jesting Mephistopheles, with a horror of Philistinism. The Breton was all passion and melancholy; the Hamburger all fancy and satire. Neither developed freely nor normally. Both of them, because of an initial mistake, threw themselves into an endless quarrel with the world. Both were revolutionists. They were not fighting for the good cause, for impersonal truth; both were rather the champions of their own pride. Both suffered greatly, and died isolated, repudiated, and reviled. Men of magnificent talents, both of them, but men of small wisdom, who did more harm than good to themselves and to others! It is a lamentable existence which wears itself out in maintaining a first antagonism, or a first blunder. The greater a man's intellectual power, the more dangerous is it for him to make a false start and to begin life badly.

July 20, 1869.—I have been reading over again five or six chapters, here and there, of Renan's "St. Paul." Analyzed to the bottom, the writer is a freethinker, but a free thinker whose flexible imagination still allows him the delicate epicurism of religious emotion. In his eyes the man who will not lend himself to these graceful fancies is vulgar, and the man who takes them seriously is prejudiced. He is entertained by the variations of conscience, but he is too clever to laugh at them. The true critic neither concludes nor excludes; his pleasure is to understand without believing, and to profit by the results of enthusiasm, while still maintaining a free mind, unembarrassed by illusion. Such a mode of proceeding has a look of dishonesty; it is nothing, however, but the good-tempered irony of a highly-cultivated mind, which will neither be ignorant of anything nor duped by anything. It is the dilettantism of the Renaissance in its perfection. At the same time what innumerable proofs of insight and of exultant scientific power!

August 14, 1869.—In the name of heaven, who art thou? what wilt thou—wavering inconstant creature? What future lies before thee? What duty or what hope appeals to thee?

My longing, my search is for love, for peace, for something to fill my heart; an idea to defend; a work to which I might devote the rest of my strength; an affection which might quench this inner thirst; a cause for which I might die with joy. But shall I ever find them? I long for all that is impossible and inaccessible: for true religion, serious sympathy, the ideal life; for paradise, immortality, holiness, faith, inspiration, and I know not what besides! What I really want is to die and to be born again, transformed myself, and in a different world. And I can neither stifle these aspirations nor deceive myself as to the possibility of satisfying them. I seem condemned to roll forever the rock of Sisyphus, and to feel that slow wearing away of the mind which befalls the man whose vocation and destiny are in perpetual conflict. "A Christian heart and a pagan head," like Jacobi; tenderness and pride; width of mind and feebleness of will; the two men of St. Paul; a seething chaos of contrasts, antinomies, and contradictions; humility and pride; childish simplicity and boundless mistrust; analysis and intuition; patience and irritability; kindness and dryness of heart; carelessness and anxiety; enthusiasm and languor; indifference and passion; altogether a being incomprehensible and intolerable to myself and to others!

Then from a state of conflict I fall back into the fluid, vague, indeterminate state, which feels all form to be a mere violence and disfigurement. All ideas, principles, acquirements, and habits are effaced in me like the ripples on a wave, like the convolutions of a cloud. My personality has the least possible admixture of individuality. I am to the great majority of men what the circle is to rectilinear figures; I am everywhere at home, because I have no particular and nominative self. Perhaps, on the whole, this defect has good in it. Though I am less of *a* man, I am perhaps nearer to *the* man; perhaps rather more *man*. There is less of the individual, but more of the species, in me. My nature, which is absolutely unsuited for practical life, shows great aptitude for psychological study. It prevents me from taking sides, but it allows me to understand all sides. It is not only indolence which prevents me from drawing conclusions; it is a sort of a secret aversion to all *intellectual proscription*. I have a feeling that something of everything is wanted to make a world, that all citizens have a right in the state, and that if every opinion is equally insignificant in itself, all opinions have some hold upon truth. To live and let live, think and let think, are maxims which are equally dear to me. My tendency is always to the whole, to the totality, to the general balance of things. What is difficult to me is to exclude, to condemn, to say no; except, indeed, in the presence of the exclusive. I am always fighting for the absent, for the defeated cause, for that portion of truth which seems to me neglected; my aim is to complete every thesis, to see round every problem, to study a thing from all its possible sides. Is this skepticism? Yes, in its result, but not in its purpose. It is rather the sense of the absolute and the infinite reducing to their proper value and relegating to their proper place the finite and the relative. But here, in the same way, my ambition is greater than my power; my philosophical perception is superior to my speculative gift. I have not the energy of my opinions; I have far greater width than inventiveness of thought, and, from timidity, I have allowed the critical intelligence in me to swallow up the creative genius. Is it indeed from timidity?

Alas! with a little more ambition, or a little more good luck, a different man might have been made out of me, and such as my youth gave promise of.

August 16, 1869.—I have been thinking over Schopenhauer. It has struck me and almost terrified me to see how well I represent Schopenhauer's typical man, for whom "happiness is a chimera and suffering a reality," for whom "the negation of will and of desire is the only road to deliverance," and "the individual life is a misfortune from which impersonal contemplation is the only enfranchisement," etc. But the principle that life is an evil and annihilation a good lies at the root of the system, and this axiom I have never dared to enunciate in any general way, although I have admitted it here and there in individual cases. What I still like in the misanthrope of Frankfort, is his antipathy to current prejudice, to European hobbies, to western hypocrisies, to the successes of the day. Schopenhauer is a man of powerful mind, who has put away from him all illusions, who professes Buddhism in the full flow of modern Germany, and absolute detachment of mind In the very midst of the nineteenth-century orgie. His great defects are barrenness of soul, a proud and perfect selfishness, an adoration of genius which is combined with complete indifference to the rest of the world, in spite of all his teaching of resignation and sacrifice. He has no sympathy, no humanity, no love. And here I recognize the unlikeness between us. Pure intelligence and solitary labor might easily lead me to his point of view; but once appeal to the heart, and I feel the contemplative attitude untenable. Pity, goodness, charity, and devotion reclaim their rights, and insist even upon the first place.

August 29, 1869.—Schopenhauer preaches impersonality, objectivity, pure contemplation, the negation of will, calmness, and disinterestedness, an aesthetic study of the world, detachment from life, the renunciation of all desire, solitary meditation, disdain of the crowd, and indifference to all that the vulgar covet. He approves all my defects, my childishness, my aversion to practical life, my antipathy to the utilitarians, my distrust of all desire. In a word, he flatters all my instincts; he caresses and justifies them.

This pre-established harmony between the theory of Schopenhauer and my own natural man causes me pleasure mingled with terror. I might indulge myself in the pleasure, but that I fear to delude and stifle conscience. Besides, I feel that goodness has no tolerance for this contemplative indifference, and that virtue consists in self-conquest.

August 30, 1869.—Still some chapters of Schopenhauer. Schopenhauer believes in the unchangeableness of innate tendencies in the individual, and in the invariability of the primitive disposition. He refuses to believe in the new man, in any real progress toward perfection, or in any positive improvement in a human being. Only the appearances are refined; there is no change below the surface.

Perhaps he confuses temperament, character, and individuality? I incline to think that individuality is fatal and primitive, that temperament reaches far back, but is alternable, and that character is more recent and susceptible of voluntary or involuntary modifications. Individuality is a matter of psychology, temperament, a matter of sensation or aesthetics; character alone is a matter of morals. Liberty and the use of it count for nothing in the first two elements of our being; character is a historical fruit, and the result of a man's biography. For Schopenhauer, character is identified with temperament just as will with passion. In short, he simplifies too much, and looks at man from that more elementary point of view which is only sufficient in the case of the animal. That spontaneity which is vital or merely chemical he already calls will. Analogy is not equation; a comparison is not reason; similes and parables are not exact language. Many of Schopenhauer's originalities evaporate when we come to translate them into a more close and precise terminology.

Later.—One has merely to turn over the "Lichtstrahlem" of Herder to feel the difference between him and Schopenhauer. The latter is full of marked features and of observations which stand out from the page and leave a clear and vivid impression. Herder is much less of a writer; his ideas are entangled in his style, and he has no brilliant condensations, no jewels, no crystals. While he proceeds by streams and sheets of thought which have no definite or individual outline, Schopenhauer breaks the current of his speculation with islands, striking, original, and picturesque, which engrave themselves in the memory. It is the same difference as there is between Nicole and Pascal, between Bayle and Satin-Simon.

What is the faculty which gives relief, brilliancy, and incisiveness to thought? Imagination. Under its influence expression becomes concentrated, colored, and strengthened, and by the power it has of individualizing all it touches, it gives life and permanence to the material on which it works. A writer of genius changes sand into glass and glass into crystal, ore into iron and iron into steel; he marks with his own stamp every idea he gets hold of. He borrows much from the common stock, and gives back nothing; but even his robberies are willingly reckoned to him as private property. He has, as it were, *carte blanche*, and public opinion allows him to take what he will.

August 31, 1869.—I have finished Schopenhauer. My mind has been a tumult of opposing systems—Stoicism, Quietism, Buddhism, Christianity. Shall I never be at peace with myself? If impersonality is a good, why am I not consistent in the pursuit of it? and if it is a temptation, why return to it, after having judged and conquered it?

Is happiness anything more than a conventional fiction? The deepest reason for my state of doubt is that the supreme end and aim of life seems to me a mere lure and deception. The individual is an eternal dupe, who never obtains what he seeks, and who is forever deceived by hope. My instinct is in harmony with the pessimism of Buddha and of Schopenhauer. It is a doubt which never leaves me even in my moments of religious fervor. Nature is indeed for me a Maia; and I look at her, as it were, with the eyes of an artist. My intelligence remains skeptical. What, then, do I believe in? I do not know. And what is it I hope for? It would be difficult to say. Folly! I believe in goodness, and I hope that good will prevail. Deep within this ironical and disappointed being of mine there is a child hidden—a frank, sad, simple creature, who believes in the ideal, in love, in holiness, and all heavenly superstitions. A whole millennium of idylls sleeps in my heart; I am a pseudo-skeptic, a pseudo-scoffer.

"Borne dans sa nature, infini dans ses voeux, L'homme est un dieu tombe qui se souvient des cieux."

October 14, 1869.—Yesterday, Wednesday, death of Sainte-Beuve. What a loss!

October 16, 1869.—*Laboremus* seems to have been the motto of Sainte-Beuve, as it was that of Septimius Severus. He died in harness, and up to the evening before his last day he still wrote, overcoming the sufferings of the body by the energy of the mind. To-day, at this very moment, they are laying him in the bosom of mother earth. He refused the sacraments of the church; he never belonged to any confession; he was one of the "great diocese"—that of the independent seekers of truth, and he allowed himself no final moment of hypocrisy. He would have nothing to do with any one except God only—or rather the mysterious Isis beyond the veil. Being unmarried, he died in the arms of his secretary. He was sixty-five years old. His power of work and of memory was immense and intact. What is Scherer thinking about this life and this death?

October 19, 1869.—An admirable article by Edmond Scherer on Sainte-Beuve in the *Temps*. He makes him the prince of French critics and the last representative of the epoch of literary taste, the future belonging to the bookmakers and the chatterers, to mediocrity and to violence. The article breathes a certain manly melancholy, befitting a funeral oration over one who was a master in the things of the mind. The fact is, that Sainte-Beuve leaves a greater void behind him than either Beranger or Lamartine; their greatness was already distant, historical; he was still helping us to think. The true critic acts as a fulcrum for all the world. He represents the public judgment, that is to say the public reason, the touchstone, the scales, the refining rod, which tests the value of every one and the merit of every work. Infallibility of judgment is perhaps rarer than anything else, so fine a balance of qualities does it demand—qualities both natural and acquired, qualities of mind and heart. What years of labor, what study and comparison, are needed to bring the critical judgment to maturity! Like Plato's sage, it is only at fifty that the critic rises to the true height of his literary priesthood, or, to put it less pompously, of his social function. By then only can he hope for insight into all the modes of being, and for mastery of all possible shades of appreciation. And Sainte-Beuve joined to this infinitely refined culture a prodigious memory, and an incredible multitude of facts and anecdotes stored up for the service of his thought.

December 8, 1869.—Everything has chilled me this morning; the cold of the season, the physical immobility around me, but, above all, Hartman's "Philosophy of the Unconscious." This book lays down the terrible thesis that creation is a mistake; being, such as it is, is not as good as non-being, and death is better than life.

I felt the same mournful impression that Obermann left upon me in my youth. The black melancholy of Buddhism encompassed and overshadowed me. If, in fact, it is only illusion which hides from us the horror of existence and makes life tolerable to us, then existence is a snare and life an evil. Like the Greek Annikeris, we ought to counsel suicide, or rather with Buddha and Schopenhauer we ought to labor for the radical extirpation of hope and desire—the causes of life and resurrection. *Not* to rise again; there is the point, and there is the difficulty. Death is simply a beginning again, whereas it is annihilation that we have to aim at. Personal consciousness being the root of all our troubles, we ought to avoid the temptation to it and the possibility of it as diabolical and abominable. What blasphemy! And yet it is all logical; it is the philosophy of happiness carried to its farthest point. Epicurism must end in despair. The philosophy of duty is less depressing. But salvation lies in the conciliation of duty and happiness, in the union of the individual will with the divine will, and in the faith that this supreme will is directed by love.

* * * * *

It is as true that real happiness is good, as that the good become better under the purification of trial. Those who have not suffered are still wanting in depth; but a man who has not got happiness cannot impart it. We can only give what we have. Happiness, grief, gayety, sadness, are by nature contagious. Bring your health and your strength to the weak and sickly, and so you will be of use to them. Give them, not your weakness, but your energy, so you will revive and lift them up. Life alone can rekindle life. What others claim from us is not our thirst and our hunger, but our bread and our gourd.

The benefactors of humanity are those who have thought great thoughts about her; but her masters and her idols are those who have flattered and despised her, those who have muzzled and massacred her, inflamed her with fanaticism or used her for selfish purposes. Her benefactors are the poets, the artists, the inventors, the apostles and all pure hearts. Her masters are the Caesars, the Constantines, the Gregory VII.'s, the Innocent III.'s, the Borgias, the Napoleons.

* * * * *

Every civilization is, as it were, a dream of a thousand years, in which heaven and earth, nature and history, appear to men illumined by fantastic light and representing a drama which is nothing but a projection of the soul itself, influenced by some intoxication—I was going to say hallucination—or other. Those who are widest awake still see the real world across the dominant illusion of their race or time. And the reason is that the deceiving light starts from our own mind: the light is our religion. Everything changes with it. It is religion which gives to our kaleidoscope, if not the material of the figures, at least their color, their light and shade, and general aspect. Every religion makes men see the world and humanity under a special light; it is a mode of apperception, which can only be scientifically handled when we have cast it aside, and can only be judged when we have replaced it by a better.

Amiel's Journal

* * * * *

February 23, 1870.—There is in man an instinct of revolt, an enemy of all law, a rebel which will stoop to no yoke, not even that of reason, duty, and wisdom. This element in us is the root of all sin—*das radicale Boese* of Kant. The independence which is the condition of individuality is at the same time the eternal temptation of the individual. That which makes us beings makes us also sinners.

Sin is, then, in our very marrow. It circulates in us like the blood in our veins, it is mingled with all our substance, [Footnote: This is one of the passages which rouses M. Renan's wonder: "Voila la grande difference," he writes, "entre l'education catholique et l'education protestante. Ceux qui comme moi ont recu une education catholique en ont garde de profonds vestiges. Mais ces vestiges ne sont pas des dogmes, ce sont des reves. Une fois ce grand rideau de drap d'or, bariole de soie, d'indienne et de calicot, par lequel le catholicisme nous masque la vue du monde, une fois, dis-je ce rideau dechire, on voit l'univers en sa splendeur infinie, la nature en sa haute et pleine majeste. Le protestant le plus libre garde souvent quelque chose de triste, un fond d'austerite intellectuelle analogue au pessimisme slave."—(*Journal des Debats*, September 30, 1884).

One is reminded of Mr. Morley's criticism of Emerson. Emerson, he points out, has almost nothing to say of death, and "little to say of that horrid burden and impediment on the soul which the churches call sin, and which, by whatever name we call it, is a very real catastrophe in the moral nature of man—the courses of nature, and the prodigious injustices of mail in society affect him with neither horror nor awe. He will see no monster if he can help it."

Here, then, we have the eternal difference between the two orders of temperament—the men whose overflowing energy forbids them to realize the ever-recurring defeat of the human spirit at the hands of circumstance, like Renan and Emerson, and the men for whom "horror and awe" are interwoven with experience, like Amiel.] Or rather I am wrong: temptation is our natural state, but sin is not necessary. Sin consists in the voluntary confusion of the independence which is good with the independence which is bad; it is caused by the half-indulgence granted to a first sophism. We shut our eyes to the beginnings of evil because they are small, and in this weakness is contained the germ of our defeat. *Principiis obsta*—this maxim dutifully followed would preserve us from almost all our catastrophes.

We will have no other master but our caprice—that is to say, our evil self will have no God, and the foundation of our nature is seditious, impious, insolent, refractory, opposed to, and contemptuous of all that tries to rule it, and therefore contrary to order, ungovernable and negative. It is this foundation which Christianity calls the natural man. But the savage which is within us, and constitutes the primitive stuff of us, must be disciplined and civilized in order to produce a man. And the man must be patiently cultivated to produce a wise man, and the wise man must be tested and tried if he is to become righteous. And the righteous man must have substituted the will of God for his individual will, if he is to become a saint. And this new man, this regenerate being, is the spiritual man, the heavenly man, of which the Vedas speak as well as the gospel, and the Magi as well as the Neo-Platonists.

March 17, 1870.—This morning the music of a brass band which had stopped under my windows moved me almost to tears. It exercised an indefinable, nostalgic power over me; it set me dreaming of another world, of infinite passion and supreme happiness. Such impressions are the echoes of paradise in the soul; memories of ideal spheres, whose sad sweetness ravishes and intoxicates the heart. O Plato! O Pythagoras! ages ago you heard these harmonies—surprised these moments of inward ecstacy—knew these divine transports! If music thus carries us to heaven, it is because music is harmony, harmony is perfection, perfection is our dream, and our dream is heaven. This world of quarrels and bitterness, of selfishness, ugliness, and misery, makes us long involuntarily for the eternal peace, for the adoration which has no limits, and the love which has no end. It is not so much the infinite as the beautiful that we yearn for. It is not being, or the limits of being, which weigh upon us; it is evil, in us and without us. It is not all necessary to be great, so long as we are in harmony with the order of the universe. Moral ambition has no pride; it only desires to fill its place, and make its note duly heard in the universal concert of the God of love.

March 30, 1870.—Certainly, nature is unjust and shameless, without probity, and without faith. Her only alternatives are gratuitous favor or mad aversion, and her only way of redressing an injustice is to commit another. The happiness of the few is expiated by the misery of the greater number. It is useless to accuse a blind force.

The human conscience, however, revolts against this law of nature, and to satisfy its own instinct of justice it has imagined two hypotheses, out of which it has made for itself a religion—the idea of an individual providence, and the hypothesis of another life.

In these we have a protest against nature, which is thus declared immoral and scandalous to the moral sense. Man believes in good, and that he may ground himself on justice he maintains that the injustice all around him is but an appearance, a mystery, a cheat, and that justice *will* be done. *Fiat justitia, pereal mundus!*

It is a great act of faith. And since humanity has not made itself, this protest has some chance of expressing a truth. If there is conflict between the natural world and the moral world, between reality and conscience, conscience must be right.

It is by no means necessary that the universe should exist, but it is necessary that justice should be done, and atheism is bound to explain the fixed obstinacy of conscience on this point. Nature is not just; we are the products of nature: why are we always claiming and prophesying justice? why does the effect rise up against its cause? It is a singular phenomenon. Does the protest come from any puerile blindness of human vanity? No, it is the deepest cry of our being, and it is for the honor of God that the cry is uttered. Heaven and earth may pass away, but good *ought* to be, and injustice ought *not* to be. Such is the creed of the human race. Nature will be conquered by spirit; the eternal will triumph over time.

April 1, 1870.—I am inclined to believe that for a woman love is the supreme authority—that which judges the rest and decides what is good or evil. For a man, love is subordinate to right. It is a great passion, but it is not the source of order, the synonym of reason, the criterion of excellence. It would seem, then, that a woman places her ideal in the perfection of love, and a man in the perfection of justice. It was in this sense that St. Paul was able to say, "The woman is the glory of the man, and the man is the glory of God." Thus the woman who absorbs herself in the object of her love is, so to speak, in the line of nature; she is truly woman, she realizes her fundamental type. On the contrary, the man who should make life consist in conjugal adoration, and who should imagine that he has lived sufficiently when he has made himself the priest of a beloved woman, such a one is but half a man; he is despised by the world, and perhaps secretly disdained by women themselves. The woman who loves truly seeks to merge her own individuality in that of the man she loves. She desires that her love should make him greater, stronger, more masculine, and more active. Thus each sex plays its appointed part: the woman is first destined for man, and man is destined for society. Woman owes herself to one, man owes himself to all; and each obtains peace and happiness only when he or she has recognized this law and accepted this balance of things. The same thing may be a good in the woman and an evil in the man, may be strength in her, weakness in him.

There is then a feminine and a masculine morality—preparatory chapters, as it were, to a general human morality. Below the virtue which is evangelical and sexless, there is a virtue of sex. And this virtue of sex is the occasion of mutual teaching, for each of the two incarnations of virtue makes it its business to convert the other, the first preaching love in the ears of justice, the second justice in the ears of love. And so there is produced an oscillation and an average which represent a social state, an epoch, sometimes a whole civilization.

Such at least is our European idea of the harmony of the sexes in a graduated order of functions. America is on the road to revolutionize this ideal by the introduction of the democratic principle of the equality of individuals in a general equality of functions. Only, when there is nothing left but a multitude of equal individualities, neither young nor old, neither men nor women, neither benefited nor benefactors—all social difference will turn upon money. The whole hierarchy will rest upon the dollar, and the most brutal, the most hideous, the most inhuman of inequalities will be the fruit of the passion for equality. What a result! Plutolatry—the worship of wealth, the madness of gold—to it will be confided the task of chastising a false principle and its followers. And plutocracy will be in its turn executed by equality. It would be a strange end for it, if Anglo-Saxon individualism were ultimately swallowed up in Latin socialism.

It is my prayer that the discovery of an equilibrium between the two principles may be made in time, before the social war, with all its terror and ruin, overtakes us. But it is scarcely likely. The masses are always ignorant and limited, and only advance by a succession of contrary errors. They reach good only by the exhaustion of evil. They discover the way out, only after having run their heads against all other possible issues.

Amiel's Journal

April 15, 1870.—*Crucifixion!* That is the word we have to meditate today. Is it not Good Friday?

To curse grief is easier than to bless it, but to do so is to fall back into the point of view of the earthly, the carnal, the natural man. By what has Christianity subdued the world if not by the apotheosis of grief, by its marvelous transmutation of suffering into triumph, of the crown of thorns into the crown of glory, and of a gibbet into a symbol of salvation? What does the apotheosis of the Cross mean, if not the death of death, the defeat of sin, the beatification of martyrdom, the raising to the skies of voluntary sacrifice, the defiance of pain? "O Death, where is thy sting? O Grave, where is thy victory?" By long brooding over this theme—the agony of the just, peace in the midst of agony, and the heavenly beauty of such peace—humanity came to understand that a new religion was born—a new mode, that is to say, of explaining life and of understanding suffering.

Suffering was a curse from which man fled; now it becomes a purification of the soul, a sacred trial sent by eternal love, a divine dispensation meant to sanctify and ennoble us, an acceptable aid to faith, a strange initiation into happiness. O power of belief! All remains the same, and yet all is changed. A new certitude arises to deny the apparent and the tangible; it pierces through the mystery of things, it places an invisible Father behind visible nature, it shows us joy shining through tears, and makes of pain the beginning of joy.

And so, for those who have believed, the tomb becomes heaven, and on the funeral pyre of life they sing the hosanna of immortality; a sacred madness has renewed the face of the world for them, and when they wish to explain what they feel, their ecstasy makes them incomprehensible; they speak with tongues. A wild intoxication of self-sacrifice, contempt for death, the thirst for eternity, the delirium of love—these are what the unalterable gentleness of the Crucified has had power to bring forth. By his pardon of his executioners, and by that unconquerable sense in him of an indissoluble union with God, Jesus, on his cross, kindled an inextinguishable fire and revolutionized the world. He proclaimed and realized salvation by faith in the infinite mercy, and in the pardon granted to simple repentance. By his saying, "There is more joy in heaven over one sinner that repenteth than over ninety and nine just persons who need no repentance," he made humility the gate of entrance into paradise.

Crucify the rebellious self, mortify yourself wholly, give up all to God, and the peace which is not of this world will descend upon you. For eighteen centuries no grander word has been spoken; and although humanity is forever seeking after a more exact and complete application of justice, yet her secret faith is not in justice but in pardon, for pardon alone conciliates the spotless purity of perfection with the infinite pity due to weakness—that is to say, it alone preserves and defends the Idea of holiness, while it allows full scope to that of love. The gospel proclaims the ineffable consolation, the good news, which disarms all earthly griefs, and robs even death of its terrors—the news of irrevocable pardon, that is to say, of eternal life. The Cross is the guarantee of the gospel.

Therefore it has been its standard.

May 7, 1870.—The faith which clings to its idols and resists all innovation is a retarding and conservative force; but it is the property of all religion to serve as a curb to our lawless passion for freedom, and to steady and quiet our restlessness of temper. Curiosity is the expansive force, which, if it were allowed an unchecked action upon us, would disperse and volatilize us; belief represents the force of gravitation and cohesion which makes separate bodies and individuals of us. Society lives by faith, develops by science. Its basis then is the mysterious, the unknown, the intangible—religion—while the fermenting principle in it is the desire of knowledge. Its permanent substance is the uncomprehended or the divine; its changing form is the result of its intellectual labor. The unconscious adhesions, the confused intuitions, the obscure presentiments, which decide the first faith of a people, are then of capital importance in its history. All history moves between the religion which is the genial instinctive and fundamental philosophy of a race, and the philosophy which is the ultimate religion—the clear perception, that is to say, of those principles which have engendered the whole spiritual development of humanity.

It is always the same thing which is, which was, and which will be; but this thing—the absolute—betrays with more or less transparency and profundity the law of its life and of its metamorphoses. In its fixed aspect it is called God; in its mobile aspect the world or nature. God is present in nature, but nature is not God; there is a nature in God, but it is not God himself. I am neither for immanence nor for transcendence taken alone.

May 9, 1870.—Disraeli, in his new novel, "Lothair," shows that the two great forces of the present are Revolution and Catholicism, and that the free nations are lost if either of these two forces triumphs. It is exactly my own idea. Only, while in France, in Belgium, in Italy, and in all Catholic societies, it is only by checking one of these forces by the other that the state and civilization can be maintained, the Protestant countries are better off; in them there is a third force, a middle faith between the two other idolatries, which enables them to regard liberty not as a neutralization of two contraries, but as a moral reality, self-subsistent, and possessing its own center of gravity and motive force. In the Catholic world religion and liberty exclude each other. In the Protestant world they accept each other, so that in the second case there is a smaller waste of force.

Liberty is the lay, the philosophical principle. It expresses the juridical and social aspiration of the race. But as there is no society possible without regulation, without control, without limitations on individual liberty, above all without moral limitations, the peoples which are legally the freest do well to take their religious consciousness for check and ballast. In mixed states, Catholic or free-thinking, the limit of action, being a merely penal one, invites incessant contravention.

The puerility of the freethinkers consists in believing that a free society can maintain itself and keep itself together without a common faith, without a religious prejudice of some kind. Where lies the will of God? Is it the common reason which expresses it, or rather, are a clergy or a church the depositories of it? So long as the response is ambiguous and equivocal in the eyes of half or the majority of consciences—and this is the case in all Catholic states—public peace is impossible, and public law is insecure. If there is a God, we must have him on our side, and if there is not a God, it would be necessary first of all to convert everybody to the same idea of the lawful and the useful, to reconstitute, that is to say, a lay religion, before anything politically solid could be built.

Liberalism is merely feeding upon abstractions, when it persuades itself that liberty is possible without free individuals, and when it will not recognize that liberty in the individual is the fruit of a foregoing education, a moral education, which presupposes a liberating religion. To preach liberalism to a population jesuitized by education, is to press the pleasures of dancing upon a man who has lost a leg. How is it possible for a child who has never been out of swaddling clothes to walk? How can the abdication of individual conscience lead to the government of individual conscience? To be free, is to guide one's self, to have attained one's majority, to be emancipated, master of one's actions, and judge of good and evil; but ultramontane Catholicism never emancipates its disciples, who are bound to admit, to believe, and to obey, as they are told, because they are minors in perpetuity, and the clergy alone possess the law of right, the secret of justice, and the measure of truth. This is what men are landed in by the idea of an exterior revelation, cleverly made use of by a patient priesthood.

But what astonishes me is the short-sight of the statesmen of the south, who do not see that the question of questions is the religious question, and even now do not recognize that a liberal state is wholly incompatible with an anti-liberal religion, and almost equally incompatible with the absence of religion. They confound accidental conquests and precarious progress with lasting results.

There is some probability that all this noise which is made nowadays about liberty may end in the suppression of liberty; it is plain that the internationals, the irreconcilables, and the ultramontanes, are, all three of them, aiming at absolutism, at dictatorial omnipotence. Happily they are not one but many, and it will not be difficult to turn them against each other.

If liberty is to be saved, it will not be by the doubters, the men of science, or the materialists; it will be by religious conviction, by the faith of individuals who believe that God wills man to be free but also pure; it will be by the seekers after holiness, by those old-fashioned pious persons who speak of immortality and eternal life, and prefer the soul to the whole world; it will be by the enfranchised children of the ancient faith of the human race.

June 5, 1870.—The efficacy of religion lies precisely in that which is not rational, philosophic, nor external; its efficacy lies in the unforeseen, the miraculous, the extraordinary. Thus religion attracts more devotion in proportion as it demands more faith—that is to say, as it becomes more incredible to the profane mind. The philosopher aspires to explain away all mysteries, to dissolve them into light. It is mystery, on the other hand, which the religious instinct demands and pursues; it is mystery which constitutes the essence of worship, the power of proselytism. When the cross became the "foolishness" of the cross, it took possession of the masses. And in our own day, those who wish to get rid of the supernatural, to enlighten religion, to economize faith, find themselves deserted, like poets who should declaim against poetry, or women who should decry love. Faith consists in the acceptance of the incomprehensible, and even in the pursuit of the impossible, and is self-intoxicated with its own sacrifices, its own repeated extravagances.

It is the forgetfulness of this psychological law which stultifies the so-called liberal Christianity. It is the realization of it which constitutes the strength of Catholicism.

Apparently no positive religion can survive the supernatural element which is the reason for its existence. Natural religion seems to be the tomb of all historic cults. All concrete religions die eventually in the pure air of philosophy. So long then as the life of nations is in need of religion as a motive and sanction of morality, as food for faith, hope, and charity, so long will the masses turn away from pure reason and naked truth, so long will they adore mystery, so long—and rightly so—will they rest in faith, the only region where the ideal presents itself to them in an attractive form.

June 9, 1870.—At bottom, everything depends upon the presence or absence of one single element in the soul—hope. All the activity of man, all his efforts and all his enterprises, presuppose a hope in him of attaining an end. Once kill this hope and his movements become senseless, spasmodic, and convulsive, like those of some one falling from a height. To struggle with the inevitable has something childish in it. To implore the law of gravitation to suspend its action would no doubt be a grotesque prayer. Very well! but when a man loses faith in the efficacy of his efforts, when he says to himself, "You are incapable of realizing your ideal; happiness is a chimera, progress is an illusion, the passion for perfection is a snare; and supposing all your ambitions were gratified, everything would still be vanity," then he comes to see that a little blindness is necessary if life is to be carried on, and that illusion is the universal spring of movement. Complete disillusion would mean absolute immobility. He who has deciphered the secret and read the riddle of finite life escapes from the great wheel of existence; he has left the world of the living—he is already dead. Is this the meaning of the old belief that to raise the veil of Isis or to behold God face to face brought destruction upon the rash mortal who attempted it? Egypt and Judea had recorded the fact, Buddha gave the key to it; the individual life is a nothing ignorant of itself, and as soon as this nothing knows itself, individual life is abolished in principle. For as soon as the illusion vanishes, Nothingness resumes its eternal sway, the suffering of life is over, error has disappeared, time and form have ceased to be for this enfranchised individuality; the colored air-bubble has burst in the infinite space, and the misery of thought has sunk to rest in the changeless repose of all-embracing Nothing. The absolute, if it were spirit, would still be activity, and it is activity, the daughter of desire, which is incompatible with the absolute. The absolute, then, must be the zero of all determination, and the only manner of being suited to it is Non-being.

July 2, 1870.—One of the vices of France is the frivolity which substitutes public conventions for truth, and absolutely ignores personal dignity and the majesty of conscience. The French are ignorant of the A B C of individual liberty, and still show an essentially catholic intolerance toward the ideas which have not attained universality or the adhesion of the majority. The nation is an army which can bring to bear mass, number, and force, but not an assembly of free men in which each individual depends for his value on himself. The eminent Frenchman depends upon others for his value; if he possess stripe, cross, scarf, sword, or robe—in a word, function and decoration—then he is held to be something, and he feels himself somebody. It is the symbol which establishes his merit, it is the public which raises him from nothing, as the sultan creates his viziers. These highly-trained and social races have an antipathy for individual independence; everything with them must be founded upon authority military, civil, or religious, and God himself is nonexistent until he has been established by decree. Their fundamental dogma is that social omnipotence which treats the pretension of truth to be true without any official stamp, as a mere usurpation and sacrilege, and scouts the claim of the individual to possess either a separate conviction or a personal value.

July 20, 1870 (*Bellalpe*).—A marvelous day. The panorama before me is of a grandiose splendor; it is a symphony of mountains, a cantata of sunny Alps.

I am dazzled and oppressed by it. The feeling uppermost is one of delight in being able to admire, of joy, that is to say, in a recovered power of contemplation which is the result of physical relief, in being able at last to forget myself and surrender myself to things, as befits a man in my state of health. Gratitude is mingled with enthusiasm. I have just spent two hours of continuous delight at the foot of the Sparrenhorn, the peak behind us. A flood of sensations overpowered me. I could only look, feel, dream, and think.

Later.—Ascent of the Sparrenhorn. The peak of it is not very easy to climb, because of the masses of loose stones and the steepness of the path, which runs between two abysses. But how great is one's reward!

The view embraces the whole series of the Valais Alps from the Furka to the Combin; and even beyond the Furka one sees a few peaks of the Ticino and the Rhaetian Alps; while if you turn you see behind you a whole polar world of snowfields and glaciers forming the southern side of the enormous Bernese group of the Finsteraarahorn, the Moench, and the Jungfrau. The near representative of the group is the Aletschhorn, whence diverge like so many ribbons the different Aletsch glaciers which wind about the peak from which I saw them. I could study the different zones, one above another—fields, woods, grassy Alps, bare rock and snow, and the principle types of mountain; the pagoda-shaped Mischabel, with its four *aretes* as flying buttresses and its staff of nine clustered peaks; the cupola of the Fletchhorn, the dome of Monte Rosa, the pyramid of the Weisshorn, the obelisk of the Cervin.

Bound me fluttered a multitude of butterflies and brilliant green-backed flies; but nothing grew except a few lichens. The deadness and emptiness of the upper Aletsch glacier, like some vast white street, called up the image of an icy Pompeii. All around boundless silence. On my way back I noticed some effects of sunshine—the close elastic mountain grass, starred with gentian, forget-me-not, and anemones, the mountain cattle standing out against the sky, the rocks just piercing the soil, various circular dips in the mountain side, stone waves petrified thousands of thousands of years ago, the undulating ground, the tender quiet of the evening; and I invoked the soul of the mountains and the spirit of the heights!

July 22, 1870 (*Bellalpe*).—The sky, which was misty and overcast this morning, has become perfectly blue again, and the giants of the Valais are bathed in tranquil light.

Whence this solemn melancholy which oppresses and pursues me? I have just read a series of scientific books (Bronn on the "Laws of Palaeontology," Karl Ritter on the "Law of Geographical Forms").

Are they the cause of this depression? or is it the majesty of this immense landscape, the splendor of this setting sun, which brings the tears to my eyes?

"Creature d'un jour qui t'agites une heure,"

what weighs upon thee—I know it well—is the sense of thine utter nothingness!... The names of great men hover before my eyes like a secret reproach, and this grand impassive nature tells me that tomorrow I shall have disappeared, butterfly that I am, without having lived. Or perhaps it is the breath of eternal things which stirs in me the shudder of Job. What is man—this weed which a sunbeam withers? What is our life in the infinite abyss? I feel a sort of sacred terror, not only for myself, but for my race, for all that is mortal. Like Buddha, I feel the great wheel turning—the wheel of universal illusion—and the dumb stupor which enwraps me is full of anguish. Isis lifts the corner of her veil, and he who perceives the great mystery beneath is struck with giddiness. I can scarcely breathe. It seems to me that I am hanging by a thread above the fathomless abyss of destiny. Is this the Infinite face to face, an intuition of the last great death?

"Creature d'un jour qui t'agites une heure, Ton ame est immortelle et tes pleurs vont finir."

Finir? When depths of ineffable desire are opening in the heart, as vast, as yawning as the immensity which surrounds us? Genius, self-devotion, love—all these cravings quicken into life and torture me at once. Like the shipwrecked sailor about to sink under the waves, I am conscious of a mad clinging to life, and at the same time of a rush of despair and repentance, which forces from me a cry for pardon. And then all this hidden agony dissolves in wearied submission. "Resign yourself to the inevitable! Shroud away out of sight the flattering delusions of youth! Live and die in the shade! Like the insects humming in the darkness, offer up your evening prayer. Be content to fade out of life without a murmur whenever the Master of life shall breathe upon your tiny flame! It is out of myriads of unknown lives that every clod of earth is built up. The infusoria do not count until they are millions upon millions. Accept your nothingness." Amen!

But there is no peace except in order, in law. Am I in order? Alas, no! My changeable and restless nature will torment me to the end. I shall never see plainly what I ought to do. The love of the better will have stood between me and the good. Yearning for the ideal will have lost me reality. Vague aspiration and undefined desire will have been enough to make my talents useless, and to neutralize my powers. Unproductive nature that I am, tortured by the belief that production was required of me, may not my very remorse be a mistake and a superfluity?

Scherer's phrase comes back to me, "We must accept ourselves as we are."

September 8, 1870 (*Zurich*).—All the exiles are returning to Paris— Edgar Quinet, Louis Blanc, Victor Hugo. By the help of their united experience will they succeed in maintaining the republic? It is to be hoped so. But the past makes it lawful to doubt. While the republic is in reality a fruit, the French look upon it as a seed-sowing. Elsewhere such a form of government presupposes free men; in France it is and must be an instrument of instruction and protection. France has once more placed sovereignty in the hands of universal suffrage, as though the multitude were already enlightened, judicious, and reasonable, and now her task is to train and discipline the force which, by a fiction, is master.

The ambition of France is set upon self-government, but her capacity for it has still to be proved. For eighty years she has confounded revolution with liberty; will she now give proof of amendment and of wisdom? Such a change is not impossible. Let us wait for it with sympathy, but also with caution.

September 12, 1870 (*Basle*).—The old Rhine is murmuring under my window. The wide gray stream rolls its great waves along and breaks against the arches of the bridge, just as it did ten years or twenty years ago; the red cathedral shoots its arrow-like spires toward heaven; the ivy on the terraces which fringe the left bank of the Rhine hangs over the walls like a green mantle; the indefatigable ferry-boat goes and comes as it did of yore; in a word, things seem to be eternal, while man's hair turns gray and his heart grows old. I came here first as a student, then as a professor. Now I return to it at the downward turn of middle age, and nothing in the landscape has changed except myself.

The melancholy of memory may be commonplace and puerile—all the same it is true, it is inexhaustible, and the poets of all times have been open to its attacks.

At bottom, what is individual life? A variation of an eternal theme—to be born, to live, to feel, to hope, to love, to suffer, to weep, to die. Some would add to these, to grow rich, to think, to conquer; but in fact, whatever frantic efforts one may make, however one may strain and excite one's self, one can but cause a greater or slighter undulation in the line of one's destiny. Supposing a man renders the series of fundamental phenomena a little more evident to others or a little more distinct to himself, what does it matter? The whole is still nothing but a fluttering of the infinitely little, the insignificant repetition of an invariable theme. In truth, whether the individual exists or no, the difference is so absolutely imperceptible in the whole of things that every complaint and every desire is ridiculous. Humanity in its entirety is but a flash in the duration of the planet, and the planet may return to the gaseous state without the sun's feeling it even for a second. The individual is the infinitesimal of nothing.

What, then, is nature? Nature is Maia—that is to say, an incessant, fugitive, indifferent series of phenomena, the manifestation of all possibilities, the inexhaustible play of all combinations.

And is Maia all the while performing for the amusement of somebody, of some spectator—Brahma? Or is Brahma working out some serious and unselfish end? From the theistic point of view, is it the purpose of God to make souls, to augment the sum of good and wisdom by the multiplication of himself in free beings—facets which may flash back to him his own holiness and beauty? This conception is far more attractive to the heart. But is it more true? The moral consciousness affirms it. If man is capable of conceiving goodness, the general principle of things, which cannot be inferior to man, must be good. The philosophy of labor, of duty, of effort, is surely superior to that of phenomena, chance, and universal indifference. If so, the whimsical Maia would be subordinate to Brahma, the eternal thought, and Brahma would be in his turn subordinate to a holy God.

October 25, 1870 (*Geneva*).—"Each function to the most worthy:" this maxim governs all constitutions, and serves to test them. Democracy is not forbidden to apply it, but democracy rarely does apply it, because she holds, for example, that the most worthy man is the man who pleases her, whereas he who pleases her is not always the most worthy, and because she supposes that reason guides the masses, whereas in reality they are most commonly led by passion. And in the end every falsehood has to be expiated, for truth always takes its revenge.

Alas, whatever one may say or do, wisdom, justice, reason, and goodness will never be anything more than special cases and the heritage of a few elect souls. Moral and intellectual harmony, excellence in all its forms, will always be a rarity of great price, an isolated *chef d'oeuvre*. All that can be expected from the most perfect institutions is that they should make it possible for individual excellence to develop itself, not that they should produce the excellent individual. Virtue and genius, grace and beauty, will always constitute a *noblesse* such as no form of government can manufacture. It is of no use, therefore, to excite one's self for or against revolutions which have only an importance of the second order—an importance which I do not wish either to diminish or to ignore, but an importance which, after all, is mostly negative. The political life is but the means of the true life.

October 26, 1870.—Sirocco. A bluish sky. The leafy crowns of the trees have dropped at their feet; the finger of winter has touched them. The errand-woman has just brought me my letters. Poor little woman, what a life! She spends her nights in going backward and forward from her invalid husband to her sister, who is scarcely less helpless, and her days are passed in labor. Resigned and indefatigable, she goes on without complaining, till she drops.

Lives such as hers prove something: that the true ignorance is moral ignorance, that labor and suffering are the lot of all men, and that classification according to a greater or less degree of folly is inferior to that which proceeds according to a greater or less degree of virtue. The kingdom of God belongs not to the most enlightened but to the best; and the best man is the most unselfish man. Humble, constant, voluntary self-sacrifice—this is what constitutes the true dignity of man. And therefore is it written, "The last shall be first." Society rests upon conscience and not upon science. Civilization is first and foremost a moral thing. Without honesty, without respect for law, without the worship of duty, without the love of one's neighbor—in a word, without virtue—the whole is menaced and falls into decay, and neither letters nor art, neither luxury nor industry, nor rhetoric, nor the policeman, nor the custom-house officer, can maintain erect and whole an edifice of which the foundations are unsound.

A state founded upon interest alone and cemented by fear is an ignoble and unsafe construction. The ultimate ground upon which every civilization rests is the average morality of the masses, and a sufficient amount of practical righteousness. Duty is what upholds all. So that those who humbly and unobtrusively fulfill it, and set a good example thereby, are the salvation and the sustenance of this brilliant world, which knows nothing about them. Ten righteous men would have saved Sodom, but thousands and thousands of good homely folk are needed to preserve a people from corruption and decay.

If ignorance and passion are the foes of popular morality, it must be confessed that moral indifference is the malady of the cultivated classes. The modern separation of enlightenment and virtue, of thought and conscience, of the intellectual aristocracy from the honest and vulgar crowd, is the greatest danger that can threaten liberty. When any society produces an increasing number of literary exquisites, of satirists, skeptics, and *beaux esprits*, some chemical disorganization of fabric may be inferred. Take, for example, the century of Augustus, and that of Louis XV. Our cynics and railers are mere egotists, who stand aloof from the common duty, and in their indolent remoteness are of no service to society against any ill which may attack it. Their cultivation consists in having got rid of feeling. And thus they fall farther and farther away from true humanity, and approach nearer to the demoniacal nature. What was it that Mephistopheles lacked? Not intelligence certainly, but goodness.

October 28, 1870.—It is strange to see how completely justice is forgotten in the presence of great international struggles. Even the great majority of the spectators are no longer capable of judging except as their own personal tastes, dislikes, fears, desires, interests, or passions may dictate—that is to say, their judgment is not a judgment at all. How many people are capable of delivering a fair verdict on the struggle now going on? Very few! This horror of equity, this antipathy to justice, this rage against a merciful neutrality, represents a kind of eruption of animal passion in man, a blind fierce passion, which is absurd enough to call itself a reason, whereas it is nothing but a force.

November 16, 1870.—We are struck by something bewildering and ineffable when we look down into the depths of an abyss; and every soul is an abyss, a mystery of love and piety. A sort of sacred emotion descends upon me whenever I penetrate the recesses of this sanctuary of man, and hear the gentle murmur of the prayers, hymns, and supplications which rise from the hidden depths of the heart. These involuntary confidences fill me with a tender piety and a religious awe and shyness. The whole experience seems to me as wonderful as poetry, and divine with the divineness of birth and dawn. Speech fails me, I bow myself and adore. And, whenever I am able, I strive also to console and fortify.

December 6, 1870.—"Dauer im Wechsel"—"Persistence in change." This title of a poem by Goethe is the summing up of nature. Everything changes, but with such unequal rapidity that one existence appears eternal to another. A geological age, for instance, compared to the duration of any living being, the duration of a planet compared to a geological age, appear eternities—our life, too, compared to the thousand impressions which pass across us in an hour. Wherever one looks, one feels one's self overwhelmed by the infinity of infinites. The universe, seriously studied, rouses one's terror. Everything seems so relative that it is scarcely possible to distinguish whether anything has a real value.

Where is the fixed point in this boundless and bottomless gulf? Must it not be that which perceives the relations of things—in other words, thought, infinite thought? The perception of ourselves within the infinite thought, the realization of ourselves in God, self-acceptance in him, the harmony of our will with his—in a word, religion—here alone is firm ground. Whether this thought be free or necessary, happiness lies in identifying one's self with it. Both the stoic and the Christian surrender themselves to the Being of beings, which the one calls sovereign wisdom and the other sovereign goodness. St. John says, "God is Light," "God is Love." The Brahmin says, "God is the inexhaustible fount of poetry." Let us say, "God is perfection." And man? Man, for all his inexpressible insignificance and frailty, may still apprehend the idea of perfection, may help forward the supreme will, and die with Hosanna on his lips!

*****

All teaching depends upon a certain presentiment and preparation in the taught; we can only teach others profitably what they already virtually know; we can only give them what they had already. This principle of education is also a law of history. Nations can only be developed on the lines of their tendencies and aptitudes. Try them on any other and they are rebellious and incapable of improvement.

* * * * *

By despising himself too much a man comes to be worthy of his own contempt.

* * * * *

Its way of suffering is the witness which a soul bears to itself.

* * * * *

The beautiful is superior to the sublime because it lasts and does not satiate, while the sublime is relative, temporary and violent.

* * * * *

February 4, 1871.—Perpetual effort is the characteristic of modern morality. A painful process has taken the place of the old harmony, the old equilibrium, the old joy and fullness of being. We are all so many fauns, satyrs, or Silenuses, aspiring to become angels; so many deformities laboring for our own embellishment; so many clumsy chrysalises each working painfully toward the development of the butterfly within him. Our ideal is no longer a serene beauty of soul; it is the agony of Laocoon struggling with the hydra of evil. The lot is cast irrevocably. There are no more happy whole-natured men among us, nothing but so many candidates for heaven, galley-slaves on earth.

"Nous ramons notre vie en attendant le port."

Moliere said that reasoning banished reason. It is possible also that the progress toward perfection we are so proud of is only a pretentious imperfection. Duty seems now to be more negative than positive; it means lessening evil rather than actual good; it is a generous discontent, but not happiness; it is an incessant pursuit of an unattainable goal, a noble madness, but not reason; it is homesickness for the impossible—pathetic and pitiful, but still not wisdom.

The being which has attained harmony, and every being may attain it, has found its place in the order of the universe, and represents the divine thought at least as clearly as a flower or a solar system. Harmony seeks nothing outside itself. It is what it ought to be; it is the expression of right, order, law, and truth; it is greater than time, and represents eternity.

February 6,1871.—I am reading Juste Olivier's "Chansons du Soir" over again, and all the melancholy of the poet seems to pass into my veins. It is the revelation of a complete existence, and of a whole world of melancholy reverie.

How much character there is in "Musette," the "Chanson de l'Alouette," the "Chant du Retour," and the "Gaite," and how much freshness in "Lina," and "A ma fille!" But the best pieces of all are "Au dela," "Homunculus," "La Trompeuse," and especially "Frere Jacques," its author's masterpiece. To these may be added the "Marionettes" and the national song, "Helvetie." Serious purpose and intention disguised in gentle gayety and childlike *badinage*, feeling hiding itself under a smile of satire, a resigned and pensive wisdom expressing itself in rustic round or ballad, the power of suggesting everything in a nothing—these are the points in which the Vaudois poet triumphs. On the reader's side there is emotion and surprise, and on the author's a sort of pleasant slyness which seems to delight in playing tricks upon you, only tricks of the most dainty and brilliant kind. Juste Olivier has the passion we might imagine a fairy to have for delicate mystification. He hides his gifts. He promises nothing and gives a great deal. His generosity, which is prodigal, has a surly air; his simplicity is really subtlety; his malice pure tenderness; and his whole talent is, as it were, the fine flower of the Vaudois mind in its sweetest and dreamiest form.

February 10, 1871.—My reading for this morning has been some vigorous chapters of Taine's "History of English Literature." Taine is a writer whose work always produces a disagreeable impression upon me, as though of a creaking of pulleys and a clicking of machinery; there is a smell of the laboratory about it. His style is the style of chemistry and technology. The science of it is inexorable; it is dry and forcible, penetrating and hard, strong and harsh, but altogether lacking in charm, humanity, nobility, and grace. The disagreeable effect which it makes on one's taste, ear, and heart, depends probably upon two things: upon the moral philosophy of the author and upon his literary principles. The profound contempt for humanity which characterizes the physiological school, and the intrusion of technology into literature inaugurated by Balzac and Stendhal, explain the underlying aridity of which one is sensible in these pages, and which seems to choke one like the gases from a manufactory of mineral products. The book is instructive in the highest degree, but instead of animating and stirring, it parches, corrodes, and saddens its reader. It excites no feeling whatever; it is simply a means of information. I imagine this kind of thing will be the literature of the future—a literature *a l'Americaine*, as different as possible from Greek art, giving us algebra instead of life, the formula instead of the image, the exhalations of the crucible instead of the divine madness of Apollo. Cold vision will replace the joys of thought, and we shall see the death of poetry, flayed and dissected by science.

February 15, 1871.—Without intending it, nations educate each other, while having apparently nothing in view but their own selfish interests. It was France who made the Germany of the present, by attempting its destruction during ten generations; it is Germany who will regenerate contemporary France, by the effort to crush her. Revolutionary France will teach equality to the Germans, who are by nature hierarchical. Germany will teach the French that rhetoric is not science, and that appearance is not as valuable as reality. The worship of prestige—that is to say, of falsehood; the passion for vainglory—that is to say, for smoke and noise; these are what must die in the interests of the world. It is a false religion which is being destroyed. I hope sincerely that this war will issue in a new balance of things better than any which has gone before—a new Europe, in which the government of the individual by himself will be the cardinal principle of society, in opposition to the Latin principle, which regards the individual as a thing, a means to an end, an instrument of the church or of the state.

In the order and harmony which would result from free adhesion and voluntary submission to a common ideal, we should see the rise of a new moral world. It would be an equivalent, expressed in lay terms, to the idea of a universal priesthood. The model state ought to resemble a great musical society in which every one submits to be organized, subordinated, and disciplined for the sake of art, and for the sake of producing a masterpiece. Nobody is coerced, nobody is made use of for selfish purposes, nobody plays a hypocritical or selfish part. All bring their talent to the common stock, and contribute knowingly and gladly to the common wealth. Even self-love itself is obliged to help on the general action, under pain of rebuff should it make itself apparent.

February 18, 1871.—It is in the novel that the average vulgarity of German society, and its inferiority to the societies of France and England, are most clearly visible. The notion of "bad taste" seems to have no place in German aesthetics. Their elegance has no grace in it; and they cannot understand the enormous difference there is between distinction (what is *gentlemanly, ladylike*), and their stiff *vornehmlichkeit*. Their imagination lacks style, training, education, and knowledge of the world; it has an ill-bred air even in its Sunday dress. The race is poetical and intelligent, but common and ill-mannered. Pliancy and gentleness, manners, wit, vivacity, taste, dignity, and charm, are qualities which belong to others.

Will that inner freedom of soul, that profound harmony of all the faculties which I have so often observed among the best Germans, ever come to the surface? Will the conquerors of to-day ever learn to civilize and soften their forms of life? It is by their future novels that we shall be able to judge. As soon as they are capable of the novel of "good society" they will have excelled all rivals. Till then, finish, polish, the maturity of social culture, are beyond them; they may have humanity of feeling, but the delicacies, the little perfections of life, are unknown to them. They may be honest and well-meaning, but they are utterly without *savoir vivre*.

February 22, 1871.—*Soiree* at the M—. About thirty people representing our best society were there, a happy mixture of sexes and ages. There were gray heads, young girls, bright faces—the whole framed in some Aubusson tapestries which made a charming background, and gave a soft air of distance to the brilliantly-dressed groups.

In society people are expected to behave as if they lived on ambrosia and concerned themselves with nothing but the loftiest interests. Anxiety, need, passion, have no existence. All realism is suppressed as brutal. In a word, what we call "society" proceeds for the moment on the flattering illusory assumption that it is moving in an ethereal atmosphere and breathing the air of the gods. All vehemence, all natural expression, all real suffering, all careless familiarity, or any frank sign of passion, are startling and distasteful in this delicate *milieu*; they at once destroy the common work, the cloud palace, the magical architectural whole, which has been raised by the general consent and effort. It is like the sharp cock-crow which breaks the spell of all enchantments, and puts the fairies to flight. These select gatherings produce, without knowing it, a sort of concert for eyes and ears, an improvised work of art. By the instinctive collaboration of everybody concerned, intellect and taste hold festival, and the associations of reality are exchanged for the associations of imagination. So understood, society is a form of poetry; the cultivated classes deliberately recompose the idyll of the past and the buried world of Astrea. Paradox or no, I believe that these fugitive attempts to reconstruct a dream whose only end is beauty represent confused reminiscences of an age of gold haunting the human heart, or rather aspirations toward a harmony of things which every day reality denies to us, and of which art alone gives us a glimpse.

April 28, 1871.—For a psychologist it is extremely interesting to be readily and directly conscious of the complications of one's own organism and the play of its several parts. It seems to me that the sutures of my being are becoming just loose enough to allow me at once a clear perception of myself as a whole and a distinct sense of my own brittleness. A feeling like this makes personal existence a perpetual astonishment and curiosity. Instead of only seeing the world which surrounds me, I analyze myself. Instead of being single, all of a piece, I become legion, multitude, a whirlwind—a very cosmos. Instead of living on the surface, I take possession of my inmost self, I apprehend myself, if not in my cells and atoms, at least so far as my groups of organs, almost my tissues, are concerned. In other words, the central monad isolates itself from all the subordinate monads, that it may consider them, and finds its harmony again in itself.

Health is the perfect balance between our organism, with all its component parts, and the outer world; it serves us especially for acquiring a knowledge of that world. Organic disturbance obliges us to set up a fresh and more spiritual equilibrium, to withdraw within the soul. Thereupon our bodily constitution itself becomes the object of thought. It is no longer we, although it may belong to us; it is nothing more than the vessel in which we make the passage of life, a vessel of which we study the weak points and the structure without identifying it with our own individuality.

Where is the ultimate residence of the self? In thought, or rather in consciousness. But below consciousness there is its germ, the *punctum saliens* of spontaneity; for consciousness is not primitive, it *becomes*. The question is, can the thinking monad return into its envelope, that is to say, into pure spontaneity, or even into the dark abyss of virtuality? I hope not. The kingdom passes; the king remains; or rather is it the royalty alone which subsists—that is to say, the idea—the personality begin in its turn merely the passing vesture of the permanent idea? Is Leibnitz or Hegel right? Is the individual immortal under the form of the spiritual body? Is he eternal under the form of the individual idea? Who saw most clearly, St. Paul or Plato? The theory of Leibnitz attracts me most because it opens to us an infinite of duration, of multitude, and evolution. For a monad, which is the virtual universe, a whole infinite of time is not too much to develop the infinite within it. Only one must admit exterior actions and influences which affect the evolution of the monad. Its independence must be a mobile and increasing quantity between zero and the infinite, without ever reaching either completeness or nullity, for the monad can be neither absolutely passive nor entirely free.

June 21, 1871.—The international socialism of the *ouvriers*, ineffectually put down in Paris, is beginning to celebrate its approaching victory. For it there is neither country, nor memories, nor property, nor religion. There is nothing and nobody but itself. Its dogma is equality, its prophet is Mably, and Baboeuf is its god.

[Footnote: Mably, the Abbe Mably, 1709-85, one of the precursors of the revolution, the professor of a cultivated and classical communism based on a study of antiquity, which Babeuf and others like him, in the following generation, translated into practical experiment. "Caius Gracchus" Babeuf, born 1764, and guillotined in 1797 for a conspiracy against the Directory, is sometimes called the first French socialist. Perhaps socialist doctrines, properly so called, may be said to make their first entry into the region of popular debate and practical agitation with his "Manifeste des Egaux," issued April 1796.]

How is the conflict to be solved, since there is no longer one single common principle between the partisans and the enemies of the existing form of society, between liberalism and the worship of equality? Their respective notions of man, duty, happiness—that is to say, of life and its end—differ radically. I suspect that the communism of the *Internationale* is merely the pioneer of Russian nihilism, which will be the common grave of the old races and the servile races, the Latins and the Slavs. If so, the salvation of humanity will depend upon individualism of the brutal American sort. I believe that the nations of the present are rather tempting chastisement than learning wisdom. Wisdom, which means balance and harmony, is only met within individuals. Democracy, which means the rule of the masses, gives preponderance to instinct, to nature, to the passions—that is to say, to blind impulse, to elemental gravitation, to generic fatality. Perpetual vacillation between contraries becomes its only mode of progress, because it represents that childish form of prejudice which falls in love and cools, adores, and curses, with the same haste and unreason. A succession of opposing follies gives an impression of change which the people readily identify with improvement, as though Enceladus was more at ease on his left side than on his right, the weight of the volcano remaining the same. The stupidity of Demos is only equaled by its presumption. It is like a youth with all his animal and none of his reasoning powers developed.

Luther's comparison of humanity to a drunken peasant, always ready to fall from his horse on one side or the other, has always struck me as a particularly happy one. It is not that I deny the right of the democracy, but I have no sort of illusion as to the use it will make of its right, so long, at any rate, as wisdom is the exception and conceit the rule. Numbers make law, but goodness has nothing to do with figures. Every fiction is self-expiating, and democracy rests upon this legal fiction, that the majority has not only force but reason on its side—that it possesses not only the right to act but the wisdom necessary for action. The fiction is dangerous because of its flattery; the demagogues have always flattered the private feelings of the masses. The masses will always be below the average. Besides, the age of majority will be lowered, the barriers of sex will be swept away, and democracy will finally make itself absurd by handing over the decision of all that is greatest to all that is most incapable. Such an end will be the punishment of its abstract principle of equality, which dispenses the ignorant man from the necessity of self-training, the foolish man from that of self-judgment, and tells the child that there is no need for him to become a man, and the good-for-nothing that self-improvement is of no account. Public law, founded upon virtual equality, will destroy itself by its consequences. It will not recognize the inequalities of worth, of merit, and of experience; in a word, it ignores individual labor, and it will end in the triumph of platitude and the residuum. The *regime* of the Parisian Commune has shown us what kind of material comes to the top in these days of frantic vanity and universal suspicion.

Still, humanity is tough, and survives all catastrophes. Only it makes one impatient to see the race always taking the longest road to an end, and exhausting all possible faults before it is able to accomplish one definite step toward improvement. These innumerable follies, that are to be and must be, have an irritating effect upon me. The more majestic is the history of science, the more intolerable is the history of politics and religion. The mode of progress in the moral world seems an abuse of the patience of God.

Enough! There is no help in misanthropy and pessimism. If our race vexes us, let us keep a decent silence on the matter. We are imprisoned on the same ship, and we shall sink with it. Pay your own debt, and leave the rest to God. Sharer, as you inevitably are, in the sufferings of your kind, set a good example; that is all which is asked of you. Do all the good you can, and say all the truth you know or believe; and for the rest be patient, resigned, submissive. God does his business, do yours.

July 29, 1871.—So long as a man is capable of self-renewal he is a living being. Goethe, Schleiermacher and Humboldt, were masters of the art. If we are to remain among the living there must be a perpetual revival of youth within us, brought about by inward change and by love of the Platonic sort. The soul must be forever recreating itself, trying all its various modes, vibrating in all its fibres, raising up new interests for itself....

The "Epistles" and the "Epigrams" of Goethe which I have been reading to-day do not make one love him. Why? Because he has so little soul. His way of understanding love, religion, duty, and patriotism has something mean and repulsive in it. There is no ardor, no generosity in him. A secret barrenness, an ill-concealed egotism, makes itself felt through all the wealth and flexibility of his talent. It is true that the egotism of Goethe has at least this much that is excellent in it, that it respects the liberty of the individual, and is favorable to all originality. But it will go out of its way to help nobody; it will give itself no trouble for anybody; it will lighten nobody else's burden; in a word, it does away with charity, the great Christian virtue. Perfection for Goethe consists in personal nobility, not in love; his standard is aesthetic, not moral. He ignores holiness, and has never allowed himself to reflect on the dark problem of evil. A Spinozist to the core, he believes in individual luck, not in liberty, nor in responsibility. He is a Greek of the great time, to whom the inward crises of the religious consciousness are unknown. He represents, then, a state of soul earlier than or subsequent to Christianity, what the prudent critics of our time call the "modern spirit;" and only one tendency of the modern spirit—the worship of nature. For Goethe stands outside all the social and political aspirations of the generality of mankind; he takes no more interest than Nature herself in the disinherited, the feeble, and the oppressed....

The restlessness of our time does not exist for Goethe and his school. It is explicable enough. The deaf have no sense of dissonance. The man who knows nothing of the voice of conscience, the voice of regret or remorse, cannot even guess at the troubles of those who live under two masters and two laws, and belong to two worlds—that of nature and that of liberty. For himself, his choice is made. But humanity cannot choose and exclude. All needs are vocal at once in the cry of her suffering. She hears the men of science, but she listens to those who talk to her of religion; pleasure attracts her, but sacrifice moves her; and she hardly knows whether she hates or whether she adores the crucifix.

Later.—Still re-reading the sonnets and the miscellaneous poems of Goethe. The impression left by this part of the "Gedichte" is much more favorable than that made upon me by the "Elegies" and the "Epigrams." The "Water Spirits" and "The Divine" are especially noble in feeling. One must never be too hasty in judging these complex natures. Completely lacking as he is in the sense of obligation and of sin, Goethe nevertheless finds his way to seriousness through dignity. Greek sculpture has been his school of virtue.

August 15, 1871.—Re-read, for the second time, Renan's "Vie de Jesus," in the sixteenth popular edition. The most characteristic feature of this analysis of Christianity is that sin plays no part at all in it. Now, if anything explains the success of the gospel among men, it is that it brought them deliverance from sin—in a word, salvation. A man, however, is bound to explain a religion seriously, and not to shirk the very center of his subject. This white-marble Christ is not the Christ who inspired the martyrs and has dried so many tears. The author lacks moral seriousness, and confounds nobility of character with holiness. He speaks as an artist conscious of a pathetic subject, but his moral sense is not interested in the question. It is not possible to mistake the epicureanism of the imagination, delighting itself in an aesthetic spectacle, for the struggles of a soul passionately in search of truth. In Renan there are still some remains of priestly *ruse*; he strangles with sacred cords. His tone of contemptuous indulgence toward a more or less captious clergy might be tolerated, but he should have shown a more respectful sincerity in dealing with the sincere and the spiritual. Laugh at Pharisaism as you will, but speak simply and plainly to honest folk. [Footnote: "'Persifflez les pharisaismes, mais parlez droit aux honnetes gens' me dit Amiel, avec une certaine aigreur. Mon Dieu, que les honnetes gens sont souvent exposes a etre des pharisiens sans le savoir!" —(M. Renan's article, already quoted).]

Later.—To understand is to be conscious of the fundamental unity of the thing to be explained—that is to say, to conceive it in its entirety both of life and development, to be able to remake it by a mental process without making a mistake, without adding or omitting anything. It means, first, complete identification of the object, and then the power of making it clear to others by a full and just interpretation. To understand is more difficult than to judge, for understanding is the transference of the mind into the conditions of the object, whereas judgment is simply the enunciation of the individual opinion.

August 25, 1871. (*Charnex-sur-Montreux*).—Magnificent weather. The morning seems bathed in happy peace, and a heavenly fragrance rises from mountain and shore; it is as though a benediction were laid upon us. No vulgar intrusive noise disturbs the religious quiet of the scene. One might believe one's self in a church—a vast temple in which every being and every natural beauty has its place. I dare not breathe for fear of putting the dream to flight—a dream traversed by angels.

"Comme autrefois j'entends dans l'ether infini La musique du temps et l'hosanna des mondes."

In these heavenly moments the cry of Pauline rises to one's lips. [Footnote: "Polyeuete," Act. V. Scene v.

"Mon epoux en mourant m'a laisse ses lumieres; Son sang dont tes bourreaux viennent de me couvrir M'a dessille les yeux et me les vient d'ouvrir. Je vois, je sais, je crois— —"]

"I feel! I believe! I see!" All the miseries, the cares, the vexations of life, are forgotten; the universal joy absorbs us; we enter into the divine order, and into the blessedness of the Lord. Labor and tears, sin, pain, and death have passed away. To exist is to bless; life is happiness. In this sublime pause of things all dissonances have disappeared. It is as though creation were but one vast symphony, glorifying the God of goodness with an inexhaustible wealth of praise and harmony. We question no longer whether it is so or not. We have ourselves become notes in the great concert; and the soul breaks the silence of ecstasy only to vibrate in unison with the eternal joy.

September 22, 1871. (*Charnex*).—Gray sky—a melancholy day. A friend has left me, the sun is unkind and capricious. Everything passes away, everything forsakes us. And in place of all we have lost, age and gray hairs! ... After dinner I walked to Chailly between two showers. A rainy landscape has a great charm for me; the dark tints become more velvety, the softer tones more ethereal. The country in rain is like a face with traces of tears upon it—less beautiful no doubt, but more expressive.

Behind the beauty which is superficial, gladsome, radiant, and palpable, the aesthetic sense discovers another order of beauty altogether, hidden, veiled, secret and mysterious, akin to moral beauty. This sort of beauty only reveals itself to the initiated, and is all the more exquisite for that. It is a little like the refined joy of sacrifice, like the madness of faith, like the luxury of grief; it is not within the reach of all the world. Its attraction is peculiar, and affects one like some strange perfume, or bizarre melody. When once the taste for it is set up the mind takes a special and keen delight in it, for one finds in it

"Son bien premierement, puis le dedain d'autrui,"

and it is pleasant to one's vanity not to be of the same opinion as the common herd. This, however, is not possible with things which are evident, and beauty which is incontestable. Charm, perhaps, is a better name for the esoteric and paradoxical beauty, which escapes the vulgar, and appeals to our dreamy, meditative side. Classical beauty belongs, so to speak, to all eyes; it has ceased to belong to itself. Esoteric beauty is shy and retiring. It only unveils itself to unsealed eyes, and bestows its favors only upon love.

This is why my friend — —, who places herself immediately in relation with the souls of those she meets, does not see the ugliness of people when once she is interested in them. She likes and dislikes, and those she likes are beautiful, those she dislikes are ugly. There is nothing more complicated in it than that. For her, aesthetic considerations are lost in moral sympathy; she looks with her heart only; she passes by the chapter of the beautiful, and goes on to the chapter of charm. I can do the same; only it is by reflection and on second thoughts; my friend does it involuntarily and at once; she has not the artistic fiber. The craving for a perfect correspondence between the inside and the outside of things—between matter and form—is not in her nature. She does not suffer from ugliness, she scarcely perceives it. As for me, I can only forget what shocks me, I cannot help being shocked. All corporal defects irritate me, and the want of beauty in women, being something which ought not to exist, shocks me like a tear, a solecism, a dissonance, a spot of ink—in a word, like something out of order. On the other hand, beauty restores and fortifies me like some miraculous food, like Olympian ambrosia.

"Que le bon soit toujours camarade du beau Des demain je chercherai femme. Mais comme le divorce entre eux n'est pas nouveau, Et que peu de beaux corps, hotes d'une belle ame, Assemblent l'un et l'autre point— —"

I will not finish, for after all one must resign one's self, A beautiful soul in a healthy body is already a rare and blessed thing; and if one finds heart, common sense, intellect, and courage into the bargain, one may well do without that ravishing dainty which we call beauty, and almost without that delicious seasoning which we call grace. We do without—with a sigh, as one does without a luxury. Happy we, to possess what is necessary.

December 29, 1871.—I have been reading Bahnsen ("Critique de l'evolutionisme de Hegel-Hartmann, au nom des principes de Schopenhauer"). What a writer! Like a cuttle-fish in water, every movement produces a cloud of ink which shrouds his thought in darkness. And what a doctrine! A thoroughgoing pessimism, which regards the world as absurd, "absolutely idiotic," and reproaches Hartmann for having allowed the evolution of the universe some little remains of logic, while, on the contrary, this evolution is eminently contradictory, and there is no reason anywhere except in the poor brain of the reasoner. Of all possible worlds that which exists is the worst. Its only excuse is that it tends of itself to destruction. The hope of the philosopher is that reasonable beings will shorten their agony and hasten the return of everything to nothing. It is the philosophy of a desperate Satanism, which has not even the resigned perspectives of Buddhism to offer to the disappointed and disillusioned soul. The individual can but protest and curse. This frantic Sivaism is developed from the conception which makes the world the product of blind will, the principle of everything.

The acrid blasphemy of the doctrine naturally leads the writer to indulge in epithets of bad taste which prevent our regarding his work as the mere challenge of a paradoxical theorist. We have really to do with a theophobist, whom faith in goodness rouses to a fury of contempt. In order to hasten the deliverance of the world, he kills all consolation, all hope, and all illusion in the germ, and substitutes for the love of humanity which inspired Cakyamouni, that Mephistophelian gall which defiles, withers, and corrodes everything it touches.

Evolutionism, fatalism, pessimism, nihilism—how strange it is to see this desolate and terrible doctrine growing and expanding at the very moment when the German nation is celebrating its greatness and its triumphs! The contrast is so startling that it sets one thinking.

This orgie of philosophic thought, identifying error with existence itself, and developing the axiom of Proudhon—"Evil is God," will bring back the mass of mankind to the Christian theodicy, which is neither optimist nor pessimist, but simply declares that the felicity which Christianity calls eternal life is accessible to man.

Self-mockery, starting from a horror of stupidity and hypocrisy, and standing in the way of all wholeness of mind and all true seriousness—this is the goal to which intellect brings us at last, unless conscience cries out.

The mind must have for ballast the clear conception of duty, if it is not to fluctuate between levity and despair.

*****

Before giving advice we must have secured its acceptance, or rather, have made it desired.

*****

If we begin by overrating the being we love, we shall end by treating it with wholesale injustice.

* * * * *

It is dangerous to abandon one's self to the luxury of grief; it deprives one of courage, and even of the wish for recovery.

* * * * *

We learn to recognize a mere blunting of the conscience in that incapacity for indignation which is not to be confounded with the gentleness of charity, or the reserve of humility.

February 7, 1872.—Without faith a man can do nothing.

But faith can stifle all science.

What, then, is this Proteus, and whence?

Faith is a certitude without proofs. Being a certitude, it is an energetic principle of action. Being without proof, it is the contrary of science. Hence its two aspects and its two effects. Is its point of departure intelligence? No. Thought may shake or strengthen faith; it cannot produce it. Is its origin in the will? No; good will may favor it, ill-will may hinder it, but no one believes by will, and faith is not a duty. Faith is a sentiment, for it is a hope; it is an instinct, for it precedes all outward instruction. Faith is the heritage of the individual at birth; it is that which binds him to the whole of being. The individual only detaches himself with difficulty from the maternal breast; he only isolates himself by an effort from the nature around him, from the love which enwraps him, the ideas in which he floats, the cradle in which he lies. He is born in union with humanity, with the world, and with God. The trace of this original union is faith. Faith is the reminiscence of that vague Eden whence our individuality issued, but which it inhabited in the somnambulist state anterior to the personal life.

Our individual life consists in separating ourselves from our *milieu*; in so reacting upon it that we apprehend it consciously, and make ourselves spiritual personalities—that is to say, intelligent and free. Our primitive faith is nothing more than the neutral matter which our experience of life and things works up a fresh, and which may be so affected by our studies of every kind as to perish completely in its original form. We ourselves may die before we have been able to recover the harmony of a personal faith which may satisfy our mind and conscience as well as our hearts. But the need of faith never leaves us. It is the postulate of a higher truth which is to bring all things into harmony. It is the stimulus of research; it holds out to us the reward, it points us to the goal. Such at least is the true, the excellent faith. That which is a mere prejudice of childhood, which has never known doubt, which ignores science, which cannot respect or understand or tolerate different convictions—such a faith is a stupidity and a hatred, the mother of all fanaticisms. We may then repeat of faith what Aesop said of the tongue—

"Quid medius lingua, lingua quid pejus eadem?"

To draw the poison-fangs of faith in ourselves, we must subordinate it to the love of truth. The supreme worship of the true is the only means of purification for all religions all confessions, all sects. Faith should only be allowed the second place, for faith has a judge—in truth. When she exalts herself to the position of supreme judge the world is enslaved: Christianity, from the fourth to the seventeenth century, is the proof of it... Will the enlightened faith ever conquer the vulgar faith? We must look forward in trust to a better future.

The difficulty, however, is this. A narrow faith has much more energy than an enlightened faith; the world belongs to will much more than to wisdom. It is not then certain that liberty will triumph over fanaticism; and besides, independent thought will never have the force of prejudice. The solution is to be found in a division of labor. After those whose business it will have been to hold up to the world the ideal of a pure and free faith, will come the men of violence, who will bring the new creed within the circle of recognized interests, prejudices, and institutions. Is not this just what happened to Christianity? After the gentle Master, the impetuous Paul and the bitter Councils. It is true that this is what corrupted the gospel. But still Christianity has done more good than harm to humanity, and so the world advances, by the successive decay of gradually improved ideals.

June 19, 1872.—The wrangle in the Paris Synod still goes on. [Footnote: A synod of the Reformed churches of France was then occupied in determining the constituent conditions of Protestant belief.] The supernatural is the stone of stumbling.

It might be possible to agree on the idea of the divine; but no, that is not the question—the chaff must be separated from the good grain. The supernatural is miracle, and miracle is an objective phenomenon independent of all preceding casuality. Now, miracle thus understood cannot be proved experimentally; and besides, the subjective phenomena, far more important than all the rest, are left out of account in the definition. Men will not see that miracle is a perception of the soul; a vision of the divine behind nature; a psychical crisis, analogous to that of Aeneas on the last day of Troy, which reveals to us the heavenly powers prompting and directing human action. For the indifferent there are no miracles. It is only the religious souls who are capable of recognizing the finger of God in certain given facts.

The minds which have reached the doctrine of immanence are incomprehensible to the fanatics of transcendence. They will never understand—these last—that the *panentheism* of Krause is ten times more religious than their dogmatic supernaturalism. Their passion for the facts which are objective, isolated, and past, prevents them from seeing the facts which are eternal and spiritual. They can only adore what comes to them from without. As soon as their dramaturgy is interpreted symbolically all seems to them lost. They must have their local prodigies—their vanished unverifiable miracles, because for them the divine is there and only there.

This faith can hardly fail to conquer among the races pledged to the Cartesian dualism, who call the incomprehensible clear, and abhor what is profound. Women also will always find local miracle more easy to understand than universal miracle, and the visible objective intervention of God more probable than his psychological and inward action. The Latin world by its mental form is doomed to petrify its abstractions, and to remain forever outside the inmost sanctuary of life, that central hearth where ideas are still undivided, without shape or determination. The Latin mind makes everything objective, because it remains outside things, and outside itself. It is like the eye which only perceives what is exterior to it, and which cannot see itself except artificially, and from a distance, by means of the reflecting surface of a mirror.

August 30, 1872.—*A priori* speculations weary me now as much as anybody. All the different scholasticisms make me doubtful of what they profess to demonstrate, because, instead of examining, they affirm from the beginning. Their object is to throw up entrenchments around a prejudice, and not to discover the truth. They accumulate that which darkens rather than that which enlightens. They are descended, all of them, from the Catholic procedure, which excludes comparison, information, and previous examination. Their object is to trick men into assent, to furnish faith with arguments, and to suppress free inquiry. But to persuade me, a man must have no *parti pris*, and must begin with showing a temper of critical sincerity; he must explain to me how the matter lies, point out to me the questions involved in it, their origin, their difficulties, the different solutions attempted, and their degree of probability. He must respect my reason, my conscience, and my liberty. All scholasticism is an attempt to take by storm; the authority pretends to explain itself, but only pretends, and its deference is merely illusory. The dice are loaded and the premises are pre-judged. The unknown is taken as known, and all the rest is deduced from it.

Philosophy means the complete liberty of the mind, and therefore independence of all social, political, or religious prejudice. It is to begin with neither Christian nor pagan, neither monarchical nor democratic, neither socialist nor individualist; it is critical and impartial; it loves one thing only—truth. If it disturbs the ready-made opinions of the church or the state—of the historical medium—in which the philosopher happens to have been born, so much the worse, but there is no help for it.

"Est ut est aut non est,"

Philosophy means, first, doubt; and afterward the consciousness of what knowledge means, the consciousness of uncertainty and of ignorance, the consciousness of limit, shade, degree, possibility. The ordinary man doubts nothing and suspects nothing. The philosopher is more cautious, but he is thereby unfitted for action, because, although he sees the goal less dimly than others, he sees his own weakness too clearly, and has no illusions as to his chances of reaching it.

The philosopher is like a man fasting in the midst of universal intoxication. He alone perceives the illusion of which all creatures are the willing playthings; he is less duped than his neighbor by his own nature. He judges more sanely, he sees things as they are. It is in this that his liberty consists—in the ability to see clearly and soberly, in the power of mental record. Philosophy has for its foundation critical lucidity. The end and climax of it would be the intuition of the universal law, of the first principle and the final aim of the universe. Not to be deceived is its first desire; to understand, its second. Emancipation from error is the condition of real knowledge. The philosopher is a skeptic seeking a plausible hypothesis, which may explain to him the whole of his experiences. When he imagines that he has found such a key to life he offers it to, but does not force it on his fellow men.

October 9, 1872.—I have been taking tea at the M's. These English homes are very attractive. They are the recompense and the result of a long-lived civilization, and of an ideal untiringly pursued. What ideal? That of a moral order, founded on respect for self and for others, and on reverence for duty—in a word, upon personal worth and dignity. The master shows consideration to his guests, the children are deferential to their parents, and every one and everything has its place. They understand both how to command and how to obey. The little world is well governed, and seems to go of itself; duty is the *genius loci*—but duty tinged with a reserve and self-control which is the English characteristic. The children are the great test of this domestic system; they are happy, smiling, trustful, and yet no trouble. One feels that they know themselves to be loved, but that they know also that they must obey. *Our* children behave like masters of the house, and when any definite order comes to limit their encroachments they see in it an abuse of power, an arbitrary act. Why? Because it is their principle to believe that everything turns round them. Our children may be gentle and affectionate, but they are not grateful, and they know nothing of self-control.

How do English mothers attain this result? By a rule which is impersonal, invariable, and firm; in other words, by law, which forms man for liberty, while arbitrary decree only leads to rebellion and attempts at emancipation. This method has the immense advantage of forming characters which are restive under arbitrary authority, and yet amenable to justice, conscious of what is due to them and what they owe to others, watchful over conscience, and practiced in self-government. In every English child one feels something of the national motto—"God and my right," and in every English household one has a sense that the home is a citadel, or better still, a ship in which every one has his place. Naturally in such a world the value set on family life corresponds with the cost of producing it; it is sweet to those whose efforts maintain it.

October 14, 1872.—The man who gives himself to contemplation looks on at, rather than directs his life, is rather a spectator than an actor, seeks rather to understand than to achieve. Is this mode of existence illegitimate, immoral? Is one bound to act? Is such detachment an idiosyncrasy to be respected or a sin to be fought against? I have always hesitated on this point, and I have wasted years in futile self-reproach and useless fits of activity. My western conscience, penetrated as it is with Christian morality, has always persecuted my oriental quietism and Buddhist tendencies. I have not dared to approve myself, I have not known how to correct myself. In this, as in all else, I have remained divided, and perplexed, wavering between two extremes. So equilibrium is somehow preserved, but the crystallization of action or thought becomes impossible.

Having early a glimpse of the absolute, I have never had the indiscreet effrontery of individualism. What right have I to make a merit of a defect? I have never been able to see any necessity for imposing myself upon others, nor for succeeding. I have seen nothing clearly except my own deficiencies and the superiority of others. That is not the way to make a career. With varied aptitudes and a fair intelligence, I had no dominant tendency, no imperious faculty, so that while by virtue of capacity I felt myself free, yet when free I could not discover what was best. Equilibrium produced indecision, and indecision has rendered all my faculties barren.

November 8, 1872. (*Friday*).—I have been turning over the "Stoics" again. Poor Louisa Siefert! [Footnote: Louise Siefert, a modern French poetess, died 1879. In addition to "Les Stoiques," she published "L'Annee Republicaine," Paris 1869, and other works.] Ah! we play the stoic, and all the while the poisoned arrow in the side pierces and wounds, *lethalis arundo*. What is it that, like all passionate souls, she really craves for? Two things which are contradictory—glory and happiness. She adores two incompatibles—the Reformation and the Revolution, France and the contrary of France; her talent itself is a combination of two opposing qualities, inwardness and brilliancy, noisy display and lyrical charm. She dislocates the rhythm of her verse, while at the same time she has a sensitive ear for rhyme. She is always wavering between Valmore and Baudelaire, between Leconte de Lisle and Sainte-

Beuve—that is to say, her taste is a bringing together of extremes. She herself has described it:

"Toujours extreme en mes desirs, Jadis, enfant joyeuse et folle, Souvent une seule parole Bouleversait tous mes plaisirs."

But what a fine instrument she possesses! what strength of soul! what wealth of imagination!

December 3, 1872.—What a strange dream! I was under an illusion and yet not under it; I was playing a comedy to myself, deceiving my imagination without being able to deceive my consciousness. This power which dreams have of fusing incompatibles together, of uniting what is exclusive, of identifying yes and no, is what is most wonderful and most symbolical in them. In a dream our individuality is not shut up within itself; it envelops, so to speak, its surroundings; it is the landscape, and all that it contains, ourselves included. But if our imagination is not our own, if it is impersonal, then personality is but a special and limited case of its general functions. *A fortiori* it would be the same for thought. And if so, thought might exist without possessing itself individually, without embodying itself in an *ego*. In other words, dreams lead us to the idea of an imagination enfranchised from the limits of personality, and even of a thought which should be no longer conscious. The individual who dreams is on the way to become dissolved in the universal phantasmagoria of Maia. Dreams are excursions into the limbo of things, a semi-deliverance from the human prison. The man who dreams is but the *locale* of various phenomena of which he is the spectator in spite of himself; he is passive and impersonal; he is the plaything of unknown vibrations and invisible sprites.

The man who should never issue from the state of dream would have never attained humanity, properly so called, but the man who had never dreamed would only know the mind in its completed or manufactured state, and would not be able to understand the genesis of personality; he would be like a crystal, incapable of guessing what crystallization means. So that the waking life issues from the dream life, as dreams are an emanation from the nervous life, and this again is the fine flower of organic life. Thought is the highest point of a series of ascending metamorphoses, which is called nature. Personality by means of thought, recovers in inward profundity what it has lost in extension, and makes up for the rich accumulations of receptive passivity by the enormous privilege of that empire over self which is called liberty. Dreams, by confusing and suppressing all limits, make us feel, indeed, the severity of the conditions attached to the higher existence; but conscious and voluntary thought alone brings knowledge and allows us to act—that is to say, is alone capable of science and of perfection. Let us then take pleasure in dreaming for reasons of psychological curiosity and mental recreation; but let us never speak ill of thought, which is our strength and our dignity. Let us begin as Orientals, and end as Westerns, for these are the two halves of wisdom.

December 11, 1872.—A deep and dreamless sleep and now I wake up to the gray, lowering, rainy sky, which has kept us company for so long. The air is mild, the general outlook depressing. I think that it is partly the fault of my windows, which are not very clean, and contribute by their dimness to this gloomy aspect of the outer world. Rain and smoke have besmeared them.

Between us and things how many screens there are! Mood, health, the tissues of the eye, the window-panes of our cell, mist, smoke, rain, dust, and light itself—and all infinitely variable! Heraclitus said: "No man bathes twice in the same river." I feel inclined to say; No one sees the same landscape twice over, for a window is one kaleidoscope, and the spectator another.

What is madness? Illusion, raised to the second power. A sound mind establishes regular relations, a *modus vivendi*, between things, men, and itself, and it is under the delusion that it has got hold of stable truth and eternal fact. Madness does not even see what sanity sees, deceiving itself all the while by the belief that it sees better than sanity. The sane mind or common sense confounds the fact of experience with necessary fact, and assumes in good faith that what is, is the measure of what may be; while madness cannot perceive any difference between what is and what it imagines—it confounds its dreams with reality.

Wisdom consists in rising superior both to madness and to common sense, and in lending one's self to the universal illusion without becoming its dupe. It is best, on the whole, for a man of taste who knows how to be gay with the gay, and serious with the serious, to enter into the game of Maia, and to play his part with a good grace in the fantastic tragi-comedy which is called the Universe. It seems to me that here intellectualism reaches its limit. [Footnote: "We all believe in duty," says M. Renan, "and in the triumph of righteousness;" but it is possible notwithstanding, "que tout le contraire soit vrai—et que le monde ne soit qu'une amusante feerie dont aucun dieu ne se soucie. Il faut donc nous arranger de maniere a ceque, dans le cas ou le seconde hypothese serait la vraie, nous n'ayons pas ete trop dupes."

This strain of remark, which is developed at considerable length, is meant as a criticism of Amiel's want of sensitiveness to the irony of things. But in reality, as the passage in the text shows, M. Renan is only expressing a feeling with which Amiel was just as familiar as his critic. Only he is delivered from this last doubt of all by his habitual seriousness; by that sense of "horror and awe" which M. Renan puts away from him. Conscience saves him "from the sorceries of Maia."] The mind, in its intellectual capacity, arrives at the intuition that all reality is but the dream of a dream. What delivers us from the palace of dreams is pain, personal pain; it is also the sense of obligation, or that which combines the two, the pain of sin; and again it is love; in short, the moral order. What saves us from the sorceries of Maia is conscience; conscience dissipates the narcotic vapors, the opium-like hallucinations, the placid stupor of contemplative indifference. It drives us into contact with the terrible wheels within wheels of human suffering and human responsibility; it is the bugle-call, the cockcrow, which puts the phantoms to flight; it is the armed archangel who chases man from an artificial paradise. Intellectualism may be described as an intoxication conscious of itself; the moral energy which replaces it, on the other hand, represents a state of fast, a famine and a sleepless thirst. Alas! Alas!

Those who have the most frivolous idea of sin are just those who suppose that there is a fixed gulf between good people and others.

* * * * *

The ideal which the wife and mother makes for herself, the manner in which she understands duty and life, contain the fate of the community. Her faith becomes the star of the conjugal ship, and her love the animating principle that fashions the future of all belonging to her. Woman is the salvation or destruction of the family. She carries its destinies in the folds of her mantle.

* * * * *

Perhaps it is not desirable that a woman should be free in mind; she would immediately abuse her freedom. She cannot become philosophical without losing her special gift, which is the worship of all that is individual, the defense of usage, manners, beliefs, traditions. Her role is to slacken the combustion of thought. It is analogous to that of azote in vital air.

* * * * *

In every loving woman there is a priestess of the past—a pious guardian of some affection, of which the object has disappeared.

January 6, 1873.—I have been reading the seven tragedies of Aeschylus, in the translation of Leconte de Lisle. The "Prometheus" and the "Eumenides" are greatest where all is great; they have the sublimity of the old prophets. Both depict a religious revolution—a profound crisis in the life of humanity. In "Prometheus" it is civilization wrenched from the jealous hands of the gods; in the "Eumenides" it is the transformation of the idea of justice, and the substitution of atonement and pardon for the law of implacable revenge. "Prometheus" shows us the martyrdom which waits for all the saviors of men; the "Eumenides" is the glorification of Athens and the Areopagus—that is to say, of a truly human civilization. How magnificent it is as poetry, and how small the adventures of individual passion seem beside this colossal type of tragedy, of which the theme is the destinies of nations!

March 31, 1873. (4 P. M.)—

"En quel songe Se plonge Mon coeur, et que veut-il?"

For an hour past I have been the prey of a vague anxiety; I recognize my old enemy.... It is a sense of void and anguish; a sense of something lacking: what? Love, peace—God perhaps. The feeling is one of pure want unmixed with hope, and there is anguish in it because I can clearly distinguish neither the evil nor its remedy.

"O printemps sans pitie, dans l'ame endolorie, Avec tes chants d'oiseaux, tes brises, ton azur, Tu creuses sourdement, conspirateur obscur, Le gouffre des langueurs et de la reverie."

Of all the hours of the day, in fine weather, the afternoon, about 3 o'clock, is the time which to me is most difficult to bear. I never feel more strongly than I do then, *"le vide effrayant de la vie,"* the stress of mental anxiety, or the painful thirst for happiness. This torture born of the sunlight is a strange phenomenon. Is it that the sun, just as it brings out the stain upon a garment, the wrinkles in a face, or the discoloration of the hair, so also it illumines with inexorable distinctness the scars and rents of the heart? Does it rouse in us a sort of shame of existence? In any case the bright hours of the day are capable of flooding the whole soul with melancholy, of kindling in us the passion for death, or suicide, or annihilation, or of driving us to that which is next akin to death, the deadening of the senses by the pursuit of pleasure. They rouse in the lonely man a horror of himself; they make him long to escape from his own misery and solitude—

"Le coeur trempe sept fois dans le neant divin."

People talk of the temptations to crime connected with darkness, but the dumb sense of desolation which is often the product of the most brilliant moment of daylight must not be forgotten either. From the one, as from the other, God is absent; but in the first case a man follows his senses and the cry of his passion; in the second, he feels himself lost and bewildered, a creature forsaken by all the world.

"En nous sont deux instincts qui bravent la raison, C'est l'effroi du bonheur et la soif du poison. Coeur solitaire, a toi prends garde!"

April 3, 1873.—I have been to see my friends ——. Their niece has just arrived with two of her children, and the conversation turned on Father Hyacinthe's lecture.

Women of an enthusiastic temperament have a curious way of speaking of extempore preachers and orators. They imagine that inspiration radiates from a crowd as such, and that inspiration is all that is wanted. Could there be a more *naif* and childish explanation of what is really a lecture in which nothing has been left to accident, neither the plan, nor the metaphors, nor even the length of the whole, and where everything has been prepared with the greatest care! But women, in their love of what is marvelous and miraculous, prefer to ignore all this. The meditation, the labor, the calculation of effects, the art, in a word, which have gone to the making of it, diminishes for them the value of the thing, and they prefer to believe it fallen from heaven, or sent down from on high. They ask for bread, but cannot bear the idea of a baker. The sex is superstitious, and hates to understand what it wishes to admire. It would vex it to be forced to give the smaller share to feeling, and the larger share to thought. It wishes to believe that imagination can do the work of reason, and feeling the work of science, and it never asks itself how it is that women, so rich in heart and imagination, have never distinguished themselves as orators—that is to say, have never known how to combine a multitude of facts, ideas, and impulses, into one complex unity. Enthusiastic women never even suspect the difference that there is between the excitement of a popular harangue, which is nothing but a mere passionate outburst, and the unfolding of a didactic process, the aim of which is to prove something and to convince its hearers. Therefore, for them, study, reflection, technique, count as nothing; the improvisatore mounts upon the tripod, Pallas all armed issues from his lips, and conquers the applause of the dazzled assembly.

Evidently women divide orators into two groups; the artisans of speech, who manufacture their laborious discourses by the aid of the midnight lamp, and the inspired souls, who simply give themselves the trouble to be born. They will never understand the saying of Quintilian, "*Fit orator, nascitur poeta.*"

The enthusiasm which acts is perhaps an enlightening force, but the enthusiasm which accepts is very like blindness. For this latter enthusiasm confuses the value of things, ignores their shades of difference, and is an obstacle to all sensible criticism and all calm judgment. The "Ewig-Weibliche" favors exaggeration, mysticism, sentimentalism—all that excites and startles. It is the enemy of clearness, of a calm and rational view of things, the antipodes of criticism and of science. I have had only too much sympathy and weakness for the feminine nature. The very excess of my former indulgence toward it makes me now more conscious of its infirmity. Justice and science, law and reason, are virile things, and they come before imagination, feeling, reverie, and fancy. When one reflects that Catholic superstition is maintained by women, one feels how needful it is not to hand over the reins to the "Eternal Womanly."

May 23, 1873.—The fundamental error of France lies in her psychology. France has always believed that to say a thing is the same as to do it, as though speech were action, as though rhetoric were capable of modifying the tendencies, habits, and character of real beings, and as though verbiage were an efficient substitute for will, conscience, and education.

France proceeds by bursts of eloquence, of cannonading, or of law-making; she thinks that so she can change the nature of things; and she produces only phrases and ruins. She has never understood the first line of Montesquieu: "Laws are necessary relations, derived from the nature of things." She will not see that her incapacity to organize liberty comes from her own nature; from the notions which she has of the individual, of society, of religion, of law, of duty—from the manner in which she brings up children. Her way is to plant trees downward, and then she is astonished at the result! Universal suffrage, with a bad religion and a bad popular education, means perpetual wavering between anarchy and dictatorship, between the red and the black, between Danton and Loyola.

How many scapegoats will Prance sacrifice before it occurs to her to beat her own breast in penitence?

August 18, 1873. (*Scheveningen*).—Yesterday, Sunday, the landscape was clear and distinct, the air bracing, the sea bright and gleaming, and of an ashy-blue color. There were beautiful effects of beach, sea, and distance; and dazzling tracks of gold upon the waves, after the sun had sunk below the bands of vapor drawn across the middle sky, and before it had disappeared in the mists of the sea horizon. The place was very full. All Scheveningen and the Hague, the village and the capital, had streamed out on to the terrace, amusing themselves at innumerable tables, and swamping the strangers and the bathers. The orchestra played some Wagner, some Auber, and some waltzes. What was all the world doing? Simply enjoying life.

A thousand thoughts wandered through my brain. I thought how much history it had taken to make what I saw possible; Judaea, Egypt, Greece, Germany, Gaul; all the centuries from Moses to Napoleon, and all the zones from Batavia to Guiana, had united in the formation of this gathering. The industry, the science, the art, the geography, the commerce, the religion of the whole human race, are repeated in every human combination; and what we see before our own eyes at any given moment is inexplicable without reference to all that has ever been. This interlacing of the ten thousand threads which necessity weaves into the production of one single phenomenon is a stupefying thought. One feels one's self in the presence of law itself—allowed a glimpse of the mysterious workshop of nature. The ephemeral perceives the eternal.

What matters the brevity of the individual span, seeing that the generations, the centuries, and the worlds themselves are but occupied forever with the ceaseless reproduction of the hymn of life, in all the hundred thousand modes and variations which make up the universal symphony? The motive is always the same; the monad has but one law: all truths are but the variation of one single truth. The universe represents the infinite wealth of the Spirit seeking in vain to exhaust all possibilities, and the goodness of the Creator, who would fain share with the created all that sleeps within the limbo of Omnipotence.

To contemplate and adore, to receive and give back, to have uttered one's note and moved one's grain of sand, is all which is expected from such insects as we are; it is enough to give motive and meaning to our fugitive apparition in existence....

After the concert was over the paved esplanade behind the hotels and the two roads leading to the Hague were alive with people. One might have fancied one's self upon one of the great Parisian boulevards just when the theaters are emptying themselves—there were so many carriages, omnibuses, and cabs. Then, when the human tumult had disappeared, the peace of the starry heaven shone out resplendent, and the dreamy glimmer of the Milky Way was only answered by the distant murmur of the ocean.

Later.—What is it which has always come between real life and me? What glass screen has, as it were, interposed itself between me and the enjoyment, the possession, the contact of things, leaving me only the role of the looker-on?

False shame, no doubt. I have been ashamed to desire. Fatal result of timidity, aggravated by intellectual delusion! This renunciation beforehand of all natural ambitions, this systematic putting aside of all longings and all desires, has perhaps been false in idea; it has been too like a foolish, self-inflicted mutilation. Fear, too, has had a large share in it—

"La peur de ce que j'aime est ma fatalite."

I very soon discovered that it was simpler for me to give up a wish than to satisfy it. Not being able to obtain all that my nature longed for, I renounced the whole *en bloc*, without even taking the trouble to determine in detail what might have attracted me; for what was the good of stirring up trouble in one's self and evoking images of inaccessible treasure?

Thus I anticipated in spirit all possible disillusions, in the true stoical fashion. Only, with singular lack of logic, I have sometimes allowed regret to overtake me, and I have looked at conduct founded upon exceptional principles with the eyes of the ordinary man. I should have been ascetic to the end; contemplation ought to have been enough for me, especially now, when the hair begins to whiten. But, after all, I am a man, and not a theorem. A system cannot suffer, but I suffer. Logic makes only one demand—that of consequence; but life makes a thousand; the body wants health, the imagination cries out for beauty, and the heart for love; pride asks for consideration, the soul yearns for peace, the conscience for holiness; our whole being is athirst for happiness and for perfection; and we, tottering, mutilated, and incomplete, cannot always feign philosophic insensibility; we stretch out our arms toward life, and we say to it under our breath, "Why—why—hast thou deceived me?"

August 19,1873. (*Scheveningen*).—I have had a morning walk. It has been raining in the night. There are large clouds all round; the sea, veined with green and drab, has put on the serious air of labor. She is about her business, in no threatening but at the same time in no lingering mood. She is making her clouds, heaping up her sands, visiting her shores and bathing them with foam, gathering up her floods for the tide, carrying the ships to their destinations, and feeding the universal life. I found in a hidden nook a sheet of fine sand which the water had furrowed and folded like the pink palate of a kitten's mouth, or like a dappled sky. Everything repeats itself by analogy, and each little fraction of the earth reproduces in a smaller and individual form all the phenomena of the planet. Farther on I came across a bank of crumbling shells, and it was borne in upon me that the sea-sand itself might well be only the detritus of the organic life of preceding eras, a vast monument or pyramid of immemorial age, built up by countless generations of molluscs who have labored at the architecture of the shores like good workmen of God. If the dunes and the mountains are the dust of living creatures who have preceded us, how can we doubt but that our death will be as serviceable as our life, and that nothing which has been lent is lost? Mutual borrowing and temporary service seem to be the law of existence. Only, the strong prey upon and devour the weak, and the concrete inequality of lots within the abstract equality of destinies wounds and disquiets the sense of justice.

Same day.—A new spirit governs and inspires the generation which will succeed me. It is a singular sensation to feel the grass growing under one's feet, to see one's self intellectually uprooted. One must address one's contemporaries. Younger men will not listen to you. Thought, like love, will not tolerate a gray hair. Knowledge herself loves the young, as Fortune used to do in olden days. Contemporary civilization does not know what to do with old age; in proportion as it defies physical experiment, it despises moral experience. One sees therein the triumph of Darwinism; it is a state of war, and war must have young soldiers; it can only put up with age in its leaders when they have the strength and the mettle of veterans.

In point of fact, one must either be strong or disappear, either constantly rejuvenate one's self or perish. It is as though the humanity of our day had, like the migratory birds, an immense voyage to make across space; she can no longer support the weak or help on the laggards. The great assault upon the future makes her hard and pitiless to all who fall by the way. Her motto is, "The devil take the hindmost."

The worship of strength has never lacked altars, but it looks as though the more we talk of justice and humanity, the more that other god sees his kingdom widen.

August 20, 1873. (*Scheveningen*).—I have now watched the sea which beats upon this shore under many different aspects. On the whole, I should class it with the Baltic. As far as color, effect, and landscape go, it is widely different from the Breton or Basque ocean, and, above all, from the Mediterranean. It never attains to the blue-green of the Atlantic, nor the indigo of the Ionian Sea. Its scale of color runs from flint to emerald, and when it turns to blue, the blue is a turquoise shade splashed with gray. The sea here is not amusing itself; it has a busy and serious air, like an Englishman or a Dutchman. Neither polyps nor jelly-fish, neither sea-weed nor crabs enliven the sands at low water; the sea life is poor and meagre. What is wonderful is the struggle of man against a miserly and formidable power. Nature has done little for him, but she allows herself to be managed. Stepmother though she be, she is accommodating, subject to the occasional destruction of a hundred thousand lives in a single inundation.

The air inside the dune is altogether different from that outside it. The air of the sea is life-giving, bracing, oxydized; the air inland is soft, relaxing, and warm. In the same way there are two Hollands in every Dutchman: there is the man of the *polder*, heavy, pale, phlegmatic, slow, patient himself, and trying to the patience of others, and there is the man of the *dune*, of the harbor, the shore, the sea, who is tenacious, seasoned, persevering, sunburned, daring. Where the two agree is in calculating prudence, and in methodical persistency of effort.

August 22, 1873. (*Scheveningen*).—The weather is rainy, the whole atmosphere gray; it is a time favorable to thought and meditation. I have a liking for such days as these; they revive one's converse with one's self and make it possible to live the inner life; they are quiet and peaceful, like a song in a minor key. We are nothing but thought, but we feel our life to its very center. Our very sensations turn to reverie. It is a strange state of mind; it is like those silences in worship which are not the empty moments of devotion, but the full moments, and which are so because at such times the soul, instead of being polarized, dispersed, localized, in a single impression or thought, feels her own totality and is conscious of herself. She tastes her own substance. She is no longer played upon, colored, set in motion, affected, from without; she is in equilibrium and at rest. Openness and self-surrender become possible to her; she contemplates and she adores. She sees the changeless and the eternal enwrapping all the phenomena of time. She is in the religious state, in harmony with the general order, or at least in intellectual harmony. For *holiness*, indeed, more is wanted—a harmony of will, a perfect self-devotion, death to self and absolute submission.

Psychological peace—that harmony which is perfect but virtual—is but the zero, the potentiality of all numbers; it is not that moral peace which is victorious over all ills, which is real, positive, tried by experience, and able to face whatever fresh storms may assail it.

The peace of fact is not the peace of principle. There are indeed two happinesses, that of nature and that of conquest—two equilibria, that of Greece and that of Nazareth—two kingdoms, that of the natural man and that of the regenerate man.

Later. (*Scheveningen*).—Why do doctors so often make mistakes? Because they are not sufficiently individual in their diagnoses or their treatment. They class a sick man under some given department of their nosology, whereas every invalid is really a special case, a unique example. How is it possible that so coarse a method of sifting should produce judicious therapeutics? Every illness is a factor simple or complex, which is multiplied by a second factor, invariably complex—the individual, that is to say, who is suffering from it, so that the result is a special problem, demanding a special solution, the more so the greater the remoteness of the patient from childhood or from country life.

The principal grievance which I have against the doctors is that they neglect the real problem, which is to seize the unity of the individual who claims their care. Their methods of investigation are far too elementary; a doctor who does not read you to the bottom is ignorant of essentials. To me the ideal doctor would be a man endowed with profound knowledge of life and of the soul, intuitively divining any suffering or disorder of whatever kind, and restoring peace by his mere presence. Such a doctor is possible, but the greater number of them lack the higher and inner life, they know nothing of the transcendent laboratories of nature; they seem to me superficial, profane, strangers to divine things, destitute of intuition and sympathy. The model doctor should be at once a genius, a saint, a man of God.

September 11, 1873. (*Amsterdam*).—The doctor has just gone. He says I have fever about me, and does not think that I can start for another three days without imprudence. I dare not write to my Genevese friends and tell them that I am coming back from the sea in a radically worse state of strength and throat than when I went there, and that I have only wasted my time, my trouble, my money, and my hopes....

This contradictory double fact—on the one side an eager hopefulness springing up afresh after all disappointments, and on the other an experience almost invariably unfavorable—can be explained like all illusions by the whim of nature, which either wills us to be deceived or wills us to act as if we were so.

Skepticism is the wiser course, but in delivering us from error it tends to paralyze life. Maturity of mind consists in taking part in the prescribed game as seriously as though one believed in it. Good-humored compliance, tempered by a smile, is, on the whole, the best line to take; one lends one's self to an optical illusion, and the voluntary concession has an air of liberty. Once imprisoned in existence, we must submit to its laws with a good grace; to rebel against it only ends in impotent rage, when once we have denied ourselves the solution of suicide.

Humility and submission, or the religious point of view; clear-eyed indulgence with a touch of irony, or the point of view of worldly wisdom—these two attitudes are possible. The second is sufficient for the minor ills of life, the other is perhaps necessary in the greater ones. The pessimism of Schopenhauer supposes at least health and intellect as means of enduring the rest of life. But optimism either of the stoical or the Christian sort is needed to make it possible for us to bear the worst sufferings of flesh, heart and soul. If we are to escape the grip of despair, we must believe either that the whole of things at least is good, or that grief is a fatherly grace, a purifying trial.

There can be no doubt that the idea of a happy immortality, serving as a harbor of refuge from the tempests of this mortal existence, and rewarding the fidelity, the patience, the submission, and the courage of the travelers on life's sea—there can be no doubt that this idea, the strength of so many generations, and the faith of the church, carries with it inexpressible consolation to those who are wearied, burdened, and tormented by pain and suffering. To feel one's self individually cared for and protected by God gives a special dignity and beauty to life. Monotheism lightens the struggle for existence. But does the study of nature allow of the maintenance of those local revelations which are called Mosaism, Christianity, Islamism? These religions founded upon an infantine cosmogony, and upon a chimerical history of humanity, can they bear confronting with modern astronomy and geology? The present mode of escape, which consists in trying to satisfy the claims of both science and faith—of the science which contradicts all the ancient beliefs, and the faith which, in the case of things that are beyond nature and incapable of verification, affirms them on her own responsibility only—this mode of escape cannot last forever. Every fresh cosmical conception demands a religion which corresponds to it. Our age of transition stands bewildered between the two incompatible methods, the scientific method and the religious method, and between the two certitudes, which contradict each other.

Surely the reconciliation of the two must be sought for in the moral law, which is also a fact, and every step of which requires for its explanation another cosmos than the cosmos of necessity. Who knows if necessity is not a particular case of liberty, and its condition? Who knows if nature is not a laboratory for the fabrication of thinking beings who are ultimately to become free creatures? Biology protests, and indeed the supposed existence of souls, independently of time, space, and matter, is a fiction of faith, less logical than the Platonic dogma. But the question remains open. We may eliminate the idea of purpose from nature, yet, as the guiding conception of the highest being of our planet, it is a fact, and a fact which postulates a meaning in the history of the universe.

My thought is straying in vague paths: why? because I have no creed. All my studies end in notes of interrogation, and that I may not draw premature or arbitrary conclusions I draw none.

Later on.—My creed has melted away, but I believe in good, in the moral order, and in salvation; religion for me is to live and die in God, in complete abandonment to the holy will which is at the root of nature and destiny. I believe even in the gospel, the good news—that is to say, in the reconciliation of the sinner with God, by faith in the love of a pardoning Father.

October 4, 1873. (*Geneva*).—I have been dreaming a long while in the moonlight, which floods my room with a radiance, full of vague mystery. The state of mind induced in us by this fantastic light is itself so dim and ghost-like that analysis loses its way in it, and arrives at nothing articulate. It is something indefinite and intangible, like the noise of waves which is made up of a thousand fused and mingled sounds. It is the reverberation of all the unsatisfied desires of the soul, of all the stifled sorrows of the heart, mingling in a vague sonorous whole, and dying away in cloudy murmurs. All those imperceptible regrets, which never individually reach the consciousness, accumulate at last into a definite result; they become the voice of a feeling of emptiness and aspiration; their tone is melancholy itself. In youth the tone of these Aeolian vibrations of the heart is all hope—a proof that these thousands of indistinguishable accents make up indeed the fundamental note of our being, and reveal the tone of our whole situation. Tell me what you feel in your solitary room when the full moon is shining in upon you and your lamp is dying out, and I will tell you how old you are, and I shall know if you are happy.

* * * * *

The best path through life is the high road, which initiates us at the right moment into all experience. Exceptional itineraries are suspicious, and matter for anxiety. What is normal is at once most convenient, most honest, and most wholesome. Cross roads may tempt us for one reason or another, but it is very seldom that we do not come to regret having taken them.

*****

Each man begins the world afresh, and not one fault of the first man has been avoided by his remotest descendant. The collective experience of the race accumulates, but individual experience dies with the individual, and the result is that institutions become wiser and knowledge as such increases; but the young man, although more cultivated, is just as presumptuous, and not less fallible to-day than he ever was. So that absolutely there is progress, and relatively there is none. Circumstances improve, but merit remains the same. The whole is better, perhaps, but man is not positively better—he is only different. His defects and his virtues change their form, but the total balance does not show him to be the richer. A thousand things advance, nine hundred and ninety-eight fall back, this is progress. There is nothing in it to be proud of, but something, after all, to console one.

February 4, 1874.—I am still reading the "Origines du Christianisme" by Ernest Havet. [Footnote: Ernest Havet, born 1813, a distinguished French scholar and professor. He became professor of Latin oratory at the College de France in 1855, and a member of the Institute in January, 1880. His admirable edition of the "Pensees de Pascal" is well-known. "Le Christianisme et ses Origines," an important book, in four volumes, was developed from a series of articles in the *Revue des deux Mondes*, and the *Revue Contemporaine*.] I like the book and I dislike it. I like it for its independence and courage; I dislike it for the insufficiency of its fundamental ideas, and the imperfection of its categories.

The author, for instance, has no clear idea of religion; and his philosophy of history is superficial. He is a Jacobin. "The Republic and Free Thought"—he cannot get beyond that. This curt and narrow school of opinion is the refuge of men of independent mind, who have been scandalized by the colossal fraud of ultramontanism; but it leads rather to cursing history than to understanding it. It is the criticism of the eighteenth century, of which the general result is purely negative. But Voltairianism is only the half of the philosophic mind. Hegel frees thought in a very different way.

Havet, too, makes another mistake. He regards Christianity as synonymous with Roman Catholicism and with the church. I know very well that the Roman Church does the same, and that with her the assimilation is a matter of sound tactics; but scientifically it is inexact. We ought not even to identify Christianity with the gospel, nor the gospel with religion in general. It is the business of critical precision to clear away these perpetual confusions in which Christian practice and Christian preaching abound. To disentangle ideas, to distinguish and limit them, to fit them into their true place and order, is the first duty of science whenever it lays hands upon such chaotic and complex things as manners, idioms, or beliefs. Entanglement is the condition of life; order and clearness are the signs of serious and successful thought.

Formerly it was the ideas of nature which were a tissue of errors and incoherent fancies; now it is the turn of moral and psychological ideas. The best issue from the present Babel would be the formation or the sketching out of a truly scientific science of man.

February 16, 1874.—The multitude, who already possess force, and even, according to the Republican view, right, have always been persuaded by the Cleons of the day that enlightenment, wisdom, thought, and reason, are also theirs. The game of these conjurors and quacks of universal suffrage has always been to flatter the crowd in order to make an instrument of it. They pretend to adore the puppet of which they pull the threads.

The theory of radicalism is a piece of juggling, for it supposes premises of which it knows the falsity; it manufactures the oracle whose revelations it pretends to adore; it proclaims that the multitude creates a brain for itself, while all the time it is the clever man who is the brain of the multitude, and suggests to it what it is supposed to invent. To reign by flattery has been the common practice of the courtiers of all despotisms, the favorites of all tyrants; it is an old and trite method, but none the less odious for that.

The honest politician should worship nothing but reason and justice, and it is his business to preach them to the masses, who represent, on an average, the age of childhood and not that of maturity. We corrupt childhood if we tell it that it cannot be mistaken, and that it knows more than its elders. We corrupt the masses when we tell them that they are wise and far-seeing and possess the gift of infallibility.

It is one of Montesquieu's subtle remarks, that the more wise men you heap together the less wisdom you will obtain. Radicalism pretends that the greater number of illiterate, passionate, thoughtless—above all, young people, you heap together, the greater will be the enlightenment resulting. The second thesis is no doubt the repartee to the first, but the joke is a bad one. All that can be got from a crowd is instinct or passion; the instinct may be good, but the passion may be bad, and neither is the instinct capable of producing a clear idea, nor the passion of leading to a just resolution.

A crowd is a material force, and the support of numbers gives a proposition the force of law; but that wise and ripened temper of mind which takes everything into account, and therefore tends to truth, is never engendered by the impetuosity of the masses. The masses are the material of democracy, but its form—that is to say, the laws which express the general reason, justice, and utility—can only be rightly shaped by wisdom, which is by no means a universal property. The fundamental error of the radical theory is to confound the right to do good with good itself, and universal suffrage with universal wisdom. It rests upon a legal fiction, which assumes a real equality of enlightenment and merit among those whom it declares electors. It is quite possible, however, that these electors may not desire the public good, and that even if they do, they may be deceived as to the manner of realizing it. Universal suffrage is not a dogma—it is an instrument; and according to the population in whose hands it is placed, the instrument is serviceable or deadly to the proprietor.

February 27, 1874.—Among the peoples, in whom the social gifts are the strongest, the individual fears ridicule above all things, and ridicule is the certain result of originality. No one, therefore, wishes to make a party of his own; every one wishes to be on the side of all the world. "All the world" is the greatest of powers; it is sovereign, and calls itself *we*. *We* dress, *we* dine, *we* walk, *we* go out, *we* come in, like this, and not like that. This *we* is always right, whatever it does. The subjects of *We* are more prostrate than the slaves of the East before the Padishah. The good pleasure of the sovereign decides every appeal; his caprice is law. What *we* does or says is called custom, what it thinks is called opinion, what it believes to be beautiful or good is called fashion. Among such nations as these *we* is the brain, the conscience, the reason, the taste, and the judgment of all. The individual finds everything decided for him without his troubling about it. He is dispensed from the task of finding out anything whatever. Provided that he imitates, copies, and repeats the models furnished by *we*, he has nothing more to fear. He knows all that he need know, and has entered into salvation.

April 29, 1874.—Strange reminiscence! At the end of the terrace of La Treille, on the eastern side, as I looked down the slope, it seemed to me that I saw once more in imagination a little path which existed there when I was a child, and ran through the bushy underwood, which was thicker then than it is now. It is at least forty years since this impression disappeared from my mind. The revival of an image so dead and so forgotten set me thinking. Consciousness seems to be like a book, in which the leaves turned by life successively cover and hide each other in spite of their semi-transparency; but although the book may be open at the page of the present, the wind, for a few seconds, may blow back the first pages into view.

And at death will these leaves cease to hide each other, and shall we see all our past at once? Is death the passage from the successive to the simultaneous—that is to say, from time to eternity? Shall we then understand, in its unity, the poem or mysterious episode of our existence, which till then we have spelled out phrase by phrase? And is this the secret of that glory which so often enwraps the brow and countenance of those who are newly dead? If so, death would be like the arrival of a traveler at the top of a great mountain, whence he sees spread out before him the whole configuration of the country, of which till then he had had but passing glimpses. To be able to overlook one's own history, to divine its meaning in the general concert and in the divine plan, would be the beginning of eternal felicity. Till then we had sacrificed ourselves to the universal order, but then we should understand and appreciate the beauty of that order. We had toiled and labored under the conductor of the orchestra; and we should find ourselves become surprised and delighted hearers. We had seen nothing but our own little path in the mist; and suddenly a marvelous panorama and boundless distances would open before our dazzled eyes. Why not?

May 31, 1874.—I have been reading the philosophical poems of Madame Ackermann. She has rendered in fine verse that sense of desolation which has been so often stirred in me by the philosophy of Schopenhauer, of Hartmann, Comte, and Darwin. What tragic force and power! What thought and passion! She has courage for everything, and attacks the most tremendous subjects.

Science is implacable; will it suppress all religions? All those which start from a false conception of nature, certainly. But if the scientific conception of nature proves incapable of bringing harmony and peace to man, what will happen? Despair is not a durable situation. We shall have to build a moral city without God, without an immortality of the soul, without hope. Buddhism and stoicism present themselves as possible alternatives.

But even if we suppose that there is no finality in the cosmos, it is certain that man has ends at which he aims, and if so the notion of end or purpose is a real phenomenon, although a limited one. Physical science may very well be limited by moral science, and *vice versa*. But if these two conceptions of the world are in opposition, which must give way?

I still incline to believe that nature is the virtuality of mind—that the soul is the fruit of life, and liberty the flower of necessity—that all is bound together, and that nothing can be done without. Our modern philosophy has returned to the point of view of the Ionians, the [Greek: *physikoi*], or naturalist thinkers. But it will have to pass once more through Plato and through Aristotle, through the philosophy of "goodness" and "purpose," through the science of mind.

July 3, 1874.—Rebellion against common sense is a piece of childishness of which I am quite capable. But it does not last long. I am soon brought back to the advantages and obligations of my situation; I return to a calmer self-consciousness. It is disagreeable to me, no doubt, to realize all that is hopelessly lost to me, all that is now and will be forever denied to me; but I reckon up my privileges as well as my losses—I lay stress on what I have, and not only on what I want. And so I escape from that terrible dilemma of "all or nothing," which for me always ends in the adoption of the second alternative. It seems to me at such times that a man may without shame content himself with being *some* thing and *some* one—

"Ni si haut, ni si bas...."

These brusque lapses into the formless, indeterminate state, are the price of my critical faculty. All my former habits become suddenly fluid; it seems to me that I am beginning life over again, and that all my acquired capital has disappeared at a stroke. I am forever new-born; I am a mind which has never taken to itself a body, a country, an avocation, a sex, a species. Am I even quite sure of being a man, a

European, an inhabitant of this earth? It seems to me so easy to be something else, that to be what I am appears to me a mere piece of arbitrary choice. I cannot possibly take an accidental structure of which the value is purely relative, seriously. When once a man has touched the absolute, all that might be other than what it is seems to him indifferent. All these ants pursuing their private ends excite his mirth. He looks down from the moon upon his hovel; he beholds the earth from the heights of the sun; he considers his life from the point of view of the Hindoo pondering the days of Brahma; he sees the finite from the distance of the infinite, and thenceforward the insignificance of all those things which men hold to be important makes effort ridiculous, passion burlesque, and prejudice absurd.

August 7, 1874. (*Clarens*).—A day perfectly beautiful, luminous, limpid, brilliant.

I passed the morning in the churchyard; the "Oasis" was delightful. Innumerable sensations, sweet and serious, peaceful and solemn, passed over me.... Around me Russians, English, Swedes, Germans, were sleeping their last sleep under the shadow of the Cubly. The landscape was one vast splendor; the woods were deep and mysterious, the roses full blown; all around me were butterflies—a noise of wings—the murmur of birds. I caught glimpses through the trees of distant mists, of soaring mountains, of the tender blue of the lake.... A little conjunction of things struck me. Two ladies were tending and watering a grave; two nurses were suckling their children. This double protest against death had something touching and poetical in it. "Sleep, you who are dead; we, the living, are thinking of you, or at least carrying on the pilgrimage of the race!" such seemed to me the words in my ear. It was clear to me that the Oasis of Clarens is the spot in which I should like to rest. Here I am surrounded with memories; here death is like a sleep—a sleep instinct with hope.

* * * * *

Hope is not forbidden us, but peace and submission are the essentials.

September 1, 1874. (*Clarens*).—On waking it seemed to me that I was staring into the future with wide startled eyes. Is it indeed to *me* that these things apply. [Footnote: Amiel had just received at the hands of his doctor the medical verdict, which was his *arret de mort*.]

Incessant and growing humiliation, my slavery becoming heavier, my circle of action steadily narrower!... What is hateful in my situation is that deliverance can never be hoped for, and that one misery will succeed another in such a way as to leave me no breathing space, not even in the future, not even in hope. All possibilities are closed to me, one by one. It is difficult for the natural man to escape from a dumb rage against inevitable agony.

Noon.—An indifferent nature? A Satanic principle of things? A good and just God? Three points of view. The second is improbable and horrible. The first appeals to our stoicism. My organic combination has never been anything but mediocre; it has lasted as long as it could. Every man has his turn, and all must submit. To die quickly is a privilege; I shall die by inches. Well, submit. Rebellion would be useless and senseless. After all, I belong to the better-endowed half of human-kind, and my lot is superior to the average.

But the third point of view alone can give joy. Only is it tenable? Is there a particular Providence directing all the circumstances of our life, and therefore imposing all our trials upon us for educational ends? Is this heroic faith compatible with our actual knowledge of the laws of nature? Scarcely; But what this faith makes objective we may hold as subjective truth. The moral being may moralize his sufferings by using natural facts for his own inner education. What he cannot change he calls the will of God, and to will what God wills brings him peace.

To nature both our continued existence and our morality are equally indifferent. But God, on the other hand, if God is, desires our sanctification; and if suffering purifies us, then we may console ourselves or suffering. This is what makes the great advantage of the Christian faith; it is the triumph over pain, the victory over death. There is but one thing necessary—death unto sin, the immolation of our selfish will, the filial sacrifice of our desires. Evil consists in living for *self*—that is to say, for one's own vanity, pride, sensuality, or even health. Righteousness consists in willingly accepting one's lot, in submitting to, and espousing the destiny assigned us, in willing what God commands, in renouncing what he forbids us, in consenting to what he takes from us or refuses us.

In my own particular case, what has been taken from me is health— that is to say, the surest basis of all independence; but friendship and material comfort are still left to me; I am neither called upon to bear the slavery of poverty nor the hell of absolute isolation.

Health cut off, means marriage, travel, study, and work forbidden or endangered. It means life reduced in attractiveness and utility by five-sixths.

Thy will be done!

September 14, 1874. (*Charnex*).—A long walk and conversation with ——. We followed a high mountain path. Seated on the turf, and talking with open heart, our eyes wandered over the blue immensity below us, and the smiling outlines of the shore. All was friendly, azure-tinted, caressing, to the sight. The soul I was reading was profound and pure. Such an experience is like a flight into paradise. A few light clouds climbed the broad spaces of the sky, steamers made long tracks upon the water at our feet, white sails were dotted over the vast distance of the lake, and sea-gulls like gigantic butterflies quivered above its rippling surface.

September 21, 1874. (*Charnex*).—A wonderful day! Never has the lake been bluer, or the landscape softer. It was enchanting. But tragedy is hidden under the eclogue; the serpent crawls under the flowers. All the future is dark. The phantoms which for three or four weeks I have been able to keep at bay, wait for me behind the door, as the Eumenides waited for Orestes. Hemmed in on all sides!

"On ne croit plus a son etoile, On sent que derriere la toile Sont le deuil, les maux et la mort."

For a fortnight I have been happy, and now this happiness is going.

There are no more birds, but a few white or blue butterflies are still left. Flowers are becoming rare—a few daisies in the fields, some blue or yellow chicories and colchicums, some wild geraniums growing among fragments of old walls, and the brown berries of the privet—this is all we were able to find. In the fields they are digging potatoes, beating down the nuts, and beginning the apple harvest. The leaves are thinning and changing color; I watch them turning red on the pear-trees, gray on the plums, yellow on the walnut-trees, and tinging the thickly-strewn turf with shades of reddish-brown. We are nearing the end of the fine weather; the coloring is the coloring of late autumn; there is no need now to keep out of the sun.

Everything is soberer, more measured, more fugitive, less emphatic. Energy is gone, youth is past, prodigality at an end, the summer over. The year is on the wane and tends toward winter; it is once more in harmony with my own age and position, and next Sunday it will keep my birthday. All these different consonances form a melancholy harmony.

* * * * *

The distinguishing mark of religion is not so much liberty as obedience, and its value is measured by the sacrifices which it can extract from the individual.

* * * * *

A young girl's love is a kind of piety. We must approach it with adoration if we are not to profane it, and with poetry if we are to understand it. If there is anything in the world which gives us a sweet, ineffable impression, of the ideal, it is this trembling modest love. To deceive it would be a crime. Merely to watch its unfolding life is bliss to the beholder; he sees in it the birth of a divine marvel. When the garland of youth fades on our brow, let us try at least to have the virtues of maturity; may we grow better, gentler, graver, like the fruit of the vine, while its leaf withers and falls.

* * * * *

To know how to grow old is the master work of wisdom, and one of the most difficult chapters in the great art of living.

* * * * *

He who asks of life nothing but the improvement of his own nature, and a continuous moral progress toward inward contentment and religious submission, is less liable than any one else to miss and waste life.

January 2, 1875. (*Hyeres.*)—In spite of my sleeping draught I have had a bad night. Once it seemed as if I must choke, for I could breathe neither way.

Could I be more fragile, more sensitive, more vulnerable! People talk to me as if there were still a career before me, while all the time I know that the ground is slipping from under me, and that the defense of my health is already a hopeless task. At bottom, I am only living on out of complaisance and without a shadow of self-delusion. I know that not one of my desires will be realized, and for a long time I have had no desires at all. I simply accept what comes to me as though it were a bird perching on my window. I smile at it, but I know very well that my visitor has wings and will not stay long. The resignation which comes from despair has a kind of melancholy sweetness. It looks at life as a man sees it from his death-bed, and judges it without bitterness and without vain regrets.

I no longer hope to get well, or to be useful, or to be happy. I hope that those who have loved me will love me to the end; I should wish to have done them some good, and to leave them a tender memory of myself. I wish to die without rebellion and without weakness; that is about all. Is this relic of hope and of desire still too much? Let all be as God will. I resign myself into his hands.

January 22, 1875. (*Hyeres*).—The French mind, according to Gioberti, apprehends only the outward form of truth, and exaggerates it by isolating it, so that it acts as a solvent upon the realities with which it works. It takes the shadow for the substance, the word for the thing, appearance for reality, and abstract formula for truth. It lives in a world of intellectual *assignats*. If you talk to a Frenchman of art, of language, of religion, of the state, of duty, of the family, you feel in his way of speaking that his thought remains outside the subject, that he never penetrates into its substance, its inmost core. He is not striving to understand it in its essence, but only to say something plausible about it. On his lips the noblest words become thin and empty; for example—mind, idea, religion. The French mind is superficial and yet not comprehensive; it has an extraordinarily fine edge, and yet no penetrating power. Its desire is to enjoy its own resources by the help of things, but it has none of the respect, the disinterestedness, the patience, and the self-forgetfulness, which, are indispensable if we wish to see things as they are. Far from being the philosophic mind, it is a mere counterfeit of it, for it does not enable a man to solve any problem whatever, and remains incapable of understanding all that is living, complex, and concrete. Abstraction is its original sin, presumption its incurable defect, and plausibility its fatal limit.

The French language has no power of expressing truths of birth and germination; it paints effects, results, the *caput mortuum*, but not the cause, the motive power, the native force the development of any phenomenon whatever. It is analytic and descriptive, but it explains nothing, for it avoids all beginnings and processes of formation. With it crystallization is not the mysterious act itself by which a substance passes from the fluid state to the solid state. It is the product of that act.

The thirst for truth is not a French passion. In everything appearance is preferred to reality, the outside to the inside, the fashion to the material, that which shines to that which profits, opinion to conscience. That is to say, the Frenchman's center of gravity is always outside him—he is always thinking of others, playing to the gallery. To him individuals are so many zeros; the unit which turns them into a number must be added from outside; it may be royalty, the writer of the day, the favorite newspaper, or any other temporary master of fashion. All this is probably the result of an exaggerated sociability, which weakens the soul's forces of resistance, destroys its capacity for investigation and personal conviction, and kills in it the worship of the ideal.

January 27, 1875. (*Hyeres*).—The whole atmosphere has a luminous serenity, a limpid clearness. The islands are like swans swimming in a golden stream. Peace, splendor, boundless space!... And I meanwhile look quietly on while the soft hours glide away. I long to catch the wild bird, happiness, and tame it. Above all, I long to share it with others. These delicious mornings impress me indescribably. They intoxicate me, they carry me away. I feel beguiled out of myself, dissolved in sunbeams, breezes, perfumes, and sudden impulses of joy. And yet all the time I pine for I know not what intangible Eden.

Lamartine in the "Preludes" has admirably described this oppressive effect of happiness on fragile human nature. I suspect that the reason for it is that the finite creature feels itself invaded by the infinite, and the invasion produces dizziness, a kind of vertigo, a longing to fling one's self into the great gulf of being. To feel life too intensely is to yearn for death; and for man, to die means to become like unto the gods—to be initiated into the great mystery. Pathetic and beautiful illusion.

Ten o'clock in the evening.—From one end to the other the day has been perfect, and my walk this afternoon to Beau Vallon was one long delight. It was like an expedition into Arcadia. Here was a wild and woodland corner, which would have made a fit setting for a dance of nymphs, and there an ilex overshadowing a rock, which reminded me of an ode of Horace or a drawing of Tibur. I felt a kind of certainty that the landscape had much that was Greek in it. And what made the sense of resemblance the more striking was the sea, which one feels to be always near, though one may not see it, and which any turn of the valley may bring into view. We found out a little tower with an overgrown garden, of which the owner might have been taken for a husbandman of the Odyssey. He could scarcely speak any French, but was not without a certain grave dignity. I translated to him the inscription on his sun-dial, "*Hora est benefaciendi,*" which is beautiful, and pleased him greatly. It would be an inspiring place to write a novel in. Only I do not know whether the little den would have a decent room, and one would certainly have to live upon eggs, milk, and figs, like Philemon. February 15, 1875. (*Hyeres*).—I have just been reading the two last "Discours" at the French Academy, lingering over every word and weighing every idea. This kind of writing is a sort of intellectual dainty, for it is the art "of expressing truth with all the courtesy and finesse possible;" the art of appearing perfectly at ease without the smallest loss of manners; of being gracefully sincere, and of making criticism itself a pleasure to the person criticized. Legacy as it is from the monarchical tradition, this particular kind of eloquence is the distinguishing mark of those men of the world who are also men of breeding, and those men of letters who are also gentlemen. Democracy could never have invented it, and in this delicate *genre* of literature France may give points to all rival peoples, for it is the fruit of that refined and yet vigorous social sense which is produced by court and drawing-room life, by literature and good company, by means of a mutual education continued for centuries. This complicated product is as original in its way as Athenian eloquence, but it is less healthy and less durable. If ever France becomes Americanized this *genre* at least will perish, without hope of revival.

April 16, 1875. (*Hyeres*).—I have already gone through the various emotions of leave-taking. I have been wandering slowly through the streets and up the castle hill, gathering a harvest of images and recollections. Already I am full of regret that I have not made a better study of the country, in which I have now spent four months and more. It is like what happens when a friend dies; we accuse ourselves of having loved him too little, or loved him ill; or it is like our own death, when we look back upon life and feel that it has been misspent.

August 16, 1875.—Life is but a daily oscillation between revolt and submission, between the instinct of the *ego*, which is to expand, to take delight in its own tranquil sense of inviolability, if not to triumph in its own sovereignty, and the instinct of the soul, which is to obey the universal order, to accept the will of God.

The cold renunciation of disillusioned reason brings no real peace. Peace is only to be found in reconciliation with destiny, when destiny seems, in the religious sense of the word, *good*; that is to say, when man feels himself directly in the presence of God. Then, and then only, does the will acquiesce. Nay more, it only completely acquiesces when it adores. The soul only submits to the hardness of fate by virtue of its discovery of a sublime compensation—the loving kindness of the Almighty. That is to say, it cannot resign itself to lack or famine, it shrinks from the void around it, and the happiness either of hope or faith is essential to it. It may very well vary its objects, but some object it must have. It may renounce its former idols, but it will demand another cult. The soul hungers and thirsts after happiness, and it is in vain that everything deserts it—it will never submit to its abandonment.

August 28, 1875. (*Geneva*).—A word used by Sainte-Beuve a propos of Benjamin Constant has struck me: it is the word *consideration*. To possess or not to possess *consideration* was to Madame de Stael a matter of supreme importance—the loss of it an irreparable evil, the acquirement of it a pressing necessity. What, then, is this good thing? The esteem of the public. And how is it gained? By honorable character and life, combined with a certain aggregate of services rendered and of successes obtained. It is not exactly a good conscience, but it is something like it, for it is the witness from without, if not the witness from within. *Consideration* is not reputation, still less celebrity, fame, or glory; it has nothing to do with *savoir faire*, and is not always the attendant of talent or genius. It is the reward given to constancy in duty, to probity of conduct. It is the homage rendered to a life held to be irreproachable. It is a little more than esteem, and a little less than admiration. To enjoy public consideration is at once a happiness and a power. The loss of it is a misfortune and a source of daily suffering. Here am I, at the age of fifty-three, without ever having given this idea the smallest place in my life. It is curious, but the desire for consideration has been to me so little of a motive that I have not even been conscious of such an idea at all. The fact shows, I suppose, that for me the audience, the gallery, the public, has never had more than a negative importance. I have neither asked nor expected anything from it, not even justice; and to be a dependent upon it, to solicit its suffrages and its good graces, has always seemed to me an act of homage and flunkeyism against which my pride has instinctively rebelled. I have never even tried to gain the good will of a *coterie* or a newspaper, nor so much as the vote of an elector. And yet it would have been a joy to me to be smiled upon, loved, encouraged, welcomed, and to obtain what I was so ready to give, kindness and good will. But to hunt down consideration and reputation—to force the esteem of others—seemed to me an effort unworthy of myself, almost a degradation. I have never even thought of it.

Perhaps I have lost consideration by my indifference to it. Probably I have disappointed public expectation by thus allowing an oversensitive and irritable consciousness to lead me into isolation and retreat. I know that the world, which is only eager to silence you when you do speak, is angry with your silence as soon as its own action has killed in you the wish to speak. No doubt, to be silent with a perfectly clear conscience a man must not hold a public office. I now indeed say to myself that a professor is morally bound to justify his position by publication; that students, authorities, and public are placed thereby in a healthier relation toward him; that it is necessary for his good repute in the world, and for the proper maintenance of his position. But this point of view has not been a familiar one to me. I have endeavored to give conscientious lectures, and I have discharged all the subsidiary duties of my post to the best of my ability; but I have never been able to bend myself to a struggle with hostile opinion, for all the while my heart has been full of sadness and disappointment, and I have known and felt that I have been systematically and deliberately isolated. Premature despair and the deepest discouragement have been my constant portion. Incapable of taking any interest in my talents for my own sake, I let everything slip as soon as the hope of being loved for them and by them had forsaken me. A hermit against my will, I have not even found peace in solitude, because my inmost conscience has not been any better satisfied than my heart.

Does not all this make up a melancholy lot, a barren failure of a life? What use have I made of my gifts, of my special circumstances, of my half-century of existence? What have I paid back to my country? Are all the documents I have produced, taken together, my correspondence, these thousands of journal pages, my lectures, my articles, my poems, my notes of different kinds, anything better than withered leaves? To whom and to what have I been useful? Will my name survive me a single day, and will it ever mean anything to anybody? A life of no account! A great many comings and goings, a great many scrawls—for nothing. When all is added up—nothing! And worst of all, it has not been a life used up in the service of some adored object, or sacrificed to any future hope. Its sufferings will have been vain, its renunciations useless, its sacrifices gratuitous, its dreariness without reward.... No, I am wrong; it will have had its secret treasure, its sweetness, its reward. It will have inspired a few affections of great price; it will have given joy to a few souls; its hidden existence will have had some value. Besides, if in itself it has been nothing, it has understood much. If it has not been in harmony with the great order, still it has loved it. If it has missed happiness and duty, it has at least felt its own nothingness, and implored its pardon.

Later on.—There is a great affinity in me with the Hindoo genius—that mind, vast, imaginative, loving, dreamy, and speculative, but destitute of ambition, personality, and will. Pantheistic disinterestedness, the effacement of the self in the great whole, womanish gentleness, a horror of slaughter, antipathy to action—these are all present in my nature, in the nature at least which has been developed by years and circumstances. Still the West has also had its part in me. What I have found difficult is to keep up a prejudice in favor of any form, nationality, or individuality whatever. Hence my indifference to my own person, my own usefulness, interest, or opinions of the moment. What does it all matter? *Omnis determinatio est negatio.* Grief localizes us, love particularizes us, but thought delivers us from personality.... To be a man is a poor thing, to be a man is well; to be *the* man—man in essence and in principle—that alone is to be desired.

Yes, but in these Brahmanic aspirations what becomes of the subordination of the individual to duty? Pleasure may lie in ceasing to be individual, but duty lies in performing the microscopic task allotted to us. The problem set before us is to bring our daily task into the temple of contemplation and ply it there, to act as in the presence of God, to interfuse one's little part with religion. So only can we inform the detail of life, all that is passing, temporary, and insignificant, with beauty and nobility. So may we dignify and consecrate the meanest of occupations. So may we feel that we are paying our tribute to the universal work and the eternal will. So are we reconciled with life and delivered from the fear of death. So are we in order and at peace.

September 1, 1875.—I have been working for some hours at my article on Mme. de Stael, but with what labor, what painful effort! When I write for publication every word is misery, and my pen stumbles at every line, so anxious am I to find the ideally best expression, and so great is the number of possibilities which open before me at every step.

Composition demands a concentration, decision, and pliancy which I no longer possess. I cannot fuse together materials and ideas. If we are to give anything a form, we must, so to speak, be the tyrants of it. [Footnote: Compare this paragraph from the "Pensees of a new writer, M. Joseph Roux, a country cure, living in a remote part of the *Bas Limousin*, whose thoughts have been edited and published this year by M. Paul Marieton (Paris: Alphonse Lemerre):

"Le verbe ne souffre et ne connait que la volonte qui le dompte, et n'emporte loin sans peril que l'intelligence qui lui menage avec empire l'eperon et le frein."]

We must treat our subject brutally, and not be always trembling lest we are doing it a wrong. We must be able to transmute and absorb it into our own substance. This sort of confident effrontery is beyond me: my whole nature tends to that impersonality which respects and subordinates itself to the object; it is love of truth which holds me back from concluding and deciding. And then I am always retracing my steps: instead of going forward I work in a circle: I am afraid of having forgotten a point, of having exaggerated an expression, of having used a word out of place, while all the time I ought to have been thinking of essentials and aiming at breadth of treatment. I do not know how to sacrifice anything, how to give up anything whatever. Hurtful timidity, unprofitable conscientiousness, fatal slavery to detail!

In reality I have never given much thought to the art of writing, to the best way of making an article, an essay, a book, nor have I ever methodically undergone the writer's apprenticeship; it would have been useful to me, and I was always ashamed of what was useful. I have felt, as it were, a scruple against trying to surprise the secret of the masters of literature, against picking *chef-d'oeuvres* to pieces. When I think that I have always postponed the serious study of the art of writing, from a sort of awe of it, and a secret love of its beauty,

Amiel's Journal

I am furious with my own stupidity, and with my own respect. Practice and routine would have given me that ease, lightness, and assurance, without which the natural gift and impulse dies away. But on the contrary, I have developed two opposed habits of mind, the habit of scientific analysis which exhausts the material offered to it, and the habit of immediate notation of passing impressions. The art of composition lies between the two; you want for it both the living unity of the thing and the sustained operation of thought.

October 25, 1875.—I have been listening to M. Taine's first lecture (on the "Ancien Regime") delivered in the university hall. It was an extremely substantial piece of work—clear, instructive, compact, and full of matter. As a writer he shows great skill in the French method of simplifying his subject by massing it in large striking divisions; his great defect is a constant straining after points; his principal merit is the sense he has of historical reality, his desire to see things as they are. For the rest, he has extreme openness of mind, freedom of thought, and precision of language. The hall was crowded.

October 26, 1875.—All origins are secret; the principle of every individual or collective life is a mystery—that is to say, something irrational, inexplicable, not to be defined. We may even go farther and say, Every individuality is an insoluble enigma, and no beginning explains it. In fact, all that has *become* may be explained retrospectively, but the beginning of anything whatever did not *become*. It represents always the *"fiat lux,"* the initial miracle, the act of creation; for it is the consequence of nothing else, it simply appears among anterior things which make a *milieu*, an occasion, a surrounding for it, but which are witnesses of its appearance without understanding whence it comes.

Perhaps also there are no true individuals, and, if so, no beginning but one only, the primordial impulse, the first movement. All men on this hypothesis would be but *man* in two sexes; man again might be reduced to the animal, the animal to the plant, and the only individuality left would be a living nature, reduced to a living matter, to the hylozoism of Thales. However, even upon this hypothesis, if there were but one absolute beginning, relative beginnings would still remain to us as multiple symbols of the absolute. Every life, called individual for convenience sake and by analogy, would represent in miniature the history of the world, and would be to the eye of the philosopher a microscopic compendium of it.

The history of the formation of ideas is what, frees the mind.

* * * * *

A philosophic truth does not become popular until some eloquent soul has humanized it or some gifted personality has translated and embodied it. Pure truth cannot be assimilated by the crowd; it must be communicated by contagion.

January 30, 1876.—After dinner I went two steps off, to Marc Monnier's, to hear the "Luthier de Cremone," a one-act comedy in verse, read by the author, Francois Coppee.

It was a feast of fine sensations, of literary dainties. For the little piece is a pearl. It is steeped in poetry, and every line is a fresh pleasure to one's taste.

This young *maestro* is like the violin he writes about, vibrating and passionate; he has, besides delicacy, point, grace, all that a writer wants to make what is simple, naive, heartfelt, and out of the beaten track, acceptable to a cultivated society.

How to return to nature through art: there is the problem of all highly composite literatures like our own. Rousseau himself attacked letters with all the resources of the art of writing, and boasted the delights of savage life with a skill and adroitness developed only by the most advanced civilization. And it is indeed this marriage of contraries which charms us; this spiced gentleness, this learned innocence, this calculated simplicity, this yes and no, this foolish wisdom. It is the supreme irony of such combinations which tickles the taste of advanced and artificial epochs, epochs when men ask for two sensations at once, like the contrary meanings fused by the smile of La Gioconda. And our satisfaction, too, in work of this kind is best expressed by that ambiguous curve of the lip which says: I feel your charm, but I am not your dupe; I see the illusion both from within and from without; I yield to you, but I understand you; I am complaisant, but I am proud; I am open to sensations, yet not the slave of any; you have talent, I have subtlety of perception; we are quits, and we understand each other.

February 1, 1876.—This evening we talked of the infinitely great and the infinitely small. The great things of the universe are for——so much easier to understand than the small, because all greatness is a multiple of herself, whereas she is incapable of analyzing what requires a different sort of measurement.

It is possible for the thinking being to place himself in all points of view, and to teach his soul to live under the most different modes of being. But it must be confessed that very few profit by the possibility. Men are in general imprisoned, held in a vice by their circumstances almost as the animals are, but they have very little suspicion of it because they have so little faculty of self-judgment. It is only the critic and the philosopher who can penetrate into all states of being, and realize their life from within.

When the imagination shrinks in fear from the phantoms which it creates, it may be excused because it is imagination. But when the intellect allows itself to be tyrannized over or terrified by the categories to which itself gives birth, it is in the wrong, for it is not allowed to intellect—the critical power of man—to be the dupe of anything.

Now, in the superstition of size the mind is merely the dupe of itself, for it creates the notion of space. The created is not more than the creator, the son not more than the father. The point of view wants rectifying. The mind has to free itself from space, which gives it a false notion of itself, but it can only attain this freedom by reversing things and by learning to see space in the mind instead of the mind in space. How can it do this? Simply by reducing space to its virtuality. Space is dispersion; mind is concentration.

And that is why God is present everywhere, without taking up a thousand millions of cube leagues, nor a hundred times more nor a hundred times less.

In the state of thought the universe occupies but a single point; but in the state of dispersion and analysis this thought requires the heaven of heavens for its expansion.

In the same way, time and number are contained in the mind. Man, as mind, is not their inferior, but their superior.

It is true that before he can reach this state of freedom his own body must appear to him at will either speck or world—that is to say, he must be independent of it. So long as the self still feels itself spatial, dispersed, corporeal, it is but a soul, it is not a mind; it is conscious of itself only as the animal is, the impressionable, affectionate, active and restless animal.

The mind being the subject of phenomena cannot be itself phenomenal; the mirror of an image, if it was an image, could not be a mirror. There can be no echo without a noise. Consciousness means some one who experiences something. And all the somethings together cannot take the place of the some one. The phenomenon exists only for a point which is not itself, and for which it is an object. The perceptible supposes the perceiver.

May 15, 1876.—This morning I corrected the proofs of the "Etrangeres." [Footnote: *Les Etrangeres: Poesies traduites de diverses litteratures*, par H. F. Amiel, 1876.] Here at least is one thing off my hands. The piece of prose theorizing which ends the volume pleased and satisfied me a good deal more than my new meters. The book, as a whole, may be regarded as an attempt to solve the problem of French verse-translation considered as a special art. It is science applied to poetry. It ought not, I think, to do any discredit to a philosopher, for, after all, it is nothing but applied psychology.

Do I feel any relief, any joy, pride, hope? Hardly. It seems to me that I feel nothing at all, or at least my feeling is so vague and doubtful that I cannot analyze it. On the whole, I am rather tempted to say to myself, how much labor for how small a result—*Much ado about nothing!* And yet the work in itself is good, is successful. But what does verse-translation matter? Already my interest in it is fading; my mind and my energies clamor for something else.

What will Edmond Scherer say to the volume?

* * * * *

To the inmost self of me this literary attempt is quite indifferent—a Lilliputian affair. In comparing my work with other work of the same kind, I find a sort of relative satisfaction; but I see the intrinsic futility of it, and the insignificance of its success or failure. I do not believe in the public; I do not believe in my own work; I have no ambition, properly speaking, and I blow soap-bubbles for want of something to do.

"Car le neant peut seul bien cacher l'infini."

Self-satire, disillusion, absence of prejudice, may be freedom, but they are not strength.

July 12, 1876.—Trouble on trouble. My cough has been worse than ever. I cannot see that the fine weather or the holidays have made any change for the better in my state of health. On the contrary, the process of demolition seems more rapid. It is a painful experience, this premature decay!... *"Apres tant de malheurs, que vous reste-t-il? Moi."* This *"moi"* is the central consciousness, the trunk of all the branches which have been cut away, that which bears every successive mutilation. Soon I shall have nothing else left than bare intellect. Death reduces us to the mathematical "point;" the destruction which precedes it forces us back, as it were, by a series of ever-narrowing concentric circles to this last inaccessible refuge. Already I have a foretaste of that zero in which all forms and all modes are extinguished. I see how we return into the night, and inversely I understand how we issue from it. Life is but a meteor, of which the whole brief course is before me. Birth, life, death assume a fresh meaning to us at each phase of our existence. To see one's self as a firework in the darkness—to become a witness of one's own fugitive phenomenon—this is practical psychology. I prefer indeed the spectacle of the world, which is a vaster and more splendid firework; but when illness narrows my horizon and makes me dwell perforce upon my own miseries, these miseries are still capable of supplying food for my psychological curiosity. What interests me in myself, in spite of my repulsions is, that I find in my own case a genuine example of human nature, and therefore a specimen of general value. The sample enables me to understand a multitude of similar situations, and numbers of my fellow-men.

To enter consciously into all possible modes of being would be sufficient occupation for hundreds of centuries—at least for our finite intelligences, which are conditioned by time. The progressive happiness of the process, indeed may be easily poisoned and embittered by the ambition which asks for everything at once, and clamors to reach the absolute at a bound. But it may be answered that aspirations are necessarily prophetic, for they could only have come into being under the action of the same cause which will enable them to reach their goal. The soul can only imagine the absolute because the absolute exists; our consciousness of a possible perfection is the guarantee that perfection will be realized.

Thought itself is eternal. It is the consciousness of thought which is gradually achieved through the long succession of ages, races, and humanities. Such is the doctrine of Hegel. The history of the mind is, according to him one of approximation to the absolute, and the absolute differs at the two ends of the story. It *was* at the beginning; it *knows itself* at the end. Or rather it advances in the possession of itself with the gradual unfolding of creation. Such also was the conception of Aristotle.

If the history of the mind and of consciousness is the very marrow and essence of being, then to be driven back on psychology, even personal psychology, is to be still occupied with the main question of things, to keep to the subject, to feel one's self in the center of the universal drama. There is comfort in the idea. Everything else may be taken away from us, but if thought remains we are still connected by a magic thread with the axis of the world. But we may lose thought and speech. Then nothing remains but simple feeling, the sense of the presence of God and of death in God—the last relic of the human privilege, which is to participate in the whole, to commune with the absolute.

"Ta vie est un eclair qui meurt dans son nuage, Mais l'eclair t'a sauve s'il t'a fait voir le ciel."

July 26, 1876.—A private journal is a friend to idleness. It frees us from the necessity of looking all round a subject, it puts up with every kind of repetition, it accompanies all the caprices and meanderings of the inner life, and proposes to itself no definite end. This journal of mine represents the material of a good many volumes: what prodigious waste of time, of thought, of strength! It will be useful to nobody, and even for myself—it has rather helped me to shirk life than to practice it. A journal takes the place of a confidant, that is, of friend or wife; it becomes a substitute for production, a substitute for country and public. It is a grief-cheating device, a mode of escape and withdrawal; but, factotum as it is, though it takes the place of everything, properly speaking it represents nothing at all....

What is it which makes the history of a soul? It is the stratification of its different stages of progress, the story of its acquisitions and of the general course of its destiny. Before my history can teach anybody anything, or even interest myself, it must be disentangled from its materials, distilled and simplified. These thousands of pages are but the pile of leaves and bark from which the essence has still to be extracted. A whole forest of cinchonas are worth but one cask of quinine. A whole Smyrna rose-garden goes to produce one vial of perfume.

This mass of written talk, the work of twenty-nine years, may in the end be worth nothing at all; for each is only interested in his own romance, his own individual life. Even I perhaps shall never have time to read them over myself. So—so what? I shall have lived my life, and life consists in repeating the human type, and the burden of the human song, as myriads of my kindred have done, are doing, and will do, century after century. To rise to consciousness of this burden and this type is something, and we can scarcely achieve anything further. The realization of the type is more complete, and the burden a more joyous one, if circumstances are kind and propitious, but whether the puppets have done this or that—

"Trois p'tits tours et puis s'en vont!"

everything falls into the same gulf at last, and comes to very much the same thing.

To rebel against fate—to try to escape the inevitable issue—is almost puerile. When the duration of a centenarian and that of an insect are quantities sensibly equivalent—and geology and astronomy enable us to regard such durations from this point of view—what is the meaning of all our tiny efforts and cries, the value of our anger, our ambition, our hope? For the dream of a dream it is absurd to raise these make-believe tempests. The forty millions of infusoria which make up a cube-inch of chalk—do they matter much to us? and do the forty millions of men who make up France matter any more to an inhabitant of the moon or Jupiter?

To be a conscious monad—a nothing which knows itself to be the microscopic phantom of the universe: this is all we can ever attain to.

September 12, 1876.—What is your own particular absurdity? Why, simply that you exhaust yourself in trying to understand wisdom without practicing it, that you are always making preparations for nothing, that you live without living. Contemplation which has not the courage to be purely contemplative, renunciation which does not renounce completely, chronic contradiction—there is your case. Inconsistent skepticism, irresolution, not convinced but incorrigible, weakness which will not accept itself and cannot transform itself into strength—there is your misery.

The comic side of it lies in capacity to direct others, becoming incapacity to direct one's self, in the dream of the infinitely great stopped short by the infinitely little, in what seems to be the utter uselessness of talent. To arrive at immobility by excess of motion, at zero from abundance of numbers, is a strange farce, a sad comedy; the poorest gossip can laugh at its absurdity.

September 19, 1876.—My reading to-day has been Doudan's "Lettres et Melanges." [Footnote: Ximenes Doudan, born in 1800, died 1872, the brilliant friend and tutor of the De Broglie family, whose conversation was so much sought after in life, and whose letters have been so eagerly read in France since his death. Compare M. Scherer's two articles on Doudan's "Lettres" and "Pensees" in his last published volume of essays.] A fascinating book! Wit, grace, subtlety, imagination, thought—these letters possess them all. How much I regret that I never knew the man himself. He was a Frenchman of the best type, *un delicat ne sublime*, to quote Sainte-Beuve's expression. Fastidiousness of temper, and a too keen love of perfection, led him to withhold his talent from the public, but while still living, and within his own circle, he was the recognized equal of the best. He scarcely lacked anything except that fraction of ambition, of brutality and material force which are necessary to success in this world; but he was appreciated by the best society of Paris, and he cared for nothing else. He reminds me of Joubert.

September 20th.—To be witty is to satisfy another's wits by the bestowal on him of two pleasures, that of understanding one thing and that of guessing another, and so achieving a double stroke.

Thus Doudan scarcely ever speaks out his thought directly; he disguises and suggests it by imagery, allusion, hyperbole; he overlays it with light irony and feigned anger, with gentle mischief and assumed humility. The more the thing to be guessed differs from the thing said, the more pleasant surprise there is for the interlocutor or the correspondent concerned. These charming and delicate ways of expression allow a man to teach what he will without pedantry, and to venture what he will without offense. There is something Attic and aerial in them; they mingle grave and gay, fiction and truth, with a light grace of touch such as neither La Fontaine nor Alcibiades would have been ashamed of. Socratic *badinage* like this presupposes a free and equal mind, victorious over physical ill and inward discontents. Such delicate playfulness is the exclusive heritage of those rare natures in whom subtlety is the disguise of superiority, and taste its revelation. "What balance of faculties and cultivation it requires! What personal distinction it shows! Perhaps only a valetudinarian would have been capable of this *morbidezza* of touch, this marriage of virile thought and feminine caprice. If there is excess anywhere, it lies perhaps in a certain effeminacy of sentiment. Doudan can put up with nothing but what is perfect—nothing but what is absolutely harmonious; all that is rough, harsh, powerful, brutal, and unexpected, throws him into convulsions. Audacity—boldness of all kinds—repels him. This Athenian of the Roman time is a true disciple of Epicurus in all matters of sight, hearing, and intelligence—a crumpled rose-leaf disturbs him.

"Une ombre, un souffle, un rien, tout lui donnait la fievre."

What all this softness wants is strength, creative and muscular force. His range is not as wide as I thought it at first. The classical world and the Renaissance—that is to say, the horizon of La Fontaine—is his horizon. He is out of his element in the German or Slav literatures. He knows nothing of Asia. Humanity for him is not much larger than France, and he has never made a bible of Nature. In music and painting he is more or less exclusive. In philosophy he stops at Kant. To sum up: he is a man of exquisite and ingenious taste, but he is not a first-rate critic, still less a poet, philosopher, or artist. He was an admirable talker, a delightful letter writer, who might have become an author had he chosen to concentrate himself. I must wait for the second volume in order to review and correct this preliminary impression.

Midday.—I have now gone once more through the whole volume, lingering over the Attic charm of it, and meditating on the originality and distinction of the man's organization. Doudan was a keen penetrating psychologist, a diviner of aptitudes, a trainer of minds, a man of infinite taste and talent, capable of every *nuance* and of every delicacy; but his defect was a want of persevering energy of thought, a lack of patience in execution. Timidity, unworldliness, indolence, indifference, confined him to the role of the literary counsellor and made him judge of the field in which he ought rather to have fought. But do I mean to blame him?—no indeed! In the first place, it would be to fire on my allies; in the second, very likely he chose the better part.

Was it not Goethe who remarked that in the neighborhood of all famous men we find men who never achieve fame, and yet were esteemed by those who did, as their equals or superiors? Descartes, I think, said the same thing. Fame will not run after the men who are afraid of her. She makes mock of those trembling and respectful lovers who deserve but cannot force her favors. The public is won by the bold, imperious talents—by the enterprising and the skillful. It does not believe in modesty, which it regards as a device of impotence. The golden book contains but a section of the true geniuses; it names those only who have taken glory by storm.

November 15, 1876.—I have been reading "L'Avenir Religieux des Peuples Civilises," by Emile de Laveleye. The theory of this writer is that the gospel, in its pure form, is capable of providing the religion of the future, and that the abolition of all religious principle, which is what the socialism of the present moment demands, is as much to be feared as Catholic superstition. The Protestant method, according to him, is the means of transition whereby sacerdotal Christianity passes into the pure religion of the gospel. Laveleye does not think that civilization can last without the belief in God and in another life. Perhaps he forgets that Japan and China prove the contrary. But it is enough to determine him against atheism if it can be shown that a general atheism would bring about a lowering of the moral average. After all, however, this is nothing but a religion of utilitarianism. A belief is not true because it is useful. And it is truth alone—scientific, established, proved, and rational truth—which is capable of satisfying nowadays the awakened minds of all classes. We may still say perhaps, "faith governs the world"—but the faith of the present is no longer in revelation or in the priest—it is in reason and in science. Is there a science of goodness and happiness?—that is the question. Do justice and goodness depend upon any particular religion? How are men to be made free, honest, just, and good?— there is the point.

On my way through the book I perceived many new applications of my law of irony. Every epoch has two contradictory aspirations which are logically antagonistic and practically associated. Thus the philosophic materialism of the last century was the champion of liberty. And at the present moment we find Darwinians in love with equality, while Darwinism itself is based on the right of the stronger.

Absurdity is interwoven with life: real beings are animated contradictions, absurdities brought into action. Harmony with self would mean peace, repose, and perhaps immobility By far the greater number of human beings can only conceive action, or practice it, under the form of war—a war of competition at home, a bloody war of nations abroad, and finally war with self. So that life is a perpetual combat; it wills that which it wills not, and wills not that it wills. Hence what I call the law of irony—that is to say, the refutation of the self by itself, the concrete realization of the absurd.

Is such a result inevitable? I think not. Struggle is the caricature of harmony, and harmony, which is the association of contraries, is also a principle of movement. War is a brutal and fierce means of pacification; it means the suppression of resistance by the destruction or enslavement of the conquered. Mutual respect would be a better way out of difficulties. Conflict is the result of the selfishness which will acknowledge no other limit than that of external force. The laws of animality govern almost the whole of history. The history of man is essentially zoological; it becomes human late in the day, and then only in the beautiful souls, the souls alive to justice, goodness, enthusiasm, and devotion. The angel shows itself rarely and with difficulty through the highly-organized brute. The divine aureole plays only with a dim and fugitive light around the brows of the world's governing race.

The Christian nations offer many illustrations of the law of irony. They profess the citizenship of heaven, the exclusive worship of eternal good; and never has the hungry pursuit of perishable joys, the love of this world, or the thirst for conquest, been stronger or more active than among these nations. Their official motto is exactly the reverse of their real aspiration. Under a false flag they play the smuggler with a droll ease of conscience. Is the fraud a conscious one? No—it is but an application of the law of irony. The deception is so common a one that the delinquent becomes unconscious of it. Every nation gives itself the lie in the course of its daily life, and not one feels the ridicule of its position. A man must be a Japanese to perceive the burlesque contradictions of the Christian civilization. He must be a native of the moon to understand the stupidity of man and his state of constant delusion. The philosopher himself falls under the law of irony, for after having mentally stripped himself of all prejudice—having, that is to say, wholly laid aside his own personality, he finds himself slipping back perforce into the rags he had taken off, obliged to eat and drink, to be hungry, cold, thirsty, and to behave like all other mortals, after having for a moment behaved like no other. This is the point where the comic poets are lying in wait for him; the animal needs revenge themselves for his flight into the Empyrean, and mock him by their cry: *Thou art dust, thou art nothing, than art man!*

November 26, 1876.—I have just finished a novel of Cherbuliez, "Le fiance de Mademoiselle de St. Maur." It is a jeweled mosaic of precious stones, sparkling with a thousand lights. But the heart gets little from it. The Mephistophelian type of novel leaves one sad. This subtle, refined world is strangely near to corruption; these artificial women have an air of the Lower Empire. There is not a character who is not witty, and neither is there one who has not bartered conscience for cleverness. The elegance of the whole is but a mask of immorality. These stories of feeling in which there is no feeling make a strange and painful impression upon me.

December 4, 1876.—I have been thinking a great deal of Victor Cherbuliez. Perhaps his novels make up the most disputable part of his work—they are so much wanting in simplicity, feeling, reality. And yet what knowledge, style, wit, and subtlety—how much thought everywhere, and what mastery of language! He astonishes one; I cannot but admire him.

Cherbuliez's mind is of immense range, clear-sighted, keen, full of resource; he is an Alexandrian exquisite, substituting for the feeling which makes men earnest the irony which leaves them free. Pascal would say of him—"He has never risen from the order of thought to the order of charity." But we must not be ungrateful. A Lucian is not worth an Augustine, but still he is Lucian. Those who enfranchise the mind render service to man as well as those who persuade the heart. After the leaders come the liberators, and the negative and critical minds have their place and function beside the men of affirmation, the convinced and inspired souls. The positive element in Victor Cherbuliez's work is beauty, not goodness, not moral or religious life. Aesthetically he is serious; what he respects is style. And therefore he has found his vocation; for he is first and foremost a writer—a consummate, exquisite, and model writer. He does not win our love, but he claims our homage.

In every union there is a mystery—a certain invisible bond which must not be disturbed. This vital bond in the filial relation is respect; in friendship, esteem; in marriage, confidence; in the collective life, patriotism; in the religious life, faith. Such points are best left untouched by speech, for to touch them is almost to profane them.

* * * * *

Men of genius supply the substance of history, while the mass of men are but the critical filter, the limiting, slackening, passive force needed for the modification of the ideas supplied by genius. Stupidity is dynamically the necessary balance of intellect. To make an atmosphere which human life can breathe, oxygen must be combined with a great deal—with three-fourths—of azote. And so, to make history, there must be a great deal of resistance to conquer and of weight to drag.

January 5, 1877.—This morning I am altogether miserable, half-stifled by bronchitis—walking a difficulty—the brain weak—this last the worst misery of all, for thought is my only weapon against my other ills. Rapid deterioration of all the bodily powers, a dull continuous waste of vital organs, brain decay: this is the trial laid upon me, a trial that no one suspects! Men pity you for growing old outwardly; but what does that matter?—nothing, so long as the faculties are intact. This boon of mental soundness to the last has been granted to so many students that I hoped for it a little. Alas, must I sacrifice that too? Sacrifice is almost easy when we believe it laid upon us, asked of us, rather, by a fatherly God and a watchful Providence; but I know nothing of this religious joy. The mutilation of the self which is going on in me lowers and lessens me without doing good to anybody. Supposing I became blind, who would be the gainer? Only one motive remains to me—that of manly resignation to the inevitable—the wish to set an example to others—the stoic view of morals pure and simple.

This moral education of the individual soul—is it then wasted? When our planet has accomplished the cycle of its destinies, of what use will it have been to any one or anything in the universe? Well, it will have sounded its note in the symphony of creation. And for us, individual atoms, seeing monads, we appropriate a momentary consciousness of the whole and the unchangeable, and then we disappear. Is not this enough? No, it is not enough, for if there is not progress, increase, profit, there is nothing but a mere chemical play and balance of combinations. Brahma, after having created, draws his creation back into the gulf. If we are a laboratory of the universal mind, may that mind at least profit and grow by us! If we realize the supreme will, may God have the joy of it! If the trustful humility of the soul rejoices him more than the greatness of intellect, let us enter into his plan, his intention. This, in theological language, is to live to the glory of God. Religion consists in the filial acceptance of the divine will whatever it be, provided we see it distinctly. Well, can we doubt that decay, sickness, death, are in the programme of our existence? Is not destiny the inevitable? And is not destiny the anonymous title of him or of that which the religions call God? To descend without murmuring the stream of destiny, to pass without revolt through loss after loss, and diminution after diminution, with no other limit than zero before us—this is what is demanded of us. Involution is as natural as evolution. We sink gradually back into the darkness, just as we issued gradually from it. The play of faculties and organs, the grandiose apparatus of life, is put back bit by bit into the box. We begin by instinct; at the end comes a clearness of vision which we must learn to bear with and to employ without murmuring upon our own failure and decay. A musical theme once exhausted, finds its due refuge and repose in silence.

February 6, 1877.—I spent the evening with the — —, and we talked of the anarchy of ideas, of the general want of culture, of what it is which keeps the world going, and of the assured march of science in the midst of universal passion and superstition.

What is rarest in the world is fair-mindedness, method, the critical view, the sense of proportion, the capacity for distinguishing. The common state of human thought is one of confusion, incoherence, and presumption, and the common state of human hearts is a state of passion, in which equity, impartiality, and openness to impressions are unattainable. Men's wills are always in advance of their intelligence, their desires ahead of their will, and accident the source of their desires; so that they express merely fortuitous opinions which are not worth the trouble of taking seriously, and which have no other account to give of themselves than this childish one: I am, because I am. The art of finding truth is very little practiced; it scarcely exists, because there is no personal humility, nor even any love of truth among us. We are covetous enough of such knowledge as may furnish weapons to our hand or tongue, as may serve our vanity or gratify our craving for power; but self-knowledge, the criticism of our own appetites and prejudices, is unwelcome and disagreeable to us.

Man is a willful and covetous animal, who makes use of his intellect to satisfy his inclinations, but who cares nothing for truth, who rebels against personal discipline, who hates disinterested thought and the idea of self-education. Wisdom offends him, because it rouses in him disturbance and confusion, and because he will not see himself as he is.

The great majority of men are but tangled skeins, imperfect keyboards, so many specimens of restless or stagnant chaos—and what makes their situation almost hopeless is the fact that they take pleasure in it. There is no curing a sick man who believes himself in health.

April 5, 1877.—I have been thinking over the pleasant evening of yesterday, an experience in which the sweets of friendship, the charm of mutual understanding, aesthetic pleasure, and a general sense of comfort, were happily combined and intermingled. There was not a crease in the rose-leaf. Why? Because "all that is pure, all that is honest, all that is excellent, all that is lovely and of good report," was there gathered together. "The incorruptibility of a gentle and quiet spirit," innocent mirth, faithfulness to duty, fine taste and sympathetic imagination, form an attractive and wholesome *milieu* in which the soul may rest.

The party—which celebrated the last day of vacation—gave much pleasure, and not to me only. Is not making others happy the best happiness? To illuminate for an instant the depths of a deep soul, to cheer those who bear by sympathy the burdens of so many sorrow-laden hearts and suffering lives, is to me a blessing and a precious privilege. There is a sort of religious joy in helping to renew the strength and courage of noble minds. We are surprised to find ourselves the possessors of a power of which we are not worthy, and we long to exercise it purely and seriously.

I feel most strongly that man, in all that he does or can do which is beautiful, great, or good is but the organ and the vehicle of something or some one higher than himself. This feeling is religion. The religious man takes part with a tremor of sacred joy in these phenomena of which he is the intermediary but not the source, of which he is the scene, but not the author, or rather, the poet. He lends them voice, and will, and help, but he is respectfully careful to efface himself, that he may alter as little as possible the higher work of the genius who is making a momentary use of him. A pure emotion deprives him of personality and annihilates the self in him. Self must perforce disappear when it is the Holy Spirit who speaks, when it is God who acts. This is the mood in which the prophet hears the call, the young mother feels the movement of the child within, the preacher watches the tears of his audience. So long as we are conscious of self we are limited, selfish, held in bondage; when we are in harmony with the universal order, when we vibrate in unison with God, self disappears. Thus, in a perfectly harmonious choir, the individual cannot hear himself unless he makes a false note. The religious state is one of deep enthusiasm, of moved contemplation, of tranquil ecstasy. But how rare a state it is for us poor creatures harassed by duty, by necessity, by the wicked world, by sin, by illness! It is the state which produces inward happiness; but alas! the foundation of existence, the common texture of our days, is made up of action, effort, struggle, and therefore dissonance. Perpetual conflict, interrupted by short and threatened truces—there is a true picture of our human condition.

Let us hail, then, as an echo from heaven, as the foretaste of a more blessed economy, these brief moments of perfect harmony, these halts between two storms. Peace is not in itself a dream, but we know it only as the result of a momentary equilibrium—an accident. "Happy are the peacemakers, for they shall be called the children of God."

April 26, 1877.—I have been turning over again the "Paris" of Victor Hugo (1867). For ten years event after event has given the lie to the prophet, but the confidence of the prophet in his own imaginings is not therefore a whit diminished. Humility and common sense are only fit for Lilliputians. Victor Hugo superbly ignores everything that he has not foreseen. He does not see that pride is a limitation of the mind, and that a pride without limitations is a littleness of soul. If he could but learn to compare himself with other men, and France with other nations, he would see things more truly, and would not fall into these mad exaggerations, these extravagant judgments. But proportion and fairness will never be among the strings at his command. He is vowed to the Titanic; his gold is always mixed with lead, his insight with childishness, his reason with madness. He cannot be simple; the only light he has to give blinds you like that of a fire. He astonishes a reader and provokes him, he moves him and annoys him. There is always some falsity of note in him, which accounts for the *malaise* he so constantly excites in me. The great poet in him cannot shake off the charlatan.

A few shafts of Voltairean irony would have shriveled the inflation of his genius and made it stronger by making it saner. It is a public misfortune that the most powerful poet of a nation should not have better understood his role, and that, unlike those Hebrew prophets who scourged because they loved, he should devote himself proudly and systematically to the flattery of his countrymen. France is the world; Paris is France; Hugo is Paris; peoples, bow down!

May 2, 1877.—Which nation is best worth belonging to? There is not one in which the good is not counterbalanced by evil. Each is a caricature of man, a proof that no one among them deserves to crush the others, and that all have something to learn from all. I am alternately struck with the qualities and with the defects of each, which is perhaps lucky for a critic. I am conscious of no preference for the defects of north or south, of west or east; and I should find a difficulty in stating my own predilections. Indeed I myself am wholly indifferent in the matter, for to me the question is not one of liking or of blaming, but of understanding. My point of view is philosophical—that is to say, impartial and impersonal. The only type which pleases me is perfection—*man*, in short, the ideal man. As for the national man, I bear with and study him, but I have no admiration for him. I can only admire the fine specimens of the race, the great men, the geniuses, the lofty characters and noble souls, and specimens of these are to be found in all the ethnographical divisions. The "country of my choice" (to quote Madame de Stael) is with the chosen souls. I feel no greater inclination toward the French, the Germans, the Swiss, the English, the Poles, the Italians, than toward the Brazilians or the Chinese. The illusions of patriotism, of Chauvinist, family, or professional feeling, do not exist for me. My tendency, on the contrary, is to feel with increased force the lacunas, deformities, and imperfections of the group to which I belong. My inclination is to see things as they are, abstracting my own individuality, and suppressing all personal will and desire; so that I feel antipathy, not toward this or that, but toward error, prejudice, stupidity, exclusiveness, exaggeration. I love only justice and fairness. Anger and annoyance are with me merely superficial; the fundamental tendency is toward impartiality and detachment. Inward liberty and aspiration toward the true—these are what I care for and take pleasure in.

June 4, 1877.—I have just heard the "Romeo and Juliet" of Hector Berlioz. The work is entitled "Dramatic symphony for orchestra, with choruses." The execution was extremely good. The work is interesting, careful, curious, and suggestive, but it leaves one cold. When I come to reason out my impression I explain it in this way. To subordinate man to things—to annex the human voice, as a mere supplement, to the orchestra—is false in idea. To make simple narrative out of dramatic material, is a derogation, a piece of levity. A Romeo and Juliet in which there is no Romeo and no Juliet is an absurdity. To substitute the inferior, the obscure, the vague, for the higher and the clear, is a challenge to common sense. It is a violation of that natural hierarchy of things which is never violated with impunity. The musician has put together a series of symphonic pictures, without any inner connection, a string of riddles, to which a prose text alone supplies meaning and unity. The only intelligible voice which is allowed to appear in the work is that of Friar Laurence: his sermon could not be expressed in chords, and is therefore plainly sung. But the moral of a play is not the play, and the play itself has been elbowed out by recitative.

The musician of the present day, not being able to give us what is beautiful, torments himself to give us what is new. False originality, false grandeur, false genius! This labored art is wholly antipathetic to me. Science simulating genius is but a form of quackery.

Berlioz as a critic is cleverness itself; as a musician he is learned, inventive, and ingenious, but he is trying to achieve the greater when he cannot compass the lesser.

Thirty years ago, at Berlin, the same impression was left upon me by his "Infancy of Christ," which I heard him conduct himself. His art seems to me neither fruitful nor wholesome; there is no true and solid beauty in it.

I ought to say, however, that the audience, which was a fairly full one, seemed very well satisfied.

July 17, 1877.—Yesterday I went through my La Fontaine, and noticed the omissions in him. He has neither butterfly nor rose. He utilizes neither the crane, nor the quail, nor the dromedary, nor the lizard. There is not a single echo of chivalry in him. For him, the history of France dates from Louis XIV. His geography only ranges, in reality, over a few square miles, and touches neither the Rhine nor the Loire, neither the mountains nor the sea. He never invents his subjects, but indolently takes them ready-made from elsewhere. But with all this what an adorable writer, what a painter, what an observer, what a humorist, what a story-teller! I am never tired of reading him, though I know half his fables by heart. In the matter of vocabulary, turns, tones, phrases, idioms, his style is perhaps the richest of the great period, for it combines, in the most skillful way, archaism and classic finish, the Gallic and the French elements. Variety, satire, *finesse*, feeling, movement, terseness, suavity, grace, gayety, at times even nobleness, gravity, grandeur—everything—is to be found in him. And then the happiness of the epithets, the piquancy of the sayings, the felicity of his rapid sketches and unforeseen audacities, and the unforgettable sharpness of phrase! His defects are eclipsed by his immense variety of different aptitudes.

One has only to compare his "Woodcutter and Death" with that of Boileau in order to estimate the enormous difference between the artist and the critic who found fault with his work. La Fontaine gives you a picture of the poor peasant under the monarchy; Boileau shows you nothing but a man perspiring under a heavy load. The first is a historical witness, the second a mere academic rhymer. From La Fontaine it is possible to reconstruct the whole society of his epoch, and the old Champenois with his beasts remains the only Homer France has ever possessed. He has as many portraits of men and women as La Bruyere, and Moliere is not more humorous.

His weak side is his epicureanism, with its tinge of grossness. This, no doubt, was what made Lamartine dislike him. The religious note is absent from his lyre; there is nothing in him which shows any contact with Christianity, any knowledge of the sublimer tragedies of the soul. Kind nature is his goddess, Horace his prophet, and Montaigne his gospel. In other words, his horizon is that of the Renaissance. This pagan island in the full Catholic stream is very curious; the paganism of it is so perfectly sincere and naive. But indeed, Reblais, Moliere, Saint Evremond, are much more pagan than Voltaire. It is as though, for the genuine Frenchman, Christianity was a mere pose or costume—something which has nothing to do with the heart, with the real man, or his deeper nature. This division of things is common in Italy too. It is the natural effect of political religions: the priest becomes separated from the layman, the believer from the man, worship from sincerity.

July 18, 1877.—I have just come across a character in a novel with a passion for synonyms, and I said to myself: Take care—that is your weakness too. In your search for close and delicate expression, you run through the whole gamut of synonyms, and your pen works too often in series of three. Beware! Avoid mannerisms and tricks; they are signs of weakness. Subject and occasion only must govern the use of words. Procedure by single epithet gives strength; the doubling of a word gives clearness, because it supplies the two extremities of the series; the trebling of it gives completeness by suggesting at once the beginning, middle, and end of the idea; while a quadruple phrase may enrich by force of enumeration.

Indecision being my principal defect, I am fond of a plurality of phrases which are but so many successive approximations and corrections. I am especially fond of them in this journal, where I write as it comes. In serious composition *two* is, on the whole, my category. But it would be well to practice one's self in the use of the single word—of the shaft delivered promptly and once for all. I should have indeed to cure myself of hesitation first. I see too many ways of saying things; a more decided mind hits on the right way at once. Singleness of phrase implies courage, self-confidence, clear-sightedness. To attain it there must he no doubting, and I am always doubting. And yet—

"Quiconque est loup agisse en loup; C'est le plus certain de beaucoup."

I wonder whether I should gain anything by the attempt to assume a character which is not mine. My wavering manner, born of doubt and scruple, has at least the advantage of rendering all the different shades of my thought, and of being sincere. If it were to become terse, affirmative, resolute, would it not be a mere imitation?

A private journal, which is but a vehicle for meditation and reverie, beats about the bush as it pleases without being hound to make for any definite end. Conversation with self is a gradual process of thought-clearing. Hence all these synonyms, these waverings, these repetitions and returns upon one's self. Affirmation maybe brief; inquiry takes time; and the line which thought follows is necessarily an irregular one.

I am conscious indeed that at bottom there is but one right expression; [Footnote: Compare La Bruyere:

"Entre toutes les differentes expressions qui peuvent rendre une seule de nos pensees il n'y en a qu'une qui soit la bonne; on ne la rencontre pas toujours en parlant ou en ecrivant: il est vray neanmoins qu'elle existe, que tout ce qui ne l'est point est foible, et ne satisfait point un homme d'esprit qui veut se faire entendre."] but in order to find it I wish to make my choice among all that are like it; and my mind instinctively goes through a series of verbal modulations in search of that shade which may most accurately render the idea. Or sometimes it is the idea itself which has to be turned over and over, that I may know it and apprehend it better. I think, pen in hand; it is like the disentanglement, the winding-off of a skein. Evidently the corresponding form of style cannot have the qualities which belong to thought which is already sure of itself, and only seeks to communicate itself to others. The function of the private journal is one of observation, experiment, analysis, contemplation; that of the essay or article is to provoke reflection; that of the book is to demonstrate.

July 21, 1877.—A superb night—a starry sky—Jupiter and Phoebe holding converse before my windows. Grandiose effects of light and shade over the courtyard. A sonata rose from the black gulf of shadow like a repentant prayer wafted from purgatory. The picturesque was lost in poetry, and admiration in feeling.

July 30, 1877.— ... makes a very true remark about Renan, *a propos* of the volume of "Les Evangiles." He brings out the contradiction between the literary taste of the artist, which is delicate, individual, and true, and the opinions of the critic, which are borrowed, old-fashioned and wavering. This hesitancy of choice between the beautiful and the true, between poetry and prose, between art and learning, is, in fact, characteristic. Renan has a keen love for science, but he has a still keener love for good writing, and, if necessary, he will sacrifice the exact phrase to the beautiful phrase. Science is his material rather than his object; his object is style. A fine passage is ten times more precious in his eyes than the discovery of a fact or the rectification of a date. And on this point I am very much with him, for a beautiful piece of writing is beautiful by virtue of a kind of truth which is truer than any mere record of authentic facts. Rousseau also thought the same. A chronicler may be able to correct Tacitus, but Tacitus survives all the chroniclers. I know well that the aesthetic temptation is the French temptation; I have often bewailed it, and yet, if I desired anything, it would be to be a writer, a great writer. Te leave a monument behind, *aere perennius*, an imperishable work which might stir the thoughts, the feelings, the dreams of men, generation after generation—this is the only glory which I could wish for, if I were not weaned even from this wish also. A book would be my ambition, if ambition were not vanity and vanity of vanities.

August 11, 1877.—The growing triumph of Darwinism—that is to say of materialism, or of force—threatens the conception of justice. But justice will have its turn. The higher human law cannot be the offspring of animality. Justice is the right to the maximum of individual independence compatible with the same liberty for others; in other words, it is respect for man, for the immature, the small, the feeble; it is the guarantee of those human collectivities, associations, states, nationalities—those voluntary or involuntary unions—the object of which is to increase the sum of happiness, and to satisfy the aspiration of the individual. That some should make use of others for their own purposes is an injury to justice. The right of the stronger is not a right, but a simple fact, which obtains only so long as there is neither protest nor resistance. It is like cold, darkness, weight, which tyrannize over man until he has invented artificial warmth, artificial light, and machinery. Human industry is throughout an emancipation from brute nature, and the advances made by justice are in the same way a series of rebuffs inflicted upon the tyranny of the stronger. As the medical art consists in the conquest of disease, so goodness consists in the conquest of the blind ferocities and untamed appetites of the human animal. I see the same law throughout—increasing emancipation of the individual, a continuous ascent of being toward life, happiness, justice, and wisdom. Greed and gluttony are the starting-point, intelligence and generosity the goal.

August 21, 1877. (Baths of Ems).—In the *salon* there has been a performance in chorus of "Lorelei" and other popular airs. What in our country is only done for worship is done also in Germany for poetry and music. Voices blend together; art shares the privilege of religion. It is a trait which is neither French nor English, nor, I think, Italian. The spirit of artistic devotion, of impersonal combination, of common, harmonious, disinterested action, is specially German; it makes a welcome balance to certain clumsy and prosaic elements in the race.

Later.—Perhaps the craving for independence of thought—the tendency to go back to first principles—is really proper to the Germanic mind only. The Slavs and the Latins are governed rather by the collective wisdom of the community, by tradition, usage, prejudice, fashion; or, if they break through these, they are like slaves in revolt, without any real living apprehension of the law inherent in things—the true law, which is neither written, nor arbitrary, nor imposed. The German wishes to get at nature; the Frenchman, the Spaniard, the Russian, stop at conventions. The root of the problem is in the question of the relations between God and the world. Immanence or transcendence—that, step by step, decides the meaning of everything else. If the mind is radically external to things, it is not called upon to conform to them. If the mind is destitute of native truth, it must get its truth from outside, by revelations. And so you get thought despising nature, and in bondage to the church—so you have the Latin world!

November 6, 1877. (*Geneva*).—We talk of love many years before we know anything about it, and we think we know it because we talk of it, or because we repeat what other people say of it, or what books tell us about it. So that there are ignorances of different degrees, and degrees of knowledge which are quite deceptive. One of the worst plagues of society is this thoughtless inexhaustible verbosity, this careless use of words, this pretense of knowing a thing because we talk about it—these counterfeits of belief, thought, love, or earnestness, which all the while are mere babble. The worst of it is, that as self-love is behind the babble, these ignorances of society are in general ferociously affirmative; chatter mistakes itself for opinion, prejudice poses as principle. Parrots behave as though they were thinking beings; imitations give themselves out as originals; and politeness demands the acceptance of the convention. It is very wearisome.

Language is the vehicle of this confusion, the instrument of this unconscious fraud, and all evils of the kind are enormously increased by universal education, by the periodical press, and by all the other processes of vulgarization in use at the present time. Every one deals in paper money; few have ever handled gold. We live on symbols, and even on the symbols of symbols; we have never grasped or verified things for ourselves; we judge everything, and we know nothing.

How seldom we meet with originality, individuality, sincerity, nowadays!—with men who are worth the trouble of listening to! The true self in the majority is lost in the borrowed self. How few are anything else than a bundle of inclinations—anything more than animals—whose language and whose gait alone recall to us the highest rank in nature!

The immense majority of our species are candidates for humanity, and nothing more. Virtually we are men; we might be, we ought to be, men; but practically we do not succeed in realizing the type of our race. Semblances and counterfeits of men fill up the habitable earth, people the islands and the continents, the country and the town. If we wish to respect men we must forget what they are, and think of the ideal which they carry hidden within them, of the just man and the noble, the man of intelligence and goodness, inspiration and creative force, who is loyal and true, faithful and trustworthy, of the higher man, in short, and that divine thing we call a soul. The only men who deserve the name are the heroes, the geniuses, the saints, the harmonious, puissant, and perfect samples of the race.

Very few individuals deserve to be listened to, but all deserve that our curiosity with regard to them should be a pitiful curiosity—that the insight we bring to bear on them should be charged with humility. Are we not all shipwrecked, diseased, condemned to death? Let each work out his own salvation, and blame no one but himself; so the lot of all will be bettered. Whatever impatience we may feel toward our neighbor, and whatever indignation our race may rouse in us, we are chained one to another, and, companions in labor and misfortune, have everything to lose by mutual recrimination and reproach. Let us be silent as to each other's weakness, helpful, tolerant, nay, tender toward each other! Or, if we cannot feel tenderness, may we at least feel pity! May we put away from us the satire which scourges and the anger which brands; the oil and wine of the good Samaritan are of more avail. We may make the ideal a reason for contempt; but it is more beautiful to make it a reason for tenderness.

December 9, 1877.—The modern haunters of Parnassus [Footnote: Amiel's expression is *Les Parnassieus*, an old name revived, which nowadays describes the younger school of French poetry represented by such names as Theophile Gautier, Leconte de Lisle, Theodore de Bauville, and Baudelaire. The modern use of the word dates from the publication of "La Parnasse Contemporain" (Lemerre, 1866).] carve urns of agate and of onyx, but inside the urns what is there?—ashes. Their work lacks feeling, seriousness, sincerity, and pathos—in a word, soul and moral life. I cannot bring myself to sympathize with such a way of understanding poetry. The talent shown is astonishing, but stuff and matter are wanting. It is an effort of the imagination to stand alone—a substitute for everything else. We find metaphors, rhymes, music, color, but not man, not humanity. Poetry of this factitious kind may beguile one at twenty, but what can one make of it at fifty? It reminds me of Pergamos, of Alexandria, of all the epochs of decadence when beauty of form hid poverty of thought and exhaustion of feeling. I strongly share the repugnance which this poetical school arouses in simple people. It is as though it only cared to please the world-worn, the over-subtle, the corrupted, while it ignores all normal healthy life, virtuous habits, pure affections, steady labor, honesty, and duty. It is an affectation, and because it is an affectation the school is struck with sterility. The reader desires in the poet something better than a juggler in rhyme, or a conjurer in verse; he looks to find in him a painter of life, a being who thinks, loves, and has a conscience, who feels passion and repentance.

* * * * *

Composition is a process of combination, in which thought puts together complementary truths, and talent fuses into harmony the most contrary qualities of style.

So that there is no composition without effort, without pain even, as in all bringing forth. The reward is the giving birth to something living—something, that is to say, which, by a kind of magic, makes a living unity out of such opposed attributes as orderliness and spontaneity, thought and imagination, solidity and charm.

The true critic strives for a clear vision of things as they are—for justice and fairness; his effort is to get free from himself, so that he may in no way disfigure that which he wishes to understand or reproduce. His superiority to the common herd lies in this effort, even when its success is only partial. He distrusts his own senses, he sifts his own impressions, by returning upon them from different sides and at different times, by comparing, moderating, shading, distinguishing, and so endeavoring to approach more and more nearly to the formula which represents the maximum of truth.

* * * * *

Is it not the sad natures who are most tolerant of gayety? They know that gayety means impulse and vigor, that generally speaking it is disguised kindliness, and that if it were a mere affair of temperament and mood, still it is a blessing.

*****

The art which is grand and yet simple is that which presupposes the greatest elevation both in artist and in public.

How much folly is compatible with ultimate wisdom and prudence? It is difficult to say. The cleverest folk are those who discover soonest how to utilize their neighbor's experience, and so get rid in good time of their natural presumption.

We must try to grasp the spirit of things, to see correctly, to speak to the point, to give practicable advice, to act on the spot, to arrive at the proper moment, to stop in time. Tact, measure, occasion—all these deserve our cultivation and respect.

*****

April 22, 1878.—Letter from my cousin Julia. These kind old relations find it very difficult to understand a man's life, especially a student's life. The hermits of reverie are scared by the busy world, and feel themselves out of place in action. But after all, we do not change at seventy, and a good, pious old lady, half-blind and living in a village, can no longer extend her point of view, nor form any idea of existences which have no relation with her own.

What is the link by which these souls, shut in and encompassed as they are by the details of daily life, lay hold on the ideal? The link of religious aspiration. Faith is the plank which saves them. They know the meaning of the higher life; their soul is athirst for heaven. Their opinions are defective, but their moral experience is great; their intellect is full of darkness but their souls is full of light. We scarcely know how to talk to them about the things of earth, but they are ripe and mature in the things of the heart. If they cannot understand us, it is for us to make advances to them, to speak their language, to enter into their range of ideas, their modes of feeling. We must approach them on their noble side, and, that we may show them the more respect, induce them to open to us the casket of their most treasured thoughts. There is always some grain of gold at the bottom of every honorable old age. Let it be our business to give it an opportunity of showing itself to affectionate eyes.

May 10, 1878.—I have just come back from a solitary walk. I heard nightingales, saw white lilac and orchard trees in bloom. My heart is full of impressions showered upon it by the chaffinches, the golden orioles, the grasshoppers, the hawthorns, and the primroses. A dull, gray, fleecy sky brooded with a certain melancholy over the nuptial splendors of vegetation. Many painful memories stirred afresh in me; at Pre l'Eveque, at Jargonnant, at Villereuse, a score of phantoms —phantoms of youth—rose with sad eyes to greet me. The walls had changed, and roads which were once shady and dreamy I found now waste and treeless. But at the first trills of the nightingale a flood of tender feeling filled my heart. I felt myself soothed, grateful, melted; a mood of serenity and contemplation took possession of me. A certain little path, a very kingdom of green, with fountain, thickets, gentle ups and downs, and an abundance of singing-birds, delighted me, and did me inexpressible good. Its peaceful remoteness brought back the bloom of feeling. I had need of it.

May 19, 1878.—Criticism is above all a gift, an intuition, a matter of tact and *flair*; it cannot be taught or demonstrated—it is an art. Critical genius means an aptitude for discerning truth under appearances or in disguises which conceal it; for discovering it in spite of the errors of testimony, the frauds of tradition, the dust of time, the loss or alteration of texts. It is the sagacity of the hunter whom nothing deceives for long, and whom no ruse can throw off the trail. It is the talent of the *Juge d'Instruction*, who knows how to interrogate circumstances, and to extract an unknown secret from a thousand falsehoods. The true critic can understand everything, but he will be the dupe of nothing, and to no convention will he sacrifice his duty, which is to find out and proclaim truth. Competent learning, general cultivation, absolute probity, accuracy of general view, human sympathy and technical capacity—how many things are necessary to the critic, without reckoning grace, delicacy, *savoir vivre*, and the gift of happy phrase-making!

July 26, 1878.—Every morning I wake up with the same sense of vain struggle against a mountain tide which is about to overwhelm me. I shall die by suffocation, and the suffocation has begun; the progress it has already made stimulates it to go on.

How can one make any plans when every day brings with it some fresh misery? I cannot even decide on a line of action in a situation so full of confusion and uncertainty in which I look forward to the worst, while yet all is doubtful. Have I still a few years before me or only a few months? Will death be slow or will it come upon me as a sudden catastrophe? How am I to bear the days as they come? how am I to fill them? How am I to die with calmness and dignity? I know not. Everything I do for the first time I do badly; but here everything is new; there can be no help from experience; the end must be a chance! How mortifying for one who has set so great a price upon independence—to depend upon a thousand unforeseen contingencies! He knows not how he will act or what he will become; he would fain speak of these things with a friend of good sense and good counsel—but who? He dares not alarm the affections which are most his own, and he is almost sure that any others would try to distract his attention, and would refuse to see the position as it is.

And while I wait (wait for what?—certainty?) the weeks flow by like water, and strength wastes away like a smoking candle....

Is one free to let one's self drift into death without resistance? Is self-preservation a duty? Do we owe it to those who love us to prolong this desperate struggle to its utmost limit? I think so, but it is one fetter the more. For we must then feign a hope which we do not feel, and hide the absolute discouragement of which the heart is really full. Well, why not? Those who succumb are bound in generosity not to cool the ardor of those who are still battling, still enjoying.

Two parallel roads lead to the same result; meditation paralyzes me, physiology condemns me. My soul is dying, my body is dying. In every direction the end is closing upon me. My own melancholy anticipates and endorses the medical judgment which says, "Your journey is done." The two verdicts point to the same result—that I have no longer a future. And yet there is a side of me which says, "Absurd!" which is incredulous, and inclined to regard it all as a bad dream. In vain the reason asserts it; the mind's inward assent is still refused. Another contradiction!

I have not the strength to hope, and I have not the strength to submit. I believe no longer, and I believe still. I feel that I am dying, and yet I cannot realize that I am dying. Is it madness already? No, it is human nature taken in the act; it is life itself which is a contradiction, for life means an incessant death and a daily resurrection; it affirms and it denies, it destroys and constructs, it gathers and scatters, it humbles and exalts at the same time. To live is to die partially—to feel one's self in the heart of a whirlwind of opposing forces—to be an enigma.

If the invisible type molded by these two contradictory currents—if this form which presides over all my changes of being—has itself general and original value, what does it matter whether it carries on the game a few months or years longer, or not? It has done what it had to do, it has represented a certain unique combination, one particular expression of the race. These types are shadows—*manes*. Century after century employs itself in fashioning them. Glory—fame—is the proof that one type has seemed to the other types newer, rarer, and more beautiful than the rest. The common types are souls too, only they have no interest except for the Creator, and for a small number of individuals.

To feel one's own fragility is well, but to be indifferent to it is better. To take the measure of one's own misery is profitable, but to understand its *raison d'etre* is still more profitable. To mourn for one's self is a last sign of vanity; we ought only to regret that which has real values, and to regret one's self, is to furnish involuntary evidence that one had attached importance to one's self. At the same time it is a proof of ignorance of our true worth and function. It is not necessary to live, but it is necessary to preserve one's type unharmed, to remain faithful to one's idea, to protect one's monad against alteration and degradation.

November 7, 1878.—To-day we have been talking of realism in painting, and, in connection with it, of that poetical and artistic illusion which does not aim at being confounded with reality itself. Realism wishes to entrap sensation; the object of true art is only to charm the imagination, not to deceive the eye. When we see a good portrait we say, "It is alive!"—in other words, our imagination lends it life. On the other hand, a wax figure produces a sort of terror in us; its frozen life-likeness makes a deathlike impression on us, and we say, "It is a ghost!" In the one case we see what is lacking, and demand it; in the other we see what is given us, and we give on our side. Art, then, addresses itself to the imagination; everything that appeals to sensation only is below art, almost outside art. A work of art ought to set the poetical faculty in us to work, it ought to stir us to imagine, to complete our perception of a thing. And we can only do this when the artist leads the way. Mere copyist's painting, realistic reproduction, pure imitation, leave us cold because their author is a machine, a mirror, an iodized plate, and not a soul.

Art lives by appearances, but these appearances are spiritual visions, fixed dreams. Poetry represents to us nature become con-substantial with the soul, because in it nature is only a reminiscence touched with emotion, an image vibrating with our own life, a form without weight—in short, a mode of the soul. The poetry which is most real and objective is the expression of a soul which throws itself into things, and forgets itself in their presence more readily than others; but still, it is the expression of the soul, and hence what we call style. Style may be only collective, hieratic, national, so long as the artist is still the interpreter of the community; it tends to become personal in proportion as society makes room for individuality and favors its expansion.

* * * * *

There is a way of killing truth by truths. Under the pretense that we want to study it more in detail we pulverize the statue—it is an absurdity of which our pedantry is constantly guilty. Those who can only see the fragments of a thing are to me *esprits faux*, just as much as those who disfigure the fragments. The good critic ought to be master of the three capacities, the three modes of seeing men and things—he should be able simultaneously to see them as they are, as they might be, and as they ought to be.

* * * * *

Modern culture is a delicate electuary made up of varied savors and subtle colors, which can be more easily felt than measured or defined. Its very superiority consists in the complexity, the association of contraries, the skillful combination it implies. The man of to-day, fashioned by the historical and geographical influences of twenty countries and of thirty centuries, trained and modified by all the sciences and all the arts, the supple recipient of all literatures, is an entirely new product. He finds affinities, relationships, analogies everywhere, but at the same time he condenses and sums up what is elsewhere scattered. He is like the smile of La Gioconda, which seems to reveal a soul to the spectator only to leave him the more certainly under a final impression of mystery, so many different things are expressed in it at once.

* * * * *

To understand things we must have been once in them and then have come out of them; so that first there must be captivity and then deliverance, illusion followed by disillusion, enthusiasm by disappointment. He who is still under the spell, and he who has never felt the spell, are equally incompetent. We only know well what we have first believed, then judged. To understand we must be free, yet not have been always free. The same truth holds, whether it is a question of love, of art, of religion, or of patriotism. Sympathy is a first condition of criticism; reason and justice presuppose, at their origin, emotion.

*****

What is an intelligent man? A man who enters with ease and completeness into the spirit of things and the intention of persons, and who arrives at an end by the shortest route. Lucidity and suppleness of thought, critical delicacy and inventive resource, these are his attributes.

*****

Analysis kills spontaneity. The grain once ground into flour springs and germinates no more.

*****

January 3, 1879.—Letter from——. This kind friend of mine has no pity.... I have been trying to quiet his over-delicate susceptibilities.... It is difficult to write perfectly easy letters when one finds them studied with a magnifying glass, and treated like monumental inscriptions, in which each character has been deliberately engraved with a view to an eternity of life. Such disproportion between the word and its commentary, between the playfulness of the writer and the analytical temper of the reader, is not favorable to ease of style. One dares not be one's natural self with these serious folk who attach importance to everything; it is difficult to write open-heartedly if one must weigh every phrase and every word.

Esprit means taking things in the sense which they are meant to have, entering into the tone of other people, being able to place one's self on the required level; *esprit* is that just and accurate sense which divines, appreciates, and weighs quickly, lightly, and well. The mind must have its play, the Muse is winged—the Greeks knew it, and Socrates.

January 13, 1879.—It is impossible for me to remember what letters I wrote yesterday. A single night digs a gulf between the self of yesterday and the self of to-day. My life is without unity of action, because my actions themselves are escaping from the control of memory. My mental power, occupied in gaining possession of itself under the form of consciousness, seems to be letting go its hold on all that generally peoples the understanding, as the glacier throws off the stones and fragments fallen into its crevasses, that it may remain pure crystal. The philosophic mind is both to overweight itself with too many material facts or trivial memories. Thought clings only to thought—that is to say, to itself, to the psychological process. The mind's only ambition is for an enriched experience. It finds its pleasure in studying the play of its own facilities, and the study passes easily into an aptitude and habit. Reflection becomes nothing more than an apparatus for the registration of the impressions, emotions, and ideas which pass across the mind. The whole moulting process is carried on so energetically that the mind is not only unclothed, but stripped of itself, and, so to speak, *desubstantiated*. The wheel turns so quickly that it melts around the mathematical axis, which alone remains cold because it is impalpable, and has no thickness. All this is natural enough, but very dangerous.

So long as one is numbered among the living—so long, that is to say, as one is still plunged in the world of men, a sharer of their interests, conflicts, vanities, passions, and duties, one is bound to deny one's self this subtle state of consciousness; one must consent to be a separate individual, having one's special name, position, age, and sphere of activity. In spite of all the temptations of impersonality, one must resume the position of a being imprisoned within certain limits of time and space, an individual with special surroundings, friends, enemies, profession, country, bound to house and feed himself, to make up his accounts and look after his affairs; in short, one must behave like all the world. There are days when all these details seem to me a dream—when I wonder at the desk under my hand, at my body itself—when I ask myself if there is a street before my house, and if all this geographical and topographical phantasmagoria is indeed real. Time and space become then mere specks; I become a sharer in a purely spiritual existence; I see myself *sub specie oeternitatis*.

Is not mind simply that which enables us to merge finite reality in the infinite possibility around it? Or, to put it differently, is not mind the universal virtuality, the universe latent? If so, its zero would be the germ of the infinite, which is expressed mathematically by the double zero (00).

Deduction: that the mind may experience the infinite in itself; that in the human individual there arises sometimes the divine spark which reveals to him the existence of the original, fundamental, principal Being, within which all is contained like a series within its generating formula. The universe is but a radiation of mind; and the radiations of the Divine mind are for us more than appearances; they have a reality parallel to our own. The radiations of our mind are imperfect reflections from the great show of fireworks set in motion by Brahma, and great art is great only because of its conformities with the Divine order—with that which is.

Ideal conceptions are the mind's anticipation of such an order. The mind is capable of them because it is mind, and, as such, perceives the Eternal. The real, on the contrary, is fragmentary and passing. Law alone is eternal. The ideal is then the imperishable hope of something better—the mind's involuntary protest against the present, the leaven of the future working in it. It is the supernatural in us, or rather the super-animal, and the ground of human progress. He who has no ideal contents himself with what is; he has no quarrel with facts, which for him are identical with the just, the good, and the beautiful.

But why is the divine radiation imperfect? Because it is still going on. Our planet, for example, is in the mid-course of its experience. Its flora and fauna are still changing. The evolution of humanity is nearer its origin than its close. The complete spiritualization of the animal element in nature seems to be singularly difficult, and it is the task of our species. Its performance is hindered by error, evil, selfishness, and death, without counting telluric catastrophes. The edifice of a common happiness, a common science of morality and justice, is sketched, but only sketched. A thousand retarding and perturbing causes hinder this giant's task, in which nations, races, and continents take part. At the present moment humanity is not yet constituted as a physical unity, and its general education is not yet begun. All our attempts at order as yet have been local crystallizations. Now, indeed, the different possibilities are beginning to combine (union of posts and telegraphs, universal exhibitions, voyages round the globes, international congresses, etc.). Science and common interest are binding together the great fractions of humanity, which religion and language have kept apart. A year in which there has been talk of a network of African railways, running from the coast to the center and bringing the Atlantic, the Mediterranean, and the Indian Ocean into communication with each other—such a year is enough to mark a new epoch. The fantastic has become the conceivable, the possible tends to become the real; the earth becomes the garden of man. Man's chief problem is how to make the cohabitation of the individuals of his species possible; how, that is to say, to secure for each successive epoch the law, the order, the equilibrium which befits it. Division of labor allows him to explore in every direction at once; industry, science, art, law, education, morals, religion, politics, and economical relations—all are in process of birth.

Thus everything may be brought back to zero by the mind, but it is a fruitful zero—a zero which contains the universe and, in particular, humanity. The mind has no more difficulty in tracking the real within the innumerable than in apprehending infinite possibility. 00 may issue from 0, or may return to it.

January 19, 1879.—Charity—goodness—places a voluntary curb on acuteness of perception; it screens and softens the rays of a too vivid insight; it refuses to see too clearly the ugliness and misery of the great intellectual hospital around it. True goodness is loth to recognize any privilege in itself; it prefers to be humble and charitable; it tries not to see what stares it in the face—that is to say, the imperfections, infirmities, and errors of humankind; its pity puts on airs of approval and encouragement. It triumphs over its own repulsions that it may help and raise.

It has often been remarked that Vinet praised weak things. If so, it was not from any failure in his own critical sense; it was from charity. "Quench not the smoking flax,"—to which I add, "Never give unnecessary pain." The cricket is not the nightingale; why tell him so? Throw yourself into the mind of the cricket—the process is newer and more ingenious; and it is what charity commands.

Intellect is aristocratic, charity is democratic. In a democracy the general equality of pretensions, combined with the inequality of merits, creates considerable practical difficulty; some get out of it by making their prudence a muzzle on their frankness; others, by using kindness as a corrective of perspicacity. On the whole, kindness is safer than reserve; it inflicts no wound, and kills nothing.

Charity is generous; it runs a risk willingly, and in spite of a hundred successive experiences, it thinks no evil at the hundred-and-first. We cannot be at the same time kind and wary, nor can we serve two masters—love and selfishness. We must be knowingly rash, that we may not be like the clever ones of the world, who never forget their own interests. We must be able to submit to being deceived; it is the sacrifice which interest and self-love owe to conscience. The claims of the soul must be satisfied first if we are to be the children of God.

Was it not Bossuet who said, "It is only the great souls who know all the grandeur there is in charity?"

January 21, 1879.—At first religion holds the place of science and philosophy; afterward she has to learn to confine herself to her own domain—which is in the inmost depths of conscience, in the secret recesses of the soul, where life communes with the Divine will and the universal order. Piety is the daily renewing of the ideal, the steadying of our inner being, agitated, troubled, and embittered by the common accidents of existence. Prayer is the spiritual balm, the precious cordial which restores to us peace and courage. It reminds us of pardon and of duty. It says to us, "Thou art loved—love; thou hast received—give; thou must die—labor while thou canst; overcome anger by kindness; overcome evil with good. What does the blindness of opinion matter, or misunderstanding, or ingratitude? Thou art neither bound to follow the common example nor to succeed. *Fais ce que dois, advienne que pourra.* Thou hast a witness in thy conscience; and thy conscience is God speaking to thee!"

March 3, 1879.—The sensible politician is governed by considerations of social utility, the public good, the greatest attainable good; the political windbag starts from the idea of the rights of the individual—abstract rights, of which the extent is affirmed, not demonstrated, for the political right of the individual is precisely what is in question. The revolutionary school always forgets that right apart from duty is a compass with one leg. The notion of right inflates the individual fills him with thoughts of self and of what others owe him, while it ignores the other side of the question, and extinguishes his capacity for devoting himself to a common cause. The state becomes a shop with self-interest for a principle—or rather an arena, in which every combatant fights for his own hand only. In either case self is the motive power.

Church and state ought to provide two opposite careers for the individual; in the state he should be called on to give proof of merit—that is to say, he should earn his rights by services rendered; in the church his task should be to do good while suppressing his own merits, by a voluntary act of humility.

Extreme individualism dissipates the moral substance of the individual. It leads him to subordinate everything to himself, and to think the world; society, the state, made for him. I am chilled by its lack of gratitude, of the spirit of deference, of the instinct of solidarity. It is an ideal without beauty and without grandeur.

But, as a consolation, the modern zeal for equality makes a counterpoise for Darwinism, just as one wolf holds another wolf in check. Neither, indeed, acknowledges the claim of duty. The fanatic for equality affirms his right not to be eaten by his neighbor; the Darwinian states the fact that the big devour the little, and adds—so much the better. Neither the one nor the other has a word to say of love, of eternity, of kindness, of piety, of voluntary submission, of self-surrender.

All forces and all principles are brought into action at once in this world. The result is, on the whole, good. But the struggle itself is hateful because it dislocates truth and shows us nothing but error pitted against error, party against party; that is to say, mere halves and fragments of being—monsters against monsters. A nature in love with beauty cannot reconcile itself to the sight; it longs for harmony, for something else than perpetual dissonance. The common condition of human society must indeed be accepted; tumult, hatred, fraud, crime, the ferocity of self-interest, the tenacity of prejudice, are perennial; but the philosopher sighs over it; his heart is not in it; his ambition is to see human history from a height; his ear is set to catch the music of the eternal spheres.

March 15, 1879.—I have been turning over "Les histories de mon Parrain" by Stahl, and a few chapters of "Nos Fils et nos Filles" by Legouve. These writers press wit, grace, gayety, and charm into the service of goodness; their desire is to show that virtue is not so dull nor common sense so tiresome as people believe. They are persuasive moralists, captivating story-tellers; they rouse the appetite for good. This pretty manner of theirs, however, has its dangers. A moral wrapped up in sugar goes down certainly, but it may be feared that it only goes down because of its sugar. The

Sybarites of to-day will tolerate a sermon which is delicate enough to flatter their literary sensuality; but it is their taste which is charmed, not their conscience which is awakened; their principle of conduct escapes untouched.

Amusement, instruction, morals, are distinct *genres*. They may no doubt be mingled and combined, but if we wish to obtain direct and simple effects, we shall do best to keep them apart. The well-disposed child, besides, does not like mixtures which have something of artifice and deception in them. Duty claims obedience; study requires application; for amusement, nothing is wanted but good temper. To convert obedience and application into means of amusement is to weaken the will and the intelligence. These efforts to make virtue the fashion are praiseworthy enough, but if they do honor to the writers, on the other hand they prove the moral anaemia of society. When the digestion is unspoiled, so much persuading is not necessary to give it a taste for bread.

May 22,1879. (Ascension Day).—Wonderful and delicious weather. Soft, caressing sunlight—the air a limpid blue—twitterings of birds; even the distant voices of the city have something young and springlike in them. It is indeed a new birth. The ascension of the Saviour of men is symbolized by this expansion, this heavenward yearning of nature.... I feel myself born again; all the windows of the soul are clear. Forms, lines, tints, reflections, sounds, contrasts, and harmonies, the general play and interchange of things—it is all enchanting! The atmosphere is steeped in joy. May is in full beauty.

In my courtyard the ivy is green again, the chestnut tree is full of leaf, the Persian lilac beside the little fountain is flushed with red, and just about to flower; through the wide openings to the right and left of the old College of Calvin I see the Saleve above the trees of St. Antoine, the Voiron above the hill of Cologny; while the three flights of steps which, from landing to landing, lead between two high walls from the Rue Verdaine to the terrace of the Tranchees, recall to one's imagination some old city of the south, a glimpse of Perugia or of Malaga.

All the bells are ringing. It is the hour of worship. A historical and religious impression mingles with the picturesque, the musical, the poetical impressions of the scene. All the peoples of Christendom— all the churches scattered over the globe—are celebrating at this moment the glory of the Crucified.

And what are those many nations doing who have other prophets, and honor the Divinity in other ways?—the Jews, the Mussulmans, the Buddhists, the Vishnuists, the Guebers? They have other sacred days, other rites, other solemnities, other beliefs. But all have some religion, some ideal end for life—all aim at raising man above the sorrows and smallnesses of the present, and of the individual existence. All have faith in something greater than themselves, all pray, all bow, all adore; all see beyond nature, Spirit, and beyond evil, Good. All bear witness to the Invisible. Here we have the link which binds all peoples together. All men are equally creatures of sorrow and desire, of hope and fear. All long to recover some lost harmony with the great order of things, and to feel themselves approved and blessed by the Author of the universe. All know what suffering is, and yearn for happiness. All know what sin is, and feel the need of pardon.

Christianity reduced to its original simplicity is the reconciliation of the sinner with God, by means of the certainty that God loves in spite of everything, and that he chastises because he loves. Christianity furnished a new motive and a new strength for the achievement of moral perfection. It made holiness attractive by giving to it the air of filial gratitude.

June 28, 1879.—Last lecture of the term and of the academic year. I finished the exposition of modern philosophy, and wound up my course with the precision I wished. The circle has returned upon itself. In order to do this I have divided my hour into minutes, calculated my material, and counted every stitch and point. This, however, is but a very small part of the professorial science, It is a more difficult matter to divide one's whole material into a given number of lectures, to determine the right proportions of the different parts, and the normal speed of delivery to be attained. The ordinary lecturer may achieve a series of complete *seances*—the unity being the *seance*. But a scientific course ought to aim at something more—at a general unity of subject and of exposition.

Has this concise, substantial, closely-reasoned kind of work been useful to my class? I cannot tell. Have my students liked me this year? I am not sure, but I hope so. It seems to me they have. Only, if I have pleased them, it cannot have been in any case more than a *succes d'estime*; I have never aimed at any oratorical success. My only object is to light up for them a complicated and difficult subject. I respect myself too much, and I respect my class too much, to attempt rhetoric. My role is to help them to understand. Scientific lecturing ought to be, above all things, clear, instructive, well put together, and convincing. A lecturer has nothing to do with paying court to the scholars, or with showing off the master; his business is one of serious study and impersonal exposition. To yield anything on this point would seem to me a piece of mean utilitarianism. I hate everything that savors of cajoling and coaxing. All such ways are mere attempts to throw dust in men's eyes, mere forms of coquetry and stratagem. A professor is the priest of his subject; he should do the honors of it gravely and with dignity.

September 9, 1879.—"Non-being is perfect. Being, imperfect:" this horrible sophism becomes beautiful only in the Platonic system, because there Non-being is replaced by the Idea, which is, and which is divine.

The ideal, the chimerical, the vacant, should not be allowed to claim so great a superiority to the Real, which, on its side, has the incomparable advantage of existing. The Ideal kills enjoyment and content by disparaging the present and actual. It is the voice which says No, like Mephistopheles. No, you have not succeeded; no, your work is not good; no, you are not happy; no, you shall not find rest—all that you see and all that you do is insufficient, insignificant, overdone, badly done, imperfect. The thirst for the ideal is like the goad of Siva, which only quickens life to hasten death. Incurable longing that it is, it lies at the root both of individual suffering and of the progress of the race. It destroys happiness in the name of dignity.

The only positive good is order, the return therefore to order and to a state of equilibrium. Thought without action is an evil, and so is action without thought. The ideal is a poison unless it be fused with the real, and the real becomes corrupt without the perfume of the ideal. Nothing is good singly without its complement and its contrary. Self-examination is dangerous if it encroaches upon self-devotion; reverie is hurtful when it stupefies the will; gentleness is an evil when it lessens strength; contemplation is fatal when it destroys character. "Too much" and "too little" sin equally against wisdom. Excess is one evil, apathy another. Duty may be defined as energy tempered by moderation; happiness, as inclination calmed and tempered by self-control.

Just as life is only lent us for a few years, but is not inherent in us, so the good which is in us is not our own. It is not difficult to think of one's self in this detached spirit. It only needs a little self-knowledge, a little intuitive preception of the ideal, a little religion. There is even much sweetness in this conception that we are nothing of ourselves, and that yet it is granted to us to summon each other to life, joy, poetry and holiness.

Another application of the law of irony: Zeno, a fatalist by theory, makes his disciples heroes; Epicurus, the upholder of liberty, makes his disciples languid and effeminate. The ideal pursued is the decisive point; the stoical ideal is duty, whereas the Epicureans make an ideal out of an interest. Two tendencies, two systems of morals, two worlds. In the same way the Jansenists, and before them the great reformers, are for predestination, the Jesuits for free-will—and yet the first founded liberty, the second slavery of conscience. What matters then is not the theoretical principle; it is the secret tendency, the aspiration, the aim, which is the essential thing.

* * * * *

At every epoch there lies, beyond the domain of what man knows, the domain of the unknown, in which faith has its dwelling. Faith has no proofs, but only itself, to offer. It is born spontaneously in certain commanding souls; it spreads its empire among the rest by imitation and contagion. A great faith is but a great hope which becomes certitude as we move farther and farther from the founder of it; time and distance strengthen it, until at last the passion for knowledge seizes upon it, questions, and examines it. Then all which had once made its strength becomes its weakness; the impossibility of verification, exaltation of feeling, distance.

* * * * *

At what age is our view clearest, our eye truest? Surely in old age, before the infirmities come which weaken or embitter. The ancients were right. The old man who is at once sympathetic and disinterested, necessarily develops the spirit of contemplation, and it is given to the spirit of contemplation to see things most truly, because it alone perceives them in their relative and proportional value.

January 2, 1880.—A sense of rest, of deep quiet even. Silence within and without. A quietly-burning fire. A sense of comfort. The portrait of my mother seems to smile upon me. I am not dazed or stupid, but only happy in this peaceful morning. Whatever may be the charm of emotion, I do not know whether it equals the sweetness of those hours of silent meditation, in which we have a glimpse and foretaste of the contemplative joys of paradise. Desire and fear, sadness and care, are done away. Existence is reduced to the simplest form, the most ethereal mode of being, that is, to pure self-consciousness. It is a state of harmony, without tension and without disturbance, the dominical state of the soul, perhaps the state which awaits it beyond the grave. It is happiness as the orientals understand it, the happiness of the anchorite, who neither struggles nor wishes any more, but simply adores and enjoys. It is difficult to find words in which to express this moral situation, for our languages can only render the particular and localized vibrations of life; they are incapable of expressing this motionless concentration, this divine quietude, this state of the resting ocean, which reflects the sky, and is master of its own profundities. Things are then re-absorbed into their principles; memories are swallowed up in memory; the soul is only soul, and is no longer conscious of itself in its individuality and separateness. It is something which feels the universal life, a sensible atom of the Divine, of God. It no longer appropriates anything to itself, it is conscious of no void. Only the Yogis and Soufis perhaps have known in its profundity this humble and yet voluptuous state, which combines the joys of being and of non-being, which is neither reflection nor will, which is above both the moral existence and the intellectual existence, which is the return to unity, to the pleroma, the vision of Plotinus and of Proclus—Nirvana in its most attractive form.

It is clear that the western nations in general, and especially the Americans, know very little of this state of feeling. For them life is devouring and incessant activity. They are eager for gold, for power, for dominion; their aim is to crush men and to enslave nature. They show an obstinate interest in means, and have not a thought for the end. They confound being with individual being, and the expansion of the self with happiness—that is to say, they do not live by the soul; they ignore the unchangeable and the eternal; they live at the periphery of their being, because they are unable to penetrate to its axis. They are excited, ardent, positive, because they are superficial. Why so much effort, noise, struggle, and greed?—it is all a mere stunning and deafening of the self. When death comes they recognize that it is so—why not then admit it sooner? Activity is only beautiful when it is holy—that is to say, when it is spent in the service of that which passeth not away.

February 6, 1880.—A feeling article by Edmond Scherer on the death of Bersot, the director of the "Ecole Normale," a philosopher who bore like a stoic a terrible disease, and who labored to the last without a complaint.... I have just read the four orations delivered over his grave. They have brought the tears to my eyes. In the last days of this brave man everything was manly, noble, moral, and spiritual. Each of the speakers paid homage to the character, the devotion, the constancy, and the intellectual elevation of the dead. "Let us learn from him how to live and how to die." The whole funeral ceremony had an antique dignity.

February 7, 1880.—Hoar-frost and fog, but the general aspect is bright and fairylike, and has nothing in common with the gloom in Paris and London, of which the newspapers tell us.

This silvery landscape has a dreamy grace, a fanciful charm, which are unknown both to the countries of the sun and to those of coal-smoke. The trees seem to belong to another creation, in which white has taken the place of green. As one gazes at these alleys, these clumps, these groves and arcades, these lace-like garlands and festoons, one feels no wish for anything else; their beauty is original and self-sufficing, all the more because the ground powdered with snow, the sky dimmed with mist, and the smooth soft distances, combine to form a general scale of color, and a harmonious whole, which charms the eye. No harshness anywhere—all is velvet. My enchantment beguiled me out both before and after dinner. The impression is that of a *fete*, and the subdued tints are, or seem to be, a mere coquetry of winter which has set itself to paint something without sunshine, and yet to charm the spectator.

February 9, 1880,—Life rushes on—so much the worse for the weak and the stragglers. As soon as a man's *tendo Achillis* gives way he finds himself trampled under foot by the young, the eager, the voracious. "*Vae victis, vae debilibus!*" yells the crowd, which in its turn is storming the goods of this world. Every man is always in some other man's way, since, however small he may make himself, he still occupies some space, and however little he may envy or possess, he is still sure to be envied and his goods coveted by some one else. Mean world!—peopled by a mean race! To console ourselves we must think of the exceptions—of the noble and generous souls. There are such. What do the rest matter! The traveler crossing the desert feels himself surrounded by creatures thirsting for his blood; by day vultures fly about his head; by night scorpions creep into his tent, jackals prowl around his camp-fire, mosquitoes prick and torture him with their greedy sting; everywhere menace, enmity, ferocity. But far beyond the horizon, and the barren sands peopled by these hostile hordes, the wayfarer pictures to himself a few loved faces and kind looks, a few true hearts which follow him in their dreams—and smiles. When all is said, indeed, we defend ourselves a greater or lesser number of years, but we are always conquered and devoured in the end; there is no escaping the grave and its worm. Destruction is our destiny, and oblivion our portion....

How near is the great gulf! My skiff is thin as a nutshell, or even more fragile still. Let the leak but widen a little and all is over for the navigator. A mere nothing separates me from idiocy, from madness, from death. The slightest breach is enough to endanger all this frail, ingenious edifice, which calls itself my being and my life.

Not even the dragonfly symbol is enough to express its frailty; the soap-bubble is the best poetical translation of all this illusory magnificence, this fugitive apparition of the tiny self, which is we, and we it.

... A miserable night enough. Awakened three or four times by my bronchitis. Sadness—restlessness. One of these winter nights, possibly, suffocation will come. I realize that it would be well to keep myself ready, to put everything in order.... To begin with, let me wipe out all personal grievances and bitternesses; forgive all, judge no one; in enmity and ill-will, see only misunderstanding. "As much as lieth in you, be at peace with all men." On the bed of death the soul should have no eyes but for eternal things. All the littlenesses of life disappear. The fight is over. There should be nothing left now but remembrance of past blessings—adoration of the ways of God. Our natural instinct leads us back to Christian humility and pity. "Father, forgive us our trespasses, as we forgive them who trespass against us."

Prepare thyself as though the coming Easter were thy last, for thy days henceforward shall be few and evil.

February 11, 1880.—Victor de Laprade [Footnote: Victor de Laprade, born 1812, first a disciple and imitator of Edgar Quinet, then the friend of Lamartine, Lamennais, George Sand, Victor Hugo; admitted to the Academy in 1857 in succession to Alfred de Musset. He wrote "Parfums de Madeleine," 1839; "Odes et Poemes," 1843; "Poemes Evangeliques," 1852; "Idylles Heroiques," 1858, etc. etc.] has elevation, grandeur, nobility, and harmony. What is it, then, that he lacks? Ease, and perhaps humor. Hence the monotonous solemnity, the excess of emphasis, the over-intensity, the inspired air, the statue-like gait, which annoy one in him. His is a muse which never lays aside the *cothurnus*, and a royalty which never puts off its crown, even in sleep. The total absence in him of playfulness, simplicity, familiarity, is a great defect. De Laprade is to the ancients as the French tragedy is to that of Euripides, or as the wig of Louis XIV. to the locks of Apollo. His majestic airs are wearisome and factitious. If there is not exactly affectation in them, there is at least a kind of theatrical and sacerdotal posing, a sort of professional attitudinizing. Truth is not as fine as this, but it is more living, more pathetic, more varied. Marble images are cold. Was it not Musset who said, "If De Laprade is a poet, then I am not one?"

February 27, 1880.—I have finished translating twelve or fourteen little poems by Petoefi. They have a strange kind of savor. There is something of the Steppe, of the East, of Mazeppa, of madness, in these songs, which seem to go to the beat of a riding-whip. What force and passion, what savage brilliancy, what wild and grandiose images, there are in them! One feels that the Magyar is a kind of Centaur, and that he is only Christian and European by accident. The Hun in him tends toward the Arab.

March 20, 1880.—I have been reading "La Banniere Bleue"—a history of the world at the time of Genghis Khan, under the form of memoirs. It is a Turk, Ouigour, who tells the story. He shows us civilization from the wrong side, or the other side, and the Asiatic nomads appear as the scavengers of its corruptions.

Genghis proclaimed himself the scourge of God, and he did in fact realize the vastest empire known to history, stretching from the Blue Sea to the Baltic, and from the vast plains of Siberia to the banks of the sacred Ganges. The most solid empires of the ancient world were overthrown by the tramp of his horsemen and the shafts of his archers. From the tumult into which he threw the western continent there issued certain vast results: the fall of the Byzantine empire, involving the Renaissance, the voyages of discovery in Asia, undertaken from both sides of the globe—that is to say, Gama and Columbus; the formation of the Turkish empire; and the preparation of the Russian empire. This tremendous hurricane, starting from the high Asiatic tablelands, felled the decaying oaks and worm-eaten buildings of the whole ancient world. The descent of the yellow, flat-nosed Mongols upon Europe is a historical cyclone which devastated and purified our thirteenth century, and broke, at the two ends of the known world, through two great Chinese walls—that which protected the ancient empire of the Center, and that which made a barrier of ignorance and superstition round the little world of Christendom. Attila, Genghis, Tamerlane, ought to range in the memory of men with Caesar, Charlemagne, and Napoleon. They roused whole peoples into action, and stirred the depths of human life, they powerfully affected ethnography, they let loose rivers of blood, and renewed the face of things. The Quakers will not see that there is a law of tempests in history as in nature. The revilers of war are like the revilers of thunder, storms, and volcanoes; they know not what they do. Civilization tends to corrupt men, as large towns tend to vitiate the air.

"Nos patimur longae pacis mala."

Catastrophes bring about a violent restoration of equilibrium; they put the world brutally to rights. Evil chastises itself, and the tendency to ruin in human things supplies the place of the regulator who has not yet been discovered. No civilization can bear more than a certain proportion of abuses, injustice, corruption, shame, and crime. When this proportion has been reached, the boiler bursts, the palace falls, the scaffolding breaks down; institutions, cities, states, empires, sink into ruin. The evil contained in an organism is a virus which preys upon it, and if it is not eliminated ends by destroying it. And as nothing is perfect, nothing can escape death.

May 19, 1880.—*Inadaptibility*, due either to mysticism or stiffness, delicacy or disdain, is the misfortune or at all events the characteristic of my life. I have not been able to fit myself to anything, to content myself with anything. I have never had the quantum of illusion necessary for risking the irreparable. I have made use of the ideal itself to keep me from any kind of bondage. It was thus with marriage: only perfection would have satisfied me; and, on the other hand, I was not worthy of perfection.... So that, finding no satisfaction in things, I tried to extirpate desire, by which things enslave us. Independence has been my refuge; detachment my stronghold. I have lived the impersonal life—in the world, yet not in it, thinking much, desiring nothing. It is a state of mind which corresponds with what in women is called a broken heart; and it is in fact like it, since the characteristic common to both is despair. When one knows that one will never possess what one could have loved, and that one can be content with nothing less, one has, so to speak, left the world, one has cut the golden hair, parted with all that makes human life—that is to say, illusion—the incessant effort toward an apparently attainable end. May 31, 1880.—Let us not be overingenious. There is no help to be got out of subtleties. Besides, one must live. It is best and simplest not to quarrel with any illusion, and to accept the inevitable good-temperedly. Plunged as we are in human existence, we must take it as it comes, not too bitterly, nor too tragically, without horror and without sarcasm, without misplaced petulance or a too exacting expectation; cheerfulness, serenity, and patience, these are best—let us aim at these. Our business is to treat life as the grandfather treats his granddaughter, or the grandmother her grandson; to enter into the pretenses of childhood and the fictions of youth, even when we ourselves have long passed beyond them. It is probable that God himself looks kindly upon the illusions of the human race, so long as they are innocent. There is nothing evil but sin—that is, egotism and revolt. And as for error, man changes his errors frequently, but error of some sort is always with him. Travel as one may, one is always somewhere, and one's mind rests on some point of truth, as one's feet rest upon some point of the globe.

Society alone represents a more or less complete unity. The individual must content himself with being a stone in the building, a wheel in the immense machine, a word in the poem. He is a part of the family, of the state, of humanity, of all the special fragments formed by human interests, beliefs, aspirations, and labors. The loftiest souls are those who are conscious of the universal symphony, and who give their full and willing collaboration to this vast and complicated concert which we call civilization.

In principle the mind is capable of suppressing all the limits which it discovers in itself, limits of language, nationality, religion, race, or epoch. But it must be admitted that the more the mind spiritualizes and generalizes itself, the less hold it has on other minds, which no longer understand it or know what to do with it. Influence belongs to men of action, and for purposes of action nothing is more useful than narrowness of thought combined with energy of will.

The forms of dreamland are gigantic, those of action are small and dwarfed. To the minds imprisoned in things, belong success, fame, profit; a great deal no doubt; but they know nothing of the pleasures of liberty or the joy of penetrating the infinite. However, I do not mean to put one class before another; for every man is happy according to his nature. History is made by combatants and specialists; only it is perhaps not a bad thing that in the midst of the devouring activities of the western world, there should be a few Brahmanizing souls.

... This soliloquy means—what? That reverie turns upon itself as dreams do; that impressions added together do not always produce a fair judgment; that a private journal is like a good king, and permits repetitions, outpourings, complaint.... These unseen effusions are the conversation of thought with itself the arpeggios involuntary but not unconscious, of that aeolian harp we bear within us. Its vibrations compose no piece, exhaust no theme, achieve no melody, carry out no programme, but they express the innermost life of man.

June 1, 1880.—Stendhal's "La Chartreuse de Parme." A remarkable book. It is even typical, the first of a class. Stendhal opens the series of naturalist novels, which suppress the intervention of the moral sense, and scoff at the claim of free-will. Individuals are irresponsible; they are governed by their passions, and the play of human passions is the observer's joy, the artist's material. Stendhal is a novelist after Taine's heart, a faithful painter who is neither touched nor angry, and whom everything amuses—the knave and the adventuress as well as honest men and women, but who has neither faith, nor preference, nor ideal. In him literature is subordinated to natural history, to science. It no longer forms part of the humanities, it no longer gives man the honor of a separate rank. It classes him with the ant, the beaver, and the monkey. And this moral indifference to morality leads direct to immorality.

The vice of the whole school is cynicism, contempt for man, whom they degrade to the level of the brute; it is the worship of strength, disregard of the soul, a want of generosity, of reverence, of nobility, which shows itself in spite of all protestations to the contrary; in a word, it is *inhumanity*. No man can be a naturalist with impunity: he will be coarse even with the most refined culture. A free mind is a great thing no doubt, but loftiness of heart, belief in goodness, capacity for enthusiasm and devotion, the thirst after perfection and holiness, are greater things still.

June 7, 1880.—I am reading Madame Necker de Saussure [Footnote: Madame Necker de Saussure was the daughter of the famous geologist, De Saussure; she married a nephew of Jacques Necker, and was therefore cousin by marriage of Madame de Stael. She is often supposed to be the original of Madame de Cerlebe in "Delphine," and the *Notice sur le Caractere et les Ecrits de Mdme. de Stael,* prefixed to the authoritative edition of Madame de Stael's collected works, is by her. Philanthropy and education were her two main interests, but she had also a very large amount of general literary cultivation, as was proved by her translation of Schlegel's "Lectures on Dramatic Literature."] again. "L'Education progressive" is an admirable book. What moderation and fairness of view, what reasonableness and dignity of manner! Everything in it is of high quality—observation, thought, and style. The reconciliation of science with the ideal, of philosophy with religion, of psychology with morals, which the book attempts, is sound and beneficent. It is a fine book—a classic—and Geneva may be proud of a piece of work which shows such high cultivation and so much solid wisdom. Here we have the true Genevese literature, the central tradition of the country.

Later.—I have finished the third volume of Madame Necker. The elevation and delicacy, the sense and seriousness, the beauty and perfection of the whole are astonishing. A few harshnesses or inaccuracies of language do not matter. I feel for the author a respect mingled with emotion. How rare it is to find a book in which everything is sincere and everything is true!

June 26, 1880.—Democracy exists; it is mere loss of time to dwell upon its absurdities and defects. Every *regime* has its weaknesses, and this *regime* is a lesser evil than others. On things its effect is unfavorable, but on the other hand men profit by it, for it develops the individual by obliging every one to take interest in a multitude of questions. It makes bad work, but it produces citizens. This is its excuse, and a more than tolerable one; in the eyes of the philanthropist, indeed, it is a serious title to respect, for, after all, social institutions are made for man, and not *vice versa.*

June 27, 1880.—I paid a visit to my friends—, and we resumed the conversation of yesterday. We talked of the ills which threaten democracy and which are derived from the legal fiction at the root of it. Surely the remedy consists in insisting everywhere upon the truth which democracy systematically forgets, and which is its proper makeweight—on the inequalities of talent, of virtue, and merit, and on the respect due to age, to capacity, to services rendered. Juvenile arrogance and jealous ingratitude must be resisted all the more strenuously because social forms are in their favor; and when the institutions of a country lay stress only on the rights of the individual, it is the business of the citizen to lay all the more stress on duty. There must be a constant effort to correct the prevailing tendency of things. All this, it is true, is nothing but palliative, but in human society one cannot hope for more.

Later.—Alfred de Vigny is a sympathetic writer, with a meditative turn of thought, a strong and supple talent. He possesses elevation, independence, seriousness, originality, boldness and grace; he has something of everything. He paints, describes, and judges well; he thinks, and has the courage of his opinions. His defect lies in an excess of self-respect, in a British pride and reserve which give him a horror of familiarity and a terror of letting himself go. This tendency has naturally injured his popularity as a writer with a public whom he holds at arm's length as one might a troublesome crowd. The French race has never cared much about the inviolability of personal conscience; it does not like stoics shut up in their own dignity as in a tower, and recognizing no master but God, duty or faith. Such strictness annoys and irritates it; it is merely piqued and made impatient by anything solemn. It repudiated Protestantism for this very reason, and in all crises it has crushed those who have not yielded to the passionate current of opinion.

July 1, 1880. (*Three o'clock*).—The temperature is oppressive; I ought to be looking over my notes, and thinking of to-morrow's examinations. Inward distaste—emptiness—discontent. Is it trouble of conscience, or sorrow of heart? or the soul preying upon itself? or merely a sense of strength decaying and time running to waste? Is sadness—or regret—or fear—at the root of it? I do not know; but this dull sense of misery has danger in it; it leads to rash efforts and mad decisions. Oh, for escape from self, for something to stifle the importunate voice of want and yearning! Discontent is the father of temptation. How can we gorge the invisible serpent hidden at the bottom of our well—gorge it so that it may sleep?

At the heart of all this rage and vain rebellion there lies—what? Aspiration, yearning! We are athirst for the infinite—for love—for I know not what. It is the instinct of happiness, which, like some wild animal, is restless for its prey. It is God calling-God avenging himself.

July 4, 1880. (*Sunday, half-past eight in the morning*).—The sun has come out after heavy rain. May one take it as an omen on this solemn day? The great voice of Clemence has just been sounding in our ears. The bell's deep vibrations went to my heart. For a quarter of an hour the pathetic appeal went on—"Geneva, Geneva, remember! I am called *Clemence*—I am the voice of church and of country. People of Geneva, serve God and be at peace together." [Footnote: A law to bring about separation between Church and State, adopted by the Great Council, was on this day submitted to the vote of the Genevese people. It was rejected by a large majority (9,306 against 4,044).—[S.]]

Seven o'clock in the evening.—Clemence has been ringing again, during the last half-hour of the *scrutin*. Now that she has stopped, the silence has a terrible seriousness, like that which weighs upon a crowd when it is waiting for the return of the judge and the delivery of the death sentence. The fate of the Genevese church and country is now in the voting box.

Eleven o'clock in the evening.—Victory along the whole line. The Ayes have carried little more than two-sevenths of the vote. At my friend ——'s house I found them all full of excitement, gratitude, and joy.

July 5, 1880.—There are some words which have still a magical virtue with the mass of the people: those of State, Republic, Country, Nation, Flag, and even, I think, Church. Our skeptical and mocking culture knows nothing of the emotion, the exaltation, the delirium, which these words awaken in simple people. The blases of the world have no idea how the popular mind vibrates to these appeals, by which they themselves are untouched. It is their punishment; it is also their infirmity. Their temper is satirical and separatist; they live in isolation and sterility.

I feel again what I felt at the time of the Rousseau centenary; my feeling and imagination are chilled and repelled by those Pharisaical people who think themselves too good to associate with the crowd.

At the same time, I suffer from an inward contradiction, from a two-fold, instinctive repugnance—an aesthetic repugnance toward vulgarity of every kind, a moral repugnance toward barrenness and coldness of heart.

So that personally I am only attracted by the individuals of cultivation and eminence, while on the other hand nothing is sweeter to me than to feel myself vibrating in sympathy with the national spirit, with the feeling of the masses. I only care for the two extremes, and it is this which separates me from each of them.

Our everyday life, split up as it is into clashing parties and opposed opinions, and harassed by perpetual disorder and discussion, is painful and almost hateful to me. A thousand things irritate and provoke me. But perhaps it would be the same elsewhere. Very likely it is the inevitable way of the world which displeases me—the sight of what succeeds, of what men approve or blame, of what they excuse or accuse. I need to admire, to feel myself in sympathy and in harmony with my neighbor, with the march of things, and the tendencies of those around me, and almost always I have had to give up the hope of it. I take refuge in retreat, to avoid discord. But solitude is only a *pis-aller*.

July 6, 1880.—Magnificent weather. The college prize-day. [Footnote: The prize-giving at the College of Geneva is made the occasion of a national festival.] Toward evening I went with our three ladies to the plain of Plainpalais. There was an immense crowd, and I was struck with the bright look of the faces. The festival wound up with the traditional fireworks, under a calm and starry sky. Here we have the republic indeed, I thought as I came in. For a whole week this people has been out-of-doors, camping, like the Athenians on the Agora. Since Wednesday lectures and public meetings have followed one another without intermission; at home there are pamphlets and the newspapers to be read; while speech-making goes on at the clubs. On Sunday, *plebiscite*; Monday, public procession, service at St. Pierre, speeches on the Molard, festival for the adults. Tuesday, the college fete-day. Wednesday, the fete-day of the primary schools.

Geneva is a caldron always at boiling-point, a furnace of which the fires are never extinguished. Vulcan had more than one forge, and Geneva is certainly one of those world-anvils on which the greatest number of projects have been hammered out. When one thinks that the martyrs of all causes have been at work here, the mystery is explained a little; but the truest explanation is that Geneva—republican, protestant, democratic, learned, and enterprising Geneva—has for centuries depended on herself alone for the solution of her own difficulties. Since the Reformation she has been always on the alert, marching with a lantern in her left hand and a sword in her right. It pleases me to see that she has not yet become a mere copy of anything, and that she is still capable of deciding for herself. Those who say to her, "Do as they do at New York, at Paris, at Rome, at Berlin," are still in the minority. The *doctrinaires* who would split her up and destroy her unity waste their breath upon her. She divines the snare laid for her and turns away. I like this proof of vitality. Only that which is original has a sufficient reason for existence. A country in which the word of command comes from elsewhere is nothing more than a province. This is what our Jacobins and our Ultramontanes never will recognize. Neither of them understand the meaning of self-government, and neither of them have any idea of the dignity of a historical state and an independent people.

Our small nationalities are ruined by the hollow cosmopolitan formulae which have an equally disastrous effect upon art and letters. The modern *isms* are so many acids which dissolve everything living and concrete. No one achieves a masterpiece, nor even a decent piece of work, by the help of realism, liberalism, or romanticism. Separatism has even less virtue than any of the other *isms*, for it is the abstraction of a negation, the shadow of a shadow. The various *isms* of the present are not fruitful principles: they are hardly even explanatory formulae. They are rather names of disease, for they express some element in excess, some dangerous and abusive exaggeration. Examples: empiricism, idealism, radicalism. What is best among things and most perfect among beings slips through these categories. The man who is perfectly well is neither sanguineous—[to use the old medical term]—nor bilious nor nervous. A normal republic contains opposing parties and points of view, but it contains them, as it were, in a state of chemical combination. All the colors are contained in a ray of light, while red alone does not contain a sixth part of the perfect ray.

July 8, 1880.—It is thirty years since I read Waagen's book on "Museums," which my friend —— is now reading. It was in 1842 that I was wild for pictures; in 1845 that I was studying Krause's philosophy; in 1850 that I became professor of aesthetics. —— may be the same age as I am; it is none the less true that when a particular stage has become to me a matter of history, he is just arriving at it. This impression of distance and remoteness is a strange one. I begin to realize that my memory is a great catacomb, and that below my actual standing-ground there is layer after layer of historical ashes.

Is the life of mind something like that of great trees of immemorial growth? Is the living layer of consciousness super-imposed upon hundreds of dead layers? *Dead?* No doubt this is too much to say, but still, when memory is slack the past becomes almost as though it had never been. To remember that we did know once is not a sign of possession but a sign of loss; it is like the number of an engraving which is no longer on its nail, the title of a volume no longer to be found on its shelf. My mind is the empty frame of a thousand vanished images. Sharpened by incessant training, it is all culture, but it has retained hardly anything in its meshes. It is without matter, and is only form. It no longer has knowledge; it has become method. It is etherealized, algebraicized. Life has treated it as death treats other minds; it has already prepared it for a further metamorphosis. Since the age of sixteen onward I have been able to look at things with the eyes of a blind man recently operated upon — that is to say, I have been able to suppress in myself the results of the long education of sight, and to abolish distances; and now I find myself regarding existence as though from beyond the tomb, from another world; all is strange to me; I am, as it were, outside my own body and individuality; I am *depersonalized*, detached, cut adrift. Is this madness? No. Madness means the impossibility of recovering one's normal balance after the mind has thus played truant among alien forms of being, and followed Dante to invisible worlds. Madness means incapacity for self-judgment and self-control. Whereas it seems to me that my mental transformations are but philosophical experiences. I am tied to none. I am but making psychological investigations. At the same time I do not hide from myself that such experiences weaken the hold of common sense, because they act as solvents of all personal interests and prejudices. I can only defend myself against them by returning to the common life of men, and by bracing and fortifying the will.

July 14, 1880. — What is the book which, of all Genevese literature, I would soonest have written? Perhaps that of Madame Necker de Saussure, or Madame de Stael's "L'Allemagne." To a Genevese, moral philosophy is still the most congenial and remunerative of studies. Intellectual seriousness is what suits us least ill. History, politics, economical science, education, practical philosophy — these are our subjects. We have everything to lose in the attempt to make ourselves mere Frenchified copies of the Parisians: by so doing we are merely carrying water to the Seine. Independent criticism is perhaps easier at Geneva than at Paris, and Geneva ought to remain faithful to her own special line, which, as compared with that of France, is one of greater freedom from the tyranny of taste and fashion on the one hand, and the tyranny of ruling opinion on the other—of Catholicism or Jacobinism. Geneva should be to *La Grande Nation* what Diogenes was to Alexander; her role is to represent the independent thought and the free speech which is not dazzled by prestige, and does not blink the truth. It is true that the role is an ungrateful one, that it lends itself to sarcasm and misrepresentation—but what matter?

July 28, 1880.—This afternoon I have had a walk in the sunshine, and have just come back rejoicing in a renewed communion with nature. The waters of the Rhone and the Arve, the murmur of the river, the austerity of its banks, the brilliancy of the foliage, the play of the leaves, the splendor of the July sunlight, the rich fertility of the fields, the lucidity of the distant mountains, the whiteness of the glaciers under the azure serenity of the sky, the sparkle and foam of the mingling rivers, the leafy masses of the La Batie woods—all and everything delighted me. It seemed to me as though the years of strength had come back to me. I was overwhelmed with sensations. I was surprised and grateful. The universal life carried me on its breast; the summer's caress went to my heart. Once more my eyes beheld the vast horizons, the soaring peaks, the blue lakes, the winding valleys, and all the free outlets of old days. And yet there was no painful sense of longing. The scene left upon me an indefinable impression, which was neither hope, nor desire, nor regret, but rather a sense of emotion, of passionate impulse, mingled with admiration and anxiety. I am conscious at once of joy and of want; beyond what I possess I see the impossible and the unattainable; I gauge my own wealth and poverty; in a word, I am and I am not—my inner state is one of contradiction, because it is one of transition. The ambiguity of it is characteristic of human nature, which is ambiguous, because it is flesh becoming spirit, space changing into thought, the Finite looking dimly out upon the Infinite, intelligence working its way through love and pain.

Man is the *sensorium commune* of nature, the point at which all values are interchanged. Mind is the plastic medium, the principle, and the result of all; at once material and laboratory, product and formula, sensation, expression, and law; that which is, that which does, that which knows. All is not mind, but mind is in all, and contains all. It is the consciousness of being—that is, Being raised to the second power. If the universe subsists, it is because the Eternal mind loves to perceive its own content, in all its wealth and expansion—especially in its stages of preparation. Not that God is an egotist. He allows myriads upon myriads of suns to disport themselves in his shadow; he grants life and consciousness to innumerable multitudes of creatures who thus participate in being and in nature; and all these animated monads multiply, so to speak, his divinity.

August 4, 1880.—I have read a few numbers of the *Feuille Centrale de Zofingen*. [Footnote: The journal of a students' society, drawn from the different cantons of Switzerland, which meets every year in the little town of Zofingen] It is one of those perpetual new beginnings of youth which thinks it is producing something fresh when it is only repeating the old.

Nature is governed by continuity—the continuity of repetition; it is like an oft-told tale, or the recurring burden of a song. The rose-trees are never tired of rose-bearing, the birds of nest-building, young hearts of loving, or young voices of singing the thoughts and feelings which have served their predecessors a hundred thousand times before. Profound monotony in universal movement—there is the simplest formula furnished by the spectacle of the world. All circles are alike, and every existence tends to trace its circle.

How, then, is *fastidium* to be avoided? By shutting our eyes to the general uniformity, by laying stress upon the small differences which exist, and then by learning to enjoy repetition. What to the intellect is old and worn-out is perennially young and fresh to the heart; curiosity is insatiable, but love is never tired. The natural preservative against satiety, too, is work. What we do may weary others, but the personal effort is at least useful to its author. Where every one works, the general life is sure to possess charm and savor, even though it repeat forever the same song, the same aspirations, the same prejudices, and the same sighs. "To every man his turn," is the motto of mortal beings. If what they do is old, they themselves are new; when they imitate, they think they are inventing. They have received, and they transmit. *E sempre bene!*

August 24, 1880.—As years go on I love the beautiful more than the sublime, the smooth more than the rough, the calm nobility of Plato more than the fierce holiness of the world's Jeremiahs. The vehement barbarian is to me the inferior of the mild and playful Socrates. My taste is for the well-balanced soul and the well-trained heart—for a liberty which is not harsh and insolent, like that of the newly enfranchised slave, but lovable. The temperament which charms me is that in which one virtue leads naturally to another. All exclusive and sharply-marked qualities are but so many signs of imperfection.

August 29, 1880.—To-day I am conscious of improvement. I am taking advantage of it to go back to my neglected work and my interrupted habits; but in a week I have grown several months older—that is easy to see. The affection of those around me makes them pretend not to see it; but the looking-glass tells the truth. The fact does not take away from the pleasure of convalescence; but still one hears in it the shuttle of destiny, and death seems to be nearing rapidly, in spite of the halts and truces which are granted one. The most beautiful existence, it seems to me, would be that of a river which should get through all its rapids and waterfalls not far from its rising, and should then in its widening course form a succession of rich valleys, and in each of them a lake equally but diversely beautiful, to end, after the plains of age were past, in the ocean where all that is weary and heavy-laden comes to seek for rest. How few there are of these full, fruitful, gentle lives! What is the use of wishing for or regretting them? It is Wiser and harder to see in one's own lot the best one could have had, and to say to one's self that after all the cleverest tailor cannot make us a coat to fit us more closely than our skin.

"Le vrai nom du bonheur est le contentement."

... The essential thing, for every one is to accept his destiny. Fate has deceived you; you have sometimes grumbled at your lot; well, no more mutual reproaches; go to sleep in peace.

August 30, 1880. (*Two o'clock*).—Rumblings of a grave and distant thunder. The sky is gray but rainless; the sharp little cries of the birds show agitation and fear; one might imagine it the prelude to a symphony or a catastrophe.

"Quel eclair te traverse, o mon coeur soucieux?"

Strange—all the business of the immediate neighborhood is going on; there is even more movement than usual; and yet all these noises are, as it were, held suspended in the silence—in a soft, positive silence, which they cannot disguise—silence akin to that which, in every town, on one day of the week, replaces the vague murmur of the laboring hive. Such silence at such an hour is extraordinary. There is something expectant, contemplative, almost anxious in it. Are there days on which "the little breath" of Job produces more effect than tempest? on which a dull rumbling on the distant horizon is enough to suspend the concert of voices, like the roaring of a desert lion at the fall of night?

September 9, 1880.—It seems to me that with the decline of my active force I am becoming more purely spirit; everything is growing transparent to me. I see the types, the foundation of beings, the sense of things.

All personal events, all particular experiences, are to me texts for meditation, facts to be generalized into laws, realities to be reduced to ideas. Life is only a document to be interpreted, matter to be spiritualized. Such is the life of the thinker. Every day he strips himself more and more of personality. If he consents to act and to feel, it is that he may the better understand; if he wills, it is that he may know what will is. Although it is sweet to him to be loved, and he knows nothing else so sweet, yet there also he seems to himself to be the occasion of the phenomenon rather than its end. He contemplates the spectacle of love, and love for him remains a spectacle. He does not even believe his body his own; he feels the vital whirlwind passing through him—lent to him, as it were, for a moment, in order that he may perceive the cosmic vibrations. He is a mere thinking subject; he retains only the form of things; he attributes to himself the material possession of nothing whatsoever; he asks nothing from life but wisdom. This temper of mind makes him incomprehensible to all that loves enjoyment, dominion, possession. He is fluid as a phantom that we see but cannot grasp; he resembles a man, as the *manes* of Achilles or the shade of Creusa resembled the living. Without having died, I am a ghost. Other men are dreams to me, and I am a dream to them.

Later—Consciousness in me takes no account of the category of time, and therefore all the partitions which tend to make of life a palace with a thousand rooms, do not exist in my case; I am still in the primitive unicellular state. I possess myself only as Monad and as Ego, and I feel my faculties themselves reabsorbed into the substance which they have individualized. All the endowment of animality is, so to speak, repudiated; all the produce of study and of cultivation is in the same way annulled; the whole crystallization is redissolved into fluid; the whole rainbow is withdrawn within the dewdrop; consequences return to the principle, effects to the cause, the bird to the egg, the organism to its germ.

This psychological reinvolution is an anticipation of death; it represents the life beyond the grave, the return to school, the soul fading into the world of ghosts, or descending into the region of *Die Muetter*; it implies the simplification of the individual who, allowing all the accidents of personality to evaporate, exists henceforward only in the indivisible state, the state of point, of potentiality, of pregnant nothingness. Is not this the true definition of mind? Is not mind, dissociated from space and time, just this? Its development, past or future, is contained in it just as a curve is contained in its algebraical formula. This nothing is an all. This *punctum* without dimensions is a *punctum saliens*. What is the acorn but the oak which has lost its branches, its leaves, its trunk, and its roots—that is to say, all its apparatus, its forms, its particularities—but which is still present in concentration, in essence, in a force which contains the possibility of complete revival?

This impoverishment, then, is only superficially a loss, a reduction. To be reduced to those elements in one which are eternal, is indeed to die but not to be annihilated: it is simply to become virtual again.

October 9, 1880. (*Clarens*).—A walk. Deep feeling and admiration. Nature was so beautiful, so caressing, so poetical, so maternal. The sunlight, the leaves, the sky, the bells, all said to me—"Be of good strength and courage, poor bruised one. This is nature's kindly season; here is forgetfulness, calm, and rest. Faults and troubles, anxieties and regrets, cares and wrongs, are but one and the same burden. We make no distinctions; we comfort all sorrows, we bring peace, and with us is consolation. Salvation to the weary, salvation to the afflicted, salvation to the sick, to sinners, to all that suffer in heart, in conscience, and in body. We are the fountain of blessing; drink and live! God maketh his sun to rise upon the just and upon the unjust. There is nothing grudging in his munificence; he does not weigh his gifts like a moneychanger, or number them like a cashier. Come—there is enough for all!"

October 29, 1880. (*Geneva*).—The ideal which a man professes may itself be only a matter of appearance—a device for misleading his neighbor, or deluding himself. The individual is always ready to claim for himself the merits of the badge under which he fights; whereas, generally speaking, it is the contrary which happens. The nobler the badge, the less estimable is the wearer of it. Such at least is the presumption. It is extremely dangerous to pride one's self on any moral or religious specialty whatever. Tell me what you pique yourself upon, and I will tell you what you are not.

But how are we to know what an individual is? First of all by his acts; but by something else too—something which is only perceived by intuition. Soul judges soul by elective affinity, reaching through and beyond both words and silence, looks and actions.

The criterion is subjective, I allow, and liable to error; but in the first place there is no safer one, and in the next, the accuracy of the judgment is in proportion to the moral culture of the judge. Courage is an authority on courage, goodness on goodness, nobleness on nobleness, loyalty on uprightness. We only truly know what we have, or what we have lost and regret, as, for example, childish innocence, virginal purity, or stainless honor. The truest and best judge, then, is Infinite Goodness, and next to it, the regenerated sinner or the saint, the man tried by experience or the sage. Naturally, the touchstone in us becomes finer and truer the better we are.

November 3, 1880.—What impression has the story I have just read made upon me? A mixed one. The imagination gets no pleasure out of it, although the intellect is amused. Why? Because the author's mood is one of incessant irony and *persiflage*. The Voltairean tradition has been his guide—a great deal of wit and satire, very little feeling, no simplicity. It is a combination of qualities which serves eminently well for satire, for journalism, and for paper warfare of all kinds, but which is much less suitable to the novel or short story, for cleverness is not poetry, and the novel is still within the domain of poetry, although on the frontier. The vague discomfort aroused in one by these epigrammatic productions is due probably to a confusion of kinds. Ambiguity of style keeps one in a perpetual state of tension and self-defense; we ought not to be left in doubt whether the speaker is jesting or serious, mocking or tender. Moreover, banter is not humor, and never will be. I think, indeed, that the professional wit finds a difficulty in being genuinely comic, for want of depth and disinterested feeling. To laugh at things and people is not really a joy; it is at best but a cold pleasure. Buffoonery is wholesomer, because it is a little more kindly. The reason why continuous sarcasm repels us is that it lacks two things—humanity and seriousness. Sarcasm implies pride, since it means putting one's self above others—and levity, because conscience is allowed no voice in controlling it. In short, we read satirical books, but we only love and cling to the books in which there is *heart*.

November 22, 1880.—How is ill-nature to be met and overcome? First, by humility: when a man knows his own weaknesses, why should he be angry with others for pointing them out? No doubt it is not very amiable of them to do so, but still, truth is on their side. Secondly, by reflection: after all we are what we are, and if we have been thinking too much of ourselves, it is only an opinion to be modified; the incivility of our neighbor leaves us what we were before. Above all, by pardon: there is only one way of not hating those who do us wrong, and that is by doing them good; anger is best conquered by kindness. Such a victory over feeling may not indeed affect those who have wronged us, but it is a valuable piece of self-discipline. It is vulgar to be angry on one's own account; we ought only to be angry for great causes. Besides, the poisoned dart can only be extracted from the wound by the balm of a silent and thoughtful charity. Why do we let human malignity embitter us? why should ingratitude, jealousy—perfidy even—enrage us? There is no end to recriminations, complaints, or reprisals. The simplest plan is to blot everything out. Anger, rancor, bitterness, trouble the soul. Every man is a dispenser of justice; but there is one wrong that he is not bound to punish—that of which he himself is the victim. Such a wrong is to be healed, not avenged. Fire purifies all.

"Mon ame est comme un feu qui devore et parfume Ce qu'on jette pour le ternir."

December 27, 1880—In an article I have just read, Biedermann reproaches Strauss with being too negative, and with having broken with Christianity. The object to be pursued, according to him, should be the freeing of religion from the mythological element, and the substitution of another point of view for the antiquated dualism of orthodoxy—this other point of view to be the victory over the world, produced by the sense of divine sonship.

It is true that another question arises: has not a religion which has separated itself from special miracle, from local interventions of the supernatural, and from mystery, lost its savor and its efficacy? For the sake of satisfying a thinking and instructed public, is it wise to sacrifice the influence of religion over the multitude? Answer. A pious fiction is still a fiction. Truth has the highest claim. It is for the world to accommodate itself to truth, and not *vice versa*. Copernicus upset the astronomy of the Middle Ages—so much the worse for it! The Eternal Gospel revolutionizes modern churches—what matter! When symbols become transparent, they have no further binding force. We see in them a poem, an allegory, a metaphor; but we believe in them no longer. Yes, but still a certain esotericism is inevitable, since critical, scientific, and philosophical culture is only attainable by a minority. The new faith must have its symbols too. At present the effect it produces on pious souls is a more or less profane one; it has a disrespectful, incredulous, frivolous look, and it seems to free a man from traditional dogma at the cost of seriousness of conscience. How are sensitiveness of feeling, the sense of sin, the desire for pardon, the thirst for holiness, to be preserved among us, when the errors which have served them so long for support and food have been eliminated? Is not illusion indispensable? is it not the divine process of education?

Perhaps the best way is to draw a deep distinction between opinion and belief, and between belief and science. The mind which discerns these different degrees may allow itself imagination and faith, and still remain within the lines of progress.

December 28, 1880.—There are two modes of classing the people we know: the first is utilitarian—it starts from ourselves, divides our friends from our enemies, and distinguishes those who are antipathetic to us, those who are indifferent, those who can serve or harm us; the second is disinterested—it classes men according to their intrinsic value, their own qualities and defects, apart from the feelings which they have for us, or we for them.

My tendency is to the second kind of classification. I appreciate men less by the special affection which they show to me than by their personal excellence, and I cannot confuse gratitude with esteem. It is a happy thing for us when the two feelings can be combined; and nothing is more painful than to owe gratitude where yet we can feel neither respect nor confidence.

I am not very willing to believe in the permanence of accidental states. The generosity of a miser, the good nature of an egotist, the gentleness of a passionate temperament, the tenderness of a barren nature, the piety of a dull heart, the humility of an excitable self-love, interest me as phenomena—nay, even touch me if I am the object of them, but they inspire me with very little confidence. I foresee the end of them too clearly. Every exception tends to disappear and to return to the rule. All privilege is temporary, and besides, I am less flattered than anxious when I find myself the object of a privilege.

A man's primitive character may be covered over by alluvial deposits of culture and acquisition—none the less is it sure to come to the surface when years have worn away all that is accessory and adventitious. I admit indeed the possibility of great moral crises which sometimes revolutionize the soul, but I dare not reckon on them. It is a possibility—not a probability. In choosing one's friends we must choose those whose qualities are inborn, and their virtues virtues of temperament. To lay the foundations of friendship on borrowed or added virtues is to build on an artificial soil; we run too many risks by it.

Exceptions are snares, and we ought above all to distrust them when they charm our vanity. To catch and fix a fickle heart is a task which tempts all women; and a man finds something intoxicating in the tears of tenderness and joy which he alone has had the power to draw from a proud woman. But attractions of this kind are deceptive. Affinity of nature founded on worship of the same ideal, and perfect in proportion to perfectness of soul, is the only affinity which is worth anything. True love is that which ennobles the personality, fortifies the heart, and sanctifies the existence. And the being we love must not be mysterious and sphinx-like, but clear and limpid as a diamond; so that admiration and attachment may grow with knowledge.

* * * * *

Jealousy is a terrible thing. It resembles love, only it is precisely love's contrary. Instead of wishing for the welfare of the object loved, it desires the dependence of that object upon itself, and its own triumph. Love is the forgetfulness of self; jealousy is the most passionate form of egotism, the glorification of a despotic, exacting, and vain *ego*, which can neither forget nor subordinate itself. The contrast is perfect.

* * * * *

Austerity in women is sometimes the accompaniment of a rare power of loving. And when it is so their attachment is strong as death; their fidelity as resisting as the diamond; they are hungry for devotion and athirst for sacrifice. Their love is a piety, their tenderness a religion, and they triple the energy of love by giving to it the sanctity of duty.

* * * * *

To the spectator over fifty, the world certainly presents a good deal that is new, but a great deal more which is only the old furbished up—mere plagiarism and modification, rather than amelioration. Almost everything is a copy of a copy, a reflection of a reflection, and the perfect being is as rare now as he ever was. Let us not complain of it; it is the reason why the world lasts. Humanity improves but slowly; that is why history goes on.

Is not progress the goad of Siva? It excites the torch to burn itself away; it hastens the approach of death. Societies which change rapidly only reach their final catastrophe the sooner. Children who are too precocious never reach maturity. Progress should be the aroma of life, not its substance.

* * * * *

Man is a passion which brings a will into play, which works an intelligence—and thus the organs which seem to be in the service of intelligence, are in reality only the agents of passion. For all the commoner sorts of being, determinism is true: inward liberty exists only as an exception and as the result of self-conquest. And even he who has tasted liberty is only free intermittently and by moments. True liberty, then, is not a continuous state; it is not an indefeasible and invariable quality. We are free only so far as we are not dupes of ourselves, our pretexts, our instincts, our temperament. We are freed by energy and the critical spirit—that is to say, by detachment of soul, by self-government. So that we are enslaved, but susceptible of freedom; we are bound, but capable of shaking off our bonds. The soul is caged, but it has power to flutter within its cage.

* * * * *

Material results are but the tardy sign of invisible activities. The bullet has started long before the noise of the report has reached us. The decisive events of the world take place in the intellect.

* * * * *

Sorrow is the most tremendous of all realities in the sensible world, but the transfiguration of sorrow after the manner of Christ is a more beautiful solution of the problem than the extirpation of sorrow, after the method of Cakyamouni.

* * * * *

Life should be a giving birth to the soul, the development of a higher mode of reality. The animal must be humanized; flesh must be made spirit; physiological activity must be transmuted into intellect and conscience, into reason, justice, and generosity, as the torch is transmuted into life and warmth. The blind, greedy, selfish nature of man must put on beauty and nobleness. This heavenly alchemy is what justifies our presence on the earth: it is our mission and our glory.

* * * * *

To renounce happiness and think only of duty, to put conscience in the place of feeling—this voluntary martyrdom has its nobility. The natural man in us flinches, but the better self submits. To hope for justice in the world is a sign of sickly sensibility; we must be able to do without it. True manliness consists in such independence. Let the world think what it will of us, it is its own affair. If it will not give us the place which is lawfully ours until after our death, or perhaps not at all, it is but acting within its right. It is our business to behave as though our country were grateful, as though the world were equitable, as though opinion were clear-sighted, as though life were just, as though men were good.

* * * * *

Death itself may become matter of consent, and therefore a moral act. The animal expires; man surrenders his soul to the author of the soul.

Amiel's Journal

[With the year 1881, beginning with the month of January, we enter upon the last period of Amiel's illness. Although he continued to attend to his professional duties, and never spoke of his forebodings, he felt himself mortally ill, as we shall see by the following extracts from the Journal. Amiel wrote up to the end, doing little else, however, toward the last than record the progress of his disease, and the proofs of interest and kindliness which he received. After weeks of suffering and pain a state of extreme weakness gradually gained upon him. His last lines are dated the 29th of April; it was on the 11th of May that he succumbed, without a struggle, to the complicated disease from which he suffered.—S.]

January 5, 1881.—I think I fear shame more than death. Tacitus said: *Omnia serviliter pro dominatione.* My tendency is just the contrary. Even when it is voluntary, dependence is a burden to me. I should blush to find myself determined by interest, submitting to constraint, or becoming the slave of any will whatever. To me vanity is slavery, self-love degrading, and utilitarianism meanness. I detest the ambition which makes you the liege man of something or someone—I desire to be simply my own master.

If I had health I should be the freest man I know. Although perhaps a little hardness of heart would be desirable to make me still more independent.

Let me exaggerate nothing. My liberty is only negative. Nobody has any hold over me, but many things have become impossible to me, and if I were so foolish as to wish for them, the limits of my liberty would soon become apparent. Therefore I take care not to wish for them, and not to let my thoughts dwell on them. I only desire what I am able for, and in this way I run my head against no wall, I cease even to be conscious of the boundaries which enclose me. I take care to wish for rather less than is in my power, that I may not even be reminded of the obstacles in my way. Renunciation is the safeguard of dignity. Let us strip ourselves if we would not be stripped. He who has freely given up his life may look death in the face: what more can it take away from him? Do away with desire and practice charity—there you have the whole method of Buddha, the whole secret of the great Deliverance....

It is snowing, and my chest is troublesome. So that I depend on nature and on God. But I do not depend on human caprice; this is the point to be insisted on. It is true that my chemist may make a blunder and poison me, my banker may reduce me to pauperism, just as an earthquake may destroy my house without hope of redress. Absolute independence, therefore, is a pure chimera. But I do possess relative independence—that of the stoic who withdraws into the fortress of his will, and shuts the gates behind him.

"Jurons, excepte Dieu, de n'avoir point de maitre."

This oath of old Geneva remains my motto still.

January 10, 1881.—To let one's self be troubled by the ill-will, the ingratitude, the indifference, of others, is a weakness to which I am very much inclined. It is painful to me to be misunderstood, ill-judged. I am wanting in manly hardihood, and the heart in me is more vulnerable than it ought to be. It seems to me, however, that I have grown tougher in this respect than I used to be. The malignity of the world troubles me less than it did. Is it the result of philosophy, or an effect of age, or simply caused by the many proofs of respect and attachment that I have received? These proofs were just what were wanting to inspire me with some self-respect. Otherwise I should have so easily believed in my own nullity and in the insignificance of all my efforts. Success is necessary for the timid, praise is a moral stimulus, and admiration a strengthening elixir. We think we know ourselves, but as long as we are ignorant of our comparative value, our place in the social assessment, we do not know ourselves well enough. If we are to act with effect, we must count for something with our fellow-men; we must feel ourselves possessed of some weight and credit with them, so that our effort may be rightly proportioned to the resistance which has to be overcome. As long as we despise opinion we are without a standard by which to measure ourselves; we do not know our relative power. I have despised opinion too much, while yet I have been too sensitive to injustice. These two faults have cost me dear. I longed for kindness, sympathy, and equity, but my pride forbade me to ask for them, or to employ any address or calculation to obtain them.... I do not think I have been wrong altogether, for all through I have been in harmony with my best self, but my want of adaptability has worn me out, to no purpose. Now, indeed, I am at peace within, but my career is over, my strength is running out, and my life is near its end.

"Il n'est plus temps pour rien excepte pour mourir."

This is why I can look at it all historically.

January 23, 1881.—A tolerable night, but this morning the cough has been frightful. Beautiful weather, the windows ablaze with sunshine. With my feet on the fender I have just finished the newspaper.

At this moment I feel well, and it seems strange to me that my doom should be so near. Life has no sense of kinship with death. This is why, no doubt, a sort of mechanical instinctive hope is forever springing up afresh in us, troubling our reason, and casting doubt on the verdict of science. All life is tenacious and persistent. It is like the parrot in the fable, who, at the very moment when its neck is being wrung, still repeats with its last breath:

"Cela, cela, ne sera rien."

The intellect puts the matter at its worst, but the animal protests. It will not believe in the evil till it comes. Ought one to regret it? Probably not. It is nature's will that life should defend itself against death; hope is only the love of life; it is an organic impulse which religion has taken under its protection. Who knows? God may save us, may work a miracle. Besides, are we ever sure that there is no remedy? Uncertainty is the refuge of hope. We reckon the doubtful among the chances in our favor. Mortal frailty clings to every support. How be angry with it for so doing? Even with all possible aids it hardly ever escapes desolation and distress. The supreme solution is, and always will be, to see in necessity the fatherly will of God, and so to submit ourselves and bear our cross bravely, as an offering to the Arbiter of human destiny. The soldier does not dispute the order given him: he obeys and dies without murmuring. If he waited to understand the use of his sacrifice, where would his submission be?

It occurred to me this morning how little we know of each other's physical troubles; even those nearest and dearest to us know nothing of our conversations with the King of Terrors. There are thoughts which brook no confidant: there are griefs which cannot be shared. Consideration for others even bids us conceal them. We dream alone, we suffer alone, we die alone, we inhabit the last resting-place alone. But there is nothing to prevent us from opening our solitude to God. And so what was an austere monologue becomes dialogue, reluctance becomes docility, renunciation passes into peace, and the sense of painful defeat is lost in the sense of recovered liberty.

"Vouloir ce que Dieu veut est la seule science Qui nous met en repos."

None of us can escape the play of contrary impulse; but as soon as the soul has once recognized the order of things and submitted itself thereto, then all is well.

"Comme un sage mourant puissions nous dire en paix: J'ai trop longtemps erre, cherche; je me trompais: Tout est bien, mon Dieu m'enveloppe."

January 28, 1881.—A terrible night. For three or four hours I struggled against suffocation and looked death in the face.... It is clear that what awaits me is suffocation—asphyxia. I shall die by choking.

I should not have chosen such a death; but when there is no option, one must simply resign one's self, and at once.... Spinoza expired in the presence of the doctor whom he had sent for. I must familiarize myself with the idea of dying unexpectedly, some fine night, strangled by laryngitis. The last sigh of a patriarch surrounded by his kneeling family is more beautiful: my fate indeed lacks beauty, grandeur, poetry; but stoicism consists in renunciation. *Abstine et sustine.*

I must remember besides that I have faithful friends; it is better not to torment them. The last journey is only made more painful by scenes and lamentations: one word is worth all others—"Thy will, not mine, be done!" Leibnitz was accompanied to the grave by his servant only. The loneliness of the deathbed and the tomb is not an evil. The great mystery cannot be shared. The dialogue between the soul and the King of Terrors needs no witnesses. It is the living who cling to the thought of last greetings. And, after all, no one knows exactly what is reserved for him. What will be will be. We have but to say, "Amen."

February 4, 1881.—It is a strange sensation that of laying one's self down to rest with the thought that perhaps one will never see the morrow. Yesterday I felt it strongly, and yet here I am. Humility is made easy by the sense of excessive frailty, but it cuts away all ambition.

"Quittez le long espoir et les vastes pensees."

Amiel's Journal

A long piece of work seems absurd—one lives but from day to day.

When a man can no longer look forward in imagination to five years, a year, a month, of free activity—when he is reduced to counting the hours, and to seeing in the coming night the threat of an unknown fate—it is plain that he must give up art, science, and politics, and that he must be content to hold converse with himself, the one possibility which is his till the end. Inward soliloquy is the only resource of the condemned man whose execution is delayed. He withdraws upon the fastnesses of conscience. His spiritual force no longer radiates outwardly; it is consumed in self-study. Action is cut off—only contemplation remains. He still writes to those who have claims upon him, but he bids farewell to the public, and retreats into himself. Like the hare, he comes back to die in his form, and this form is his consciousness, his intellect—the journal, too, which has been the companion of his inner life. As long as he can hold a pen, as long as he has a moment of solitude, this echo of himself still claims his meditation, still represents to him his converse with his God.

In all this, however, there is nothing akin to self-examination: it is not an act of contrition, or a cry for help. It is simply an Amen of submission—"My child, give me thy heart!"

Renunciation and acquiescence are less difficult to me than to others, for I desire nothing. I could only wish not to suffer, but Jesus on Gethesemane allowed himself to make the same prayer; let us add to it the words that he did: "Nevertheless, not my will, but thine, be done,"—and wait.

... For many years past the immanent God has been more real to me than the transcendent God, and the religion of Jacob has been more alien to me than that of Kant, or even Spinoza. The whole Semitic dramaturgy has come to seem to me a work of the imagination. The apostolic documents have changed in value and meaning to my eyes. Belief and truth have become distinct to me with a growing distinctness. Religious psychology has become a simple phenomenon, and has lost its fixed and absolute value. The apologetics of Pascal, of Leibnitz, of Secretan, are to me no more convincing than those of the Middle Ages, for they presuppose what is really in question—a revealed doctrine, a definite and unchangeable Christianity. It seems to me that what remains to me from all my studies is a new phenomenology of mind, an intuition of universal metamorphosis. All particular convictions, all definite principles, all clear-cut formulas and fixed ideas, are but prejudices, useful in practice, but still narrownesses of the mind. The absolute in detail is absurd and contradictory. All political, religious, aesthetic, or literary parties are protuberances, misgrowths of thought. Every special belief represents a stiffening and thickening of thought; a stiffening, however, which is necessary in its time and place. Our monad, in its thinking capacity, overleaps the boundaries of time and space and of its own historical surroundings; but in its individual capacity, and for purposes of action, it adapts itself to current illusions, and puts before itself a definite end. It is lawful to be *man*, but it is needful also to be *a* man, to be an individual. Our role is thus a double one. Only, the philosopher is specially authorized to develop the first role, which the vast majority of humankind neglects.

February 7, 1881.—Beautiful sunshine to-day. But I have scarcely spring enough left in me to notice it. Admiration, joy, presuppose a little relief from pain. Whereas my neck is tired with the weight of my head, and my heart is wearied with the weight of life; this is not the aesthetic state.

I have been thinking over different things which I might have written. But generally speaking we let what is most original and best in us be wasted. We reserve ourselves for a future which never comes. *Omnis mortar.*

February 14, 1881.—Supposing that my weeks are numbered, what duties still remain to me to fulfill, that I may leave all in order? I must give every one his due; justice, prudence, kindness must be satisfied; the last memories must be sweet ones. Try to forget nothing useful, nor anybody who has a claim upon thee! February 15, 1881.— I have, very reluctantly, given up my lecture at the university, and sent for my doctor. On my chimney-piece are the flowers which — — has sent me. Letters from London, Paris, Lausanne, Neuchatel ... They seem to me like wreaths thrown into a grave.

Mentally I say farewell to all the distant friends whom I shall never see again.

February 18, 1881.—Misty weather. A fairly good night. Still, the emaciation goes on. That is to say, the vulture allows me some respite, but he still hovers over his prey. The possibility of resuming my official work seems like a dream to me.

Although just now the sense of ghostly remoteness from life which I so often have is absent, I feel myself a prisoner for good, a hopeless invalid. This vague intermediate state, which is neither death nor life, has its sweetness, because if it implies renunciation, still it allows of thought. It is a reverie without pain, peaceful and meditative. Surrounded with affection and with books, I float down the stream of time, as once I glided over the Dutch canals, smoothly and noiselessly. It is as though I were once more on board the *Treckschute*. Scarcely can one hear even the soft ripple of the water furrowed by the barge, or the hoof of the towing horse trotting along the sandy path. A journey under these conditions has something fantastic in it. One is not sure whether one still exists, still belongs to earth. It is like the *manes*, the shadows, flitting through the twilight of the *inania regna*. Existence has become fluid. From the standpoint of complete personal renunciation I watch the passage of my impressions, my dreams, thoughts, and memories.... It is a mood of fixed contemplation akin to that which we attribute to the seraphim. It takes no interest in the individual self, but only in the specimen monad, the sample of the general history of mind. Everything is in everything, and the consciousness examines what it has before it. Nothing is either great or small. The mind adopts all modes, and everything is acceptable to it. In this state its relations with the body, with the outer world, and with other individuals, fade out of sight. *Selbst-bewusstsein* becomes once more impersonal *Bewusstsein*, and before personality can be reacquired, pain, duty, and will must be brought into action.

Are these oscillations between the personal and the impersonal, between pantheism and theism, between Spinoza and Leibnitz, to be regretted? No, for it is the one state which makes us conscious of the other. And as man is capable of ranging the two domains, why should he mutilate himself?

February 22, 1881.—The march of mind finds its typical expression in astronomy—no pause, but no hurry; orbits, cycles, energy, but at the same time harmony; movement and yet order; everything has its own weight and its relative weight, receives and gives forth light. Cannot this cosmic and divine become oars? Is the war of all against all, the preying of man upon man, a higher type of balanced action? I shrink form believing it. Some theorists imagine that the phase of selfish brutality is the last phase of all. They must be wrong. Justice will prevail, and justice is not selfishness. Independence of intellect, combined with goodness of heart, will be the agents of a result, which will be the compromise required.

March 1, 1881.—I have just been glancing over the affairs of the world in the newspaper. What a Babel it is! But it is very pleasant to be able to make the tour of the planet and review the human race in an hour. It gives one a sense of ubiquity. A newspaper in the twentieth century will be composed of eight or ten daily bulletins—political, religious, scientific, literary, artistic, commercial, meteorological, military, economical, social, legal, and financial; and will be divided into two parts only—*Urbs* and *Orbis*. The need of totalizing, of simplifying, will bring about the general use of such graphic methods as permit of series and comparisons. We shall end by feeling the pulse of the race and the globe as easily as that of a sick man, and we shall count the palpitations of the universal life, just as we shall hear the grass growing, or the sunspots clashing, and catch the first stirrings of volcanic disturbances. Activity will become consciousness; the earth will see herself. Then will be the time for her to blush for her disorders, her hideousness, her misery, her crime and to throw herself at last with energy and perseverance into the pursuit of justice. When humanity has cut its wisdom-teeth, then perhaps it will have the grace to reform itself, and the will to attempt a systematic reduction of the share of the evil in the world. The *Weltgeist* will pass from the state of instinct to the moral state. War, hatred, selfishness, fraud, the right of the stronger, will be held to be old-world barbarisms, mere diseases of growth. The pretenses of modern civilization will be replaced by real virtues. Men will be brothers, peoples will be friends, races will sympathize one with another, and mankind will draw from love a principle of emulation, of invention, and of zeal, as powerful as any furnished by the vulgar stimulant of interest. This millennium—will it ever be? It is at least an act of piety to believe in it.

March 14, 1881.—I have finished Merimee's letters to Panizzi. Merimee died of the disease which torments me—"*Je tousse, et j'etouffe.*" Bronchitis and asthma, whence defective assimilation, and finally exhaustion. He, too, tried arsenic, wintering at Cannes, compressed air. All was useless. Suffocation and inanition carried off the author of "Colomba." *Hic tua res agitur*. The gray, heavy sky is of the same color as my thoughts. And yet the irrevocable has its own sweetness and serenity. The fluctuations of illusion, the uncertainties of desire, the leaps and bounds of hope, give place to tranquil resignation. One feels as though one were already beyond the grave.

It is this very week, too, I remember, that my corner of ground in the Oasis is to be bought. Everything draws toward the end. *Festinat ad eventum.*

March 15, 1881.—The "Journal" is full of details of the horrible affair at Petersburg. How clear it is that such catastrophes as this, in which the innocent suffer, are the product of a long accumulation of iniquities. Historical justice is, generally speaking, tardy—so tardy that it becomes unjust. The Providential theory is really based on human solidarity. Louis XVI. pays for Louis XV., Alexander II. for Nicholas. We expiate the sins of our fathers, and our grandchildren will be punished for ours. A double injustice! cries the individual. And he is right if the individualist principle is true. But is it true? That is the point. It seems as though the individual part of each man's destiny were but one section of that destiny. Morally we are responsible for what we ourselves have willed, but socially, our happiness and unhappiness depend on causes outside our will. Religion answers— "Mystery, obscurity, submission, faith. Do your duty; leave the rest to God."

March 16, 1881.—A wretched night. A melancholy morning.... The two stand-bys of the doctor, digitalis and bromide, seem to have lost their power over me. Wearily and painfully I watch the tedious progress of my own decay. What efforts to keep one's self from dying! I am worn out with the struggle.

Useless and incessant struggle is a humiliation to one's manhood. The lion finds the gnat the most intolerable of his foes. The natural man feels the same. But the spiritual man must learn the lesson of gentleness and long-suffering. The inevitable is the will of God. We might have preferred something else, but it is our business to accept the lot assigned us.... One thing only is necessary—

"Garde en mon coeur la foi dans ta volonte sainte, Et de moi fais, o Dieu, tout ce que tu voudras."

Later.—One of my students has just brought me a sympathetic message from my class. My sister sends me a pot of azaleas, rich in flowers and buds;——sends roses and violets: every one spoils me, which proves that I am ill.

March 19, 1881.—Distaste—discouragement. My heart is growing cold. And yet what affectionate care, what tenderness, surrounds me!... But without health, what can one do with all the rest? What is the good of it all to me? What was the good of Job's trials? They ripened his patience; they exercised his submission.

Come, let me forget myself, let me shake off this melancholy, this weariness. Let me think, not of all that is lost, but of all that I might still lose. I will reckon up my privileges; I will try to be worthy of my blessings.

March 21, 1881.—This invalid life is too Epicurean. For five or six weeks now I have done nothing else but wait, nurse myself, and amuse myself, and how weary one gets of it! What I want is work. It is work which gives flavor to life. Mere existence without object and without effort is a poor thing. Idleness leads to languor, and languor to disgust. Besides, here is the spring again, the season of vague desires, of dull discomforts, of dim aspirations, of sighs without a cause. We dream wide-awake. We search darkly for we know not what; invoking the while something which has no name, unless it be happiness or death.

March 28, 1881.—I cannot work; I find it difficult to exist. One may be glad to let one's friends spoil one for a few months; it is an experience which is good for us all; but afterward? How much better to make room for the living, the active, the productive.

"Tircis, voici le temps de prendre sa retraite."

Is it that I care so much to go on living? I think not. It is health that I long for—freedom from suffering.

And this desire being vain, I can find no savor in anything else. Satiety. Lassitude. Renunciation. Abdication. "In your patience possess ye your souls."

April 10, 1881. (*Sunday*).—Visit to — —. She read over to me letters of 1844 to 1845—letters of mine. So much promise to end in so meager a result! What creatures we are! I shall end like the Rhine, lost among the sands, and the hour is close by when my thread of water will have disappeared.

Afterward I had a little walk in the sunset. There was an effect of scattered rays and stormy clouds; a green haze envelops all the trees—

"Et tout renait, et deja l'aubepine A vu l'abeille accourir a ses fleurs,"

—but to me it all seems strange already.

Later.—What dupes we are of our own desires!... Destiny has two ways of crushing us—by refusing our wishes and by fulfilling them. But he who only wills what God wills escapes both catastrophes. "All things work together for his good."

April 14, 1881.—Frightful night; the fourteenth running, in which I have been consumed by sleeplessness....

April 15, 1881.—To-morrow is Good Friday, the festival of pain. I know what it is to spend days of anguish and nights of agony. Let me bear my cross humbly.... I have no more future. My duty is to satisfy the claims of the present, and to leave everything in order. Let me try to end well, seeing that to undertake and even to continue, are closed to me.

April 19, 1881.—A terrible sense of oppression. My flesh and my heart fail me.

"Que vivre est difficile, o mon coeur fatigue!"